Unifying Theories of Programming

Series editors: Tony Hoare and Richard Bird

APT, K.R., *From Logic Programming to Prolog*
ARNOLD, A., *Finite Transition Systems*
ARNOLD, A. and GUESSARIAN, I., *Mathematics for Computer Science*
BARR, M. and WELLS, C., *Category Theory for Computing Science (2nd edn)*
BEN-ARI, M., *Principles of Concurrent and Distributed Programming*
BEN-ARI, M., *Mathematical Logic for Computer Science*
BEST, E., *Semantics of Sequential and Parallel Programs*
BIRD, R., and DE MOOR, O., *The Algebra of Programming*
BIRD, R., and WADLER, P., *Introduction to Functional Programming*
BOMAN, M., BUBENCKO, JR, J.A., JOHANNESSON, P. and WANGLER, B., *Conceptual Modelling*
BOVET, D.P. and CRESCENZI, P., *Introduction to the Theory of Complexity*
DE BROCK, B., *Foundations of Semantic Databases*
BRODA, EISENBACK, KHOSHNEVISAN and VICKERS, *Reasoned Programming*
BRUNS, G., *Distributed Systems Analysis with CCS*
BURKE, E. and FOXLEY, E., *Logic and Its Applications*
DAHL, O.-J., *Verifiable Programming*
ELDER, J., *Compiler Construction*
FREEMAN, T.L. and PHILLIPS, R.C., *Parallel Numerical Algorithms*
GOLDSCHLAGER, L. and LISTER, A., *Computer Science: A modern introduction (2nd edn)*
HAYES, I. (ed.), *Specification Case Studies (2nd edn)*
HINCHEY, M.G. and BOWEN, J.P., *Applications of Formal Methods*
HOARE, C.A.R., *Communicating Sequential Processes*
HOARE, C.A.R. and GORDON, M.J.C., *Mechanized Reasoning and Hardware Design*
HOARE, C.A.R. and JONES, C.B. (eds), *Essays in Computing Science*
HUGHES, J.G., *Database Technology: A software engineering approach*
HUGHES, J.G., *Object-oriented Databases*
INMOS LTD, *Occam 2 Reference Manual*
JONES, C.B. and SHAW, R.C.F. (eds), *Case Studies in Systematic Software Development*
JONES, G., *Programming in Occam*
JONES, G. and GOLDSMITH, M., *Programming in Occam 2*
JONES, N.D., GOMARD, C.K. and SESTOFT, P., *Partial Evaluation and Automatic Program Generation*
JOSEPH, M., PRASAD, V.R., and NATARAJAN, N., *A Multiprocessor Operating System*
JOSEPH, M. (ed.), *Real-time Systems: Specification, verification and analysis*
KALDEWAIJ, A., *Programming: The derivation of algorithms*
KING, P.J.B., *Computer and Communications Systems Performance Modelling*
LALEMENT, R., *Computation as Logic*
McCABE, F.G., *High-level Programmer's Guide to the 68000*
MEYER, B., *Object-oriented Software Construction*
MILNER, R., *Communication and Concurrency*
MORGAN, C., *Programming from Specifications (2nd edn)*
NISSANKE, N., *Realtime Systems*
OMONDI, A.R., *Computer Arithmetic Systems*
PATON, COOPER, WILLIAMS and TRINDER, *Database Programming Languages*
PEYTON-JONES, S.L., *The Implementation of Functional Programming Languages*
PEYTON-JONES, S. and LESTER, D., *Implementing Functional Languages*
POTTER, B., SINCLAIR, J. and TILL, D., *An Introduction to Formal Specification and Z (2nd edn)*
ROSCOE, A.W. (ed.), *A Classical Mind: Essays in honour of C.A.R. Hoare*
ROSCOE, A.W., *The Theory and Practice of Concurrency*
ROZENBERG, G. and SALOMAA, A., *Cornerstones of Undecidability*
SLOMAN, M. and KRAMER, J., *Distributed Systems and Computer Networks*
SHARP, R., *Principles of Protocol Design*

Series listing continued at back of book

Unifying Theories of Programming

C.A.R. Hoare and He Jifeng

Oxford University Computing Laboratory

Prentice Hall

London New York Toronto Sydney Tokyo Singapore
Madrid Mexico City Munich Paris

First published 1998 by
Prentice Hall Europe
Campus 400, Maylands Avenue
Hemel Hempstead
Hertfordshire, HP2 7EZ
A division of
Simon & Schuster International Group

Printed and bound in Great Britain by
Redwood Books, Trowbridge, Wiltshire

Library of Congress Cataloging-in-Publication Data

Hoare, C. A. R. (Charles Anthony Richard), 1934–
Unifying theories of programming / C.A.R. Hoare and He Jifeng.
p. cm.
Includes bibliographical references and index.
ISBN 0-13-458761-8 (alk. paper)
1. Electronic digital computers—Programming. I. He, Jifeng, 1943– . II. Title.
QA76.6..H5735 1998
005.1′01—dc21 98–10608
CIP

British Library Cataloguing in Publication Data

A catalogue record for this book is available from
the British Library

ISBN 0-13-458761-8

---

1 2 3 4 5 02 01 00 99 98

Contents

Preface

A theory of programming explores the principles that underlie the successful practice of software engineering. As in all branches of engineering, the practice comes first, both in importance and in historical order. The rapidly spreading benefits of computer application in modern society are largely due to the efforts and intuitive genius of teams of programmers, who have gained their skills and understanding the hard way, by long practice and experience. But now there is another complementary way for practising software engineers. A study of the relevant scientific theory can enhance their skills, broaden their range, deepen their understanding and strengthen their confidence in the accuracy and reliability of their designs and products. Understanding of a common theory enables experience gained in one language or application to be generalised rapidly to new applications and to new developments in technology or fashion; and it is the theory that maintains the intellectual interest of professional activity throughout a lifetime of achievement. But best of all, development of a comprehensive and comprehensible theory encapsulates the best of the state of the art in the subject, and makes it more readily available to the next generation of entrants to the profession.

The key to further progress is education; that is the goal of this book. It aims to attract and inform a class of student who are committed to practical engineering ideals, and who wish to devote their efforts to study of the relevant scientific foundation. They will probably have exposure already to one or more programming languages, and expect to meet more in their professional careers. An understanding of the basic concepts which underlie this variety will assist in mastery of new methods and notations, and in transfer of hard-won experience from one field of application to another. In a university curriculum, the book may find a place on a course entitled "principles of programming languages" or "programming language semantics". It would be a useful technical basis for a course on program verification, or on a software engineering course which takes seriously the normal engineering concerns of quality, reliability and safety. If such courses do not exist now, perhaps this book will eventually inspire the development of courses entirely devoted to the theory of programming. An introductory course can be based on the first six chapters or so; the remaining chapters lead to the edge of current research.

The book may also attract the interest of students and researchers in mathematics, who look to computing science as a source of new applications and examples, and as a source of new research problems of relevance to the modern world. Those who have already made a contribution to theoretical computing science may be inspired to contribute further towards the ideal of unification. It is certain that progress towards a deeper and broader understanding will depend on the commitment, cooperation, and further major discoveries by specialists in many diverse fields of research.

The book is wide ranging not only in its subject matter but also in its approach and style. The early chapters take a rather general philosophical approach, and the early sections of each chapter devote attention to general background and motivation. The definitions are accompanied by examples and the theorems by meticulous proof. The reader is strongly encouraged to skip the elements that are found uninteresting or incomprehensible; there is a strong possibility that further reading will solve both these problems. Sections marked with an asterisk may be profitably omitted on first reading. The following summary is a further guide to judicious skipping.

The first five chapters justify and introduce the main concepts and methods used throughout the rest of the book. Chapter 0 relates the goal of unification to the achievements of other branches of science and mathematics. It surveys the range of programming methods and languages, and the axes along which they are classified. It summarises the main methods and conclusions of the book, in a manner suitable for readers who enjoy prior acquaintance with programming semantics. It ends with a summary of major challenges which have been left for future research. Chapter 1 draws similar inspiration from a study of general methods of engineering design, which are found to follow exactly the principles of logical reasoning familiar in other mathematical and scientific disciplines. The chapter ends with a summary of the many personal and professional qualities required of the successful engineer, apart from an understanding of the relevant theory and its practice.

Both these chapters may be lightly skipped by a reader who wants to get on to the real substance, which begins in Chapter 2. This is a presentation within predicate calculus of Tarski's theory of relations, enriched with his fixed point theory, and applied to Dijkstra's simple non-deterministic sequential programming language. This language will prove adequate as a framework within which all more complex languages can be defined. But first, a small inconsistency between relation theory and practice must be resolved. This is done in Chapter 3, where *designs* are introduced as a subclass of relations which can be decomposed into the familiar precondition–postcondition pair of programming calculi like VDM. Chapter 4 develops some of the more elegant general results used in the rest of the book. Chapter 5 presents a complete algebra for the sequential programming language, and derives a normal form theorem.

The remaining chapters of the book introduce more advanced programming language features one by one. They may be studied in almost any combination and to any depth, with cross references followed at will. Chapter 6 deals with labels, jumps and machine code, and expounds the principles of correct compilation from a high level language. Chapter 7 introduces parallel processing based on the shared-store paradigm. It gives a common parameterised definition of parallel composition that is reused in the following chapters. Chapter 8 introduces reactive processes, which allow interaction and communication not only on termination of a program but also at intermediate stable states while it is running. Chapter 9 deals with programs that manipulate programs as data. It includes declarative programming, as incorporated in modern functional and logical programming languages. Chapter 10 unifies the general theory of programming with a popular mode of presentation in the form of an operational semantics.

Note: A prerequisite for private reading of the book is some acquaintance with propositional calculus, predicate notation and the concepts of discrete mathematics. In the interests of standardisation, and for the general benefit of software engineers, the mathematical notations are taken largely from the draft international standards for Z and VDM.

Tony Hoare
He Jifeng

Oxford, July 1997

Acknowledgements

The ideas put forward in this book have been inspired or derived from the work of many earlier researchers. The references are a partial acknowledgement of the work that has been most influential on the thinking of the authors; they are not necessarily the earliest source of the ideas.

The following have performed a sterling service to the reader by comments on earlier drafts of this work: R. Backhouse, J. Baeten, J.W. de Bakker, J.A. Bergstra, O.-J. Dahl, E.W. Dijkstra, P. Gardiner, M. Hennessy, R. Joshi, B. von Karger, H. Langmaack, G. Lowe, G. McCusker, A.J.R.G. Milner, J. Misra, C.C. Morgan, O. Owe, F. Page, J. Parrow, G.D. Plotkin, A. Ravn, W.P. de Roever, A.W. Roscoe, A. Sampaio, S.A. Schneider, D.S. Scott, M. Sintzoff, A. Stevens, F. Vaandrager.

The research reported in this book was supported by EPSRC research grant GR/K58708 "Linking theories for computing science", the ESPRIT Basic Research Actions 3104 and 7071 ProCoS and 3006 CONCUR, and the Admiral B.R. Inman Centennial Chair in Computing Theory at the University of Texas at Austin, and the Newton Institute Seminar on the Semantics of Programming Languages, and the James Martin Chair of Computing at the University of Oxford.

Glossary of Notations

Cross references

Section 3.2	Chapter 3 Section 2
3.2L1	Law 1 in Section 3.2
Theorem 3.2.3	Theorem 3 in Section 3.2
Lemma 3.2.7	Lemma 7 in Section 3.2
Example 3.2.5	Example 5 in Section 3.2
Table 3.2.4	Table 4 in Section 3.2
Diagram 3.2.8	Diagram 8 in Section 3.1
Exercise 3.2.10	Exercise 10 in Section 3.1
$\square$	end of an example or proof

Logic

$=$	equals
$\neq$	is distinct from
$=_{df}$	is defined by
iff	if and only if
$[P]$	P is true for all values of variables in its alphabet
$P \wedge Q$	P and Q (both true)
$P \vee Q$	P or Q (one or both true)
$\neg P$	not P (P is not true)
$P \Rightarrow Q$	if P then Q

$P \equiv Q$	P if and only if Q
$\exists x : T \bullet P$	there exists an x in set T such that P
$\forall x : T \bullet P$	for all x in set T, P
$P \vdash Q$	Q can be validly deduced from P
$P \dashv\vdash Q$	$P \vdash Q$ and $Q \vdash P$

Sets

$\in$	is a member of
$\notin$	is not a member of
$\{\}$	the empty set
$\{a\}$	the singleton set containing only a
$\{x : T \mid P(x)\}$	the set of all x in T such that $P(x)$
$\{f(x) \mid P(x)\}$	the set of all the values $f(x)$ such that $P(x)$
$S \cup T$	S union T
$S \cap T$	S intersect T
$S \setminus T$	S minus T
$S \subseteq T$	S is contained in T
$S \supseteq T$	S contains T
$\mathcal{N}$	the set of natural numbers
$\bigcup C$	union of collection C of sets
$\bigcap C$	intersection of collection C of sets

Sequences

$<>$	the empty sequence
$<a>$	the sequence containing only a
$s\,\hat{}\,t$	catenation of sequences s and t
s_0	the head of sequence s
$tail(s)$	the tail of sequence s
$\#s$	the length of s
A^*	set of all sequences with elements from set A
$s \downarrow E$	the subsequence of s omitting elements outside E
$s \vert\vert\vert t$	the set of all interleavings of sequences s and t

Functions

id_S	the identity function on set S
$\{i \mapsto e\}$	the singleton function that maps i to e
$F : S \to T$	F is a total mapping from S to T
$domain(F)$	the domain of function F
$image(F)$	the image of function F
$X \lhd F$	function F with domain restricted to set X
$F(x)$	the member of T to which F maps x
F^{-1}	inverse of F
$F \circ G$	F composed with G, mapping x to $F(G(x))$
$\lambda x : S \bullet F(x)$	the function that maps each x in S to $F(x)$
$F \oplus G$	the function $\lambda x \bullet (G(x)$ if $x \in domain(G)$ else $F(x))$
or_P	the function $\lambda X \bullet (P \vee X)$
and_Q	the function $\lambda X \bullet (Q \wedge X)$
pre_J	the function $\lambda X \bullet (J; X)$
$post_K$	the function $\lambda X \bullet (X; K)$
imp_P	the function $\lambda X \bullet (P \Rightarrow X)$

Alphabets

1.1	αP	the alphabet of relation P
1.3	$in\alpha P$	the input alphabet of relation P
1.3	$out\alpha P$	the output alphabet of relation P
6.1	$\alpha l P$	the set of continuations of program P
6.4	$\alpha l_0 P$	the set of entry points of labelled program P
6.4	$\alpha l' P$	the set of exit points of labelled program P
8.0	$\mathcal{A}P$	the set of all actions possible for process P
8.3	$inchan\ P$	the set of input channels of process P
8.3	$outchan\ P$	the set of output channels of process P

Observations

1.1	x	the initial value of variable x
1.1	x'	the final value of variable x

3.0	ok	the program has started
3.0	ok'	the program has reached a stable state
6.1	l	control variable of the execution mechanism
7.6	q	the initial observation of a logic program (called a question)
7.6	a'	the resulting sequence of answers
8.0	tr	an arbitrary trace of the specified process
8.0	ref	an arbitrary refusal of the specified process
8.0	$wait$	the specified process is in an intermediate observable state

Relations

1.5	$[P \Rightarrow Q]$	P implies Q (everywhere)
2.4	**true**	the universal relation
2.5	$P \sqcup Q$	intersection of P and Q
2.5	$\top$	miracle (the top of the lattice)
2.5	**false**	the empty relation
2.6	$\mu X_{\mathbf{S}} \bullet P(X)$	the weakest solution in $\mathbf{S}$ of $X = P(X)$
2.7	$\nu X_{\mathbf{S}} \bullet P(X)$	the strongest solution in $\mathbf{S}$ of $X = P(X)$
2.8	$p\{Q\}r$	Hoare triple: on precondition p, execution of Q ensures postcondition r
2.8	$b_\perp$	assertion b
2.8	$b^\top$	assumption b
2.9	**var** x	declaration of variable x
2.9	**end** x	termination of the scope of variable x
2.9	P_{+x}	P with its alphabet augmented by x and x'
3.1	$P \vdash Q$	the relation $ok \wedge P \Rightarrow ok' \wedge Q$
3.1	$\mathcal{D}e$	expression e is defined
4.0	$P \sqsupseteq Q$	P is a refinement of Q, i.e. $[P \Rightarrow Q]$
4.3	P/Q	the weakest prespecification of Q through P
4.3	$Q \backslash P$	the weakest postspecification of Q through P
10.1	$\rightarrow$	step relation on machine states
10.2	$\sim_s$	strong bisimulation
10.2	$\approx_w$	weak bisimulation

10.3	$\xrightarrow{*}$	the reflexive transitive closure of $\rightarrow$
10.3	$(\mathtt{s},\ \mathtt{P}) \uparrow$	$(\mathtt{s},\ \mathtt{P})$ is a divergent machine state
10.3	$(\mathtt{s},\ \mathtt{P}) \sqsubseteq (\mathtt{t},\ \mathtt{Q})$	$(\mathtt{t},\ \mathtt{Q})$ refines $(\mathtt{s},\ \mathtt{P})$
10.3	$\mathtt{P} \sim \mathtt{Q}$	$\mathtt{P}$ simulates $\mathtt{Q}$ and vice versa
10.4	$\xrightarrow{a}$	step accompanied by action a

Sequential programming language

2.1	$P \lhd b \rhd Q$	P if b else Q
2.2	$P;Q$	P then Q
2.3	$x := e$	assign value of e to variable x
2.3	II	skip (do nothing, but terminate)
2.4	$P \sqcap Q$	non-deterministic choice of P and Q
2.4	$\bot$	abort

Labelled programming language

6.1	P^*	repeated execution of the step relation P
6.1	$P\Vert Q$	assembly of step relations P and Q
6.2	$\langle s,\ P,\ f\rangle$	the target code: $\mathbf{var}\, l; (l = s)^\top; P^*; (l = f)_\bot; \mathbf{end}\, l$
6.3	P	text of program P
6.4	$P : S \Rightarrow F$	P with S as its entries and F as its exits
6.4	$P^{\backslash H}$	P without the exit labels in H
6.4	${}^{H/}P$	P without the entry labels in H

Concurrent programming language

7.1	$l : P(x)$	the relation $P(l.x)$, with observations labelled by l
7.1	$P \mid\mid Q$	disjoint parallel composition of P and Q
7.2	$\mid\mid_M$	parallel composition with the merge operation M

Logic programming language

7.6	**no**	always gives an empty sequence of answers
7.6	**yes**	the program which copies the question as its answer
7.6	$K \mid\mid\mid L$	interleaves the answers produced by K and L

7.6	K **or** L	catenates the answers produced by K and L
7.6	L^*	apply L to each of the questions and catenate all the answers
7.6	K **and** L	feed the answers produced by K to L^*
7.6	!	cut : take the first answer
7.6	$\neg L$	**yes** if L has no answer, else **no**

ACP (Algebra of Communicating Processes)

8.1	δ	the deadlocked process
8.1	$\mathbf{do}_A(a)$	do a then terminate (abbreviated to a)
8.1	$a; P$	do a then P
8.1	$P + Q$	P choice Q
8.1	$\Sigma_{i \in I} P_i$	choice from the family $\{P_i \mid i \in I\}$
8.1	$P\|\|\|Q$	P interleave Q
8.1	$P\|\|_{ACP}Q$	P in parallel with Q, with selective synchronisation
8.1	$\varrho_E P$	process P without events in E (encapsulation)

CSP (Communicating Sequential Processes)

8.2	$SKIP$	the process which does nothing but terminate successfully
8.2	$STOP$	the deadlocked process
8.2	$CHAOS$	the worst process, whose behaviour is unpredictable
8.2	$a \to P$	a then P
8.2	$P \talloblong Q$	P choice Q
8.2	$P\|\|\|Q$	P interleave Q
8.2	$P\|\|_{CSP}Q$	P in parallel with Q, with synchronisation of identical actions
8.2	$P \backslash E$	P with events in E hidden
8.2	$P \gg Q$	P chained to Q
8.2	$P \oslash Q$	the composite choice $(P \talloblong Q) \sqcap Q$

Data flow

8.3	$c.m$	communication of value m on channel c
8.3	$\mathcal{A}_c(P)$	the set of messages which P can communicate on c
8.3	$[P]$	P with each of its channels buffered

8.3	$a?x \leadsto P$	wait for an input from channel a then P
8.3	$c!e \leadsto P$	output e on channel c then P
8.3	$P/a.m$	P after input of m from channel a
8.3	$P\|_{DF}Q$	parallel composition of data flow processes P and Q

High order programming

9.1	$\{\![P]\!\}$	predicate P named as a constant
9.3	$\tau\ res \bullet P$	the res such that P (unique description)
9.4	$P^{\bullet}\!\| Q$	P if it does not stop, else Q (priority choice)

Precedence

arithmetic operators	bind tightest
;	
$\lhd b \rhd$	
$\wedge$, $\vee$, $\sqcap$, $\sqcup$	
$\cap$, $\cup$	
$\Rightarrow$, $\equiv$	bind loosest

Chapter 0

The Challenge of Unification

The study of science has long been split into many branches, and within each branch there are many specialisations. Each specialisation concentrates on some narrowly defined natural process, and hopes to discover the laws which govern it. In the early days of a new branch of science, these laws are very specific to the outcome of a particular experiment, but as the range of experiment broadens, a collection of laws are found to be special cases of some more general theory, and in turn these theories are comprehended within some theory of yet greater generality. This constant tendency in science towards unifying theories has as ultimate goal the discovery of a clear and convincing explanation of the entire working of the natural universe.

A classical example of a unifying theory is Newton's theory of gravitation, which assimilates the motion of the moon or planets in the sky with the trajectories of apples or cannon balls falling to earth. Unification often begins more simply than that, with just a humble classification: Mendeleev's periodic table of elements classified them by their chemical properties, and these were only later explained by the unifying theory of atomic valences. A unifying theory is usually complementary to the theories that it links, and does not seek to replace them. Physicists still hope to find a Grand Unified Theory, which underlies the four known fundamental forces of nature; when found, this will further reinforce our understanding of the separate theories. It certainly will not replace them by abolishing the forces or repealing the laws that govern them.

The drive towards unification of theories that has been so successful in science has achieved equal success in revealing the clear structure of modern mathematics. For example, topology brings order to the study of continuity in all the many forms and applications discovered by analysis. Algebra classifies and generalises the many properties shared by familiar number systems, and succinctly codifies their differences. Logic and set theory formalise the common principles that govern mathematical reasoning in all branches of the subject. Category theory makes yet further abstraction from logic, set theory, algebra and topology. Computing science is a new subject, and we have not yet achieved the unification of theories that should support a proper understanding of its structure. In meeting this challenge, we may find inspiration and guidance even from quite superficial analogies with better established branches of knowledge. Our main appeal will be to thought experiments rather than physical observation; this suggests that mathematics will provide closer analogies than the physical sciences.

A proposed unification of theories occasionally receives spectacular confirmation and reward by the prediction and subsequent discovery of new planets, of new elements or of new particles. In the timespan of decades and centuries, the resulting improvement of understanding may lead to new branches of technology, with new processes and products contributing to the health and prosperity of mankind. But at the start of the research and on initial study of its results, such benefits are purely speculative, and are best left unspoken. The real driving force for the scientist is wonderment about the complexity of the world we live in, and the hope that it can be described simply enough for us to understand, and elegantly enough to admire and enjoy. Computing scientists need no excuse to indulge and cultivate their genuine curiosity about the complex world of computers, and the languages in which their programs are written.

In satisfying this curiosity, we face the challenge of building a coherent structure for the intellectual discipline of computing science, and in particular for the theory of programming. Such a comprehensive theory must include a convincing approach to the study of the range of languages in which computer programs may be expressed. It must introduce basic concepts and properties which are common to the whole range of programming methods and languages. Then it must deal separately with the additions and variations which are particular to specific groups of related programming languages. The aim throughout should be to treat each aspect and feature in the simplest possible fashion and in isolation from all the other features with which it may be combined or confused. Just as the study of chemical molecules is based upon an understanding of their constituent atoms, the study of programming languages should be based on a prior analysis of their constituent features. Simplification and isolation are the very essence of scientific method, and need no apology.

On the other hand, any practical programming language must include a great many features, together with many *ad hoc* compromises needed to reconcile them with efficient implementation and to maintain compatibility with many previously released implementations. The construction of an effective conceptual framework to understand and control the complexity of currently fashionable programming languages is a continuing challenge and stimulus to productive research. If progress is slow, this should be remedied by more rigorous isolation of the fundamental and more general issues. By concentrating on theory, the pursuit of pure science aims to convey a broader and deeper understanding of the whole range of the subject, and to contribute a foundation, a structure and an intellectual framework for further and more specialised studies of its individual branches.

In this introductory chapter we survey the immensity of the task of unification, and the general methods proposed for tackling it. Theories of programming may be classified along three independent axes.

1. Firstly, there is the vast number of programming languages already invented and yet to come. They can be classified under a smaller range of general computational paradigms, based on the structure and technology of their implementation.
2. Each of these paradigms can be described at different levels of abstraction or detail, with a corresponding trade-off between simplicity and accuracy.
3. Finally, there is a choice of mathematical technique for presenting the foundations of each theory in a simple and convincing fashion.

Unification of theories must study their variation along all these axes. To characterise a particular theory in programming (as in science generally), we need to describe the primitive concepts of the theory, and the way that these are related to the real world by observation or experiment. The technical terms chosen to denote these concepts are called the *alphabet* of the theory. Next, there is a choice of primitive statements of the theory and methods of combining them into more complex descriptions of experiments and products. The symbols chosen for this purpose are called the *signature* of the theory. Finally, the results of a theory are expressed by a set of equations or other *laws* that are both mathematically provable and useful in the design of programs and prediction of the results of their execution. Theories are unified by sharing elements of their alphabet, signature and laws. They are differentiated by what they do not share.

This introductory chapter concludes with a survey of challenging tasks which have not been completed in this book, and which are recommended as topics for future research and development.

0.1 Programming paradigms

Programming languages may be classified in accordance with their basic control structures, or computational *paradigm*. The earliest and most widespread paradigm is that of conventional *imperative* programming. Design of an imperative program requires planned reuse of computer storage by assigning new values to its individual locations. Examples of imperative languages are machine code, FORTRAN, COBOL, ALGOL 60, PASCAL and C. The *functional* programming paradigm makes no reference to updatable storage. It specifies a function by a formula that describes how to compute its result from its arguments. This paradigm is embodied in the languages LISP [122], ML [128, 182] and Haskell [95]. The *logical* paradigm specifies the answer to a question by defining the predicates which the answer must satisfy; search for an answer may involve backtracking, as in the language PROLOG [115], or in more recent constraint logic languages such as CLP [100] and CHIP [53].

The *parallel* programming paradigm permits a program to exploit the power of many processing units operating concurrently and cooperating in the solution of the same problem. There are many variations of this paradigm; they correspond to the different kinds of mechanism which are implemented in hardware for the connection of separate processors, and the different kinds of channel through which they communicate and interact with each other. Many of the fastest computers are designed with multiple processing units working out of a single homogeneously addressed main store. In the study of program complexity, this is known as the PRAM model [58], and it is finding application in BSP (the Bulk Synchronous Paradigm) [123, 183] for high performance computing; its characteristic feature is an occasional global synchronisation. At a much lower level of granularity, a similar kind of lockstep progression is standard in hardware design, and its theory is embodied in SCCS [125].

The other main class of parallel programming paradigm is suited to *distributed* systems. It replaces shared storage by communication of messages, output by one process and input by another. An early example was the *actor* paradigm [8, 9], in which any message output by any process could be collected at any subsequent time by any other process, or even by the same one. A similar scheme underlies Linda [63, 65, 64]. Most subsequent message passing models require them to be directed through *channels*, which connect exactly two processes. In the *data flow* variation [33, 75, 106, 107], messages which have been output by one process will be stored in the correct sequence until the inputting process calls for them. In versions designed for *asynchronous* hardware design [105, 181], the wires have no storage, so the outputting process must undertake not to send a second message until the first has been consumed. Finally, the most widely researched variant is that of fully *synchronised* communication, where the output and input of a message occur virtually simultaneously, as in the theories CCS [125, 126], ACP [23] and CSP [88], and in the programming language occam [97]. The component processes of a distributed parallel program play the role of objects in the *object-oriented* programming paradigm [41, 44, 74, 124].

Certain language properties and features can be included or omitted from any language, independently of its underlying paradigm. For example, *non-determinism* is a property of a language by which a program leaves unspecified the exact actions to be performed, or the exact result produced [50, 83, 137]. Non-determinism tends to arise implicitly in parallel languages, but it is easier to study in isolation as an explicit choice operator, independent of the language in which it is embedded.

Another capability is that of *higher order* [154] programming, which allows a program to treat other programs as data or results. It is a common feature of a functional programming language. Data structures containing programs provide another approach to object-oriented programming, and communication of such data models the program distribution capability of Java [12]. *Timing* [10] can be introduced as a facility for synchronising with a clock, measuring either resource usage or the passage of real or simulated time, and *hybrid* systems [71] include an element of continuous change, perhaps modelling an analog computer or even the real world. A surprisingly powerful feature in programming is *probability* [54], which permits the actions of a computer to be selected by random choice with specified (or unspecified) probabilities. This is widely used in simulation studies; it also promises to solve problems of fault tolerance and self-stabilisation, particularly in distributed systems.

0.2 Levels of abstraction

This survey of the branches and specialisations in the science of programming has classified them according to their choice of paradigm, language and feature. Classification by topic of study is characteristic of any branch of science in its early stages. But as our understanding matures, there often appears an orthogonal classification, by which the same materials and phenomena are treated by different theories, at different scales and different levels of complexity or abstraction. The most mature branch of science is physics, which explains the properties of matter by theories at four (or more) levels: chromodynamics deals with the interactions of quarks, quantum theory with elementary particles, nuclear physics with atoms and molecular dynamics with molecules. Above this, the theories of chemistry begin to diversify according to the choice of material studied. At each level the theory is self-contained, and can be studied in isolation. But the most spectacular achievement of physics is the discovery that the theory at each level can in principle be fully justified by embedding it in the theory below: with the aid of plausible definitions of its concepts, its laws are provable at least as approximations to the underlying reality. The necessary calculations have been checked in detail for the case of the simpler particles and atoms, and there is no reason to doubt the scientists' faith in extrapolation of their results to the cases that are too complicated for practical computation. Clarification of the hierarchical structure of physical theories is what gives the study of physics its pride of place among all the branches of science.

A similar hierarchy of theories is evident in mathematics, where set theory is the basis of topology, which provides a foundation for analysis; in its turn, analysis derives and justifies the laws of the differential calculus, which are then applied to the solution of practical problems by engineers and scientists from a broad range of disciplines. Different concepts, notations, theorems and problem solving methods are available at each of these levels. Fortunately, the successful application of each theory does not require any knowledge of its more abstract foundations.

A goal for a unified theory of programming is to suggest a very similar hierarchical approach to software engineering. Even for a single programming paradigm, a unified theory should link a family of related subtheories at various levels of abstraction. A subtheory at a macroscopic level of granularity and at a high level of abstraction will be useful for capture and analysis of the requirements of the eventual user of a software product. A theory at an intermediate level will help in the definition of the components of the product itself, and the interfaces between its subassemblies and parts. At the lowest level, a theory must fully explain the behaviour of programs written in a particular programming language. The links between all the theories at these different levels must be based on mathematical calculations and proof; without that, it is impossible to establish with confidence that the delivered program will meet the originally specified requirements.

0.3 Varieties of presentation

Even confining attention to a single theory defining a single class of phenomenon at a single level of abstraction, there is scope for wide variation in the manner in which the theory is presented. For example, the theory of gravitation may be presented in its original form as governing the effect of forces acting at a distance. A more modern presentation is in terms of field theory; yet another uses Einsteinian geodesics. All these presentations may be proved to be equally valid, because they are formally equivalent. A branch of mathematics often enjoys a similar range of styles of definition. For example, a particular topology may be defined as a family of open sets, subject to certain conditions. Alternatively it can be specified as a closure operation mapping any set onto its smallest containing closed set. Or it may be specified as a collection of neighbourhoods. Each presentation may be suitable for a different purpose; because they are known to be equivalent, an experienced mathematician will move effortlessly between them as required to solve the current problem. Understanding the relationship between the presentations ensures that the diversity is only beneficial; it is an excellent indicator of the value and maturity of the theory as a whole.

A similar diversity of presentation is seen in a theory of programming, which has to explain the meaning of the notations of a programming language. The methods of presenting such a semantic definition may be classified under three headings. The *denotational* [155, 164, 167, 172, 176] method defines each notation and formula of the language as denoting some value in a mathematical domain which is understood independently, say as a function, or as a set of trajectories, or in general as some kind of observation of the properties and behaviour of the program when executed. The *algebraic* [82, 83, 93, 137, 138, 161] style is more subtle and abstract. It does not say what programs actually mean, but if two differently written programs happen to mean the same thing, this can be proved from the equations of an algebraic presentation. An *operational* [73, 126, 151] presentation describes how a program can be executed by a series of steps of some abstract mathematical machine. As in the hardware of current general-purpose stored-program computers, the text of the program itself is often taken as part of the state of the machine.

The denotational style of definition is closest to that used most normally in mathematics, for example, to define complex numbers or matrices and operations upon them. In the case of programs and other engineering products, we can relate the definitions immediately to more or less direct observations of the execution of the program. A specification too is nothing but a description of the observations of the product which the customer will regard as acceptable. This gives an extraordinarily simple definition of the central concept of the theory, namely program correctness. To be correct, a program must be just a subset of the observations permitted by the specification. The definition of a non-deterministic union of two programs is equally simple – just the union of all the observations that might be made of either of the alternatives. Other connectives of propositional logic and predicate calculus also play an important role.

The great merit of algebra is as a powerful tool for exploring family relationships over a wide range of different theories. For example, study of the foundations of mathematics has given denotations to a wide variety of number systems – integers, reals, complex, etc. Deep distinctions are revealed in the structure and content of each kind of number so defined. It is only their algebraic properties that emphasise the family likenesses across the range of number systems. That is why we are justified in calling them all numbers, and using the same symbols for all the arithmetic operators. There are practical advantages too: the same theorems can be reused without proof in all branches of mathematics which share the same axioms. And algebra is well suited for direct use by engineers in symbolic calculation of parameters and structure of an optimal design. Algebraic proofs by term rewriting are the most promising way in which computers can assist in the process of reliable design.

The operational style of definition of a programming language is distinctive to the study of theoretical computing science, and it also plays an essential practical role. For example, the search for program efficiency and the study of abstract complexity are wholly dependent on counting the number of steps in program execution. In analysing the faults of an incorrect program, it is common to obtain information dumped from an intermediate step of the running program, and this can be interpreted only in the light of an understanding of operational semantics.

Furthermore, the existence (or at least the possibility) of implementation is the only reason for taking an interest in a particular set of notations, or dignifying them with the title of a programming language.

Each of these three styles of presentation has its distinctive advantages for a study of the theory of programming. To combine these advantages, a comprehensive theory of programming treats a programming language in all three styles, and proves that the definitions are consistent with each other in the appropriate sense. In this book, the denotational definition is given first; it provides a basis for proof of the laws needed in the algebraic presentation. At a certain stage, the laws are sufficiently powerful to derive and prove correctness of the step (transition relation) of an operational semantics. This is a natural and fairly easy progression, from abstract definitions through mathematical proof to one or more concrete implementations. But many excellent treatments of semantics [184, 73] proceed in the opposite direction, from the concrete to the abstract. Starting with an operational semantics, one can derive from it a collection of valid algebraic laws and even a denotational semantics. The derivations in this direction use methods based on the concept of simulation in automata theory. These have been further developed by computing scientists under the name *bisimulation*; this has been very successfully applied in the context of CCS [126], and can be extended to other languages.

Caution: The original presentations of the denotational semantics of a programming language made clear a notational distinction between its syntax and its semantics, and the semantics was wholly presented within the mathematical domain of partial functions. These characteristics came to be regarded by later authors as definitive of the nature of denotational semantics. The style which we call denotational has been given many alternative names: "predicative" [77, 90], "specification-oriented" [139], "application-oriented", "observational" or even "relational" [16, 117]. A pioneer of our direct style of denotational definition is Mosses [132]. The decision to return to the original term "denotational" is justified by appeal to its original significance [172, 173]:

1. Each component of the program has a meaning which is independent of its text or the manner of its execution.
2. The meaning of a larger program can be determined as a mathematical function of the *meaning* of its syntactic constituents, not of their syntactic form.

0.4 Alphabets

Our primary subject of study is a new branch of science, the science of computer programming. Like other sciences, its study requires a specialised language for describing the class of relevant phenomena arising from a well-conducted experiment, and introduces a formal framework for deducing consequences from these descriptions. In well-established branches of natural science, the observable results of an experiment are described by a collection of equations or inequations or other mathematical relations. These descriptions will be called by the general logical term *predicate*. The theory of programming uses predicates in the same way as a scientific theory, to describe the observable behaviour of a program when it is executed by computer. In fact, we will define the *meaning* of a program as a predicate which describes as exactly as possible the full range of its possible behaviour, when executed in any possible environment of its use.

Scientific predicates contain many mathematical symbols whose meaning has been defined by pure mathematicians; the laws of reasoning that govern them are ultimately based on the axioms of set theory and logic. But any scientifically meaningful predicate also contains free variables like $x, y, v, \dot{v}$, standing for possible results of measurements taken from an experiment in the real world; for example, the position of some particle, its velocity and acceleration. The relationship between these free variables and the method of observing their values can never be formalised: an understanding can be conveyed only by informal description and practical demonstration. Theories developed for individual branches of science are differentiated by their selection of relevant observations, measurements and naming conventions; the chosen collection of names will be called the *alphabet* of the theory. It is by their alphabets that we shall relate our various theories of programming. Obviously, we will choose the same names for observations that are the same in all the different theories.

Predicates are used in engineering not just to describe the behaviour of an existing product that has already been designed, produced, delivered and put into service. They are also used to specify the requirements on a new product that has not yet even been designed. Such a specification will use the agreed alphabet of free variables to describe the desired behaviour of the eventual product. It may also use any other concept that has a clearly defined or axiomatised mathematical meaning; in software engineering, we may include even the notations of the eventual programming language. The eventual program is, of course, wholly restricted to these notations. The program is *correct* if its interpretation as a predicate describing its behaviour on execution logically implies its original specification. That will ensure that no execution of the program can ever give rise to an observation that violates the specification.

Observations of an experiment may be made at various times during its progress; but the most important time is at the beginning, when the initial settings are made for the controlled variables. We adopt the convention that any observation made at this time will be denoted by an *undecorated* variable $(x, y, ok, trace)$, whereas observations made on later occasions will be *decorated*. For example, the variable x may stand for the initial value of a global variable updated by the program, and the final value of that variable on termination will be denoted x'.

Once an experiment has started, it is usual to wait for some initial transient behaviour to stabilise before making any further observation, and under certain initial conditions, this may never happen. To represent this possibility, we introduce a Boolean variable *ok* (and its decorated version *ok'*), which takes the value *true* just when the program has reached a stable and therefore observable state. Consequently, *ok* is true of any program that has started, and *ok'* is true of any program that has successfully terminated. In a simple theory of sequential programming, initiation and termination are the only occasions on which the state of executing mechanism may be observed.

A programming language is called *reactive* if the behaviour of its programs can be observed or even altered at stable states intermediate between initiation and termination. To distinguish intermediate states from final ones, we introduce another Boolean variable *wait*, which is true when the program is in a stable intermediate state, and which is false if the program has terminated; after termination, further intermediate observations are of course impossible. A sequential language does not need a *wait* variable, because there are no intermediate observations, and so it would always be false.

We take a view shared with quantum theory that each intermediate observation is an event that may change the subsequent behaviour both of the experiment and of the observer. We introduce the name $\mathcal{A}$ to stand for the set of all possible events that may occur at intermediate stages of the program execution, together with any values that may be measured or observed on that occasion. A typical event may be the exchange of some message with the environment within which the program is running. The value of the message will be observed and recorded, together with the identity of the channel along which it is communicated. $\mathcal{A}$ contains or consists of the set of all such records of communication events.

We use the name *trace* to stand for a cumulative record of all observations that have been made of a program so far. This may be organised as a finite sequence of observations from it, corresponding to the temporal order of occurrence of these events: simultaneous events have to be recorded in arbitrary order. In theories of so-called *true concurrency*, strict interleaving is not needed because the trace is regarded as partially rather than totally ordered. For reasoning about fairness, infinite traces also have to be admitted.

Programming languages of the reactive class offer a facility for synchronisation with the observer on the occasion of each observation. When the program has reached a stable intermediate state (i.e. *wait* is true), it will remain in this state until the environment actually makes the relevant observation, for example by accepting an output message or providing an input message. But not all observations are always possible: on any given occasion, a certain subset of events will be *refused*, even if the environment is ready and willing to engage in them. Such a subset of events is known as a *refusal*. Constraints on the refusal set permit an analysis of the responsiveness or liveness of a distributed system.

The lowest level of programming language is known as *machine code*, because its programs are directly executed by a particular brand of computing machinery. Execution of the program is controlled by the value of a program pointer held in a special hardware sequence control register. This will be denoted by the special global variable *control*, ranging over values in a set αl. This set contains the location numbers of those memory cells which actually store the binary instructions of a given segment of the machine code program. By convention, termination of the program results whenever *control* first takes a value outside αl. The *control* variable is also relevant in a higher level language with jumps and labels. In this case, αl contains the symbolic names of all the labels placed within the program text. We use the control constants *start* and *finish* to stand for implicit labels placed before the beginning and after the end of the program. They are the initial value and final value taken by *control* when the program starts and finishes smoothly, without a jump.

One of the main goals of programming theory is to abstract from the notion of real time; this ensures that the correctness of a program will be unaffected by running it on a faster computer or even a slower one. For many important programs known as *real-time* programs, this abstraction is impossible, because the speed of response is part of the very specification of the program. For describing the behaviour of these programs, we use the variable *clock* (or c) to stand for the real global time at which an observation is made. Real time is distinguished from *resource* time, which keeps a record of the utilisation of processor cycles during the execution of a program; in general, it does not increase while the program is waiting. In a multiprocessor implementation *resource* is a vector quantity, recording utilisation of the various resources available.

That concludes our survey of the main common naming conventions for observations that can be made before, during and after execution of a program. Just as in other branches of science, a specialised theory will select as its alphabet only a subset of all possible observations of the world, as summarised in Appendix 0. At the same time specialisation restricts the range of experimental designs to ensure that all the relevant phenomena can still be predicted within its deliberately limited conceptual framework. In the case of a programming language, a successful restriction will guarantee that programs and their components can be safely specified and designed and proved correct within the restricted alphabet, in confidence that the delivered program will not fail as a result of factors left out of consideration. The benefit of ignoring irrelevant concerns is an obvious gain in simplicity of reasoning but it may also bring benefits in efficiency of implementation of the program and of the more restricted programming language.

The remaining sections of this chapter summarise the methods and conclusions of this book for the benefit of readers who already have some exposure to the mathematical treatment of programming. Other readers may prefer to return to them at a later stage, say after Chapter 4.

0.5 Signatures

Suppose a fixed alphabet has been selected for investigation of a particular programming language. The first task of the theory is to define the meaning of every program in the language as a predicate, with free variables restricted to the alphabet of the language. The predicate should describe as accurately as desired the entire range of observations that could be made of the program when executed. The primitive statements of the language are defined directly by such a predicate. A composite program is built from simpler components by means of the various operators of the language. Each programming operator is therefore defined as an operator on the predicates that describe its operands; this delivers a predicate that describes, again with all appropriate accuracy, the observations of an execution of the larger composite program; each such observation is usually an amalgam of single observations derived from each of the component programs.

The set of operators and atomic components (constants) of a programming theory are known as its *signature*. Essentially, the signature defines the *syntax* of a simple programming language, though a practical language based on the theory may have a much more elaborate syntax, with convenient abbreviations for a number of common idioms. There is a close correlation between the choice of a signature of a theory and its alphabet. Choice of a smaller alphabet restricts the choice of operators to those that can be defined and explained by predicates using only the restricted alphabet.

The concept of a signature is one that is familiar to students of algebra. The signature is the first part of the definition of which branch of algebra is selected for study. For example, the first four rows of Table 0.5.1 contain the operators and constants relevant to lattice theory. The columns of the table give alternative notations which are used in different applications of the algebra, for example propositional calculus or set theory. (Note that the square operators are the other way up from the angular and round ones.) These examples happen also to be Boolean algebras, in which negation is also a valid operation (row 5). A complete lattice is one in which even infinite sets have bounds; they are denoted by the limit operators of rows 6 and 7. They correspond to existential and universal quantification in the predicate calculus. The last three rows of the table extend the signature to that of a relational algebra. Relational algebra lies at the basis of our unification of theories of programming, and its mathematical properties are common to all branches.

1 greatest lower bound	$\sqcap$	$\vee$	$\cup$	union
2 least upper bound	$\sqcup$	$\wedge$	$\cap$	intersection
3 bottom	$\perp$	*true*	U	universe
4 top	$\top$	*false*	$\{\}$	empty
5 negation		$\neg$	overbar	complement
6 lower limit	$\bigsqcap$	$\exists$	$\bigcup$	join
7 upper limit	$\bigsqcup$	$\forall$	$\bigcap$	meet
8 composition	;			product
9 converse	$\smile$			
10 unit, skip	$\mathit{\Pi}$	$1'$		identity

Table 0.5.1 Signatures for relations/predicates/sets

A predicate used for specification may be structured with the aid of any of these operators, and indeed any other operator definable in mathematics. Any mathematically sound proof technique may be applied to reasoning about specifications, but there is considerable advantage in restricting predicates to those expressed in smaller sets of notations. This is because notationally restricted predicates are susceptible to a more powerful range of simpler proof techniques. These include familiar methods of symbolic calculation using just the algebraic properties of the chosen operators. Sometimes the algebra permits reduction to a *normal form*; perhaps there is even a decision procedure that can be implemented on a computer. The need for a proof is strongest in the design phase of a project. A language intended for this phase will therefore omit some of the symbols of a specification language. Negation is usually the first operator to go, together with the infinitary limit operators. At the same time, a design calculus introduces other operators which begin to model the global structure of the eventual target program, and thereby provide facilities for programming-in-the-large. These new operators can be defined with the aid of the more abstract operators, even ones that have been deliberately excluded from the signature. However, the excluded operators are used in carefully disciplined ways that do not invalidate the more powerful proof techniques of the design calculus.

In the design of a programming language there is an even stronger reason for restricting the signature of permitted operators yet further: all expressible programs must be computable in the sense of Turing and Church, and preferably they should be implemented with reasonable efficiency on available computing equipment. This requires the exclusion not only of negation but also of conjunction and **false**, for **false** cannot correctly describe any system whatsoever.

The signature of a programming theory at the lowest level of abstraction must obviously include all the notations and operators for the target programming language. Table 0.5.2 gives the signature of basic notations common to nearly all languages treated in this book. Again, they can all be defined in terms of the more abstract operators that have been excluded from the language, but again they use them in such a disciplined way that computability is preserved.

$x := e$	assignment of the value of expression e to the variable x
$P; Q$	sequential composition: Q is executed after P has terminated
$P \lhd b \rhd Q$	conditional: P is executed if b is true initially, otherwise Q
$P \sqcap Q$	non-determinism: P or Q is executed, but it is not specified which
$\|\|$	parallel execution of processes with disjoint alphabets
var x	introduces a new variable x
end x	terminates the scope of the variable x
$\mu X \bullet F(X)$	call a recursive procedure which has name X and body $F(X)$

Table 0.5.2 Signature of a programming language

In general programming theory, each program and each part of a program may have its own different alphabet selected from the alphabet of the theory. For example, we have already seen that each block of program has its own local variables; each process in a distributed system has a different set $\mathcal{A}$ of events in which it can participate; and in machine code, each segment of the program *must* have a disjoint set αl of locations in which its instructions are stored. In principle, each constant and operator of the signature should be subscripted by the alphabets of its operands and of its results, giving a *heterogeneous* or multi-sorted algebra [42]. In practice the alphabets are omitted, but in a way that permits a compiler to restore them automatically from the context. In exploring the theory, a knowledge of the alphabet is sometimes essential to a definition of the meaning, especially of primitive components like assignments.

Parallel programming languages are those that provide some mechanism for executing two or more programs at the same time, in a way that permits them to interact by sharing one or more global variables in their alphabet. But there is considerable variation in the ways in which the components P and Q may be connected together for mutual interaction. We therefore give a general definition of parallel composition as a *ternary* operator $(P \|_M Q)$, where M is a third predicate describing the way in which observations of P and Q are merged to give an observation of their parallel execution. For example, a particular choice of M will give the independent interleaving operator ($|||$ of CSP), and others will give the more tightly coupled parallel composition ($|$) of CCS or ACP. A reactive parallel language will also provide an external choice operator $[\!]$ (or $+$), which enables the choice between two alternative courses of action to be taken by other processes running in parallel.

$\|_M$	parallel composition of type M	$\|, \|$
$[\!]$	external choice	$+$
$c?x$	input a new value of x from channel c	$c.x$
$c!e$	output the value of e on channel x	$\bar{c}.e$
$\|\|\|$	parallelism with interleaving of actions	

Table 0.5.3 Parallelism and communication in CSP and CCS

A selection from the signatures of these more complex programming languages is given in Table 0.5.3. Each of these new operators is definable in terms of the more basic notations of Table 0.5.2. The definitions involve reference and assignment to special observational variables, such as *trace*, *refusal* or *wait*, which are included in the alphabet of the language. It is essential, both to the theory and to its implementation, that these variables are manipulated *only* by means of the operators of the signature. The programmer cannot be allowed to access or change these variables by arbitrary assignment, because it would be clearly impossible to implement (for example) an assignment that moves time backwards or cancels an event that has already occurred. The more complex languages, which need a larger alphabet of concepts to capture and reason about specifications, also need a larger signature of operators to conceal this alphabet from the programmer. But when the definitions of the operators are expanded, it turns out that the complex programs are just a subset of programs expressible in the simple language, in the same way that programs are just a subset of the predicates expressible in a design language or a specification.

0.6 Laws

The main purpose of the mathematical definition of a programming operator is to deduce its interesting mathematical properties. These are most elegantly expressed as algebraic laws – equations usually, but sometimes inequations, with implication between predicates rather than equivalence. For a newly defined binary operator, the first questions are: Is it associative or commutative? Does it have a unit or a zero? And how does it distribute through other operators? Sequential composition clearly should be associative; it has $I\!I$ as its unit and distributes through disjunction. Many forms of parallel composition share these properties, and are also commutative.

The primary goal of theorists at this stage is to prove a collection of laws which is sufficiently comprehensive that any other true inequation between programs can be derived from the laws alone by algebraic reasoning, without ever again expanding the definition of the operators. This is achieved by defining a highly restricted subset of the programming language, known as a *normal form*; such a form may be defined by excluding many of the operators of the language, and requiring a fixed order of application of the others. Then a proof is given that every program in the language can be reduced by the laws to a normal form (though in practice it is more usually an expansion).

An important goal of a normal form is to help in a test whether two arbitrary programs are equal (or related by implication). Suppose a simple test is available for comparing normal forms. Then the test may be applied to any pair of programs, by first reducing them both to normal form. The reduction may be within the capability of a computer. For human benefit, the task of understanding the whole theory is simplified by separately understanding the simple normal form and the laws by which it may be derived.

The laws for a language may be powerful enough for reduction to several different normal forms, each of them useful for a different purpose. One important purpose of an algebraic transformation is to match the structure of a program to the architecture of the computer on which it will be executed. This is done by a compiler for the language whenever it translates a high level program to machine code. All the control structures of the program are translated to jumps, the data structures are replaced by single-dimensional array references, the local data are held in machine registers, and the expressions and assignments are translated to sequences of commands selected from the very limited range of available machine instructions. Defining this as the normal form, a proof that every program can be transformed to it is simultaneously a proof of correctness of a compiling algorithm that carries out the transformation.

A final advantage to be derived from a normal form is an easy proof of certain additional algebraic properties that are true for all normal forms, and therefore for all programs reducible to that kind of normal form. But such laws are not true for all predicates in general. A predicate that happens to satisfy such a law is called *healthy*, and the law is called a *healthiness condition*. Predicates expressed in intermediate design languages tend to satisfy many but not all of the healthiness conditions of the eventual target programs.

There are often sound physical reasons why programs will always satisfy a given healthiness condition. For example, no program can ever make time go backwards or change the history of what happens before it starts. Let B be a predicate describing all physically possible observations, for example

$$B \;=\; (clock \le clock') \;\wedge\; (trace \le trace') \;\wedge \ldots$$

No physically realisable program P can ever give rise to an observation that violates this, a fact that is expressed by the healthiness condition

$$P \Rightarrow B \quad \text{(or equivalently } P \;=\; P \wedge B\text{)}, \qquad \text{for all programs } P$$

At the other extreme, there are certain observations that a given theory regards as irrelevant. They are perfectly feasible, and nothing can prevent such observations being made: they just violate the rules of experimentation that make the theory applicable. Typical examples could be observations made before the program starts, or observations taken when the program is still in a transient or unstable state. Let T be a predicate describing all such improper observations. Since they cannot be prevented, every program must allow them, as expressed in the healthiness condition

$$T \Rightarrow \; P \quad \text{(or equivalently } P = T \vee P\text{)}, \qquad \text{for all programs } P$$

Clearly T and B are a new top and bottom of the lattice of those predicates which satisfy both conditions.

Similarly, let J be a description of the way a program should be initialised, and let K be a description of the way in which the final observation of the program should be taken. Let us suppose (not unreasonably) that repeated initialisation or finalisation has the same effect as just once, that is

$$J = J; J \quad \text{and} \quad K = K; K$$

Since every program P should have been properly initialised and finalised, it must satisfy the healthiness conditions

$$P = J; P \quad \text{and} \quad P = P; K$$

Healthiness conditions play much the same role in programming theory as principles of symmetry and conservation in science. They are not themselves testable by experiment; they are accepted because they are preserved by all known theories that do predict testable results. A well-established principle is then used as a preliminary screen to prevent waste of time considering a theory that violates it. Similarly, a healthiness condition can be used to test a specification or design for *feasibility*, and reject it if it makes implementation demonstrably impossible in the target programming language.

All the healthiness conditions described above have the same general shape

$$P = P \odot X \qquad (\text{or } P = X \odot P)$$

where $\odot$ is an associative operator (e.g. $\sqcap$, $\sqcup$, ;) and X itself satisfies the same healthiness condition

$$X = X \odot X$$

As a consequence of this idempotence principle for X, an arbitrary predicate P can be made more healthy by application of the function

$$\phi(P) =_{df} P \odot X$$

Such a function is called a *coercion*, and it plays an important role in linking theories, which may be ranked according to the healthiness conditions that they satisfy. At a level closer to specification they satisfy few; at a level close to the program they satisfy all. Coercions are potentially helpful in making the transition between the stages of a design project, to transform a design document from one level to the next in the hierarchy.

Healthiness conditions are summarised in Appendix 3. They have an important role in unification of theories of programming. They are used to differentiate programming paradigms, to classify them in families, and to clarify the choices that should be made by a programming language designer. The observance of healthiness conditions is the main cause and motivation for complexity in the definitions of a programming theory, and their isolation for independent study is a vital contribution to mastering this complexity.

0.7 Challenges that remain

Unifying theories of programming is an activity that has dominated the authors' research for over ten years. This book concentrates on those theories that have been found most amenable to unification. The study is far from complete. So far, it uses only the simplest methods to treat the most elementary aspects of the basic programming paradigms. To complete the study will require the dedicated cooperation of many theorists, exploring more deeply and far more widely the topics in which they have specialist skills and interests. To bring the results of the study to bear upon the practical problems of software engineering will require long term investment from the builders and suppliers of design automation tools. This section suggests a number of the important challenges that remain.

The first challenge is to extend the range of programming paradigms and features defined and studied within the unifying network. The omissions of this book include: the actor paradigm for parallel programming [8, 9], the process algebra CCS [126], and all varieties of temporal logic [113, 118, 136, 152]. *True concurrency* [146, 147, 148] and *fairness* [60, 144] have been unfairly neglected. The treatment of time and object orientation [10, 41, 44, 73, 74, 84] is only cursory, and the probabilistic paradigm [54] is altogether omitted. No attempt has been made to pursue analogies with computer hardware design, which offers an excellent example of a design hierarchy, ranging over transistor switching circuits, asynchronous circuits, combinational logic, and clocked sequential circuits. A good test for a unifying theory would be to formalise and validate all these interfaces. A more demanding test is to integrate them with the underlying continuous universe at one end [61], and the discrete world of programming at the other [62]. The results could be beneficial to reliable design of hybrid systems, involving a mixture of hardware, software and real-world components.

There are also many newer programming languages, practices and concepts which have not yet been investigated by programming theory. These include languages designed for more specific tasks, such as the calculation and display of spreadsheets, the control of graphical interfaces, the generation of menus, or the maintenance and interrogation of large scale data bases. Many critical computing systems are already implemented in these languages, possibly in combination with each other or with some general-purpose language. As in other branches of engineering, it is such combination of technologies that can present the gravest problems of design and maintenance. The responsible engineer needs to understand the science which underlies each of the pure technologies, as well as that which explains the possible interactions across their interfaces, because the interfaces provide a breeding ground for the most elusive, costly and persistent errors. Avoidance of such errors may be a long term benefit from study of the common theory which underlies all the technologies involved.

The level of exposition in this book is essentially introductory. Each new feature and concept is treated in isolation and in the simplest possible approach, ignoring many known complexities and perhaps some unknown ones as well. These complexities will be discovered, studied and hopefully remedied by those who take up the challenge of applying the theories in combination to complete programming languages. Priority should be given to languages that are already supported by recognised design methods and widely used support tools. Examples from hardware are Verilog [141] and VHDL [163]. On the software side, similar support is given by state charts for embedded systems, SDL [36, 37] for telecommunications, and UML (Unified Modeling Language) [59] for general data processing.

The mathematical methods used in the book are taken from logic, algebra and discrete mathematics. The only real novelty is that these branches of pure mathematics have been turned into applied mathematics. This has been accompanied by a shift in emphasis away from the pure functions that feature so strongly in mathematical tradition. Their primary role has been taken over by the more general concept of a relation. But for deeper investigation of programming theory, mathematicians and computing scientists have developed a range of more sophisticated techniques. Examples from this book include operational semantics, bisimulation and predicate transformers. Further contributions to unifying theories may be expected from the π-calculus [127], from type theory [39, 166], and from game-theoretic modelling [4]. Of particular promise are the classificatory concepts of abstract algebra and category theory [22, 96, 116, 170].

The final and most critical challenge is to bring the contributions of the theory of programming to the aid of programmers engaged in the almost impossible task of reliable design, development and maintenance of computer systems. Such aid is especially needed for very large programs, and for applications in which the consequences of design error could be critical. But first, the methods recommended by the theory should be widely tested on much smaller case studies. These should still be large enough that it is realistic to formalise a specification at a higher level of abstraction than the eventual implementation. The real benefit of a unifying theory will be most appropriately tested if there is more than one stage of design, or more than one implementation paradigm, selected as alternatives or even used in combination. Such case studies are completely absent from this book. The largest example program is about three lines. Fortunately, this does not detract from the value of the theory, which is inherently scalable. Its results are expressed as formulae with variables ranging over all programs, with no limit to their size. The glory of all of mathematics is that its truths are independent of the magnitude and accuracy of numbers, the dimensions of matrices, or the complexity of functions.

But when mathematics first finds application in industry, the problem of scale cannot be ignored. With increasing complexity of case studies, and even more in live application, the size of the programs, formulae and proofs are such that computer assistance is needed to manage them. In hardware design, the use of a range of design automation tools is now considered essential to the production of ever more complex devices at ever shortening intervals, with ever increasing requirement for accuracy. Software design is more complex and less generally well understood, and the state of the art is well behind that of hardware. Nevertheless, there are very promising developments. A good example is provided by symbolic algebra systems (Maple [3], Mathematica [186]), which are routinely used for continuous mathematical symbol processing in science and engineering. In hardware design, new and improved model-checkers (SPIN [94], FDR [159]) are capable of detecting errors in high level algorithms well in advance of implementation. Term rewriting systems (OBJ3 [67]) can reliably calculate the details of a transition from one level of abstraction to another, or reliably optimise a design at a single level. Decision procedures (PVS [143]) can check the validity of the individual steps of a design at the time that they are taken. More difficult tasks can be delegated to a proof search engine [56]. Increased hardware speeds and main store sizes are reinforcing the benefits of improved algorithms for symbol manipulation, and the rate of progress is not decreasing.

At present, the main available mechanised mathematical tools are programmed for use in isolation, and many of them are targeted towards general use in logical and mathematical proof. To extend them to meet the needs of software engineering, it will be necessary to build within each tool a structured library of programming design aids which take the advantage of the particular strengths of that tool. To ensure that the tools may safely be used in combination, it is essential that these theories be unified. In the long run, the tools also should be unified. Only then will we overcome the main barrier to industrial acceptance of both tools and theories: that there are too many of them and they all compete for attention by individual claims of universal applicability, exclusive of all the others. Achievement of a proper balance of healthy competition with eager cooperation of specialist researchers and schools has always been necessary for progress in science, and it has often been the result of unifying previously unconnected theories. Let it be so for programming too.

Chapter 1

The Logic of Engineering Design

A scientific theory takes the form of an equation or a set of equations and inequation, usually expressed in the language of mathematics. We will use the general logical term *predicate* to stand for such mathematical descriptions. The purpose of the predicate is to describe and therefore predict all possible observations that can be made directly or indirectly of any system from a given reproducible class. The values obtained by physical measurement are denoted by free variables occurring in the formulae. An example is Einstein's famous equation

$$e = mc^2$$

where	e	is the energy of the system
	m	is its mass
and	c	is the speed of light.

Considerable familiarity with physics is needed to correlate the variables e and m and the constant c with the physical reality which they refer to. Nothing but confusion would result if the names of these variables were replaced by arbitrary alternatives, for example: $f = nd^2$.

The same physical system may be described at many different levels of abstraction and granularity; for example, physics can describe the material world as a collection of interacting quarks, or elementary particles, or atoms, or molecules, or crystal structures. All these descriptions lie well below the common-sense level of the physical objects which we see and touch in the everyday world. Science has discovered independent theories for reasoning at each of these levels of abstraction. But even more impressive is the demonstration that each theory is logically based on the more detailed theory below it. This is the strongest argument for the soundness of each separate theory, and also for the coherence of the entire intellectual structure of modern physics.

Mathematical theories expressed as predicates play an equally decisive role in engineering. A significant engineering project begins with a specification describing as directly as possible the observable properties and behaviour of the desired product. The design documents, formulated at various stages of the project, are indirect descriptions of the same behaviour. They are expressed in some restricted notation, at a level of abstraction appropriate to guide the physical implementation. This implementation is correct if its detailed description logically implies its specification; for then any observation of the product will be among those described and therefore permitted by the specification. The success of the whole project depends not only on correct reasoning at each level of design, but also on the soundness of the transition between the decreasing levels of abstraction appropriate to the successive stages of specification, design and implementation.

An engineering product is usually delivered as an assembly of components, which in general operate concurrently. The operation of each component can be described scientifically by a specific predicate, describing all its possible behaviours, including all its possible interactions with any other components which may be connected to it in an assembly. For this reason, the joint behaviour of many components in the assembly can often be described by the conjunction of these predicates describing the components separately. If some aspect of the component cannot be fully determined in advance, it may be described by the disjunction of predicates describing its alternative modes of behaviour. Finally, the links between predicates describing behaviour at different levels of granularity and abstraction can be formalised by quantification. In summary, the elementary operators of propositional and predicate logic provide all the basic concepts needed for a systematic engineering design methodology.

The goal of this book is to apply the philosophy and methods of modern science and engineering to the study and practice of computer programming. A computer program, and each of its components, is treated as a mathematical formula, describing the experimental observations which may be made by executing it in any variety of circumstances. The same phenomena may be described at several different levels of abstraction; the consistency of the various presentations can be assured by mathematical calculation and proof. The theory is developed first for a very simple programming language, which is then extended piecemeal; at each stage, it is hoped to preserve the validity and simplicity of what has gone before. The eventual goal is to develop theories which may be useful in the engineering of computer software, from specification of requirements through modular design to reliable implementation, installation and subsequent maintenance.

The full treatment of a simple programming language starts in Chapter 2. The remainder of this chapter develops the general philosophy of our approach to the science of programming and its application to software engineering.

1.1 Observations and alphabets

The first task of the scientist is to isolate some interesting class of reproducible system for detailed study. At the same time, a selection must be made of those properties which are regarded as observable or controllable or generally relevant to understanding and prediction of system behaviour. For each property, a name is chosen to denote its value, and instructions are given on how and when that property is to be observed, in what unit it is to be measured, etc. The list of names is usually accompanied by a declaration of the type of value over which each of them ranges, for example

$$x : \text{integer}, \quad y : \text{real}, \quad \ldots, \quad z : \text{Boolean}$$

This collection of names is known as an *alphabet*, and the names will occur as free variables, together with physical constants and other mathematical symbols, in any predicate describing the general properties of the system. They are called variables because their values vary from one experiment to another, conducted on a different system at a different place and time. Each theory in each branch of science is determined and delimited by its own choice of alphabet, and every formula and predicate of the theory has its free variables restricted to that alphabet.

We therefore require that every predicate P has associated with it (usually implicitly) a known set of free variables which it is allowed to contain. This is known as the *alphabet* of the predicate, abbreviated as αP. Often the predicate will contain all the variables of its alphabet, but there is no compulsion for it to do so. If the predicate has nothing to say about an observation x in its alphabet, that variable does not have to occur; or if preferred, it may be included vacuously by adding the trivial equation $(x = x)$. Of course, it is always forbidden for a predicate to contain free variables outside its alphabet.

An *observation* of a particular example of the chosen class of system can be expressed as a very limited kind of predicate. It consists only of a set of equations, ascribing particular constant values to each of the variables in the alphabet, for example

$$x = 4 \ \wedge \ y = 37.3 \ \wedge \ldots \wedge \ z = \text{false}$$

In logic, such observations are called *valuations* or *interpretations*; in computing, the instantaneous *state* of a machine executing a program is often recorded in this way as a "symbolic dump" of the values of all its variables at the time the observation is made.

Most of the dynamic variables treated in the physical sciences are functions which map a continuously varying time to a continuum of possible values. Consider for example a simple tank containing a liquid. The variables of its alphabet selected to describe the state of the system might be:

t (measured in seconds) is the time since the start of the apparatus ($t = 0$),
v_t stands for the measurable volume of liquid in the tank (in litres),
x_t is the total amount of liquid poured into the tank up to time t,
y_t is the total amount drained from the tank up to time t,
a_t is the setting of the input valve at time t (in degrees),
b_t is the setting of the output valve at time t.

The relationship between the symbolic variables and the real measurements that they denote is often illustrated by an annotated picture (Figure 1.1.1).

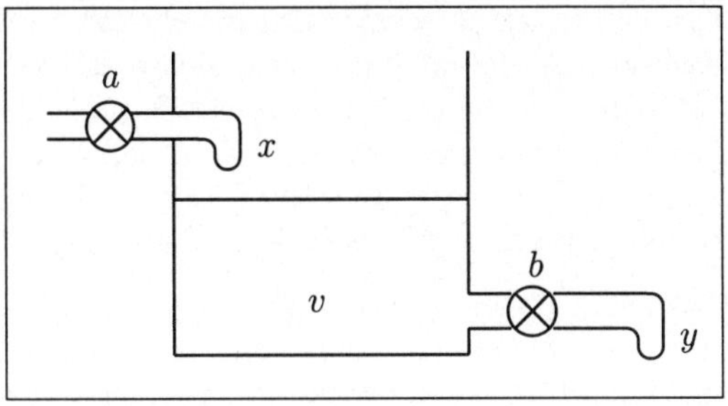

Figure 1.1.1 The water tank

In constructing a simple theory for a sequential programming language, we decide that the only relevant times at which observations can be made of its state are before the program starts and after it terminates; the decision to ignore all intermediate values of the variables is based on the reasonable hope that they will not be needed in the formulation of the theory. At the relevant times it is possible to record the values of all the global variables accessed or updated by the program. We will therefore need two names for each variable x: the final value will be recorded under the dashed name x', whereas the name x itself will stand for the initial value. An observation of a single completed execution of a particular program will give both the values observed, before and after; for example

$$x = 5 \wedge x' = 7 \wedge y = 2$$

may be an observation of a particular run of the program

$$x := x + y$$

The criterion of successful choice of an appropriate set of observations is nothing less than the success of the scientific theory that predicts their values. As Einstein remarked, it is the theory that determines what is observable. If there are too many observables, the theory gets too complicated; too few variables will make the theory inaccurate or restrict its range of application; and in general, the wrong choice will incur both penalties. In the following chapters, there will be examples of such failure, from which useful lessons will be drawn.

1.2 Behaviour and predicates

The normal discourse of scientists and engineers is wholly dependent on an agreed interpretation in reality of the alphabet of names used to describe observations or measurements. Only this makes it possible to perform experiments and record the observations against the relevant observation name. Scientific investigation often starts with a long, detailed and accurate record of particular observations of particular systems, and actual individual observations continue to play a decisive role throughout the later development of scientific knowledge. But the real purpose and goal of science are to replace this merely historical record by a theory of sufficient accuracy and power to predict the observations that will be made in experiments that remain to be performed in the future. A scientific theory is usually expressed as a mathematical *predicate* – an equation or an inequation or a collection of such formulae – which contain as *free* variables the names which have been selected to denote observations. Consider an observation

$$x = 12 \ \wedge \ y = 37.3 \ \ \wedge \ldots \wedge \ \ z = \text{ false}$$

A predicate $P(x, y, \ldots, z)$ correctly describes this particular observation if substitution of each variable by its observed value makes the predicate true (*satisfies* it)

$$P(12,\ 37.3,\ \ldots,\ \text{false})$$

But the purpose of the predicate is to describe in general a whole class of system, and it does so correctly if it describes every possible observation of every possible experiment made on any member of the class.

A useful scientific predicate is one that is as strong as possible, subject to the constraint of correctness: in general, it should be false exactly when its variables take combinations of values which in reality never occur together. This recommendation is violated by the weakest possible predicate, namely **true** (or equivalently, $x = x \wedge y = y$), which is satisfied by every conceivable observation. It therefore correctly describes every system, and it is useless because it does so. The strongest predicate **false** is equally useless for the opposite reason: there is no system which it describes. (If there were, it would necessarily have no observations, and therefore be inaccessible to science.) All of science is concerned with predicates that lie strictly between the two extremes of absolute logical truth and absolute falsity. Only such intermediate predicates convey useful information about what goes on in the world that we happen to live in.

Predicates describing the world are sometimes called Laws of Nature. They often take the form of a conservation principle or a differential equation. In the example of the water tank, the obvious law of conservation of liquid defines an invariant relationship between total inflow, total outflow and retained volume

$$x_t + v_0 = y_t + v_t \pm t \times \epsilon, \qquad \text{for all } t \geq 0$$

where $\epsilon \leq \epsilon_{max}$, the maximum rate of accumulation of errors due to seepage, evaporation, precipitation, condensation, overflow, etc.

Other physical constraints may be imposed as inequations on the setting of the valves

$$0 \leq a_t \leq amax, \qquad 0 \leq b_t \leq bmax$$

Finally, the relationship between the valve settings and the flow of liquid may be expressed by differential equations, say

$$\dot{x} = k \times a \quad \text{and} \quad \dot{y} = k \times b + \delta \times v$$

where δ accounts for extra outflow due to pressure of water in the tank, and $\dot{x}$ and $\dot{y}$ are the rates of change in x and y.

This collection of mathematical equations and inequations is strong enough to make a prediction about future water volumes, given sufficiently precise knowledge of the valve settings and the other variables and constants in the system.

The fundamental constituent of a sequential program is an assignment statement, for example

$$x := x + y$$

This causes the final value of x to be equal to the sum of the initial values of x and y. The effect is formally described by the predicate

$$x' = x + y$$

No restriction is placed on the initial or final values of any other global variables. Since no assignment is made to y, we choose to say nothing of the final value y'. Later, we will even exclude y' from the alphabet of the predicate. But still, the predicate can be used to help predict the final value of x on every single execution of the program.

A multiple assignment evaluates a list of expressions, and assigns their values to corresponding members of a list of variables; for example, the assignment

$$x, y := x + 3, \ y - x$$

is captured by the predicate

$$x' = x + 3 \ \wedge \ y' = y - x$$

This clearly states that all the expressions on the right of the assignment must be evaluated with the initial values of all the variables that they contain, and only then is it allowed to assign the new values to the variables on the left of the assignment. In the interests of consistency, we require that all the assigned variables (on the left of :=) be distinct. The simplicity of this treatment of general assignment justifies the use of undashed variables to stand for initial values, and dashed variants (which are not allowed in the programming language itself) to stand for final values.

Scientists and engineers are entirely familiar with the practice of describing systems by predicates with an understood alphabet of free variables. They habitually transform, manipulate, differentiate and integrate textual formulae containing free variables, which have an external meaning independent of the formulae in which they occur. Such practices have been decried by pure mathematicians and logicians, who tend to use bound variables and closed mathematical abstractions like sets, functions and (less commonly) relations. But the conflict is only one of style, not of substance. Every predicate $P(x, y, \ldots, z)$ can be identified with the closed set of all tuples of observations that satisfy it

$$\{(x, y, \ldots, z) \mid P(x, y, \ldots, z)\}$$

Conversely, every formula S describing a set of observations can be rewritten as a predicate

$$(x, y, \ldots, z) \in S$$

A preference for the closed or open style of presentation of theories can influence a lifelong choice between specialisation as a pure or an applied mathematician. The preferences of pure mathematicians are explained by their main concern, which is the proof of mathematical theorems – formulae without free variables which are equivalent to the predicate **true**. Since our concern is primarily with descriptions of physical systems, we shall prefer to use predicates containing free variables selected from an alphabet whose existence, composition and meaning can only be explained informally by relating them to reality. In fact we have already begun to identify systems with descriptions of their behaviour, so that we can combine, manipulate and transform the descriptions in a manner which corresponds to the assembly and use of the corresponding systems in the real world. In this, we will see that the universal truth of abstract mathematical theorems, so useless for direct description of reality, plays an essential role in validating the transformations applied to such descriptions by scientists and engineers, and among them the engineers of software.

1.3 Conjunction

Propositional logic provides many ways of constructing complex predicates from simpler ones; the first and most important of these is undoubtedly *conjunction*, which we write as $\wedge$. If it needs definition, the following will suffice:

1. An observation satisfies a conjunction $(P \wedge Q)$ **iff** it satisfies both P and Q.
2. The alphabet of $(P \wedge Q)$ is the union of the separate alphabets of P and Q.

Conjunction is extremely useful in describing the behaviour of a product that is constructed from (say) two components with known behaviour, described individually by the two predicates P and Q. Consider first the simple but important case, when the alphabets of P and Q are *disjoint*, containing no variable in common, for example $\alpha P = \{x\}$ and $\alpha Q = \{z\}$. Then their conjunction $(P \wedge Q)$ describes the behaviour of two completely separate components, the first of which is described by $P(x)$ and the second by $Q(z)$. There is no connection between the components, and no synchronisation or coordination of their behaviour. Each observation (say, $x = 7 \wedge z = 3$) of their joint behaviour can be split in two: one part $(x = 7)$ involves only variables from the alphabet of P, and this part satisfies $P(x)$; the rest of the observation $(z = 3)$ similarly satisfies $Q(z)$. That is exactly the condition under which the whole observation satisfies $(P \wedge Q)$.

As an example, consider two programs operating on entirely disjoint collections of global variables. The two programs can be executed together in either order, or even in parallel. The combined effect of their execution is most simply described as the conjunction of the separate effects of each component. We use $\|$ to denote parallel execution of two assignments

$$x := x + z \parallel y := y - w$$

Their combined behaviour is precisely described by the conjunction of their separate behaviours

$$(x' = x + z) \wedge (y' = y - w)$$

It can be seen that the effect is the same as the multiple assignment

$$x, y := x + z,\ y - w$$

In most cases of interest, components of an engineering product are connected together in such a way that they can interact and thereby affect each other's behaviour. In principle, such an interaction can also be observed from the outside, and the observation can be recorded in some variable, say y. The interaction and its observation belong simultaneously to the behaviour of *both* the components which participate in it. The physical possibility of interaction is therefore represented by the fact that the variable y belongs to the alphabet of *both* of the predicates P and Q that describe them. In order for an observation (say, $x = 7 \wedge y = 12$) of one component P to be coupled with an observation (say, $y = 12 \wedge z = 3$) from the other component Q, it is essential that both observations give the *same* value to all the variables they share (in this case, just y), so that the coupling gives (say) $x = 7 \wedge y = 12 \wedge z = 3$. Such a coupled observation can still be split into two overlapping parts, one of which contains only the variables in the alphabet of

P, and this part satisfies $P(x, y)$; and the same for the other part, which satisfies $Q(y, z)$. That is the exact condition for the whole observation to satisfy the conjunction $(P(x, y) \wedge Q(y, z))$ of the component descriptions; its alphabet is clearly still the union of their separate alphabets.

A simple example of conjunction has already been given in the previous section. The three components of the water system are the tank, which obeys the conservation law, and the input valve and output valve, which regulate the flow in accordance with separate differential equations. The behaviour of the whole system is described exactly by the conjunction of the predicates describing the behaviour of its components. The variables in common to the three parts must obviously take the same value wherever they occur.

Conjunction is the general method of modelling connection and interaction in an assembly constructed from two or more components. But in practice, not all combinations of predicates are physically realisable in the available technology, for example by connection of wires in hardware, or by execution of programs in some software system. Any scientific theory which is to be useful in engineering practice must clearly state the general conditions under which assembly of components with non-disjoint alphabets will be physically realisable. If these conditions are violated, the resulting conjunction of specifications could be contradictory, yielding the predicate **false**, which is a logical impossibility and could never be implemented in practice. Avoidance of such inconsistency is a necessary goal of the more complex theories described later in this book.

A very effective way of achieving the necessary consistency is to distinguish which variables in the alphabet of each subsystem are "controlled" by that subsystem itself, rather than the environment in which it may be connected. These are called *dependent variables* or *outputs*, and form the *output alphabet* ($out\alpha P$) of the subsystem P. The necessary constraint is that each variable of a complete subsystem can be controlled by only one of its components. So the conjunction $(P \wedge Q)$ is forbidden unless the output alphabets are disjoint

$$out\alpha P \cap out\alpha Q \quad = \quad \{\}$$

A variable controlled by any subsystem is controlled in the combined system

$$out\alpha(P \wedge Q) \quad = \quad out\alpha P \cup out\alpha Q$$

The *input alphabet* is just defined as the rest of the variables, often called *independent variables*, controlled by the experimenter or the environment of the system

$$in\alpha P \quad = \quad \alpha P \setminus out\alpha P$$

The output alphabet of a sequential program consists of all its dashed variables; that is those that are allowed to appear on the left of an assignment within it. The restriction on sharing the output variables is sufficient to ensure consistency of the conjunction of the predicates describing any two parallel programs. We can therefore relax the usual constraint against one component using variables updated by another parallel component. For example, we can allow

$$(x := x - y \parallel y := 2 \times y) \quad = \quad (x' = x - y) \ \wedge \ (y' = 2 \times y)$$

This again gives the same result as a multiple assignment. When one of the component expressions refers to a variable (e.g. y) updated by the other, our theory requires that it is the *initial* value of that variable that is obtained. In general, an implementation might have to make a private copy of such variables before executing the programs in parallel, as is standard when forking a process in UNIX^{TM} [157]. Consequently in this theory parallel components can never interact with each other by shared variables. We will see that such interactions can lead to highly non-deterministic effects. These may well be worth avoiding, even at the cost of extra copying (which is needed anyway on a distributed implementation, one with disjoint stores). A general theory for parallel programs which interact by updating the same variables is considerably more complicated, because it needs to take into account the intermediate values of program variables during execution.

1.4 Specifications

We have seen the role of predicates in describing the actual behaviour of individual components of an assembly. In suitable circumstances, the behaviour of the whole assembly is described by the conjunction of the predicates describing its components. The result can be used by the scientist to predict or even control the outcome of individual experiments on the assembly. But once the theory has been confirmed by experiment, it has an even more valuable role in reasoning about much more general properties of much wider classes of system: there is no longer any need to amass more data by individual experiment. In software engineering, lengthy experimentation is the usual method to determine the properties of a program – it is called program testing. As in natural science, the main reason for theoretical studies is to replace the bulk of tests by mathematical calculations based on the theory, and verified by just a few crucial experiments.

In engineering practice, predicates have an additional role as *specifications*, which define the purpose of a product by describing the desired properties of a system which does not yet exist in the real world, but some client, with money to pay, would like to see it brought into existence. A predicate used as a specification should describe the desired system as clearly and directly as possible, in terms of what behaviour is to be exhibited and what is to be avoided. The specification often defines part of a formal or informal contract between the client and the team engaged on implementation of the product.

In an industrial control system, a primary requirement is to hold some controlled variable within certain safety limits. In the example of the water tank, we impose a lower limit *minv* and an upper limit *maxv* on the volume of liquid held

$$minv \leq v_t \leq maxv, \qquad \text{for all } t$$

These express absolute limits on v, which must be maintained at all times.

Sometimes there are undesirable states which are permitted occasionally, but only for a relatively short proportion of the total time. For example, we may wish that the volume should not be above $(maxv - \delta)$ for more than 10% of any consecutive interval of ten seconds. The undesirable condition can be defined as a Boolean function of time (taking values 0,1)

$$\text{risk}_t \;=_{df}\; (v_t + \delta > maxv)$$

Now the requirement is expressed using integrals

$$\textstyle\int_t^{t+10} \text{risk}_x dx \leq 1, \qquad \text{for all t}$$

The overall safety specification includes the conjunction of the two requirements displayed above. A complete specification will usually be a conjunction of a much larger number of separately expressible requirements.

Another lesson that may be drawn from this example is that, in the formalisation of a specification, one should not hesitate to use notations like those of real numbers and integrals, chosen from the entire conceptual armoury of mathematics: whatever will express the intention as clearly and directly as possible. Often, the notations cannot be executed or even represented on a computer, but they are well understood by the process physicists and control engineers, who must carry the ultimate responsibility for approving the statement of requirements before implementation begins.

An example more familiar to programmers is *sorting*. One of the requirements of a program that sorts data held in an array A is that the result A' should be sorted in ascending order of key. An array is regarded as a function from its indices to its elements. Let *key* be the function which maps each element to its key. The desired condition is

$$(key \circ A') \text{ is monotonic}$$

where $\circ$ denotes function composition. A second requirement on the program is that the result should be a permutation of the initial value

$$(\exists p : p \text{ is a permutation} \bullet A' = A \circ p)$$

The overall specification is the conjunction of these two requirements. Note that the alphabet constraints described in the previous section prevent the program from being implemented as a conjunction of components which meet the two requirements separately.

Again, this example uses fairly sophisticated concepts from pure mathematics to achieve brevity at a high level of abstraction. For example, one must know the definition of a monotonic function, that it preserves the ordering of its arguments

$$x \leq y \Rightarrow A'(x) \leq A'(y), \qquad \text{for all } x, y \text{ in the domain of } A'$$

Other more diffuse formulations of the sorting concept may be shown to be equivalent to it. And they should be, if that increases confidence that the specification describes exactly what the customer has in mind. Even when safety is not involved, it is extremely wasteful and embarrassing to implement and deliver a product which turns out to do what was never wanted.

Knuth has claimed that every interesting concept in computing science can be illuminated by the example of the greatest common divisor [111]. The most direct way of specifying the greatest common divisor z of two numbers x and y is that it must be a divisor of both its operands, and the greatest such. This can be formalised as

$$\begin{aligned} x, y \geq 1 \Rightarrow \quad & x \bmod z = 0 \land \\ & y \bmod z = 0 \land \\ & (\forall w : x \bmod w = y \bmod w = 0 \bullet w \leq z) \end{aligned}$$

This specification has the form of an implication, where the antecedent $(x, y \geq 1)$ states the general condition under which it is reasonable to ask for calculation of the greatest common divisor. The user of the product must undertake to make the antecedent true, because if it fails, there is no constraint whatsoever on the behaviour of the product.

In all the examples described above, individual requirements placed on the system have been formalised as separate predicates; like the components of an assembly, these are collected together by simple conjunction, but now unrestricted by the constraints of implementation technology. As a result, the conjunctive structure of a clear specification is usually orthogonal to the structure of its eventual implementation. The essential intellectual content of engineering design lies in correctly transforming the conjunctive structure of a specification to the orthogonally structured conjunction of components assembled to implement the specification. Engineering would be essentially trivial if a fast and economical product could be assembled from two components, one of which was fast and the other one economical.

1.5 Correctness

The previous two sections have shown both systems and specifications are (conjunctions of) predicates, describing all actual behaviour and all desired behaviour respectively. This gives a particularly convenient definition of the concept of correctness: it is just logical implication. Let S be a specification, composed perhaps as a conjunction of many individual requirements placed on the behaviour of a system yet to be delivered. Let P be a description of all the possible behaviours of the eventually delivered implementation, composed perhaps as the conjunction of the description of its many components. Assume that P and S have the same alphabet of variables, standing for the same observations. We want assurance that the delivered implementation meets its specification, in the sense that none of the possible observations of the implementation could ever violate the specification. In other words, every observation that satisfies P must also satisfy S. This is expressed formally by universally quantified implication

$$\forall v, w, \cdots \bullet \; P \Rightarrow S$$

where $v, w, \cdots$ are all the variables of the alphabet. Dijkstra and Scholten [52] abbreviate this using square brackets to denote universal quantification over all variables in the alphabet

$$[P \Rightarrow S]$$

Logical implication is the fundamental concept of all mathematical reasoning; it plays a crucial role in deducing testable consequences from scientific theories, so it should not be a matter of surprise or regret that it is the basis of all correct design and implementation in engineering practice.

As a trivial example, consider the specification

$$x' > x \;\wedge\; y' = y \qquad \ldots S$$

which specifies that the value of x is to be increased, and the value of y is to remain the same. No restriction is placed on changes to any other variable. There are many programs that satisfy this specification, including the assignment

$$x, y := x + 1, y \qquad \ldots P$$

Correctness of a program means that every possible observation of any run of the program will yield values which make the specification true; for example, the specification is satisfied by the observation $(x = 4 \wedge x' = 5 \wedge y' = y = 7)$, because the predicate S is true when its free variables are replaced by their observed values

$$5 > 4 \;\wedge\; 7 = 7$$

In fact, the specification is satisfied not just by this single observation but by every possible observation of every possible run of the program

$$[(x, y := x + 1, y) \;\Rightarrow\; x' > x \;\wedge\; y' \;=\; y]$$

This mixture of programming with mathematical notations may seem unfamiliar; it is justified by the identification of each program with the predicate describing exactly its range of possible behaviours. Both programs and specifications are predicates over the same set of free variables, and that is why the concept of program correctness can be so simply explained as universally quantified logical implication between them.

Logical implication is equally interesting as a relation between two products or between two specifications. If S and T are specifications, $[S \Rightarrow T]$ means that T is a more general or abstract specification than S, and at least as easy to implement. Indeed, by transitivity of implication, any product that correctly implements S will serve as an implementation of T, though not necessarily the other way round. So a logically weaker specification is easier to implement, and the easiest of all is the predicate **true**, which can be implemented by anything.

Similarly, if P and Q are products, $[P \;\Rightarrow\; Q]$ means that P is a more specific or determinate product than Q, and it is (in general) more useful. Indeed, by transitivity of implication, any specification met by Q will be met by P, though not necessarily the other way round. So for any given purpose a logically weaker product is less likely to be any good, and the weakest product **true** is the most useless of all.

Explanation of correctness as implication gives a strangely simple treatment of the perplexing topic of non-determinism. Let P and Q be product descriptions with the same alphabet. Their disjunction $(P \vee Q)$ may behave like P or it may behave like Q, with no indication which it will be. In order to be sure that this is correct, both P and Q must be correct. Fortunately, this is also a sufficient condition; this is justified by appeal to the fundamental logical property of disjunction as the least upper bound of the implication ordering

$$[P \vee Q \Rightarrow S] \quad \textbf{iff} \quad [P \Rightarrow S] \text{ and } [Q \Rightarrow S]$$

The progress of a complex engineering project is often split into a number of design stages. The transition between successive stages is marked by signing off a document, produced in the earlier stage and used in the later stage. A design document D can also be regarded as a predicate: it describes directly or indirectly the general properties of all products conforming to the design. But before embarking on final implementation, it is advisable to ensure the correctness of the design by proving the implication

$$[D \;\Rightarrow\; S]$$

Now the implementation of the product itself reduces to the simpler task of finding a predicate P, expressed in technologically feasible notations, which satisfies the implication

$$[P \Rightarrow D]$$

Transitivity of implication then ensures the validity of the original goal that the product should meet the starting specification

$$[P \Rightarrow S]$$

This is a very simple justification of the widespread engineering practice of stepwise design. It is also a vindication of our philosophy of interpreting specifications, designs and implementations all as predicates describing the same kind of observable phenomena. However, these predicates are usually expressed in very different notations at each different stage of the engineering process. For example, the notations of a programming language are deliberately restricted in the interests of feasibility and efficiency of implementation. Satisfaction of notational constraints is an essential feature also for the solution of any mathematically defined problem: the answer must be expressed in notations essentially more primitive than the problem, for example as numerals rather than formulae, as explicit functions rather than differential equations. Otherwise a trivial restatement of the problem itself could be offered as a solution.

Stepwise design is even more effective if it is accompanied by decomposition of complex tasks into simpler subtasks. Let D and E be designs of components that will be assembled to meet specification S. The correctness of the designs can be checked before their implementation by proof of the implication

$$[D \land E \Rightarrow S]$$

The two designs can then be separately implemented as products P and Q that conform individually to the two design descriptions

$$[P \Rightarrow D] \quad \text{and} \quad [Q \Rightarrow E]$$

Their assembly will then necessarily satisfy the original specification

$$[P \land Q \Rightarrow S]$$

The correctness of the final step does not depend on lengthy integration testing after assembly of the components, but rather on a mathematical proof completed before starting to implement the components. The validity of the method of stepwise decomposition follows from a fundamental property of conjunction: that it is monotonic in the implication ordering.

The principle of monotonicity plays an essential role in engineering practice. Let X stand for a component, and let Y stand for a component that is claimed to be better than X in all relevant respects: as explained above, this can be expressed formally as an implication between their descriptions

$$[Y \Rightarrow X]$$

Now let $F(X)$ be a description of the behaviour of an assembly in which X has been inserted as a component. Replacement of component X by Y in the physical assembly corresponds to replacement of the description of X by the description of Y, and the resulting overall description is therefore $F(Y)$. If Y is really better than X, the engineer would expect the resulting assembly to be better too. This expectation is expressed by the implication

$$[Y \Rightarrow X] \Rightarrow [F(Y) \Rightarrow F(X)]$$

But this is exactly what is meant by the statement that F is monotonic.

For any theory to be useful in engineering, all methods of connection of components into an assembly should be monotonic in this sense. Of course, in practice, the principle will occasionally be violated, in cases when a supposed local improvement leads to worse global performance. This kind of failure is one of the most worrying problems to the engineer, because it is not just a failure of a single component or a single product, but rather a failure in the underlying theory on which its whole design has been based. Until the theory has been mended, there is no reason to suppose that the design can be.

A major problem in the account we have given of stepwise decomposition is that the designer must simultaneously formalise the designs of *both* the components D and E. That is like trying to split an integer s into two integer factors before the invention of division: it was necessary then to guess *both* the factors d and e, checking the guesses by multiplication

$$d \times e = s$$

But after the invention of long division, all that is needed is to guess only one of the numbers, say d; the other can be calculated by the formula

$$e = s \div d$$

Provided there is no remainder (which is also checked by calculation), this is guaranteed to give the other factor. Fortunately, a similar principle is in general available in engineering design.

The principle is especially helpful in planning the reuse of existing assemblies and designs. Suppose it is decided to use a known design or available component Q in the implementation of a specification S. So it remains only to design another component X which will be connected to Q, adapting its behaviour to meet this particular requirement. More formally, X must satisfy the implication

$$[X \land Q \Rightarrow S]$$

There are many answers to such an inequation, of which (X = **false**) is the most trivial. It is also the most difficult to implement — in fact impossible! There can never be any way of expressing the universally false predicate in any notation that claims to be implementable. What we want is at the other extreme, the answer that is easiest to implement, the one which preserves all design options and choices, so that these can be made later, when it is possible to assess their implications.

That is why we ask: What is the *weakest* specification [92] that should be met by the designers of X? In a top-down design, it is much better to calculate X from Q and S, rather than attempting to find it by guesswork. Fortunately, propositional calculus gives a very simple answer

$$X \;=\; \neg Q \lor S$$

This is guaranteed by the law of propositional logic

$$[X \land Q \Rightarrow S] \quad \textbf{iff} \quad [X \Rightarrow (\neg Q \lor S)]$$

The specification $(\neg Q \lor S)$ is often written as an implication $(Q \Rightarrow S)$, and will be in general easier to implement than S. The formula permits calculation rather than guesswork to aid in the top-down search for an implementation of X that works with Q to achieve S. Such replacement of guesswork by calculation is the main practical goal of the development of a mathematical theory for engineering.

1.6 Abstraction

Our simple explanation of correctness assumes that the alphabets of specification, design and implementation are all the same. In many cases, the alphabets are different, and for good reason: they reflect different levels of abstraction, granularity and scale at which the observations are made. The whole task of design and implementation is to cross these levels of abstraction, and to do so without introducing error. A simple case of abstraction is when the alphabet of the specification is a subset of that of the implementation. For example, specifications will usually exclude mention of any variable introduced to describe only the internal interactions of the components of the implementation. Such a variable serves as a *local variable* in a program, similar to a bound variable in a mathematical formula. What is observable inside the assembly is of no concern to its customer, and is usually hidden by physical enclosure in its casing. The corresponding logical operation must remove the free variable from the predicate and from its alphabet.

For the implementation to work, such a hidden variable describing an internal property must indeed have *some* value, but we do not care what it is. It should therefore be hidden by existential quantification. The quantification is justified by the ∃-introduction rule of the predicate calculus

$$[P \Rightarrow S] \quad \textbf{iff} \quad [(\exists v \bullet P) \Rightarrow S], \qquad \text{if } v \text{ does not occur in } S$$

The variable is removed from the alphabet of $(\exists v \bullet P)$. Existential quantification over internal interactions of an assembly often leads to considerable simplification of the descriptions, without affecting the range of specifications that will be satisfied.

Universal quantification plays a complementary role to the existential: it assists in the top-down design of systems with reusable components. Recall the task described at the end of the previous section, to find the weakest X such that

$$[X \wedge Q \Rightarrow S]$$

But of course the condition of implementability of the conjunction $(X \wedge Q)$ requires that X must not mention any of the output variables (say x' and y') of Q. So the answer must hold for *all* values which Q may give to them, as in the universally quantified formula

$$X \;=\; (\forall x', y' \bullet Q \Rightarrow S)$$

where $out\alpha Q = \{x', y'\}$. This answer has been called the *residual* [15] of S by Q, because it describes what remains to be implemented in order to achieve S with the aid of Q. The answer is justified again by a simple law of the predicate calculus

$$[X \wedge Q \Rightarrow S] \quad \textbf{iff} \quad [X \Rightarrow (\forall x', y' \bullet Q \Rightarrow S)]$$

whenever x', y' do not occur in X.

As an example, suppose it is required to maintain a constant value for the expression $(x - y)$. This task is expressed in the specification that its value afterwards is the same as its value before

$$S \;=\; (x' - y' = x - y)$$

Suppose for other reasons it is desirable to double the value y by

$$Q \;=\; (y := 2 \times y)$$

What simultaneous change must be made to the value of x in order to re-establish the truth of S? The required answer is given by the residual.

$$\begin{aligned}
&(\forall y' \bullet y' = 2 \times y \Rightarrow (x' - y' = x - y)) \\
= \;& (x' - 2 \times y \;=\; x - y) \\
= \;& x' \;=\; x + y \\
= \;& x := x + y
\end{aligned}$$

The answer, which is not totally obvious, has been derived by pure calculation, and has not required the dubious aid of intuition.

Of course, not all design decisions are sensible. An ill-conceived design may be expensive, difficult or even impossible to implement. Suppose the specification is to make the product of x and y into an odd number with the help of a program that doubles y. So the required residual is

$$\begin{aligned}
&(\forall y' \bullet y' = 2 \times y \;\Rightarrow\; (x' \times y' \text{ is odd})) \\
= \;& x' \times 2 \times y \text{ is odd} \\
= \;& \textbf{false}
\end{aligned}$$

This is, of course, unimplementable: there is no way that an odd product can be obtained by doubling one of the factors, and the situation cannot be remedied by changing the value of the other factor. It was clearly foolish to think that it would help to double y. Fortunately, the calculation of the residual as **false** gives clear warning of the impossibility of implementation.

In general, the transitions between engineering specifications and designs, or between various levels of design, present conceptual gaps far greater than can be bridged by just hiding some of the details of the interaction between components of the implementation. In fact, there is often an abrupt change in the nature, scale and granularity of all the observations involved and therefore of the alphabet used to denote them. We have a hierarchy of abstraction levels analogous to that found in the branches of a mature science, and there is an even more urgent practical need to demonstrate the soundness of the transitions between them.

A simple but quite general way of solving the problem is to describe mathematically the relationship between observations at the two levels, for example specification and design. At the design level, let $D(c)$ be a predicate with alphabet $\{c\}$ denoting a concrete observation relevant to implementation, and let $S(a)$ be a specification with alphabet $\{a\}$ denoting a more abstract observation relevant to the customer's use of the product (our reasoning will apply equally to much larger alphabets). The problem cannot be solved by plain universally quantified implication $[D(c) \;\Rightarrow\; S(a)]$ is equivalent to $[\exists c.D(c) \;\Rightarrow\; \forall a.S(a)]$; except in the most trivial cases this is just false, and most certainly does not define the proper notion of correctness, relating the design to the specification. The solution is to understand and formalise the relationship between an individual observation c of the design, and the corresponding values of a to which it may give rise at the higher level. This relationship can be described in the usual way by some linking predicate $L(c, a)$. Now the set of all abstract observations that may be made of the design is described by a predicate in which all concrete observations are hidden

$$\exists c \bullet D(c) \wedge L(c, a)$$

This construction lifts the abstraction level of the design to that of the specification. More precisely, it gives the strongest specification with alphabet $\{a\}$ that is satisfied by the design D. Proceeding from the top down, the specification describing the higher level observation a can be converted into a design describing the more concrete observations

$$(\forall a \bullet L(c, a) \Rightarrow S(a))$$

This actually gives the weakest design with alphabet $\{c\}$ that is guaranteed to satisfy the specification. Either the existential or the universal transformation may be used to define correctness, as shown by the equivalence

$$[(\exists c \bullet D(c) \wedge L(c, a)) \Rightarrow S(a)] \quad \textbf{iff} \quad [D(c) \Rightarrow (\forall a \bullet L(c, a) \Rightarrow S(a))]$$

Equivalences of this form are very common in constructing links between theories: the two transformations are often known as *Galois connections*. They will play a central role in the unification of theories of programming.

1.7 The ideal and the reality of engineering

The preceding sections have painted an ideal picture of an engineering project, as an abstract exercise in pure logic. It is a picture that is as far from the day-to-day reality of engineering practice as could be expected of any other branch of pure speculative philosophy. The first idealisation is that the true requirements and qualities of a product can be accurately captured in a precise logical description of the way that it should behave. Requirements capture is in fact the most challenging of all the engineers' tasks, because there is no way of checking that they describe what the customer actually is going to want when the product is actually delivered. Even the best specifications are peppered with qualifications like "reasonably" and "normally" and "approximately" and "preferably", which cannot be made more precise until much later in the investigation of the design, or even after delivery.

Another bold idealisation is that the specification, once formalised, will remain constant. In fact specifications are subject to a constant series of changes, before, during, and even after delivery of the product. In principle, the slightest change can invalidate the entire structure and all the details of the whole design, but in practice the engineer usually finds some ingenious way of preserving and maintaining the greater part of the work progressed so far. Indeed, the experienced engineer often has a way of anticipating the most likely changes from the start. Changes made even after initial delivery of the product are particularly significant in software engineering. The lifelong task of many programmers is to make a succession of adaptations to some existing program, to meet new or changing needs that were never envisaged in the original specification. In principle, the rigorous documentation of the design should be the most valuable aid in identifying where to make the necessary changes and how to make them correctly. Unfortunately, in practice the design documentation goes rapidly out of date, and even becomes too dangerous to use. The only safe way to find out what the program actually does is by testing and tracing example runs, by trial and more frequently by error.

A project that starts from scratch can suffer from even greater problems. The absence of a previous program to adapt usually means that this is the first application of some new and comparatively immature technology to a problem for which there is no current solution. These are just those cases where the standard calculations do not apply, and greatest reliance must be placed on guesswork and experimentation. In the top-down progression from specification through design, the earliest decisions on the structure of the product are the most irreversible, and yet they must be taken at the time of greatest ignorance of their consequences on the cost and performance and acceptability of the product. Mistakes are inevitable, and can be recovered only by judicious backtracking. If success is possible at all, it is only by the experience, judgement and ingenuity of the engineer. No amount of mathematical calculation or logical proof can ever be a substitute for that.

Finally, all other problems of engineering design must be subordinate to the overriding imperative to deliver the promised product at the due time, and at a cost within the allocated budget. All the ideals of philosophy and logic are of no avail if the engineer fails in this, the most important of all engineering duties. And in fact, this is where the true engineer finds his or her greatest intellectual and personal reward – not just the pursuit of an ideal of accuracy, but also a justified pride in the working product and the satisfied customer.

The stark contrast between ideals and reality has been noted and deplored by philosophers, moralists and theologians through the centuries; there is no general reconciliation, and each individual must continually find a resolution appropriate to the needs of the moment. In engineering, some will ignore theoretical ideals, and rely exclusively on experience of their craft, but others will on occasion find guidance from their understanding and pursuit of an ideal, which is shared by other members of a recognised profession. The ideal suggests an integrated approach to the overall task, and enables deviations to be isolated and controlled separately. In the longer term, a theoretical understanding provides a basis for the emergence of professional standards, methods and techniques for uniformly reliable solution of technical problems, independent of the area of application. These in turn provide material for a sound education for new entrants to the profession, who respond favourably to the inspiration of a unifying ideal, even before understanding the many compromises necessary to put it into practice.

Finally, the privilege of the purest allegiance to an ideal is that of the researcher, seeking to build a scientific foundation which will contribute simultaneously to the advancement of knowledge and education, as well as the continuous improvement of professional practice of the accredited engineer. One final appeal to an analogy with the physical sciences: it is the pursuit of an ideal of truth that in the long run has led to the development of modern technology and engineering methods, and these have been of outstanding success in solving problems which continue to face the modern world.

Chapter 2

Relations

Our treatment of the logic of engineering design has been sparsely illustrated by examples of water tanks and of computer programs, but it is applicable in principle to any branch of technology. We have allowed specifications and products to be formalised as predicates with arbitrary alphabets, and these predicates may be assembled by an arbitrary combination of the operators of the predicate calculus, including conjunction and even negation. Indeed, at the level of specifications, negation could be the most important contribution to safety of a control system; for example, a common safety requirement can be simply and most reliably expressed by stating that

"it must *not* explode".

In this chapter we begin to specialise our study to the particular classes of predicate that are relevant to the specification and development of programs in a simple sequential programming language. For a program in such a language, the relevant observations come in pairs, with one observation of the values of all global variables before program execution, and one observation of their values after termination. Any set of such pairs therefore constitutes a *relation* in the usual sense, and this is the word we choose to apply to the corresponding predicate describing program behaviour. The relational calculus provides most of the concepts and laws that we need both for sequential programming and for all the more complex programming paradigms treated in later chapters. We deliberately omit both relational converse ($^{\cup}$) and negation ($\neg$) because they are not directly implementable. The inverse of an operation cannot be computed by running a program backwards, and an explosion cannot be prevented by just negating a program which deliberately causes one.

Definition 2.0.1 (Relation)

A relation is a pair $(\alpha P, P)$, where P is a predicate containing no free variables other than those in αP, and

$$\alpha P \;=\; in\alpha P \cup out\alpha P$$

where $in\alpha P$ is a set of undashed variables standing for initial values, and $out\alpha P$ is a set of dashed variables standing for final values. □

In all familiar programming languages, the global variables observable at the start of execution of a block of program are the same as those observable at the end. In this case the output alphabet is obtained just by putting a dash on all the variables of the input alphabet, as suggested by the equation

$$out\alpha P \;=\; in\alpha' P$$

The relation is then called *homogeneous.* The classical relational calculus deals solely with homogeneous relations. Our treatment is more general, although we will not need to make explicit mention of non-homogeneous relations again until Section 9 of this chapter.

Having formally associated an alphabet with every predicate, we will adopt a number of conventions to prevent the formality from becoming too obtrusive. For example, an important class of predicates are those with no variables in their output alphabet. They are the only kind of predicate that can actually appear in a computer program: they can be tested in the initial state of the program, and will yield the value *true* or *false.* (For simplicity, we assume they never fail to terminate.) We call them *conditions*, and denote them by lower case italics

$$b, c, \ldots, \; true$$

This distinguishes them from more general predicates describing programs, which generally mention both dashed and undashed variables. These will be denoted by upper case or bold

$$P, Q, \ldots, \mathbf{true}$$

Similar remarks apply to expressions which appear on the right of assignments in a program: they have no dashed variables, their evaluation always terminates, and they are denoted by

$$e, f, g, \ldots, 37$$

These letters can also stand for *lists* of expressions. We will use the letters x, y, z, v to stand for lists of *distinct* variables in the input alphabets, and their variants x', y', z', v' to stand for the corresponding lists of dashed variables. So the form

$$x := e$$

could stand for a multiple assignment of many values to many variables, and it will be implicitly assumed that the lists are of matching length. The lists v and v' are special: they are assumed to contain *all* the variables of the input and output alphabets respectively.

Substitution will also be treated quite informally. Whenever appropriate, some or all of the free variables of a predicate, term or condition will be made explicit in brackets

$$P(x), Q(x'), e(x) \text{ or } b(x)$$

If f is now a list of expressions (of the right length, of course) then

$$P(f), Q(f), e(f) \text{ or } b(f)$$

stands for the result of replacing each occurrence of any variable in x (or x') by the expression which occupies the corresponding position in the list f. Implicitly, we ensure that there is no collision between free variables of f and bound variables in the context where f is being substituted. Sometimes we will use an explicit notation for substitution. $P[e/x]$ is the result of substituting expressions e for variables x in P.

The specialisation of the class of predicates to those which are relations is motivated by the desire to develop a theory which is relevant to computer programming. The primitive components of our programs are assignments, and these were described in the last chapter. In this chapter we will describe how larger programs are built up from the primitives by combining them in sequential compositions, conditionals and disjunctions. These operators have been selected for ease and efficiency of implementation on a sequential computer. Finally, recursion is introduced as a general method of specifying how portions of a program can be repeated, with the number of repetitions being determined by the initial values of the variables.

In the normal fashion of mathematics, each definition is followed by a collection of simple theorems that can be proved from it. These laws are intended to appeal to experienced programmers as obviously true of a tightly disciplined programming language in which all expressions terminate and none of them has side-effects; such an appeal is essential to the memorisation, recall and fluent use of the laws. It also lends credibility to the definitions on which they are based. Conversely, an obviously false law will serve like an unsuccessful scientific experiment: it will refute the theory from which it has been derived.

2.1 Conditional

Any non-trivial program requires a facility to select between alternative actions in accordance with the truth or falsity of some testable condition b. The restriction that b contains no dashed variables ensures that it can be tested before starting either of the actions. If P and Q are predicates describing two fragments of program with the same alphabet, then the conditional

$$P \lhd b \rhd Q$$

describes a program which behaves like P if the initial value of b is true, or like Q if the initial value of b is false. It can be defined as a simple truth function in the propositional calculus.

Definition 2.1.1 (Conditional)

$$P \lhd b \rhd Q \; =_{df} \; (b \wedge P) \vee (\neg b \wedge Q), \quad \text{if } \alpha b \subseteq \alpha P = \alpha Q$$
$$\alpha(P \lhd b \rhd Q) \; =_{df} \; \alpha P \qquad \square$$

The more usual notation for a conditional is

if b **then** P **else** Q

We have chosen an infix notation $\lhd b \rhd$ because it simplifies expression of the relevant algebraic laws.

L1 $P \lhd b \rhd P = P$ (cond idemp)

L2 $P \lhd b \rhd Q = Q \lhd \neg b \rhd P$ (cond symm)

L3 $(P \lhd b \rhd Q) \lhd c \rhd R = P \lhd b \wedge c \rhd (Q \lhd c \rhd R)$ (cond assoc)

L4 $P \lhd b \rhd (Q \lhd c \rhd R) = (P \lhd b \rhd Q) \lhd c \rhd (P \lhd b \rhd R)$ (cond distr)

L5 $P \lhd \mathit{true} \rhd Q = P = Q \lhd \mathit{false} \rhd P$ (cond unit)

Proof These laws can be proved by propositional calculus; the easiest way is to consider separately the case when b is true and when b is false. $\square$

The laws have been named by descriptions of familiar algebraic properties. A binary operator is *idempotent* when application to two identical operands gives a result equal to both of them, as shown in the first law. An operator is *symmetric* when an exchange of its two operands does not change the result. However, in the case of **L2**, the operator also has to be changed by negating the condition, so the symmetry is *skewed.* An *associative* operator is one that permits rearrangement of its brackets when applied twice. **L3** gives a slightly stronger form of this property for the conditional. The fourth law states the distribution of any conditional choice operator $\lhd b \rhd$ through the conditional $\lhd c \rhd$, for any condition c. The final law clearly expresses the criterion for making a choice between two alternatives of a conditional based on the value of the condition. It is called a *unit* law, because it indicates the operand (the unit) for which the application of the operator makes no difference. These laws are strong enough to prove additional useful laws, as shown below.

L6 $P \lhd b \rhd (Q \lhd b \rhd R) = P \lhd b \rhd R$

Proof

$$\begin{aligned} & LHS && \{\mathbf{L2}\} \\ = \;& (Q \lhd b \rhd R) \lhd \neg b \rhd P && \{\mathbf{L3}\} \\ = \;& Q \lhd \mathit{false} \rhd (R \lhd \neg b \rhd P) && \{\mathbf{L2}\text{ and }\mathbf{L5}\} \\ = \;& RHS && \square \end{aligned}$$

L7 $P \lhd b \rhd (P \lhd c \rhd Q) = P \lhd b \vee c \rhd Q$

Proof

$$\begin{aligned} & LHS && \{\mathbf{L2}\} \\ = \;& (Q \lhd \neg c \rhd P) \lhd \neg b \rhd P && \{\mathbf{L3}\text{ and }\mathbf{L1}\} \\ = \;& Q \lhd \neg c \wedge \neg b \rhd P && \{\mathbf{L2}\} \\ = \;& RHS && \square \end{aligned}$$

These laws would be just as easy to prove directly by the propositional calculus. The algebraic style of proof has been preferred, because it reveals something of the structure of our theory, with only a few laws taken as basic, and many more derivable as theorems. This has the advantage that both axioms and theorems can often be used again in other mathematical theories, even those that use different definitions of the operators involved.

Exercise 2.1.2 (Mutual distribution)

For any truth-functional operator $\odot$, prove that

$$(P \odot Q) \lhd b \rhd (R \odot S) \;=\; (P \lhd b \rhd R) \odot (Q \lhd b \rhd S)$$

A similar principle of mutual distribution is called the *interchange law* in category theory [116] or the *abides* principle in functional programming [26]. □

2.2 Composition

The most characteristic combinator of a sequential programming language is sequential composition, often denoted by semicolon. If P and Q are predicates describing behaviours of two programs, their sequential composition

$$P; Q$$

describes a program which may be executed by first executing P, and when P terminates then Q is started. The final state of P is passed on as the initial state of Q, but this is only an intermediate state of $(P;Q)$, and cannot be directly observed. All we know is that it exists. The formal definition of composition therefore uses existential quantification to hide the intermediate observation, and to remove the variables which record it from the list of free variables of the predicate. In order to do this, we need to introduce a fresh set of variables v_0 to denote the hidden observation. These replace the output variables v' of P and the input variables v of Q, so these lists must correspond exactly in length and in type.

Definition 2.2.1 (Sequential composition)

$$\begin{aligned} P(v'); Q(v) &=_{df} \exists v_0 \bullet P(v_0) \wedge Q(v_0), \quad \text{provided } out\alpha P = in\alpha' Q = \{v'\} \\ in\alpha(P(v'); Q(v)) &=_{df} in\alpha P \\ out\alpha(P(v'); Q(v)) &=_{df} out\alpha Q \end{aligned}$$ □

The bound variables v_0 record the intermediate values of the program variables v, and so represent the intermediate state as control passes from P to Q. But this operational explanation is far more detailed than necessary. A clever implementation is allowed to achieve the defined effect by more direct means, without ever passing through any of the possible intermediate states. That is the whole purpose of a more abstract definition of the programming language.

In spite of the complexity of its definition, sequential composition obeys some simple, familiar and obvious algebraic laws. For example, it is associative; to execute three programs in order, one can either execute the first program followed by the other two, or the first two programs followed by the third. Finally, sequential composition distributes leftward (but not rightward) over the conditional. This asymmetry arises because the condition b is allowed to mention only the initial values of the variables, and not the final (dashed) variables.

L1 $P;(Q;R) = (P;Q);R$ (; assoc)

L2 $(P \lhd b \rhd Q);R = (P;R) \lhd b \rhd (Q;R)$ (;-cond left distr)

Proof Hint: Move the existential quantifier outward over predicates that do not contain the quantified variable. □

2.3 Assignment

The assignment is the basic action in all procedural programming languages. Its meaning was explained in the previous chapter, but here we deal more carefully with the phenomenon of alphabets. Every assignment should technically be marked by its alphabet A, which is needed to define an important part of its meaning – that all the variables not mentioned on the left hand side remain unchanged.

Definition 2.3.1 (Assignment)

Let $A = \{x, y, \ldots, z, x', y', \ldots, z'\}$, and let $\alpha e \subseteq A$.

$$x :=_A e \;=_{df}\; (x' = e \wedge y' = y \wedge \ldots \wedge z' = z)$$
$$\alpha(x :=_A e) \;=_{df}\; A \qquad \Box$$

Having introduced the complexity of alphabets, we will very seldom subscript an assignment.

The following laws express the basic properties of assignment: that variables not mentioned on the left of := remain unchanged, that the order of the listing is immaterial, and that evaluation of an expression or a condition uses the value most recently assigned to its variables.

L1 $(x := e) \;=\; (x, y := e, y)$

L2 $(x, y, z := e, f, g) \;=\; (y, x, z := f, e, g)$

L3 $(x := e;\; x := f(x)) \;=\; (x := f(e))$

L4 $x := e;\, (P \lhd b(x) \rhd Q) \;=\; (x := e; P) \lhd b(e) \rhd (x := e; Q)$

In most programming languages there is a command that has no effect at all! It always terminates, and leaves the values of *all* the variables unchanged. Although its lack of effect can be described fully by the assignment $x := x$, and although it is totally useless for all practical purposes, it is extremely useful for reasoning about programs. We therefore denote it by a special hollow symbol $I\!I_A$ (pronounced "skip"), where A is its alphabet.

Definition 2.3.2 (Skip)

$$I\!I_A \;=_{df}\; (v' = v), \qquad \text{where } A = \{v, v'\}$$
$$\alpha I\!I_A \;=_{df}\; A \qquad \Box$$

The ineffectiveness of $I\!I$ is neatly captured by its most important algebraic property: that it is the unit for sequential composition.

L5 $P; I\!I_{\alpha P} \;=\; P \;=\; I\!I_{\alpha P}; P$ (; unit)

In future, we will drop the alphabet subscript on $I\!I$, on the grounds that it can be restored in any way that satisfies the constraints imposed by the definition of the neighbouring operators and operands, including the constraint that both sides of an equation or inequation must have the same alphabet.

Assignment to a subscripted variable has the same form as assignment to a simple variable. If w is an array-valued variable (single dimensional for simplicity)

$$w[i] := e$$

denotes an assignment of the value of e to just the ith element of the array. Because this is the only element that changes, implementation is easy and efficient. But in principle, the value of an array variable is a finite function from its index range to its element type, and the change to the value of a single element changes the value of the whole array. The new function is quite similar to the old: it maps all the indices except one to the same value, and just the assigned index is mapped to a new value. Such a change is described by the overriding operator $\oplus$, defined by

$$(w \oplus x)[i] \;=_{df}\; x[i] \lhd i \in \mathit{domain}(x) \rhd w[i]$$

A subscripted assignment to $w[i]$ is mathematically equivalent to an assignment

$$w := w \oplus \{i \mapsto e\}$$

where $\{i \mapsto e\}$ is the singleton function with domain $\{i\}$ that maps i to e.

Definition 2.3.3 (Array assignment)

$$w[i] := e \;=_{df}\; w := w \oplus \{i \mapsto e\} \qquad \square$$

2.4 Non-determinism

Non-determinism was described in the previous chapter as simply disjunction of predicates. If P and Q are predicates describing the behaviour of programs with the same alphabet, then we introduce the notation

$$P \sqcap Q$$

to stand for a program which is executed by executing either P or Q, but with no indication which one will be chosen. The introduction of the new notation $\sqcap$ emphasises that the alphabets of both the operands must be the same.

Definition 2.4.1 (Non-deterministic choice)

$$P \sqcap Q \;=_{df}\; P \vee Q, \qquad \text{provided that } \alpha P = \alpha Q$$

$$\alpha(P \sqcap Q) \;=_{df}\; \alpha P \qquad \square$$

As an operator of our programming language, non-deterministic choice may be easily implemented by arbitrary selection of either of the operands, and the selection may be made at any time, either before or after the program is compiled or even after it starts execution. The non-deterministic choice satisfies a number of laws common to other forms of choice, including the conditional.

L1 $P \sqcap Q \ = \ Q \sqcap P$ ($\sqcap$ symm)

L2 $P \sqcap (Q \sqcap R) \ = \ (P \sqcap Q) \sqcap R$ ($\sqcap$ assoc)

L3 $P \sqcap P \ = \ P$ ($\sqcap$ idemp)

Proof From symmetry, associativity and idempotency of disjunction. □

The first law states that it does not make any difference in what order a choice is offered, that is the operator $\sqcap$ is symmetric. The second one is an associative law: a choice between three alternatives can be offered as first a choice between one alternative and the other two, followed (if necessary) by a choice between the other two; it does not matter in which way the choices are grouped. The final law says that a choice between a program and itself offers no choice at all, that is $\sqcap$ is idempotent. Using these laws we can prove that $\sqcap$ distributes through itself.

L4 $P \sqcap (Q \sqcap R) \ = \ (P \sqcap Q) \sqcap (P \sqcap R)$ ($\sqcap$ distr)

Proof

$$\begin{aligned} & RHS && \{\textbf{L1} \text{ and } \textbf{L2}\} \\ = \ & (P \sqcap P) \sqcap (Q \sqcap R) && \{\textbf{L3}\} \\ = \ & LHS && \square \end{aligned}$$

All programming combinators defined so far distribute through $\sqcap$. This means that separate consideration of each case is adequate for all reasoning about non-determinism. Finally, $\sqcap$ also distributes through the conditional.

L5 $P \lhd b \rhd (Q \sqcap R) \ = \ (P \lhd b \rhd Q) \sqcap (P \lhd b \rhd R)$ (cond-$\sqcap$ distr)

L6 $(P \sqcap Q); R \ = \ (P; R) \sqcap (Q; R)$ (;-$\sqcap$ left distr)

L7 $P; (Q \sqcap R) \ = \ (P; Q) \sqcap (P; R)$ (;-$\sqcap$ right distr)

L8 $P \sqcap (Q \lhd b \rhd R) \ = \ (P \sqcap Q) \lhd b \rhd (P \sqcap R)$ ($\sqcap$-cond distr)

Proof Propositional and predicate calculus. □

As a consequence of distribution through the non-deterministic choice, all program combinators defined so far are monotonic in all arguments; for example,

$$[X; Y \Rightarrow X'; Y'] \text{ whenever } [X \Rightarrow X'] \text{ and } [Y \Rightarrow Y']$$

A further consequence is that all functions defined solely in terms of these programming operators will be monotonic. But not all monotonic operators distribute through $\sqcap$. Consider an operator which executes its argument more than once, for example a squaring operator defined by

$$P^2 =_{df} P; P$$

This is certainly monotonic. But if it is applied to a non-deterministic argument, a different choice may be made when each copy of the argument is executed. Expansion of the definition and distribution of ; through $\sqcap$ gives

$$\begin{aligned}(Q \sqcap R)^2 &= (Q;Q) \sqcap (Q;R) \sqcap (R;Q) \sqcap (R;R) \\ &= (Q^2 \sqcap R^2) \sqcap (Q;R) \sqcap (R;Q)\end{aligned}$$

This is in general weaker than $Q^2 \sqcap R^2$, but that is not surprising, because it is already known for any monotonic function F that

$$[F(P) \sqcap F(Q) \;\Rightarrow\; F(P \sqcap Q)]$$

A product or component P can be made less deterministic by adding the possibility that it behaves like Q. But in general an increase in non-determinism makes the thing worse, no matter what you want to use it for. It is harder to predict how it will behave; it is more difficult to use and control, and more likely to go wrong. This fact is expressed in the simple law

$$[P \;\Rightarrow\; (P \sqcap Q)]$$

Taking this argument to extreme, the worst component of all is totally unpredictable and totally uncontrollable; as a result, it is useless for any purpose whatever. There is no limit to the range of its possible behaviour or misbehaviour. The only predicate that it satisfies is the weakest predicate of all, the one that is always true. In a programming language, a program like this is sometimes called ABORT or CHAOS, but we will adopt a more compact notation.

Definition 2.4.2 (Abort)

$$\begin{aligned}\bot_A &=_{df} \mathbf{true} \\ \alpha\bot_A &=_{df} A\end{aligned} \qquad \square$$

The notation has been chosen as suggestive of the bottom (weakest) element of the implication ordering

$$[\bot_A \;\Leftarrow\; P], \quad \text{for all } P \text{ with alphabet } A$$

In engineering practice, it may well be impossible to find or to build a physical component or assembly whose behaviour is so totally arbitrary. But there are other ways in which a product may become totally undependable, for example foodstuff that has been mis-handled in storage, or a bottle of medicine that has lost its label. The only safe thing to do with it is to throw it away. Since there is no reason to make distinctions in uselessness, these objects may all be represented by the single mathematical abstraction $\bot$. An alternative view is that a non-deterministic product might actually be better, because at least it might exhibit a desirable behaviour which an incorrect deterministic product could never do. This view is attractive, but only because it panders to wishful thinking, a pleasant habit that cannot be allowed in the professional engineer. The only allowable view is that non-determinism is resolved by a demon which is dedicated to the implementation of Murphy's law

"if it can go wrong it will".

2.5 The complete lattice of relations

The combinator $\sqcap$ may be used to describe non-deterministic behaviour in terms of any finite set of n more deterministic behaviours

$$P_1 \sqcap P_2 \sqcap \ldots \sqcap P_n$$

The disjunction of an infinite set of predicates asserts the existence of at least one of the predicates that is true. Like existential quantification in the predicate calculus, it is impossible to define infinite disjunction in terms of the finite disjunctions of the propositional calculus. It is therefore necessary to introduce the concept by an axiom rather than a formal definition, and that is the role of **L1** below. It is one of the few laws in the book which cannot be proved from definitions, simply because no definition can be given. Fortunately, this axiom alone is strong enough for all the proofs that we need about the properties of $\sqcap$. In fact, it is so strong that there is provably at most one operator that satisfies it. Thus the axiom merely postulates the existence of the operation that it indirectly defines.

Let S_A be some set of predicates, all with alphabet A (which we will henceforth omit). Then $\bigsqcap S$ describes a system that behaves in any of the ways described by any of the relations in S. The law governing this construction applies equally to infinite and to finite non-determinism.

L1 $[P \Leftarrow \bigsqcap S]$ **iff** $([P \Leftarrow X]$ for all X in $S)$

The quantification "for all X in S" on the right hand side of this law is necessary. The square brackets mean universal quantification over all observations described by X, and denoted by free variables in the alphabet of X. Quantification over predicates like X is different; it is known as *higher order* quantification, and will be explained more fully in the next section. The law **L1** for unbounded non-determinism may be easier to understand when it is split into two parts that are together equivalent to it.

L1A $[\bigsqcap S \Leftarrow X]$ for all X in S

L1B If $[P \Leftarrow X]$ for all X in S, then $[P \Leftarrow \bigsqcap S]$

The first of these states that the disjunction of a set is a lower bound of all its members (in the implication ordering), and the second states that it is the greatest such lower bound. The least upper bound operator is often abbreviated to *glb*.

The concept of arbitrary, perhaps infinite, non-determinism has been introduced not as a programming notation but as an aid to reasoning about programs. We will see in Chapter 5 that it is actually impossible to define infinite non-determinism within the notations of a programming language, so when it is needed we cannot avoid just assuming its existence and just postulating its properties. This is done implicitly by introducing the notation in an axiom.

If infinite disjunction is not possible to implement as a program, an empty disjunction is even worse: it yields the predicate **false** which can certainly never be implemented

$$\sqcap\{\} = \mathbf{false}$$

If it did exist, it would satisfy *every* specification

$$[\mathbf{false} \Rightarrow P], \qquad \text{for all } P$$

Such a miracle we do not believe in. Indeed, it must remain forever inaccessible to science, because it can never give rise to any observation. Any theory which implies its existence must be to some degree unrealistic, and use of such a theory in engineering practice must involve some element of risk. Nevertheless the miracle is so useful as a mathematical abstraction in reasoning about programs that we give it a special symbol.

Definition 2.5.1 (Miracle)

$$\top_A =_{df} \mathbf{false}$$

$$\alpha\top_A =_{df} A \qquad \square$$

The notation suggests the top (strongest) element in the implication ordering. We will later see some intuitive content for $\top_A$: it stands for a product that can never be used, because its conditions of use are impossible to satisfy, or its instructions are impossible to carry out. Think of a computer with no on-switch, or a bottle of medicine that cannot be opened. A claim for miraculous powers of such a product would be impossible to refute.

In predicate calculus, the dual of disjunction is conjunction. Because of the danger of contradiction, this certainly cannot be included in a programming language, but in reasoning about programs, it is just as useful, and can just as usefully be extended to arbitrary sets of relations. The conjunction of all relations in a set S is denoted by $\sqcup S$, and gives the least upper bound (*lub*) of the set S. Its postulated defining property is dual to that of disjunction, with the implications in the opposite direction

$$[P \Rightarrow \sqcup S] \quad \mathbf{iff} \quad ([P \Rightarrow X] \text{ for all } X \text{ in } S)$$

A system is described by $\bigsqcup S$ just if it is described by every relation in S. The least upper bound of an empty set is the bottom of the lattice

$$\bigsqcup\{\} = \mathbf{true}$$

A mathematical space with an ordering that has the *lub* and the *glb* of all subsets of its elements is known as a *complete lattice*, and we have postulated that the space of relations deserves this title. Furthermore it is *distributive* in the sense that *finite* disjunction distributes into arbitrary conjunction.

L2 $(\bigsqcup S) \sqcap Q = \bigsqcup\{P \sqcap Q \mid P \in S\}$

Many properties of conjunction can be translated to a similar property of disjunction, by reversing the direction of implication (which leaves equations unchanged). Such a property is called *dual*, and the distribution law gives a good example.

L3 $(\bigsqcap S) \sqcup Q = \bigsqcap\{P \sqcup Q \mid P \in S\}$

These distributive properties deserve special names. A function F will be called *disjunctive* if it distributes through arbitrary disjunctions, and *conjunctive* if it distributes through arbitrary conjunctions. For example, sequential composition is disjunctive in each of its two arguments

L4 $(\bigsqcap S); Q = \bigsqcap\{P; Q \mid P \in S\}$ (; left univ disj)

L5 $R; (\bigsqcap S) = \bigsqcap\{R; P \mid P \in S\}$ (; right univ disj)

2.6 Recursion

To explain recursion, we will need to formalise a concept of quantification over variables whose values range over relations with a given alphabet A. We shall use capital letters $X_A, Y_A, \ldots$ for this purpose (but usually leave out the subscript A). Of course, the value of X_A is a relation which also contains free variables in the alphabet A. These variables stand for observations; they are written in lower case, and are subject to quantification by square brackets. In this section, we make no mention of observation variables. They are all encapsulated within a single capital letter, which is known as a *second-order variable* to indicate its purpose and status as standing for a predicate rather than an observation.

Let X be a variable to stand for a call of the recursive program which we are about to define. X is then used, perhaps more than once, to build up the body of the program, using assignments and the various combinators of the programming language. The result may be seen as a formula $F(X)$, whose value will be known as soon as the value of X is known. The engineer may prefer to think of $F(X)$ as an assembly with a vacant slot labelled X, into which some component of an appropriate kind may later be plugged. Now the magic of a recursive definition is to declare that X is just the same as the result of applying F to X itself, or in symbols, it satisfies the equation

$$X = F(X)$$

Such an X is called a *fixed point* of the function F because application of F leaves it unchanged. The same trick can be played with two or more unknowns in a definition by *mutual recursion*. This is expressed by simultaneous equations, for example

$$X = F(X, Y) \quad \text{and} \quad Y = G(X, Y)$$

But for simplicity we shall concentrate on single recursions; multiple recursion is treated fully in Section 9.4.

How does the magic work? Logicians and philosophers, ever since Aristotle, have not allowed themselves to define an unknown X in terms of itself by mentioning it on the right hand side of its own definition. Engineers are even more sceptical: How can the object $F(X)$ be plugged into itself as one of its own components? In physical reality, such feedback can lead to discontinuities, singularities, race conditions, explosions, etc.

Fortunately, computing scientists have found an effective way in practice to implement recursively defined programs by means of a stack. Even earlier, mathematicians discovered how to solve the theoretical paradox of apparently circular definition. The solution we present here is due to Tarski [175]. It depends crucially on the fact that relations are members of a complete lattice, and that all the operators that interest us are monotonic. As a result, any function F which is defined solely in terms of these operators will also be monotonic. Tarski's famous theorem shows that every such function has a fixed point, defined by a formula to be given below.

But there may well be more than one fixed point: Tarski has proved that there will be a complete lattice of them. For example, the miracle $\top$ is a fixed point of sequential composition, because it satisfies

$$X = P; X$$

Because it is the strongest of all relations, it is the strongest of all the fixed points. But we want the recursion to be implementable, which $\top$ certainly is not. We therefore take the other obvious alternative, the *weakest* of the fixed points – the one that is easiest to implement, although most difficult to use. The effect of this decision is that erroneous recursions (those that do not terminate when executed) are revealed as totally useless: they give rise to the worst of all behaviours, namely $\bot$. The weakest fixed point of a monotonic function F will be denoted by μF. It can be implemented as a single non-recursive call of a parameterless procedure with name X and with body $F(X)$. Occurrences of X within $F(X)$ are implemented as recursive calls on the same procedure. The mathematical definition is much more abstract.

Definition 2.6.1 (Weakest fixed point)

$$\mu F =_{df} \sqcap\{X \mid [X \Rightarrow F(X)]\}$$

where the join operator $\sqcap$ is applied to the set of all solutions of $[X \Rightarrow F(X)]$. A definition using the equation $[X = F(X)]$ would give the same result. □

The following laws state that this formula is indeed a fixed point of F, and that it is the weakest one.

L1 $[Y \Rightarrow \mu F]$ whenever $[Y \Rightarrow F(Y)]$ (weakest fixed point)

L2 $[F(\mu F) \equiv \mu F]$ (fixed point)

Proof of L1

$$\begin{array}{lll} & [Y \Rightarrow F(Y)] & \{\text{by set theory}\} \\ \Rightarrow & Y \in \{X \mid [X \Rightarrow F(X)]\} & \{2.5\mathbf{L1A}\} \\ \Rightarrow & [Y \Rightarrow \mu F] & \end{array}$$

The following proof for **L2** is due to Dijkstra and Scholten [52].

$$\begin{array}{lll} & \mathit{true} & \{\mathbf{L1}\} \\ \equiv & \forall X \bullet [X \Rightarrow F(X)] \Rightarrow [X \Rightarrow \mu F] & \{F \text{ is monotonic}\} \\ \equiv & \forall X \bullet [X \Rightarrow F(X)] \Rightarrow [F(X) \Rightarrow F(\mu F)] & \{\Rightarrow \text{ is transitive}\} \\ \Rightarrow & \forall X \bullet [X \Rightarrow F(X)] \Rightarrow [X \Rightarrow F(\mu F)] & \{2.5\mathbf{L1B}\} \\ \Rightarrow & [\mu F \Rightarrow F(\mu F)] & \{F \text{ is monotonic}\} \\ \Rightarrow & [\mu F \Rightarrow F(\mu F)] \wedge [F(\mu F) \Rightarrow F(F(\mu F))] & \{\mathbf{L1}, \text{ with } F(\mu F) \text{ for } Y\} \\ \Rightarrow & [\mu F \Rightarrow F(\mu F)] \wedge [F(\mu F) \Rightarrow \mu F] & \\ \equiv & [\mu F \equiv F(\mu F)] & \end{array}$$

□

The second law **L2** is a mathematical formulation of the "copy rule", which makes a copy of the whole procedure in the place of each one of its calls. This is often given as an explanation to programmers of the meaning of a procedure call. In the case of recursions that terminate properly, there is only a single fixed point, and the copy rule gives its complete meaning. But the mathematics must also deal with the risk of non-termination, because that is the only way the mathematics can help in avoiding that risk. That is why the first law is also needed.

It is usually convenient in a programming language to combine the definition of the function F with the application of the operator μ. The body of the recursive procedure is written as a program text containing occurrences of the higher order variable X

$$\ldots X \ldots X \ldots$$

A call of the corresponding procedure is obtained just by putting $\mu X \bullet$ in front of this

$$\mu X \bullet \ldots X \ldots X \ldots$$

The name X is thereby declared as the name of a recursive procedure, and its occurrences within the text are interpreted accordingly as recursive calls.

Definition 2.6.2

$$\mu X \bullet \ldots X \ldots X \ldots \;=_{df}\; \mu F$$

where $F \;=_{df}\; \lambda X \bullet \ldots X \ldots X \ldots$. □

Example 2.6.3 (Iteration)

A simple common case of recursion is the iteration or while loop. If b is a condition

$$b * P \qquad \text{(while } b \text{ do } P\text{)}$$

repeats the program P as long as b is true before each iteration. More formally, it can be defined as the recursion

$$b * P \;=_{df}\; \mu X \bullet ((P; X) \lhd b \rhd \mathit{II})$$ □

An even simpler example (but hopefully less common) is the infinite recursion which never terminates

$$\mu X \bullet X$$

This is the weakest fixed point of the identity function, or in other words, the weakest solution of the trivial equation

$$X = X$$

It is therefore the weakest of all predicates, namely **true**. In engineering practice, a non-terminating program is the worst of all programs, and must be carefully avoided by any responsible engineer. That is our justification for practical use of a theory which equates any totally non-terminating program with a totally unpredictable one, which is the weakest in the lattice ordering.

Consider now the program which starts with an infinite loop and ends with the assignment of constants to all variables.

$$(\mu X \bullet X);\ (x, y, \ldots, z := 3, 12, \ldots, 17)$$

In any normal implementation, this would fail to terminate, and so be equal to $(\mu X \bullet X)$. Unfortunately, our theory gives the unexpected result

$$x' = 3 \wedge y' = 12 \wedge \ldots \wedge z' = 17$$

This is the same as if the prior non-terminating program had been omitted. To achieve this result, an implementation would have to execute the program backwards, starting with the assignment, and stopping as soon as the values of all the variables are known. While backward execution is not impossible (indeed, it is standard for a lazy functional language, as discussed in Section 9.3), it is certainly not efficient for a normal procedural language. Since we want to allow the conventional forward execution, we are forced to accept the practical consequence that the program

$$(\mu X \bullet X);\ P$$

will fail to terminate for any program P, and the same holds for

$$P;\ (\mu X \bullet X)$$

Substituting $(\mu X \bullet X)$ by its value **true**, we observe in practice of all programs P that

$$\begin{aligned} \mathbf{true}; P &= \mathbf{true} \\ P; \mathbf{true} &= \mathbf{true} \end{aligned}$$

These laws state that **true** is a zero for sequential composition.

But these laws are certainly not valid for an arbitrary relation P (e.g. if P is **false**). As always in science, if a theory makes an incorrect prediction of the behaviour of an actual system, it is the theory that must take the blame. All the assumptions on which the theory is based may then be questioned, starting with the most questionable. In the case of recursion, the obvious first question is whether we were right to accept its definition as the *weakest* fixed point of the defining function. Maybe the *strongest* fixed point would be better.

Exercise 2.6.4

Prove the following fixed point rules [121]

(1) $\mu X \bullet F(G(X)) \;=\; F(\mu X \bullet G(F(X)))$

(2) If $[G(H(X)) \Rightarrow F(G(X))]$ for all X, then $[G(\mu H) \Rightarrow \mu F]$. □

2.7* Strongest fixed point

The strongest fixed point of a monotonic function on a complete lattice can be defined as the dual of the weakest.

Definition 2.7.1 (Strongest fixed point)

$$\nu F \;=_{df}\; \neg \mu X \bullet \neg F(\neg X) \qquad \square$$

Its properties are easily proved by duality: just reverse the direction of the arrows in the laws for the weakest fixed point.

L1 $[\nu F \Rightarrow S]$ whenever $[F(S) \Rightarrow S]$

L2 $[F(\nu F) \equiv \nu F]$

This new interpretation of recursion gives the entirely opposite view of non-termination

$$(\nu X \bullet X) = \mathbf{false}$$

This is a plausible view. One can argue that the reason why the set of observations is empty is because the implementation in practice fails to reach an observable state. Furthermore, the zero laws are immediately validated, because

L3 $\mathbf{false}; P = \mathbf{false} = P; \mathbf{false}$

A recursively defined program is much easier to prove correct using the strongest fixed point νF rather than the weakest fixed point μF. In order to prove that νF meets a specification S, all that is needed by **L1** is to prove $[F(S) \Rightarrow S]$. That is why several early theories of programming [85] have interpreted recursion as the strongest fixed point. Unfortunately the implication in 2.6**L1** for μF goes in the opposite direction. It could be used to prove that a program meets a recursively defined specification, but that is rarely what is wanted.

There are two serious objections to the use of the strongest fixed point. The first has already been mentioned: a non-terminating program implements falsity, which will satisfy *every* specification S

$$[\mathbf{false} \Rightarrow S]$$

This would invalidate the use of implication to model correctness of designs, requiring abandonment of our whole logic of engineering design. Even scientists are allowed to resist the questioning of their most basic assumptions! The second objection is more practical. It is embodied in the law

$$(\mathbf{false} \sqcap P) = P$$

This places a serious burden on the implementor of non-determinism: it requires that if one of the alternatives fails to terminate, the effect must be the same as that of the other alternative. The trouble is that it is impossible to know in advance whether or which of the programs is going to fail; an implementor must therefore execute both alternatives (e.g. by timesharing or running them in parallel), and take the result of whichever terminates first. This wastes all the computing resource allocated to the rejected alternative, and it is certainly not the intended implementation of non-determinism, which is much easier (just select the easier alternative whenever you like).

Although we reject the strongest fixed point as the proper meaning of recursion in a programming language, we can fortunately continue to use the very simple rule **L1** for proving its correctness. Of course, there is an additional proof obligation which is the subject of the remainder of this section: we need to show that the strongest and weakest fixed points are in fact the same; or in other words, that there is altogether only one fixed point. This will be the case for any recursion which is guaranteed in all circumstances to terminate.

A recursion which terminates only conditionally (on some condition C) can be proved correct in a similar way. In this case, it is sufficient to prove conditional equality of the two fixed points, that is

$$[C \wedge \mu F \equiv C \wedge \nu F]$$

This defines a concept of *approximate equality* modulo C: the two fixed points will appear equal to an observer whose observations are confined to the set C. But that is good enough if the specification itself is of the form $(C \Rightarrow S)$. The full proof rule for weakest fixed points can now be formalised.

Lemma 2.7.2

If $\quad [F(C \Rightarrow S) \;\Rightarrow\; (C \Rightarrow S)]$ and $[C \;\Rightarrow\; (\mu F \equiv \nu F)]$

then $\;[\mu F \;\Rightarrow\; (C \Rightarrow S)]$ □

The essential proof of conditional equality of fixed points is often conducted by a process of successive approximation. The condition C is expressed as an infinite disjunction of a weakening chain of predicates.

Definition 2.7.3 (Approximation chain)

A set of predicates $E = \{E_i \mid i \in \mathcal{N}\}$ is called an approximation chain for C if

$$E_0 = \mathbf{false}$$

$$[E_i \Rightarrow E_{i+1}], \quad \text{for all } i \text{ in } \mathcal{N}$$

$$C = \bigvee_i E_i$$

□

If X is any predicate, $X \wedge E_n$ is regarded as the nth approximation to $X \wedge C$, and we state the obvious lemma.

Lemma 2.7.4

If $\quad X \wedge E_n = Y \wedge E_n, \quad$ for all n in $\mathcal{N}$

then $\quad X \wedge (\bigvee_n E_n) = Y \wedge (\bigvee_n E_n)$ □

The most important use of an approximation chain E is to help in proving equality (modulo $\bigvee E$) of the strongest and weakest fixed points of a function F. For this, E must be chosen so that the $(n+1)^{\text{st}}$ approximation of $F(X)$ can be computed from just the nth approximation to X. A function with this property is said to be E-constructive, and it has at most one fixed point modulo E.

Definition 2.7.5 (E-constructive)

Let E be an approximation chain for C. A function F is E-constructive if

$$F(X) \wedge E_{n+1} = F(X \wedge E_n) \wedge E_{n+1}$$

for all X and n. □

Theorem 2.7.6

If E is an approximation chain for C, and if F is E-constructive, then

$$C \wedge \mu F = C \wedge \nu F$$

Proof By Lemma 2.7.4, it is sufficient to show that

$$E_n \wedge \mu F = E_n \wedge \nu F, \qquad \text{for all } n$$

This is done by induction on n:

$$(0) \quad E_0 \wedge \mu F \;=\; E_0 \wedge \nu F \quad \{E_0 \;=\; \mathbf{false}\}$$

$$\begin{aligned}
(1) \quad E_{n+1} \wedge \mu F &= E_{n+1} \wedge F(\mu F) && \{\text{def constructive and 2.6}\mathbf{L2}\} \\
&= E_{n+1} \wedge F(E_n \wedge \mu F) && \{\text{induction}\} \\
&= E_{n+1} \wedge F(E_n \wedge \nu F) && \{\text{def constructive and } \mathbf{L2}\} \\
&= E_{n+1} \wedge \nu F && \square
\end{aligned}$$

This theorem describes the general condition for proving the termination of a recursion. It shows the contribution of the strongest fixed point in reasoning about recursive programs. But it does not give a solution to the problem described in Section 2.6; this is postponed to the next chapter, which the keen or impatient reader could immediately skip to. As so often in science, the solution requires a slight complication of the theory, which has to recognise the relevance of additional factors, and introduce new variables to denote them. These stand for properties of the world which are perhaps not themselves directly observable. However, they can be inferred from more direct observations, and they are successful in predicting others. All the most fundamental concepts in science have been discovered in this way, as corrections to some simpler theory; examples range from friction and viscosity in mechanics to colour and charm in particle physics.

2.8* Preconditions and postconditions

A condition p has been defined as a predicate not containing dashed variables. It describes the values of global variables of a program Q before its execution starts. Such a condition is therefore called a *precondition* of the program. If r is a condition, let r' be the result of placing a dash on all its variables. As a result, r' describes the values of the variables of a program Q when it terminates. Such a condition is therefore said to be a *postcondition* for the program. Important aspects of the behaviour of a program can often be specified simply by means of a postcondition. Usually, this needs to be accompanied by a precondition, which the designer of the program has to *assume* to be satisfied at the start. The discharge of this assumption is the responsibility of the user of the program, or the designer of some previously executed part of the program, who will accept the precondition of the later part as a postcondition of the earlier part.

The overall specification of the program can often be formalised as a simple implication $(p \Rightarrow r')$. As usual, the correctness of a program Q is also interpreted as an implication, and the triple (precondition, program, postcondition) is known as a Hoare triple [85].

Definition 2.8.1 (Hoare triple)

$$p\{Q\}r =_{df} [Q \Rightarrow (p \Rightarrow r')] \qquad \square$$

This definition validates a number of classical proof rules for proving the correctness of a program.

Theorem 2.8.2 (Hoare proof rules)

L1 If $p\{Q\}r$ and $p\{Q\}s$ then $p\{Q\}(r \wedge s)$

L2 If $p\{Q\}r$ and $q\{Q\}r$ then $(p \vee q)\{Q\}r$

L3 If $p\{Q\}r$ then $(p \wedge q)\{Q\}(r \vee s)$

L4 $r(e)\{x := e\}r(x)$

L5 If $(p \wedge b)\{Q1\}r$ and $(p \wedge \neg b)\{Q2\}r$ then $p\{Q1 \lhd b \rhd Q2\}r$

L6 If $p\{Q1\}s$ and $s\{Q2\}r$ then $p\{Q1; Q2\}r$

L7 If $p\{Q1\}r$ and $p\{Q2\}r$ then $p\{Q1 \sqcap Q2\}r$

L8 If $b \wedge c\{Q\}c$ then $c\{\nu X \bullet Q; X \lhd b \rhd I\!I\}(\neg b \wedge c)$

L9 $false\{Q\}r$ and $p\{Q\}true$ and $p\{\mathbf{false}\}false$ and $p\{I\!I\}p$

Proof of L8 Let $Y =_{df} c \Rightarrow \neg b' \vee c'$. By 2.7**L1**, it is sufficient to prove

$$[(Q; Y) \lhd b \rhd I\!I \Rightarrow Y]$$

Assume the antecedents

$$
\begin{array}{lll}
 & (Q; Y \lhd b \rhd I\!I) \wedge c & \{b \wedge (P; Q) = (b \wedge p); Q\} \\
= & (b \wedge c \wedge Q); Y \vee (\neg b \wedge c \wedge I\!I) & \{b \wedge c\{Q\}c, c\{Y\}\neg b \wedge c, \textbf{L6} \text{ and } \textbf{L9}\} \\
\Rightarrow & \neg b' \wedge c' & \Box
\end{array}
$$

These proof rules use the preconditions and postconditions purely as program specifications; they permit reasoning about program correctness to be detached as quickly as possible from the text of the program. The mathematical hypotheses which need proof can be extracted mechanically with the aid of a verification condition generator (VCG) [109]. But conditions can play an even more vital role in explaining the meaning of a program if they are included at appropriate points as an integral part of the program documentation. Such a condition is asserted or expected to be true at the point at which it is written. It is known as a Floyd assertion [57]; formally, it is defined to have no effect if it is true, but to cause failure if it is false. Failure is something that everyone agrees must be avoided.

It is often important to distinguish who or what is responsible for a failure. If it is the designer or the programmer, failure should be represented by $\bot$, because this can never be proved to meet its specification. But if the failure is due to the failure of the environment to meet agreed commitments, then the appropriate representation is by $\top$. There is then no obligation on the designer to prove anything. Preconditions are a prime example of this kind of permitted assumption.

Definition 2.8.3 (Floyd assertion and assumption)

$$
\begin{array}{lll}
c_{\bot} & =_{df} \; I\!I \lhd c \rhd \bot & \text{(assertion)} \\
c^{\top} & =_{df} \; I\!I \lhd c \rhd \top & \text{(assumption)} \quad \Box
\end{array}
$$

Definition 2.8.1 of correctness can be rewritten in a number of different ways.

$$
\begin{array}{rl}
[Q \Rightarrow (p \Rightarrow r')] & = [p \Rightarrow (Q \Rightarrow r')] \\
 & = [p \Rightarrow (\forall v'. Q \Rightarrow r')] \\
 & = [p \Rightarrow \neg \exists v'(Q \wedge \neg r')] \\
 & = [p \Rightarrow \neg (Q; \neg r)]
\end{array}
$$

This last reformulation gives an answer to the question: What is the *weakest* precondition under which execution of Q is guaranteed to achieve the postcondition r' ?

Definition 2.8.4 (Weakest precondition)

$$Q\,\mathbf{wp}\,r \quad =_{df} \quad \neg(Q; \neg r) \qquad \square$$

The calculation of the weakest precondition may be assisted by the following laws.

L10 $(x := e)\,\mathbf{wp}\,r(x) \;=\; r(e)$

L11 $(P;Q)\,\mathbf{wp}\,r \;=\; P\,\mathbf{wp}\,(Q\,\mathbf{wp}\,r)$

L12 $(P \lhd b \rhd Q)\,\mathbf{wp}\,r \;=\; (P\,\mathbf{wp}\,r) \lhd b \rhd (Q\,\mathbf{wp}\,r)$

L13 $(P \sqcap Q)\,\mathbf{wp}\,r \;=\; (P\,\mathbf{wp}\,r) \wedge (Q\,\mathbf{wp}\,r)$

The weakest precondition satisfies a number of additional laws, known as *healthiness* conditions. Firstly, it is monotonic in its postcondition. An easier postcondition in general makes the precondition easier too.

L14 If $[r \Rightarrow s]$ then $[Q\,\mathbf{wp}\,r \Rightarrow Q\,\mathbf{wp}\,s]$

It is, however, *antimonotonic* in the program which is its first argument. A weaker program is less predictable, less controllable, and more likely to fail. It is therefore harder to satisfy the precondition for success of the weaker program.

L15 If $[Q \Rightarrow S]$ then $[S\,\mathbf{wp}\,r \Rightarrow Q\,\mathbf{wp}\,r]$

Antimonotonicity means that **wp** itself can never be included in an implemented programming language, and even when used in specifications or designs, it must never be involved in recursion through its first argument.

A stronger property than monotonicity is conjunctivity, defined as distribution through conjunction of an arbitrary set of postconditions.

L16 $Q\,\mathbf{wp}\,(\bigwedge R) = \bigwedge\{Q\,\mathbf{wp}\,r \mid r \in R\}$

This means that (when R is empty) our definition of **wp** differs slightly from the original definition given by Dijkstra [50], which does not satisfy

$$Q\,\mathbf{wp}\,true = true$$

This discrepancy is resolved by the method introduced in Chapter 3.

At the other extreme, one would expect that the achievement of the impossible postcondition *false* would also be impossible.

L17 $Q\,\mathbf{wp}\,false = false,$ provided $Q; \mathbf{true} = \mathbf{true}$

This is known as the law of the excluded miracle, and is usually quoted without the proviso. In the next chapter we will show that the omission of the proviso is justified, because all programs satisfy it anyway.

In specifying and designing a program, the postcondition conveys far more significant information than the precondition. It is therefore recommended practice to design a program backwards from the postcondition. Given a proposed design of a final program segment Q, it is possible (by calculation mostly) to deduce the *weakest* precondition under which Q will satisfy the postcondition r. This precondition can often be simplified by strengthening, and then it is taken as the postcondition in the design of the next preceding segment of the program. The systematic design continues until the calculated precondition is implied by the originally stated precondition for the whole program. Then the programming task is complete.

An interesting generalisation of the weakest precondition is the *weakest prespecification*. It is obtained merely by allowing the second argument of **wp** to be an arbitrary relation, containing both dashed and undashed variables. It gives an answer to the question: What is the weakest specification of a program P whose execution before Q is certain to meet specification S?

L18 $[(P;Q) \Rightarrow S]$ **iff** $[P \Rightarrow Q\,\mathbf{wp}\,S]$

The relevance of conditions in reasoning about programs was known to Turing and von Neumann [179]. They were rediscovered by Floyd (and called assertions) [57] and by Naur (and called generalised snapshots) [134]. Floyd suggested that the assertions encapsulate the meaning of a program, and Hoare suggested that the laws of reasoning with assertions should be accepted as an axiomatic definition of the meaning of the whole programming language [85]. The axiomatic approach was adopted also by Dijkstra in his development of weakest preconditions [50]. The approach of this book is not axiomatic: we prefer to prove the necessary laws as theorems based on an independent mathematical definition of the meaning of a program as a relation. In this we follow the example of standard mathematical practice, to provide a link between its purer and the more applied branches. The axioms postulated in one branch are proved as the theorems of a more basic theory.

Exercises 2.8.5

Prove the following laws for Floyd assertions and assumptions.

(1) $b_\perp ; c_\perp \;=\; (b \wedge c)_\perp \;=\; b_\perp \sqcap c_\perp$

(2) $b^\top ; c^\top \;=\; (b \wedge c)^\top \;=\; b^\top \sqcup c^\top$

(3) $b^\top ; b_\perp \;=\; b^\top$ □

2.9 Variable declarations

An essential characteristic of engineering is that the internal details of the working of its products are of no concern to their users, which is why they are usually concealed from observation and interference by an opaque casing and an instruction not to open it. In Chapter 1 it was shown that this concealment from observation is represented in the predicate calculus by quantification over the irrelevant free variables, which are then removed from the alphabet of the predicate. Section 2.2 gave an important example – the forgetting of the intermediate values of the variables on transition between the first and second operands of a sequential composition. In this section we extend the method of concealment from the temporal domain of program execution to the spatial domain of computer storage.

An essential characteristic of program design is that the efficient implementation of any non-trivial algorithm requires the invention and introduction of additional temporary variables; they store the results of intermediate calculation for repeated use on later occasions. The values of these variables are of no concern to the user of the program, and they should be concealed, as usual, by existential quantification. Since each program variable is represented in the predicate by two observational variables, one dashed and one undashed, both of these must be treated appropriately.

To introduce a new program variable x we use the form of *declaration*

$$\mathbf{var}\, x$$

which permits the variable x to be used in the portion of the program that follows it. The complementary operation (called *undeclaration*) takes the form

$$\mathbf{end}\, x$$

and terminates the region of permitted use of the variable x. The portion of program Q in which a variable x may be used is called its *scope*; it is bracketed on the left and on the right by the declaration and undeclaration

$$\mathbf{var}\, x;\ Q;\ \mathbf{end}\, x$$

In this case, x is called a *local* variable of Q, and Q is called a *block*. However, it is sometimes (e.g. in Section 4.4) beneficial both in theory and in practice to reason separately about unbracketed fragments of the form ($\mathbf{var}\, x$; Q) and (Q; $\mathbf{end}\, x$).

In programming languages, as in conventional mathematical reasoning, it is usual to associate a type T with each variable, and this is often done on the occasion of its declaration

$$\mathbf{var}\, x : T$$

The type T determines the range of possible values for the variable, and there is usually a syntactically enforceable guarantee that no assignment can take a variable's value outside its declared range. (Alternatively, such assignment is specified to lead to disaster.) In this section it is convenient to ignore all distinctions of type, so that the results will apply to languages with any kind of type structure.

Definition 2.9.1 (Declaration and undeclaration)

Let A be an alphabet which includes x and x'. Then

$$\begin{aligned} \mathbf{var}\, x &=_{df} \exists x \bullet \mathit{II}_A \\ \mathbf{end}\, x &=_{df} \exists x' \bullet \mathit{II}_A \\ \alpha(\mathbf{var}\, x) &=_{df} A \setminus \{x\} \\ \alpha(\mathbf{end}\, x) &=_{df} A \setminus \{x'\} \end{aligned}$$ □

Note that the alphabet constraints forbid the redeclaration of a variable within its own scope. For example, $\mathbf{var}\, x\, ; \mathbf{var}\, x$ is disallowed because

$$x' \in out\alpha(\mathbf{var}\, x) \quad \text{but} \quad x \notin in\alpha(\mathbf{var}\, x)$$

and as a result the composition is undefined. We shall see later how this restriction may be relaxed, to permit nested and even recursive declarations of the same variable.

Declaration and undeclaration act exactly like existential quantification over their scopes

$$\begin{aligned} \mathbf{var}\, x; Q &= \exists x \bullet Q \\ Q; \mathbf{end}\, x &= \exists x' \bullet Q \end{aligned}$$

For convenience we allow variables to be declared together in a list provided they are all distinct

$$\mathbf{var}\, x, y, \ldots, z \quad \text{instead of} \quad \mathbf{var}\, x;\ \mathbf{var}\, y;\ \ldots;\ \mathbf{var}\, z$$

We will also allow initialisation to be combined with declaration

$$\mathbf{var}\, x := e \quad \text{instead of} \quad \mathbf{var}\, x; x := e$$

The algebraic laws for declaration closely match those for existential quantification. Both declaration and undeclaration are commutative.

L1 $(\mathbf{var}\, x\, ; \mathbf{var}\, y) = (\mathbf{var}\, y\, ; \mathbf{var}\, x) = \mathbf{var}\, x,\, y$

L2 $(\mathbf{end}\, x\, ; \mathbf{end}\, y) = (\mathbf{end}\, y\, ; \mathbf{end}\, x) = \mathbf{end}\, x,\, y$

L3 $(\mathbf{var}\, x\, ; \mathbf{end}\, y) = (\mathbf{end}\, y\, ; \mathbf{var}\, x)$, provided x and y are distinct

The initial value of a declared variable is arbitrarily non-deterministic.

L4 If T is the type of x, then $\mathbf{var}\, x \;=\; \sqcap\{\mathbf{var}\, x := k \mid k \in T\}$

Declaration and undeclaration distribute through a conditional as long as no interference occurs with the condition.

L5 If x is not free in b, then

$$\begin{aligned} \mathbf{var}\, x\,;\,(P \lhd b \rhd Q) \;&=\; (\mathbf{var}\, x\,;\,P) \lhd b \rhd (\mathbf{var}\, x\,;\,Q) \\ \mathbf{end}\, x\,;\,(P \lhd b \rhd Q) \;&=\; (\mathbf{end}\, x\,;\,P) \lhd b \rhd (\mathbf{end}\, x\,;\,Q) \end{aligned}$$

$\mathbf{var}\, x$ followed by $\mathbf{end}\, x$ has no effect whatsoever. In practice, there is a risk that available computer storage may run out; such unfortunate events may be modelled within the theory by introducing variables to account for resource utilisation, as in Example 7.2.1.

L6 $\mathbf{var}\, x\,;\,\mathbf{end}\, x \;=\; I\!I$

The next law states that the sequential composition of $\mathbf{end}\, x$ with $\mathbf{var}\, x$ has no effect whenever it is followed by an update of x that does not rely on the previous value of x.

L7 $(\mathbf{end}\, x\,;\,\mathbf{var}\, x := e) = (x := e)$, provided that x does not occur in e

Assignment to a variable just before the end of its scope is irrelevant.

L8 $(x := e; \mathbf{end}\, x) = \mathbf{end}\, x$

One of the purposes of introducing local variables into a program is to break up a complex calculation into a series of simpler calculations that can be understood and performed separately. For example,

$$y := y^2 \times (6y^4 + 1)/12$$

is logically equivalent to the block

$$\mathbf{var}\, x := y^2;\; y := x \times (6 \times x^2 + 1)/12;\; \mathbf{end}\, x$$

The declaration and undeclaration of x are essential to equalise the alphabets of the two programs; without equal alphabets they cannot even be compared, let alone proved equal.

A conventional digital computer is not capable of direct execution of generally bracketed expressions of a programming language. Reduction of the complexity of expressions is one of the essential tasks in the translation of a program from its high level language to the machine code of a computer that will execute it. In fact, many computers can execute only the simplest assignments, with just two or three operands, and most of these operands must be selected from among the available machine registers. The registers are usually given names like a, b, c, which are assumed distinct from all variables of the programming language. A list of typical machine code instructions is given in Table 2.9.2.

name	effect
load x	$a, b := x, a$
store x	$x, a := a, b$
add	$a := a + b$
subtract	$a := a - b$
multiply	$a := a \times b$
divide	$a := a/b$

Table 2.9.2 Machine code instructions

In principle, the translation of a source program is accomplished by algebraic transformations, which reduce it to a form containing only instructions in the repertoire of the machine, as shown in Table 2.9.4. The registers of the machine are just components of an implementation on a particular machine. After they are hidden, the meaning of the machine code is the same as that of the high level program – or better.

Exercise 2.9.3 (Compilation of assignments)

Consider a programming language with suitable restrictions on the operations permitted in expressions. Prove that every sequence of assignments can be translated into a sequence of machine code instructions (Table 2.9.2), together with declarations of additional local variables standing for machine registers. □

var a, b; $\quad a, b := y, a$;	load y
$a, b := z, a$;	load z
$a := a \times b$;	multiply
$a, b := w, a$;	load w
$a := a + b$;	add
$x, a := a, b$	store x
end a, b	

Table 2.9.4 Machine code for $(x := y \times z + w)$

If x and x' are in the alphabet of Q, the bracketed declarations

$$\mathbf{var}\, x; Q; \mathbf{end}\, x$$

provide a means of removing these variables from the alphabet. The converse operation is defined on a program R which does not have x or x' in its alphabet, and produces a result which does. Since R certainly does not update x, it is reasonable to assume that the final value x' is the same as the initial value x.

Definition 2.9.5 (Alphabet extension)

Let $x, x' \notin \alpha R$

$$\begin{aligned} R_{+x} &=_{df} R \wedge (x' = x) \\ \alpha R_{+x} &=_{df} \alpha R + \{x, x'\} \end{aligned} \qquad \square$$

The following laws state how declaration and alphabet extension cancel each other.

L9 If R does not mention x, then

$$\mathbf{var}\, x; R_{+x}; P; \mathbf{end}\, x \;=\; R; \mathbf{var}\, x; P; \mathbf{end}\, x$$

$$\mathbf{var}\, x; P; R_{+x}; \mathbf{end}\, x \;=\; \mathbf{var}\, x; P; \mathbf{end}\, x; R$$

Alphabet extension enables sequential composition to be applied to operands with non-matching alphabets. For example, if x is in αQ but x, x' are not in αP, then $(P; Q)$ is illegal, but $(P_{+x}; Q)$ can be written instead. This alphabet extension is unavoidable if P is a call of a procedure whose body was written outside the scope of the variable x, as described in Section 9.1. In fact, it is convenient just to write the simpler illegal form, on the understanding that it should be made legal by extending the alphabets of one or both of the operands in the minimal possible way.

The most important application of alphabet extension is for the declaration of local variables within recursively defined programs, for example

$$R \;=_{df}\; (\mu X \bullet \mathbf{var}\, x; \ldots; X; \ldots; \mathbf{end}\, x)$$

Because x is a local variable of R, the alphabet of R by Definition 2.9.1 excludes x and x'. But by the fixed point property of recursion

$$R \;=\; \mathbf{var}\, x; \ldots; R; \ldots; \mathbf{end}\, x$$

Unfortunately, the right hand side of this equation is now syntactically incorrect, because the alphabet of the internal R does not match its context.

The solution is to extend the alphabet of the internal call to match the alphabet of its context

$$R \;=_{df}\; \mu X \bullet \mathbf{var}\, x; \ldots ; X_{+x}; \ldots ; \mathbf{end}\, x$$

Apart from restoring syntactic correctness, the definition of alphabet extension also states that the value of the local variable x remains unchanged, even though the recursive call declares and manipulates a local variable with the same name. The constancy of the local variable at each level of recursion is essential to the correctness of recursively defined programs, and to reasoning about it.

The rule of alphabet extension for a recursive call places a strong duty on an implementation: it must reserve separate storage for local variables at each level of recursion. The storage may be released again on exit from that level of recursion, thereby permitting an efficient implementation of storage allocation by means of a stack.

Exercise 2.9.6

Prove that

$$\begin{aligned} (\mathbf{var}\, x)\, \mathbf{wp}\, r &= \forall x \bullet r \\ (\mathbf{end}\, x)\, \mathbf{wp}\, r &= r, \qquad \text{if } x \text{ is not free in } r \end{aligned}$$ □

Chapter 3

Designs

In this chapter, we work towards a more precise characterisation of the class of relations that are most useful in program design, namely those that are expressible (or at least implementable) in the limited notations of a particular programming language. As usual, we follow the standard practice of mathematics, which is to classify the basic concepts by their most important properties. For example, among the functions of real numbers, it is useful to single out those that are integrable, or continuous, or differentiable. A similar classification of the basic concept of a relation is essential to our goal of unifying theories of programming.

A subclass of formulae may be defined in a variety of ways. Sometimes it is done by a syntactic property, for example that a function can be expressed in a certain normal form using only a limited vocabulary of operators. Sometimes the definition requires satisfaction of a particular collection of algebraic laws. And sometimes the definition is by a general mathematical property: for example, a polynomial is a function whose higher derivatives all vanish. But the most useful definitions are those that are given in many different forms, together with a proof that all of them are equivalent.

The main goal of this chapter is to solve the paradox of non-termination presented in Section 2.6. We need therefore to define a subclass of relation P which can be proved to satisfy the zero laws

$$\mathbf{true}; P \quad = \quad \mathbf{true} \quad = \quad P; \mathbf{true}$$

Clearly this class must exclude the miraculous predicate **false**, which fails to satisfy these laws; indeed

$$\mathbf{true}; \mathbf{false} \quad = \quad \mathbf{false} \quad = \quad \mathbf{false}; \mathbf{true}$$

The easiest way to define the required subclass is to use the laws themselves as the defining property. Unfortunately the class of relations that satisfy the zero laws themselves is too large, and does not have the right closure properties. It is necessary to define a slightly more restricted class of predicates by means of a slightly stronger collection of laws known as healthiness conditions. There are four laws in all, which will be numbered **H1**, **H2**, **H3** and **H4**.

Relations satisfying **H1** already satisfy the left zero law for **true**. Section 3.2 introduces the conditions **H3** and **H4**, and shows how the right zero law is also satisfied. This finally solves the outstanding problem raised in Section 2.6. Relations satisfying the first two laws can be split into two parts: an *assumption*, which a designer can assume will be satisfied before the program starts; and a *commitment*, which the program has to meet when it terminates. Such pairs of predicates are called *designs*; they are amenable to a calculus of refinement – essentially the same as that described by [14, 129, 130], or that used in the Vienna Development Method [101]. Section 3.1 shows that the definitions of these earlier calculi can be proved as theorems in the simpler calculus of relations. In this way, we achieve a unification of single-predicate theories of programming, like those based on B [7] or Z [171], with the familiar double-predicate theories of refinement; both of them can now be used interchangeably or in combination whenever this is most convenient.

The formalisation of the four healthiness conditions depends on a more explicit analysis of the phenomena of program initiation and termination, and this is what leads to a solution to the original problem of non-termination. We therefore introduce into the alphabet of our predicates a pair of Boolean variables to denote the relevant observations.

Definition 3.0.1 (ok and ok')

ok records the observation that the program has been started.

ok' records the observation that the program has terminated. Here, termination means proper normal termination, without error messages etc. □

If ok' is false, the program has not terminated and the final values of the program variables are unobservable: the predicate describing the program should make no prediction about these values. Similarly, if ok is false, the program has never started and even the initial values are unobservable. These considerations underlie the validity of the desired zero laws for sequential composition.

The variables ok and ok' are not global variables held in the store of any program, and it is assumed that they will never be mentioned in any expression or assignment of the program text. Furthermore, they will not be mentioned in any of the predicates featuring as assumptions or commitments; these are restricted to just the program variables, either in their dashed or undashed forms. However, the variables ok and ok' are *included* in the list of variables that are existentially quantified in the definition of sequential composition, and they are *included* in the list of universally quantified variables that are abbreviated by square brackets.

3.1 The refinement calculus

The purpose of the refinement calculus is to assist in the design of a complex software product. As indicated in Section 1.5, the complexity is mastered by splitting the overall task into well-defined separate subtasks, together with a proof (given in advance) that the assembly of components that fulfil the separate subtasks will meet the original overall goal. A design task is generally described by a pair of predicates: an *assumption* P which the designer can rely on when the program is initiated, and a *commitment* Q which must be true when the program terminates. The preconditions and postconditions of Section 2.8 are special cases of assumptions and commitments, but now we relax the restriction that forbids mention of dashed variables. The main achievement of the refinement calculus is to show how the assumptions made in one part of the design can be discharged by commitments made in other parts. Any outstanding assumptions are transmitted to a more global environment, or eventually to the user of the product. It is just this careful accounting of assumptions and commitments that enables a large team of engineers to collaborate successfully in the implementation of a large product.

There is one assumption that every program design must rely on, namely that the program will be started; that is that *ok* will be true. And there is one commitment that every design must make, namely that the program will terminate; that is that *ok′* will be true. If the assumption is violated, no constraint whatsoever is placed on the behaviour of the program: it may even fail to terminate. These insights permit a precise interpretation of the meaning of an assumption P and a commitment Q as parts of a single predicate describing the overall behaviour of the program. This predicate is

$$(ok \wedge P) \;\Rightarrow\; (ok' \wedge Q)$$

or in words "if the program starts in a state satisfying P, it will terminate, and on termination Q will be true".

The basic concept of a design in the refinement calculus deserves a notation of its own.

Definition 3.1.1 (Design)

Let P and Q be predicates not containing *ok* or *ok′*.

$$(P \vdash Q) \;=_{df}\; (ok \wedge P) \;\Rightarrow\; (ok' \wedge Q)$$

A *design* is a relation whose predicate is (or could be) expressed in this form. **D** will stand for the set of designs. □

In the interpretation of programs and specifications as single predicates, correctness (Section 1.5) is identified with implication. In the refinement calculus, the corresponding ordering is known as refinement. The following theorem shows that the two orderings are the same. The notation $P[e, f/x, y]$ denotes the result of simultaneously substituting e for x and f for y in P.

Theorem 3.1.2

$$[(P_1 \vdash Q_1) \Rightarrow (P_2 \vdash Q_2)] \quad \textbf{iff} \quad [P_2 \Rightarrow P_1] \text{ and } [(P_2 \wedge Q_1) \Rightarrow Q_2]$$

Proof $\quad [(P_1 \vdash Q_1) \;\Rightarrow\; (P_2 \vdash Q_2)]$ $\qquad$ {predicate calculus}

$$\begin{aligned}
\equiv\ & [(P_1 \vdash Q_1)[true,\ false/ok,\ ok'] \;\Rightarrow\; (P_2 \vdash Q_2)[true,\ false/ok,\ ok']] \wedge \\
& [(P_1 \vdash Q_1)[true,\ true/ok,\ ok'] \;\Rightarrow\; (P_2 \vdash Q_2)[true,\ true/ok,\ ok']] \wedge \\
& [(P_1 \vdash Q_1)[false/ok] \;\Rightarrow\; (P_2 \vdash Q_2)[false/ok]] && \{\text{Def. 3.1.1}\} \\
\equiv\ & [\neg P_1 \;\Rightarrow\; \neg P_2] \wedge [(P_1 \Rightarrow Q_1) \Rightarrow (P_2 \Rightarrow Q_2)] && \{\text{predicate calculus}\} \\
\equiv\ & [P_2 \;\Rightarrow\; P_1] \wedge [(P_2 \wedge Q_1) \;\Rightarrow\; Q_2] && \square
\end{aligned}$$

The message of this theorem is that $(P_1 \vdash Q_1)$ is stronger because it has a weaker assumption P_1, and so it can be used more widely; furthermore, in all circumstances where $(P_2 \vdash Q_2)$ can be used, $(P_1 \vdash Q_1)$ has a stronger commitment, so its behaviour can be more readily predicted and controlled.

Equivalence of predicate pairs is defined in the normal way by mutual implication

$$\begin{aligned}
& [(P_1 \vdash Q_1) \;\equiv\; (P_2 \vdash Q_2)] \quad \textbf{iff} \\
& [(P_1 \vdash Q_1) \;\Rightarrow\; (P_2 \vdash Q_2)] \text{ and } [(P_2 \vdash Q_2) \;\Rightarrow\; (P_1 \vdash Q_1)]
\end{aligned}$$

It follows that all equivalent predicate pairs actually denote the same predicate. This gives a degree of freedom in the expression of the commitment, which can be strengthened or weakened in accordance with the equivalences

$$[(P \vdash Q) \;\equiv\; (P \vdash P \wedge Q)] \quad \text{and} \quad [(P \vdash Q) \;\equiv\; (P \vdash P \Rightarrow Q)]$$

In fact, these examples show that $P \wedge Q$ is the strongest and $P \Rightarrow Q$ is the weakest commitment predicate for which the equivalence holds. Any other commitment R that preserves equivalence must lie between them.

$$[(P \vdash Q) \;\equiv\; (P \vdash R)] \;\; \textbf{iff} \;\; [(P \wedge Q) \;\Rightarrow\; R] \text{ and } [R \;\Rightarrow\; (P \Rightarrow Q)]$$

In the extreme case, we have two alternative characterisations of **true**, namely

$$\textbf{false} \vdash \textbf{false} \quad \text{and} \quad \textbf{false} \vdash \textbf{true}$$

The definition of design already solves the first part of the paradox of Section 2.6; the left zero law is valid for all designs.

L1 $\mathbf{true}; (P \vdash Q) \;=\; \mathbf{true}$ (**true**-; left zero)

Proof $\mathbf{true}; (P \vdash Q)$ $\{\text{def of } ;\ \text{and } \vdash\}$

$= \exists ok^0, \ldots \bullet \mathbf{true} \wedge (ok^0 \wedge P \Rightarrow ok' \wedge Q)$ $\{\text{let } ok^0 = false\}$

$= \mathbf{true}$ □

All that remains is to show that every program can be expressed as a design. Unfortunately, this is not so. The problem arises right at the beginning, with our original definition of assignment. A new definition is needed, which recognises the role of *ok* as a precondition.

Definition 3.1.3 (Assignment)

$$x := e \;=_{df}\; (\mathbf{true} \vdash x' = e \wedge y' = y \wedge \ldots \wedge z' = z)$$ □

This definition can easily be generalised to solve the postponed problem of undefined expressions in assignments. For each expression e of a reasonable programming language, it is possible to calculate a condition $\mathcal{D}e$ which is true in just those circumstances in which e can be successfully evaluated [88, 131]. For example,

$$\mathcal{D}17 \;=\; \mathcal{D}x \;=\; true$$

$$\mathcal{D}(e+f) \;=\; \mathcal{D}e \wedge \mathcal{D}f$$

$$\mathcal{D}(e/f) \;=\; \mathcal{D}e \wedge \mathcal{D}f \wedge (f \neq 0)$$

Successful execution of an assignment relies on the assumption that the expression will be successfully evaluated, so we formulate our new definition of assignment

$$x := e \;=_{df}\; (\mathcal{D}e \vdash x' = e \wedge y' = y \wedge \ldots \wedge z' = z)$$

Expressed in words, this definition states that

either the program never starts ($ok = false$) and nothing can be said about its initial and final values,

or the initial values of the variables are such that evaluation of e fails ($\neg\mathcal{D}e$), and nothing can be said about the final values,

or the program terminates ($ok' = true$), and the value of x' is e, and the final values of all the other variables are the same as their initial values.

The definition of the conditional also needs to be modified to take into account the possibility that evaluation of the condition is undefined

$$P \lhd b \rhd Q \;=_{df}\; (\mathcal{D}b \;\Rightarrow\; (b \wedge P \vee \neg b \wedge Q))$$

However, in future we will maintain the simplifying assumption that all program expressions are everywhere defined. We return to the topic of $\mathcal{D}$ in Section 9.3.

The change in the definition of assignment requires us to give a new proof of the relevant algebraic laws.

L2 $(v := e\,;\, v := f(v)) \;=\; (v := f(e))$

L3 $v := e; (P \lhd b(v) \rhd Q) \;=\; (v := e; P) \lhd b(e) \rhd (v := e; Q)$

Proof of L2 $(v := e\,;\, v := f(v))$ {Def. 3.1.3}

$= (\neg ok \vee ok' \wedge (v' = e));$

$(\neg ok \vee ok' \wedge (v' = f(v)))$ {2.4**L6** and **L7**}

$= \neg ok \vee (v' = e); (ok' \wedge (v' = f(v)))$ {def of ;}

$= \neg ok \vee ok' \wedge (v' = f(e))$ {Def. 3.1.3}

$= v := f(e)$ □

The identity element $I\!I$ was defined as a special case of assignment $(v := v)$, and therefore needs a new definition

$$I\!I \;=_{df}\; (\mathbf{true} \vdash x' = x \wedge y' = y \wedge \ldots \wedge z' = z)$$

Fortunately, $I\!I$ is the left unit of sequential composition on designs.

L4 $I\!I\,; (P \vdash Q) \;=\; (P \vdash Q)$ ($I\!I$–; left unit)

The right unit law, however, is not valid for arbitrary designs; a solution to this problem is postponed to the next section.

The redefinition of assignment (Definition 3.1.3) is fortunately the only change that needs to be made to the definitions of Chapter 2. The normal combinators of the programming language have exactly the same meaning as operators on the single predicates as they have on the double predicates of the refinement calculus.

Theorem 3.1.4

(1) $(P_1 \vdash Q_1) \sqcap (P_2 \vdash Q_2) \;=\; (P_1 \wedge P_2 \vdash Q_1 \vee Q_2)$

(2) $(P_1 \vdash Q_1) \lhd b \rhd (P_2 \vdash Q_2) \;=\; (P_1 \lhd b \rhd P_2 \vdash Q_1 \lhd b \rhd Q_2)$

(3) $(P_1 \vdash Q_1); (P_2 \vdash Q_2) \;=\; (\neg(\neg P_1; \mathbf{true}) \wedge \neg(Q_1; \neg P_2) \vdash Q_1; Q_2)$

$$
\begin{aligned}
\textbf{Proof of (3)}\quad & (P_1 \vdash Q_1)\,;\,(P_2 \vdash Q_2) && \{\text{def of };\}\\
= \quad & (P_1 \vdash Q_1)[false/ok']\,;\,(P_2 \vdash Q_2)[false/ok] \ \vee \\
& (P_1 \vdash Q_1)[true/ok']\,;\,(P_2 \vdash Q_2)[true/ok] && \{\text{Def. 3.1.1}\}\\
= \quad & (\neg ok \vee \neg P_1); \mathbf{true} \vee \\
& (\neg ok \vee \neg P_1 \vee Q_1); (P_2 \vdash Q_2)[true/ok] && \{2.4\mathbf{L6} \text{ and } \mathbf{L7}\}\\
= \quad & (\neg ok \vee \neg P_1); (\mathbf{true} \vee (P_2 \vdash Q_2)[true/ok]) \vee \\
& Q_1; (P_2 \vdash Q_2)[true/ok] && \{2.4\mathbf{L6} \text{ and } \mathbf{L7}\}\\
= \quad & \neg ok \ \vee \ (\neg P_1); \mathbf{true} \vee \\
& (Q_1; \neg P_2) \ \vee ok' \wedge (Q_1; Q_2) && \{\text{Def. 3.1.1}\}\\
= \quad & (\neg(\neg P_1; \mathbf{true}) \wedge \neg(Q_1; \neg P_2) \ \vdash \ Q_1; Q_2) && \square
\end{aligned}
$$

This theorem shows that all the combinators of the programming language map designs to designs. Since the primitive assignments have been redefined as designs, it follows that all predicates expressible as programs without recursion are also designs. This result will now be extended to recursive programs as well.

The law for disjunction (Theorem 3.1.4(1)) generalises to the union of arbitrary sets, and a similar law holds for arbitrary intersections.

Theorem 3.1.5

$$
\begin{aligned}
&(1)\ \ \textstyle\bigsqcap_i (P_i \vdash Q_i) &=&\ \ (\textstyle\bigwedge_i P_i) \vdash (\textstyle\bigvee_i Q_i)\\
&(2)\ \ \textstyle\bigsqcup_i (P_i \vdash Q_i) &=&\ \ (\textstyle\bigvee_i P_i) \vdash (\textstyle\bigwedge_i (P_i \Rightarrow Q_i)) \qquad \square
\end{aligned}
$$

This means that designs form a complete lattice under implication ordering. Like all complete lattices, it contains a bottom element $\bot_{\mathbf{D}}$, which is $(\mathbf{false} \vdash \mathbf{true})$. It also has a top element

$$\top_{\mathbf{D}} \ =_{df}\ (\mathbf{true} \vdash \mathbf{false}) \ = \ \neg ok$$

This exactly describes a program that can never be started.

The really important property of a complete lattice is that it contains the weakest fixed point of any monotonic function. We have shown that all programming operators map designs to designs, and since the ordering of designs is the same as that of relations, the operators remain monotonic. It is this that justifies recursion in expressing designs and in developing their implementations, because it ensures that the result of the recursion will still be a design. That completes a demonstration that all programs are expressible as designs. As a result, they all satisfy the left zero law **L1**.

This appeal to Tarski's theorem gives an abstract proof of the validity of μ as a design notation. The following theorem gives an explicit way of calculating the assumption and commitment of a recursively defined design. As shown in Theorems 3.1.4 and 3.1.5, any monotonic function of designs, composed solely by lattice and programming operators, can be analysed as a pair of functions applied separately to the assumption and the commitment, for example

$$(F(P, Q) \vdash G(P, Q))$$

Here, F is monotonic in P and antimonotonic in Q, whereas for G it is the other way round. The weakest fixed point is given by a mutually recursive formula.

Theorem 3.1.6

$$\begin{array}{rrcl} & \mu(X, Y) \bullet (F(X, Y) \vdash G(X, Y)) & = & (P(Q) \vdash Q) \\ \text{where} & P(Y) & = & \nu X \bullet F(X, Y) \\ \text{and} & Q & = & \mu Y \bullet (P(Y) \Rightarrow G(P(Y), Y)) \end{array}$$

Proof Here we only show that $(P(Q) \vdash Q)$ is a fixed point of the recursive equation

$$(X \vdash Y) \;=\; (F(X, Y) \vdash G(X, Y))$$

and leave to our readers the proof that the fixed point is the weakest.

$$\begin{array}{rll} & F(P(Q), Q) \vdash G(P(Q), Q) & \{\text{fixed point, def of } P\} \\ = & P(Q) \vdash G(P(Q), Q) & \{(P \vdash Q) \equiv (P \vdash (P \Rightarrow Q))\} \\ = & P(Q) \vdash (P(Q) \Rightarrow G(P(Q), Q)) & \{\text{fixed point, def of } Q\} \\ = & P(Q) \vdash Q & \Box \end{array}$$

Definition 3.1.3 and Theorems 3.1.4 to 3.1.6 of this section show that all programs of our language can be expressed solely in terms of predicate pairs, without ever translating them into single predicates by Definition 3.1.1. In a presentation of the refinement calculus for intending practitioners, these theorems are often presented as *definitions* of the notations of the programming language. There is no need then to introduce the variables *ok* and *ok'*. This overcomes a common philosophical objection to a variable like *ok'*, whose value when false will never be observed. But this objection can be countered: similar encodings, like points at infinity, are common in mathematics and science, and they can be justified if they simplify the subsequent definitions, calculations and proofs. For exploration of unified theories, simplicity is paramount, though for practical application, the more complicated two-predicate definitions are more helpful. This section has shown how to get the best of both worlds.

Exercises 3.1.7

(1) Prove that $\top_{\mathbf{D}}; (P \vdash Q) \;=\; \top_{\mathbf{D}}$.

(2) Prove that $(x := e); \mathbf{true} \;=\; \mathbf{true}; (x := e) \;=\; \mathbf{true}$. □

3.2 Healthiness conditions

The previous section has made a start on defining an interesting subclass of predicates, namely those that can be written in the form

$$(ok \wedge P) \;\Rightarrow\; (ok' \wedge Q)$$

where P and Q do not contain ok or ok'. A trivial consequence is that all designs D satisfy

$$D \;=\; (ok \;\Rightarrow\; D)$$

From this, the left zero law follows trivially. A slightly less trivial consequence is satisfaction of the left unit law (3.1**L4**)

$$D \;=\; I\!I \,;\, D$$

In this section we explore these and additional conditions that can be placed on designs, to ensure that they satisfy additional desirable laws, such as the right unit law and the right zero law. By far the easiest way of doing this is to use the laws themselves to define the desired subclasses.

Definition 3.2.1 (Four healthiness conditions)

A predicate R is said to be **H1**, **H2**, **H3** and/or **H4** according to which of the following laws it satisfies.

H1 $R \;=\; (ok \;\Rightarrow\; R)$

H2 $[R[false/ok'] \;\Rightarrow\; R[true/ok']]$

H3 $R \;=\; R; I\!I$

H4 $R; \mathbf{true} \;=\; \mathbf{true}$ □

The trouble with such abstract definitions is that it is difficult to see what they are actually saying about programs or about the observations that can be made of program behaviour. Fortunately, each of the laws can be given an intuitive explanation, obtained often by expanding the definition of the operators. For example, **H1** is the simplest: it requires that the predicate R makes no prediction about the final values (or even the initial values) of the program variables until at least the program has started. That is reasonable, because these values are actually impossible to observe: the understood condition for making the observation does not hold. The healthiness condition **H2** states formally that the predicate R is upward closed in the variable ok': as ok' changes from false to true, R cannot change from true to false. The semantic significance of the condition is not great: if R is a specification that under certain conditions allows failure to terminate, then R also allows an implementation which terminates under the same conditions. In other words, no specification can satisfy **H2** if it actually *requires* non-termination, so **H2** is a formal mathematical encoding of the fact that non-termination is something that is never wanted. Theorems 3.2.4 and 3.2.5 will give a similar interpretation of the semantic significance of **H3** and **H4**. The next two theorems describe the exact correspondence between **H1** and two of the laws that are definitely needed in any reasonable algebra for programming.

Theorem 3.2.2 (Algebraic characterisation of **H1**)

A predicate is **H1** **iff** it satisfies the left zero and left unit laws.

Proof of ($\Leftarrow$)

$$\begin{array}{lll} & R & \{\text{assumption : left unit law}\} \\ = & I\!I; R & \{\text{def of } I\!I \text{ and } 2.4\mathbf{L6}\} \\ = & \neg ok; R \ \vee\ I\!I; R & \{\neg ok; \mathbf{true} = \neg ok \text{ and left unit}\} \\ = & \neg ok; \mathbf{true}; R \ \vee\ R & \{\text{assumption : left zero law}\} \\ = & \neg ok; \mathbf{true} \ \vee\ R & \{\neg ok; \mathbf{true} = \neg ok\} \\ = & \neg ok \ \vee\ R & \end{array}$$

($\Rightarrow$)

$$\begin{array}{lll} & \mathbf{true}; R & \{R \text{ is } \mathbf{H1} \text{ and } 2.4\mathbf{L6}\} \\ = & \mathbf{true}; \neg ok \ \vee\ \mathbf{true}; R & \{\mathbf{true}; \neg ok = \mathbf{true}\} \\ = & \mathbf{true} & \end{array}$$

$$\begin{array}{lll} & I\!I; R & \{\text{def of } I\!I \text{ and } 2.4\mathbf{L6}\} \\ = & \neg ok; R \ \vee\ (ok' \wedge v' = v); R & \{\neg ok; \mathbf{true} = \neg ok\} \\ = & \neg ok; \mathbf{true}; R \ \vee\ ok \wedge R & \{\mathbf{true}; R = \mathbf{true}\} \\ = & \neg ok; \mathbf{true} \ \vee\ ok \wedge R & \{\neg ok; \mathbf{true} = \neg ok,\ R \text{ is } \mathbf{H1}\} \\ = & R & \square \end{array}$$

The next theorem states the exact correspondence between the first two healthiness conditions and the syntactic definition (Definition 3.1.1) of a design as a pair of predicates.

Theorem 3.2.3 (Healthiness of designs)

A predicate is **H1** and **H2** **iff** it is a design.

Proof of $(\Rightarrow)$

$$
\begin{array}{lll}
 & R & \{R \text{ satisfies } \mathbf{H1}\} \\
= & \neg ok \vee R & \{\text{predicate calculus}\} \\
= & \neg ok \vee (\neg ok' \wedge R[false/ok']) \vee & \\
 & (ok' \wedge R[true/ok']) & \{R \text{ satisfies } \mathbf{H2}\} \\
= & \neg ok \vee R[false/ok'] \vee R[true/ok'] \wedge ok' & \{\text{Def. 3.1.1}\} \\
= & \neg R[false/ok'] \vdash R[true/ok'] &
\end{array}
$$

Finally we need to prove that designs satisfy **H2**.

$$
\begin{array}{lll}
 & (P \vdash Q)[false/ok'] & \{\text{Def. 3.1.1}\} \\
= & \neg ok \vee \neg P & \{\text{predicate calculus}\} \\
\Rightarrow & \neg ok \vee \neg P \vee Q & \{\text{Def. 3.1.1}\} \\
= & (P \vdash Q)[true/ok'] & \square
\end{array}
$$

The general definition of the assumption in a design allows it to contain dashed variables as well as undashed variables. This is a freedom which it would be better to forego, because there is no way in which such an assumption could be discharged by other components in the program, whether they are executed previously or subsequently. And a dashed variable in an assumption makes the implementation too easy. All that is needed is to find some final value for the dashed variables that makes the assumption false, and then the specification will be trivially satisfied – but probably not in the desired way.

None of these problems arise if the assumption is a precondition, containing only undashed variables. Then the responsibility for making the assumption true can be discharged by the preceding segment of program. This sensible restriction, observed in all current program calculi, corresponds exactly to the third healthiness condition.

Theorem 3.2.4 (Assumption and precondition)

A design $P \vdash Q$ is **H3 iff** its assumption P can be expressed as a condition.

Proof

$$
\begin{array}{lll}
 & (P \vdash Q) \;=\; (P \vdash Q); \mathit{I\!I} & \{\text{Theorem 3.1.4}\} \\
\equiv & (P \vdash Q) \;=\; (\neg(\neg P; \mathbf{true}) \vdash Q) & \{\text{Theorem 3.1.2}\} \\
\equiv & \neg P \;=(\neg P); \mathbf{true} & \{\text{predicate calculus}\} \\
\equiv & P \;=\; P; \mathbf{true} & \square
\end{array}
$$

A significant benefit of **H3** is that it permits a simplification of Theorem 3.1.4(3), replacing $\neg(\neg P_1; \mathbf{true})$ simply by P_1.

If the precondition of a design $P \vdash Q$ is satisfied, the eventual program is required to terminate and deliver final values for the program variables, and these must satisfy the predicate Q. But that will be logically impossible if there are no final values which satisfy Q. This paradox is precluded by **H4**, which states that for *any* initial values of the undashed variables that satisfy P, there exist final values for the dashed variables that satisfy Q.

Theorem 3.2.5 (Feasibility)

$P \vdash Q$ satisfies **H4 iff** $[\exists ok', x', \ldots, z' \bullet (P \vdash Q)]$.

Proof Expand Definition 2.2.1 of ;. □

It is the condition **H4** that excludes the miraculous predicate $\top_{\mathbf{D}}$. **H4** is called a *feasibility* condition; all programs will be proved to satisfy it, and furthermore if a design fails to satisfy it, there is no program that could ever implement that design.

Exercises 3.2.6

(1) Prove that sequential composition, non-deterministic and conditional choices preserve the healthiness conditions.

(2) A design $b(v) \vdash Q(v, v')$ is *predeterministic* if

$$[(b(v) \wedge Q(v, v_1) \wedge Q(v, v_2)) \ \Rightarrow \ (v_1 = v_2)]$$

Prove that if both R and S are predeterministic, so are $R; S$ and $R \lhd b \rhd S$.

(3) Define a condition b to be *stable* if

$$b = b \wedge ok$$

Restrict R to healthy predicates and b to stable conditions, and prove that

$$R \ \mathbf{wp} \ b \text{ is stable}$$

and that it obeys Dijkstra's healthiness condition

$$R \ \mathbf{wp} \ false = false \qquad \text{(absence of miracle)}$$ □

Chapter 4

Linking Theories

In the preceding two chapters we have developed a theory of programming through a series of stages; each stage concentrates on a different and successively smaller class of predicate, defined by healthiness conditions of increasing strength. At each stage, Exercise 3.6.1 shows that the notations of the programming language conserve the healthiness properties of their operands. Thus each stage could be presented independently as a separate closed theory, with its own notations, definitions and theorems. Later, we could explore the mathematical relationships between theories and show that the set of predicates expressible in each theory is essentially just a subset of those of the previous theory. The subset relation is one of the simplest forms of linkage between theories, but it serves as a model for the more elaborate linkage methods introduced in this chapter.

The most general possible way of defining a link between theories is as a function L which maps all predicates from one theory into a subset of the predicates from the other. An example familiar in computing is a compiler, which translates a program in a high level language to one expressed in a lower level language, executed directly by the hardware of a machine. In addition to these practical purposes, the link can reveal a lot about the structure of the theories which it is used to compare.

We shall assume in this chapter that nearly all the theories are complete lattices, and we shall use the symbol $\sqsubseteq$ to stand for the ordering relation between their elements. The use of the form $P \sqsubseteq Q$ in place of $[Q \Rightarrow P]$ emphasises the purely algebraic nature of our definitions and theorems and their proofs; it will help to generalise the results to other kinds of lattice ordering.

In dealing with functions that link theories, we will use standard functional notations. Theories will be identified primarily by their sets of predicates, denoted by bold capitals, for example $\mathbf{S}$, $\mathbf{T}$, $\mathbf{U}$. A total function L which maps every element of $\mathbf{S}$ to some element of $\mathbf{T}$ will be declared by

$$L : \mathbf{S} \rightarrow \mathbf{T}$$

If $L : \mathbf{S} \rightarrow \mathbf{T}$ and $M : \mathbf{T} \rightarrow \mathbf{U}$, then the composition of these functions is denoted by a little circle

$$M \circ L : \mathbf{S} \rightarrow \mathbf{U}$$

It is defined by the formula

$$(M \circ L)(X) \;=\; M(L(X)), \qquad \text{for all } X \text{ in } \mathbf{S}$$

The identity function on **S** maps every element of **S** to itself

$$id_{\mathbf{S}} : \mathbf{S} \rightarrow \mathbf{S}$$

$$id_{\mathbf{S}}(X) \;=\; X, \qquad \text{for all } X \text{ in } \mathbf{S}$$

The image of a function is the set of values it can actually take

$$image(L) \;=_{df}\; \{L(X) \mid X \in \mathbf{S}\}$$

A mathematical theory is characterised not only by the set of values which form its subject matter, but also by the collection of operators that may be applied to these values. The set of symbols chosen for the operators constitute the *signature* of the theory, usually denoted Σ. Different theories often share the same symbols from Σ, and formulae using shared symbols will look the same in both theories. It is very important that a link between these theories should map a formula in one theory to the formula in the other that has the same appearance. Such a link is called a *homomorphism*, or more precisely a Σ-*homomorphism*, where Σ is the set of shared operator symbols. In theories of programming, formulae containing the least fixed point of functions expressible in the theory should also be translated without change.

In Section 4.1 we concentrate on the simple and familiar case when the predicates of one of the two theories form a subset of those of the other ($\mathbf{T} \subseteq \mathbf{S}$, say). The link function is now an *endofunction*, mapping **S** to a subset of itself, and the predicates of **T** are just those in its image. Important properties of an endofunction are monotonicity and idempotence and weakening, and these may occur in interesting combinations. For subset theories, it is important that the result of each operation of the shared signature Σ should be a member of the subset whenever all its parameters are. A link that guarantees this is called a Σ-closure. Reasoning about closure can be generalised to a parameterised family of subsets; their closure properties define a type system, of the kind that is used for checking and optimisation by compilers for many programming languages.

The more general case of a link is a function that maps between disjoint domains. Since the domains are usually lattices, monotonicity is still an important property, and so is distribution through conjunction or disjunction over sets of various sizes, finite, infinite or empty. If a function distributes through arbitrary disjunctions, it is called a *Galois connection*, as defined and described in Section 4.2; its properties are analogous to those of the subset relation, even though its image is disjoint from its domain.

The *weakest prespecification* is an interesting generalisation of the weakest precondition (Definition 2.8.4), in which the argument is an arbitrary predicate, not restricted to just a condition. It contributes to the process of top-down program decomposition by answering the question:

> Given a design Q and a specification S, what is the weakest specification X of a program to be executed before Q such that $S \sqsubseteq X; Q$?

It is an excellent example of a Galois connection, and it shares many properties with more familiar examples, such as approximate division of natural numbers and implication in logic (either classical or intuitionistic). These are the topics of Section 4.3.

The final section of the chapter deals with the case of a Galois connection that can be defined by means of a single predicate within the theory itself. This is known as a *simulation*; its purpose is to map abstract mathematical concepts onto the values which represent them concretely in the store of a computer. The simulation then provides an automatic way of transforming an abstract mathematical algorithm onto the corresponding concrete computer program. An important example is the simulation that maps the symbolic variables of a programming language to the machine addresses of the storage locations which hold their values in a computer at run time.

4.1 Subset theories

If the theory $\mathbf{T}$ is a subset of $\mathbf{S}$, there is always a very simple link from $\mathbf{T}$ to $\mathbf{S}$. It is just the identity function, whose domain has been restricted to $\mathbf{T}$.

$$R : \mathbf{T} \to \mathbf{S} \quad =_{df} \quad (\lambda X : X \in \mathbf{T} \bullet X)$$

A more interesting link is to be sought in the other direction, from the more general expressive theory to the more restricted. It is a function

$$L : \mathbf{S} \to \mathbf{S}$$

from $\mathbf{S}$ to $\mathbf{S}$ itself (an endofunction), which ranges over *all* the members of $\mathbf{T}$

$$\mathbf{T} \quad = \quad \mathit{image}(L)$$

This equation can be used to *define* the subset theory **T** from any chosen endofunction L. A nested sequence of subsets can be derived by composing a sequence of endofunctions, in the desired order.

Examples 4.1.1 (Endofunction)

Let P, Q, J and K be predicates, and let **S** be the set of predicates of a theory.

name	mapping
$id_{\mathbf{S}}$	$\lambda X : X \in \mathbf{S} \bullet X$
or_P	$\lambda X : X \in \mathbf{S} \bullet (P \vee X)$
and_Q	$\lambda X : X \in \mathbf{S} \bullet (Q \wedge X)$
$or_P \circ and_Q$	$\lambda X : X \in \mathbf{S} \bullet (P \vee (X \wedge Q))$
pre_J	$\lambda X : X \in \mathbf{S} \bullet (J; X)$
ass_e	$\lambda X : X \in \mathbf{S} \bullet (v := e\,;\, X)$
$post_K$	$\lambda X : X \in \mathbf{S} \bullet (X; K)$
imp_P	$\lambda X : X \in \mathbf{S} \bullet (P \Rightarrow X)$

□

A common property of a link, shared by all these examples, is *monotonicity*. But some important links do not possess it. In particular, a function which links a lattice of healthy predicates to a theory of feasible predicates has to map the miraculous predicate **false** to the feasible but useless predicate **true**. Such a function cannot be monotonic (unless it trivially maps everything to **true**). In this section we will *not* assume that endofunctions are monotonic; we will explore their other useful properties, particularly *weakening* and *idempotence*.

Definition 4.1.2 (Weakening and strengthening)

A function $L : \mathbf{S} \to \mathbf{S}$ is *weakening* if

$$L(X) \sqsubseteq X, \qquad \text{for all } X \in \mathbf{S}$$

The definition of *strengthening* is similar, using the inequality $\sqsupseteq$. □

Definition 4.1.3 (Idempotence)

A function $L : \mathbf{S} \to \mathbf{S}$ is *idempotent* if

$$L \circ L = L$$

□

Examples 4.1.4 (Weakening)

(1) or_P is weakening and and_Q is strengthening.

(2) If L and M are weakening, so is $L \circ M$. □

Examples 4.1.5 (Idempotent)

The following are idempotents, subject to the stated proviso, which we will assume to hold in future examples.

name	proviso
or_P	
and_Q	
pre_J	$J; J = J$
$post_K$	$K; K = K$
$or_P \circ and_Q$	
$pre_J \circ or_P$	$J; J = J$
$post_K \circ or_P$	$K; K = K$

□

In general, the composition of idempotents is not idempotent.

Counterexample 4.1.6

Let $J = (v < 0)$ and $Q = (v \geq 0)$. Then

$$\begin{aligned} & pre_J(and_Q(\mathbf{true})) \\ = \; & (v < 0) \\ \neq \; & \mathbf{false} \\ = \; & pre_J(and_Q(pre_J(and_Q(\mathbf{true})))) \end{aligned}$$

□

However, idempotence of the composition is assured in certain common cases.

Theorem 4.1.7 (Commuting idempotents)

If L and M are idempotents satisfying $L \circ M = M \circ L$, then $L \circ M$ is an idempotent. □

Examples 4.1.8

(1) pre_J commutes with $post_K$.

(2) or_P commutes with $post_K$ **iff** $P = P; K$. □

If L is an idempotent, its image is actually the same as its set of fixed points, because trivially

$$(\exists Y \bullet X \;=\; L(Y)) \quad \textbf{iff} \quad X \;=\; L(X)$$

If L is monotonic as well as idempotent, and $\mathbf{S}$ is a complete lattice, then its image $\mathbf{T}$ will also be a complete lattice. But take care: the join and meet operations in $\mathbf{T}$ will be different from those in $\mathbf{S}$ (see Example 4.1.9 and Figure 4.1.10). We will distinguish them notationally by subscripts ($\sqcap_{\mathbf{S}}$, $\sqcup_{\mathbf{T}}$), and we will similarly distinguish the fixed point operators $\mu_{\mathbf{S}}$ and $\mu_{\mathbf{T}}$. An even better way to avoid confusion is to discover the common conditions under which these distinctions are unnecessary, because the lattice operators have the same meaning in both the subset and the superset.

Example 4.1.9 ($\sqcap_{\mathbf{S}} \neq \sqcap_{\mathbf{T}}$)

Let $\mathbf{S} =_{df} \{\bot, x, y, z, \top\}$ and $\mathbf{T} =_{df} \{\bot, x, y, \top\}$. Define $L : \mathbf{S} \to \mathbf{T}$ by

$$L(z) \;=_{df}\; \bot$$

$$L(w) \;=_{df}\; w \qquad \text{if } w \neq z$$

Then (see Figure 4.1.10)

$$x \sqcap_{\mathbf{T}} y \;=\; \bot \;\neq\; z \;=\; x \sqcap_{\mathbf{S}} y$$ □

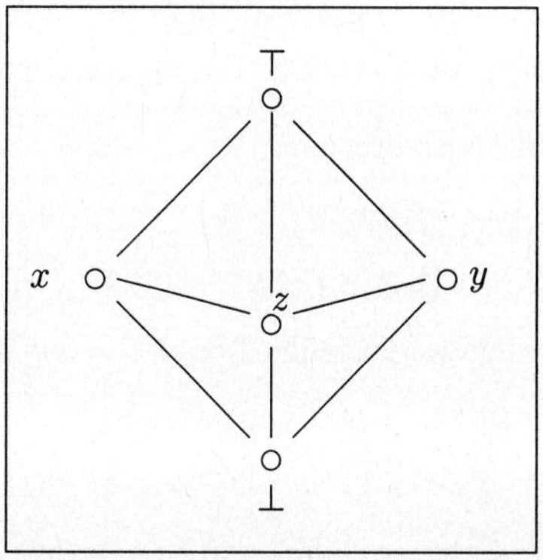

Figure 4.1.10 Not a sublattice

Definition 4.1.11 (Link and retract)

For convenience, we will reserve the term *link* for a function that is both weakening and idempotent; a *retract* is defined as a link that is monotonic as well. □

Examples 4.1.12 (retract)

(1) If $K \sqsubseteq id_{\mathbf{S}}$ then $post_K$ is a retract.

(2) If L and M are retracts, so is $L \circ M$. □

In general, a weaker theory **T** is less able to describe things accurately than a theory **S** that contains more predicates. But for any predicate P in **S**, we can single out those members X of **T** that *approximate to* P, in the sense of describing the same thing less accurately ($X \sqsubseteq P$). The *best* approximation to P is the strongest limit of this set.

Definition 4.1.13 (Approximation)

$$approx_{\mathbf{T}}^{\mathbf{S}}(P) =_{df} \bigsqcup_{\mathbf{S}} \{ X : \mathbf{T} \mid X \sqsubseteq P \}$$ □

Although in general the limit $\bigsqcup_{\mathbf{S}}$ will not be a member of **T**, we will be most interested in the cases when it is, as described in the following theorem.

Theorem 4.1.14

If $\mathbf{T} \subseteq \mathbf{S}$ and $\bigsqcup_{\mathbf{T}} = \bigsqcup_{\mathbf{S}}$, then $approx_{\mathbf{T}}^{\mathbf{S}}$ is a retract. □

Corollary $approx_{\mathbf{T}}^{\mathbf{S}}$ is the only retract linking between **S** and **T**. □

The nature of the weakest fixed point in a subset theory is explored in the following theorem, which gives the necessary assurance that the weakest fixed point exists and belongs to the subset. This is particularly important in Case (2), when L is not monotonic and the subset theory T may not even be a lattice.

Theorem 4.1.15 (Links and recursion)

Let $F : \mathbf{S} \to \mathbf{S}$ be monotonic, and $F(\mathbf{T}) \subseteq \mathbf{T}$.

Let $L : \mathbf{S} \to \mathbf{T}$ satisfy $L \circ F \sqsupseteq F \circ L$.

(1) If L is a monotonic idempotent, then $L(\mu_{\mathbf{S}} F) = \mu_{\mathbf{T}} F$

(2) If L is a link, then $L(\mu_{\mathbf{S}} F) = \mu_{\mathbf{T}} F = \mu_{\mathbf{S}} F$

Proof of (1)

$$\begin{aligned} & \mu_{\mathbf{T}} F = F(\mu_{\mathbf{T}} F) && \{\text{weakest fixed point}\} \\ \Rightarrow\ & \mu_{\mathbf{T}} F \sqsupseteq \mu_{\mathbf{S}} F && \{L \text{ is monotonic}\} \\ \Rightarrow\ & L(\mu_{\mathbf{T}} F) \sqsupseteq L(\mu_{\mathbf{S}} F) && \{L \text{ is idempotent}\} \\ \Rightarrow\ & \mu_{\mathbf{T}} F \sqsupseteq L(\mu_{\mathbf{S}} F) \end{aligned}$$

$$\begin{aligned} & L(\mu_{\mathbf{S}} F) = L(F(\mu_{\mathbf{S}} F)) && \{L \circ F \sqsupseteq F \circ L\} \\ \Rightarrow\ & L(\mu_{\mathbf{S}} F) \sqsupseteq F(L(\mu_{\mathbf{S}} F)) && \{L(\mu_{\mathbf{S}} F) \in \mathbf{T},\ \text{weakest fixed point}\} \\ \Rightarrow\ & L(\mu_{\mathbf{S}} F) \sqsupseteq \mu_{\mathbf{T}} F \end{aligned}$$

$$
\begin{array}{llr}
(2) & \mu_{\mathbf{S}}F \;=\; F(\mu_{\mathbf{S}}F) & \\
& \Rightarrow\; L(\mu_{\mathbf{S}}F) \;=\; L(F(\mu_{\mathbf{S}}F)) & \{L \circ F \sqsupseteq F \circ L\} \\
& \Rightarrow\; L(\mu_{\mathbf{S}}F) \;\sqsupseteq\; F(L(\mu_{\mathbf{S}}F)) & \{\text{weakest fixed point}\} \\
& \Rightarrow\; L(\mu_{\mathbf{S}}F) \sqsupseteq \mu_{\mathbf{S}}F & \{L(X) \sqsubseteq X\} \\
& \Rightarrow\; L(\mu_{\mathbf{S}}F) = \mu_{\mathbf{S}}F &
\end{array}
$$

This shows that $\mu_{\mathbf{S}}F$ satisfies the defining property for membership of $\mathbf{T}$. Since $\mathbf{T} \subseteq \mathbf{S}$, it is the weakest fixed point in $\mathbf{T}$ as well

$$\mu_{\mathbf{S}}F = \mu_{\mathbf{T}}F \qquad \square$$

Corollary Let L be strengthening, and satisfy $L \circ F \;\sqsubseteq\; F \circ L$; then

$$\nu_{\mathbf{S}}F \;=\; \nu_{\mathbf{T}}F \qquad \square$$

That concludes our study of the links between a theory and a subset theory, insofar as each theory is represented purely by its set of predicates. We turn next to an equally important aspect, namely the set of operators which are introduced in the theory to build up complex formulae, predicates and programs from their primitive components. Again, the subset theory will often select only a subset Σ of the operators of the larger theory, and we will assume that all the operators are monotonic.

The main reason for omitting an operator from a subset theory is that when applied to operands in the subset $\mathbf{T}$, it does not necessarily give an answer within that subset. So let us suppose that Σ excludes all such unconstrained operators. Then $\mathbf{T}$ is said to be Σ-*closed*, and the function L that defines $\mathbf{T}$ is a Σ-closure. It is sometimes adequate that the closure be merely approximate.

Definition 4.1.16 (Σ-closure with strengthening or weakening)

Let $F : \mathbf{S} \to \mathbf{S}$ be a monotonic function. L is an F-closure if

$$L \circ F \;=\; F \circ L$$

An analogous definition is given for $F_{\sqsubseteq}$-closure or $F_{\sqsupseteq}$-closure, using inequations

$$L \circ F \;\sqsubseteq\; F \circ L \qquad \text{or} \qquad L \circ F \;\sqsupseteq\; F \circ L \qquad \square$$

The definition of closure is adapted to apply to operators of less or greater arity than one. For example, if K is a constant, L is a $K_{\sqsupseteq}$-closure if

$$L(K) \;\sqsupseteq\; K$$

If G has two arguments, the condition is

$$L(G(X, Y)) \;\sqsupseteq\; G(L(X), L(Y)), \quad \text{for all } X, Y \in \mathbf{S}$$

The definition extends to all the operators of the signature.

Definition 4.1.17 (Σ-link)

A link L is called a Σ-link if it is an F-closure for all F in Σ, and similarly for a $\Sigma_{\sqsubseteq}$-link and a $\Sigma_{\sqsupseteq}$-link. □

Examples 4.1.18 (Σ-closure)

The table gives the operators in Σ for which the function is a closure or an approximate closure.

name	closure	$_{\sqsubseteq}$closure	$_{\sqsupseteq}$closure	proviso
or_P	$\sqcap$, $\triangleleft b \triangleright$		;	$P;P = P$
and_Q	$\sqcap$, $\triangleleft b \triangleright$	;		$Q;Q = Q$
pre_J	$\sqcap$		;	$J \sqsubseteq id_S$
$post_K$	$\sqcap$, $\triangleleft b \triangleright$		;	$K \sqsubseteq id_S$

□

Theorem 4.1.19

If L is a $\Sigma_{\sqsupseteq}$-link, then the set $image(L)$ is closed under all functions in Σ.

Proof For any $X \in image(L)$ and any function F in Σ

$$
\begin{array}{lll}
 & L(F(X)) & \{L \circ F \sqsupseteq F \circ L\} \\
\sqsupseteq & F(L(X)) & \{L \text{ is idempotent}\} \\
= & F(X) & \{L \text{ is weakening}\} \\
\sqsupseteq & L(F(X)) & \square
\end{array}
$$

The important property of a Σ-link is that it applies not just to the finite set of operators in Σ but also to the infinite set of all formulae definable by means of these operators: any program containing only constants and operators of Σ will always denote a predicate in the subset theory $\mathbf{T}$. But what if the program contains recursion, as most programs do? Fortunately, Theorem 4.1.15 shows that the closure property is strong enough to ensure that recursion preserves closure in $\mathbf{T}$.

A successful definition of a subset theory $\mathbf{T}$ requires a proof that $\mathbf{T}$ is Σ-closed for the desired operators in Σ. The proof involves a collection of theorems of the form

$$\text{If } X \in \mathbf{T} \text{ and } Y \in \mathbf{T} \text{ then } (X;Y) \in \mathbf{T}$$

These theorems are often presented in the notations of type theory, for example

$$X : \mathbf{T}, Y : \mathbf{T} \vdash (X;Y) : \mathbf{T}$$

Here, *membership* is represented by colon, and *and* by comma and the consequent is separated from the antecedents by $\vdash$. Nearly all the theorems of Exercise 3.2.6(1) can be cast in this form.

It is often useful to single out not just a single subset of a theory, but rather a whole family of subsets, indexed by a set of parameters that correspond to important properties of the subset. An operator applied to an operand in one member of the family may give a result which is in another member of the family, characterised by different parameters. For example,

$$\text{If } X = and_P(X) \text{ and } Y = and_Q(Y) \text{ then } (X;Y) = and_{P;Q}(X;Y)$$

In the notation of type theory, this could be rewritten

$$X : image(and_P),\ Y : image(and_Q) \vdash (X;Y) : image(and_{P;Q})$$

A collection of laws of this kind may contain enough laws to determine a type for every term in the language; it is then known as a *type system* or a *type theory.* A useful type system will permit an automatic association of a type with every term in the language – often a unique type or a minimal type of some kind. But in this book we will not be further concerned with the interesting and important techniques of automatic type inference.

As an example we will present again the theory of preconditions and postconditions (Section 2.8) in the form of a type theory. We will adopt the notation

$$X : p \rightarrow r \quad \text{instead of} \quad X \sqsupseteq (p \Rightarrow r') \quad \text{or} \quad X = (p \Rightarrow r') \wedge X$$

Theorem 4.1.20

(1) $(\mathit{\Pi} : p \rightarrow p)$, for all conditions p

(2) $X : p \rightarrow q,\ Y : q \rightarrow r \vdash (X;Y) : p \rightarrow r$

(3) $X : b \wedge p \rightarrow r,\ Y : \neg b \wedge p \rightarrow r \vdash (X \lhd b \rhd Y) : p \rightarrow r$

(4) $X : p \rightarrow r,\ Y : q \rightarrow s \vdash (X \sqcap Y) : p \wedge q \rightarrow r \vee s$

(5) If $X : p \rightarrow r$ implies $F(X) : p \rightarrow r$ for all X, then $\nu F : p \rightarrow r$

Proof of (5) From the assumption it follows that the sublattice $\mathbf{T}$ associated with the idempotent $and_{p \Rightarrow r'}$ is an F-closure. From the corollary of Theorem 4.1.15 we conclude

$$\nu F = \nu_{\mathbf{T}} F = and_{p \Rightarrow r'}(\nu_{\mathbf{T}} F) \qquad \square$$

These laws are very similar in appearance to the laws which define the algebraic concept of a *category*. The conditions p, r are the *objects* of the category, and the *arrows* are triples (p, X, r) such that $(X : p \to r)$. The first two laws give the basic properties of categorical composition. They are supplemented in category theory by the associative law for composition and by unit laws for Π, which are also true for programs. In summary, programs are arrows of a category whose objects are conditions. But no further knowledge of category theory will be used in this book.

A frequent goal in the definition of a subset theory is to ensure the validity on that subset of certain additional algebraic laws. For example, the desired law may be of the form

$$X \; = \; L(X)$$

Now if L happens to be idempotent, the goal is very simply achieved: just take the link L itself and define

$$\mathbf{T} =_{df} image(L)$$

As an additional advantage, it is frequently found that other useful laws become true in $\mathbf{T}$, as shown by the examples taken from Chapter 3.

Examples 4.1.21 (Healthiness conditions)

(1) These examples are taken from Section 3.2. Define the following retracts

$$\mathbf{H1} =_{df} or_{\neg ok}$$

$$\mathbf{H2} =_{df} post_K \quad \text{where} \quad K =_{df} (ok \Rightarrow ok') \wedge (v' = v)$$

$$\mathbf{H3} =_{df} post_{\Pi} \quad \text{where} \quad \Pi =_{df} ok \Rightarrow (ok' \wedge v' = v)$$

Then

$X \in image(\mathbf{H1})$ **iff** X satisfies the healthiness condition **H1**

$X \in image(\mathbf{H2})$ **iff** X satisfies the healthiness condition **H2**

$X \in image(\mathbf{H3})$ **iff** X satisfies the healthiness condition **H3**

(2) Let $\mathbf{H4}(X) =_{df} ((X; \mathbf{true}) \Rightarrow X)$, where X is a design. Then

(2a) the mapping **H4** is a $\Sigma_{\sqsupseteq}$-link for $\Sigma = \{\sqcap, \,;\, , \lhd b \rhd\}$, and

(2b) $X \in image(\mathbf{H4})$ **iff** X satisfies the healthiness condition **H4**. □

Exercises 4.1.22

Suppose that the following laws hold for all $X \in \{J, T, B\}$

L1 $X \;=\; X \vee T$ (new top)

L2 $X \;=\; X \wedge B$ (new bottom)

L3 $J; X \;=\; X \;=\; X; J$ (new unit)

L4 $X; X \;=\; X$ (idemp)

Prove that

(1) P satisfies the first three laws **iff** it is a fixed point of the monotonic mapping

$$L(X) \;=_{df}\; J; (T \;\vee\; B \wedge X); J$$

(2) If $B; T \;=\; B$, then all fixed points P of L satisfy the left zero law

$$B; P \;=\; B$$

□

4.2 Galois connections

One of the strongest familiar properties of a function L is that it is a *bijection.* This means that there exists a function L^{-1} which exactly reverses the effect of L, and the same reversal occurs on applying the functions in the opposite order

$$L^{-1}(L(X)) \;=\; X \quad \text{and} \quad L(L^{-1}(Y)) \;=\; Y$$

This property can be expressed more abstractly as

$$L \circ L^{-1} \;=\; id_{\mathbf{T}} \quad \text{and} \quad L^{-1} \circ L \;=\; id_{\mathbf{S}}$$

Two theories which are connected by a bijection have equal expressive power. They may have different alphabets and they may be presented in different styles; they may be implemented with differing efficiency or in different technologies. But everything that can be expressed in one theory can be expressed just as precisely in the other. In this mathematical sense, a bijection is the strongest possible kind of a function to serve as a link between the predicates of two theories. The only trouble is that theories can be *too* similar, because there is *no* interesting mathematical distinction between them.

A mathematically more interesting case is when one theory is genuinely richer than another; it contains features that cannot be exactly mapped into the weaker theory. As a result of the weakness, the function L which maps each predicate of the stronger theory to the weaker one can only give a certain *best approximation* of the same meaning in the weaker theory. So there cannot be an exact inverse for L. Nevertheless, there often exists a function R, which maps in the opposite direction (from the weaker to the stronger), and as far as possible undoes the effect of L. But there is some unavoidable weakening, so the equality which holds for a bijection has to be replaced by an inequation

$$X \sqsupseteq R(L(X))$$

However, when the two functions are applied in the opposite order, they may actually strengthen the predicate Y in the weaker theory

$$L(R(Y)) \sqsupseteq Y$$

It is this second law that ensures that the weakening caused by the function L is as small as possible. Such a pair of functions (L, R) is known as a *Galois connection.*

Definition 4.2.1 (Galois connection)

Let $\mathbf{S}$ and $\mathbf{T}$ both be complete lattices. Let L be a function from $\mathbf{S}$ to $\mathbf{T}$, and let R be a function from $\mathbf{T}$ to $\mathbf{S}$. The pair (L, R) is a *Galois connection* if for all $X \in \mathbf{S}$ and $Y \in \mathbf{T}$

$$L(X) \sqsupseteq Y \quad \textbf{iff} \quad X \sqsupseteq R(Y)$$

R is called a *weak inverse* of L, and L is called a *strong inverse* of R. (Sometimes they are called left adjoint (L) and right adjoint (R).) The restriction to complete lattices is not necessary; the definition applies to any partial order. □

Example 4.2.2 (Conjunction and implication)

Let $and_P(X) =_{df} P \wedge X$ and $imp_P(Y) =_{df} (P \Rightarrow Y)$. It is a simple fact of the predicate calculus that

$$(P \wedge X) \sqsupseteq Y \quad \textbf{iff} \quad X \sqsupseteq (P \Rightarrow Y)$$ □

In Section 1.4, this example illustrated a top-down development technique for designing a component X to fit into an assembly $L(X)$, with the goal that it should meet a specification Y. The weakest allowable specification of the component to meet that goal is calculated as $R(Y)$. The general definition of a Galois connection extends the technique of top-down development to the case when the specification Y is actually expressed in a different theory from the description of the component X. For example, the two theories may have different alphabets, as described in Section 1.6.

The following lemma gives an alternative definition for a Galois connection, which matches the alternative definition of a bijection.

Lemma 4.2.3

Let L and R be monotonic mappings. $(L,\ R)$ is a Galois connection **iff**

$$(L \circ R) \sqsupseteq id_{\mathbf{T}} \text{ and } id_{\mathbf{S}} \sqsupseteq (R \circ L) \qquad \square$$

Exercise 4.2.4

Prove that if $(L,\ R)$ is a Galois connection, then L and R are monotonic. □

This exercise shows that not all bijections are Galois connections. For example, negation is its own exact inverse, but it is far from being monotonic.

Theorem 4.2.5 (Composition of Galois connections)

If $(L_1,\ R_1)$ and $(L_2,\ R_2)$ are Galois connections, then their composition

$$(L_2 \circ L_1,\ R_1 \circ R_2)$$

is alao a Galois connection. □

As in the case of a bijection, a Galois connection is uniquely determined by either of its two components separately.

Theorem 4.2.6 (Uniqueness of adjoint)

If $(L_1,\ R_1)$ and $(L_2,\ R_2)$ both are Galois connections, then

$$(L_1 = L_2) \quad \textbf{iff} \quad (R_1 = R_2)$$

Proof First we show that $(L_1 = L_2) \Rightarrow (R_1 = R_2)$.

$$\begin{array}{lll} & X \sqsupseteq R_1(Y) & \{\text{Def. 4.2.1}\} \\ \equiv & L_1(X) \sqsupseteq Y & \{L_1 = L_2\} \\ \equiv & L2(X) \sqsupseteq Y & \{\text{Def. 4.2.1}\} \\ \equiv & X \sqsupseteq R_2(Y) & \end{array}$$

which implies that $R_1 = R_2$. In a dual way, replacing $\sqsupseteq$ with $\sqsubseteq$, we can show $(R_1 = R_2) \Rightarrow (L_1 = L_2)$. □

A Galois connection can be drawn as a picture, with **T** and **S** represented by plane figures and the functions L and R by arrows in one direction or the other. Figure 4.2.7 shows how L maps the whole of **S** to a subset in the upper areas of **T**, and R dually selects a subset towards the bottom of **S**. The connection between these two subsets is a bijection, showing that each subspace contains an exact image of the corresponding part of the other. More formally, if X is in the image of L then $L(R(X)) = X$, and if Y is in the image of R the $R(L(Y)) = Y$.

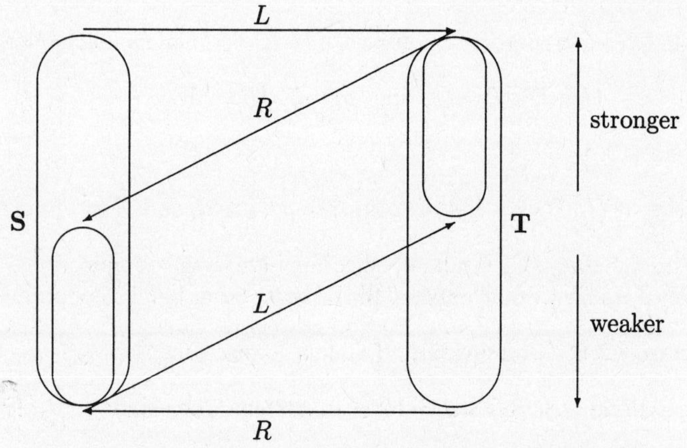

Figure 4.2.7 Galois connection

An interesting special case is when the image of L is the whole of $\mathbf{T}$, that is L is a surjection. This case is captured by a definition in terms of its most important property.

Definition 4.2.8 (Retract and coretract)

A Galois connection $(L,\ R)$ is a *retract* if

$$L \circ R \;=\; id_{\mathbf{T}}$$

It is a *coretract* if $R \circ L \;=\; id_{\mathbf{S}}$. □

A common special case of a retract is when the predicates of the weaker theory $\mathbf{T}$ are selected as a subset of the stronger theory $\mathbf{S}$. In this case, the weak inverse R is just the identity function on $\mathbf{S}$, but restricted to $\mathbf{T}$.

$$R(X) \;=\; X, \qquad \text{for all } X \text{ in } \mathbf{T}$$

Furthermore, the left inverse L is exactly the approximation $approx^{\mathbf{S}}_{\mathbf{T}}$ (Definition 4.1.13). More generally, for any Galois connection $(L,\ R)$, the function $R \circ L$ is a retract on $\mathbf{S}$. This shows the high degree of similarity between Galois connections and subsets.

In Section 2.5 we gave definitions of the conjunctive and disjunctive properties of functions. There are a number of useful weaker versions of these properties, depending on the size of the set over which the lower or upper bound is taken.

Definition 4.2.9 (Disjunctivity and conjunctivity)

Let **U** (not necessarily a lattice) be a subset of **S**. Consider the distributive laws

$$(1)\quad L(\bigsqcup \mathbf{U}) \;=\; \bigsqcup\{L(X) \mid X \in \mathbf{U}\}$$
$$(2)\quad L(\bigsqcap \mathbf{U}) \;=\; \bigsqcap\{L(X) \mid X \in \mathbf{U}\}$$

where $\bigsqcup$ and $\bigsqcap$ stand for the *least upper bound* and *greatest lower bound* operators respectively. L is said to be

- $\bigsqcup^{\infty}$ (universally conjunctive) if the first law is true for all subsets **U**.
- $\bigsqcup^{+}$ (positively conjunctive) if the first law is true for all non-empty **U**.
- $\bigsqcup^{2}$ (conjunctive) if the first law is true for all finite and non-empty **U**.
- $\bigsqcup^{0}$ (strict on bottom) if the first law is true for empty **U**.

Similarly, using the second distributive law as a criterion, we can define a function to be $\bigsqcap^{\infty}$ (universally disjunctive), $\bigsqcap^{+}$ (positively disjunctive), $\bigsqcap^{2}$ (disjunctive) and $\bigsqcap^{0}$ (strict on top). □

Examples 4.2.10 (Disjunctivity and conjunctivity)

name	disjunctivity	conjunctivity
or_P	$\bigsqcap^{+}$	$\bigsqcup^{\infty}$
and_Q	$\bigsqcap^{\infty}$	$\bigsqcup^{+}$
pre_J	$\bigsqcap^{\infty}$	
$post_K$	$\bigsqcap^{\infty}$	

Distributivity gives us an exact criterion for a Galois connection.

Theorem 4.2.11 (Distributivity and Galois connections)

(1) The weak inverse of L exists **iff** L is universally disjunctive.

(2) The strong inverse of R exists **iff** R is universally conjunctive.

Proof Assume that L has a weak inverse R. For any subset **U** of **S** and any $Y \in \mathbf{T}$

$$
\begin{array}{lll}
 & L(\bigsqcap \mathbf{U}) \sqsupseteq Y & \{\text{Def. 4.2.1}\} \\
\equiv & \bigsqcap \mathbf{U} \sqsupseteq R(Y) & \{2.5\mathbf{L1}\} \\
\equiv & \forall X \in \mathbf{U} \bullet (X \sqsupseteq R(Y)) & \{\text{Def. 4.2.1}\} \\
\equiv & \forall X \in \mathbf{U} \bullet (L(X) \sqsupseteq Y) & \{2.5\mathbf{L1}\} \\
\equiv & (\bigsqcap\{L(X) \mid X \in \mathbf{U}\}) \sqsupseteq Y &
\end{array}
$$

So L is universally disjunctive.

Suppose that L is $\sqcap^\infty$. Let $R(Y) =_{df} \sqcap\{P \mid L(P) \sqsupseteq Y\}$. This is the weakest predicate in **S** whose transform by L meets specification Y in **T**.

$$
\begin{array}{lll}
 & L(X) \sqsupseteq Y & \{\text{set theory}\} \\
\equiv & X \in \{P \mid L(P) \sqsupseteq Y\} & \{\text{def of } R\} \\
\Rightarrow & X \sqsupseteq R(Y) & \{L \text{ is mono}\} \\
\Rightarrow & L(X) \sqsupseteq L(R(Y)) & \{L \text{ is } \sqcap^\infty\} \\
\equiv & L(X) \sqsupseteq \sqcap\{L(P) \mid L(P) \sqsupseteq Y\} & \{2.5\mathbf{L1}\} \\
\Rightarrow & L(X) \sqsupseteq Y &
\end{array}
$$

The conclusion (2) can be proved in a similar way. □

Fixed points in Galois-connected theories are related in much the same way as in a subset theory: again, the theorems depend on commutativity between the link and the monotonic function in question.

Theorem 4.2.12 (μ-fusion [121])

Let F and G be monotonic functions, and let $(L,\ R)$ be a Galois connection.

(1) If $R \circ F \sqsubseteq G \circ R$, then $R(\mu F) \sqsubseteq \mu G$

(2) If $R \circ F = G \circ R$, then $R(\mu F) = \mu G$

Proof of (1)

$$
\begin{array}{lll}
 & (R \circ F) \sqsubseteq (G \circ R) & \{L \text{ is monotonic}\} \\
\Rightarrow & (L \circ R \circ F \circ L) \sqsubseteq (L \circ G \circ R \circ L) & \{\text{Lemma 4.2.3}\} \\
\Rightarrow & (F \circ L) \sqsubseteq (L \circ G) & \{\text{def of } \sqsubseteq\} \\
\Rightarrow & F(L(\mu G)) \sqsubseteq L(G(\mu G)) & \{\text{fixed point}\} \\
\equiv & F(L(\mu G)) \sqsubseteq L(\mu G) & \{\text{weakest fixed point}\} \\
\Rightarrow & \mu F \sqsubseteq L(\mu G) & \{\text{Def. 4.2.1}\} \\
\equiv & R(\mu F) \sqsubseteq \mu G &
\end{array}
$$

(2)

$$
\begin{array}{lll}
 & (R \circ F) = (G \circ R) & \{\text{Exercise 2.6.4(2)}\} \\
\Rightarrow & (R \circ F) = (G \circ R) \wedge (R(\mu F) \sqsupseteq \mu G) & \{\text{Conclusion (1)}\} \\
\Rightarrow & R(\mu F) = \mu G &
\end{array}
$$

□

It is time now to turn from the predicates of the two theories to their respective signatures $\Sigma_{\mathbf{S}}$ and $\Sigma_{\mathbf{T}}$. It is very common that these signatures should contain many or all of their symbols in common, and we will confine attention to the symbols that they share

$$\Sigma \;=\; \Sigma_{\mathbf{S}} \cap \Sigma_{\mathbf{T}}$$

In the case of a subset theory, it is reasonable to insist that the same symbol has the same meaning in both theories, and the concept of Σ-closure (Definition 4.1.16) was defined to give the necessary assurance. But in the case of a Galois connection $\mathbf{S}$ and $\mathbf{T}$ are typically disjoint sets, and no operator can have the same meaning on both of them. Nevertheless, it is possible to use the same symbol with two different meanings, and without too much confusion.

The confusion is avoided in the study of algebra by defining the appropriate properties of the function that connects the theories. In particular, it should commute with all operators in Σ.

Definition 4.2.13 (Σ-morphism)

A function $L : \mathbf{S} \to \mathbf{T}$ is an F-morphism if

$$L \circ F_{\mathbf{S}} \;=\; F_{\mathbf{T}} \circ L$$

where the subscripts emphasise (for the last time) that the operators have disjoint meanings in $\mathbf{S}$ and $\mathbf{T}$.

L is an $F_{\sqsubseteq}$-morphism if the equality above is replaced by $\sqsubseteq$, and an $F_{\sqsupseteq}$-morphism is defined similarly. The definition is easily adapted to operators of any arity. A Σ-morphism is an F-morphism for all F in Σ. □

Example 4.2.14

Let $(L,\ R)$ be a Galois connection.
Then L is a $\Sigma_{\sqsupseteq}$-morphism **iff** R is a $\Sigma_{\sqsubseteq}$-morphism. □

Exercises 4.2.15

In the following, assume that (L, R) and (L_i, R_i), for $i = 1, 2$, are Galois connections for appropriate domains and ranges. Prove the claims

(1) $L \circ R \circ L = L$ and $R \circ L \circ R = R$.

(2) Define $(L_1 \sqcap L_2)(X) =_{df} L_1(X) \sqcap L_2(X)$, and $(R_1 \sqcup R_2)(X)$ similarly. Then $(L_1 \sqcap L_2,\ R_1 \sqcup R_2)$ is a Galois connection.

(3) Define the iterates

$$L^{\Diamond}(X) =_{df} (\nu Y \bullet X \sqcap L(Y))$$
$$R^{\Box}(X) =_{df} (\mu Y \bullet X \sqcup R(Y))$$

Then $L^{\Diamond}$ is a retract, and $R^{\Box}$ a coretract.

(4) Burghard von Karger has shown that a Galois connection $(L,\ R)$ forms the basis for temporal logic [118], with the definitions [108]

$$\begin{array}{lll} \oplus P & =_{df} & L(P) & \text{forward step (next)} \\ \diamondplus P & =_{df} & L^{\diamond}(P) & \text{in the future (sometime)} \\ \ominus P & =_{df} & \neg R(\neg P) & \text{backward step (previously)} \\ \diamondminus P & =_{df} & \neg R^{\square}(\neg P) & \text{in the past (sometime)} \end{array}$$

The duals of these give the "always" operators, often written with a box

$$\boxplus(P) \ =_{df} \ \neg\diamondplus(\neg P) \qquad \text{and} \qquad \boxminus(P) \ =_{df} \ \neg\diamondminus(\neg P)$$

With these definitions, prove the following laws of temporal logic

$$\oplus P \wedge \boxplus Q \ \sqsupseteq \ \oplus(P \wedge Q)$$
$$\oplus P \wedge Q \ \sqsupseteq \ \oplus(P \wedge \ominus Q) \qquad \square$$

4.3* Prespecification and postspecification

The treatment of Galois connections in Section 4.2 dealt with functions only of a single argument. But a function with two (or more) arguments can be regarded as a single-argument function, if the values of all the other arguments are fixed. For example, the functions pre_J and $post_K$ of Section 4.1 are derived from sequential composition by fixing the first or second of its arguments to J or K respectively. Each of these functions is universally disjunctive, and so they both have approximate inverses, which form the subject of this section.

Definition 4.3.1 (Weakest prespecification and postspecification)

The weakest prespecification of K through X is denoted by X/K and is defined as the weak inverse of $post_K$

$$(X; K) \sqsupseteq Y \quad \textbf{iff} \quad X \sqsupseteq (Y/K)$$

Because $post_K$ is $\sqcap^{\infty}$, there is no need to give an explicit formula for (Y/K); the above implicit definition characterises it uniquely. The weakest postspecification is defined similarly by

$$(J; X) \sqsupseteq Y \quad \textbf{iff} \quad X \sqsupseteq (J\backslash Y) \qquad \square$$

The weakest prespecification [92] is a generalisation of the weakest precondition (Definition 2.8.4); they are almost identical when the first argument mentions only dashed variables

$$r'/K \ = \ (K \ \mathbf{wp} \ r)'$$

The following laws are generalisations of the laws 2.8**L10** to **L13**

L1 $Q(x')/(x := e) \;=\; Q(e')$

L2 $S/(P \lhd b \rhd Q) \;=\; (S/P) \lhd b' \rhd (S/Q)$

L3 $S/(P; Q) \;=\; (S/Q)/P$

L4 $S/(P \sqcap Q) \;=\; (S/P) \sqcup (S/Q)$

L5 $(R \sqcup S)/P \;=\; (R/P) \sqcup (S/P)$

L6 $P \sqsupseteq (P; Q)/Q$

L7 $(S/Q); Q \sqsupseteq S$

L8 $(S/P); (P/Q) \sqsupseteq (S/Q)$

L9 $I\!I \sqsupseteq S/S$

The laws for postspecification are exact mirror images of the laws for prespecification, for example $(Q; P)\backslash S \;=\; P\backslash(Q\backslash S)$. This is obtained from **L3** for / by reading the equation backwards, exchanging / for \ but leaving ; unchanged. The following law requires both operators and it is its own mirror image

L10 $(Q\backslash S)/P \;=\; Q\backslash(S/P)$

We have previously (Section 1.6) drawn attention to the analogy between stepwise decomposition of program designs and factorisation of natural numbers, and the same analogy extends between weakest prespecification and approximate division (discarding the remainder). The basis of the analogy is now revealed: both of them are Galois connections.

$$x \times q \le y \quad \textbf{iff} \quad x \le y \div q, \qquad \text{for } x, y \ge 0 \text{ and } q > 0$$

From this single property the following laws can be deduced in exactly the same way as the laws **L3** to **L9** for /. Here, $\sqcup$ means the lesser of its two arguments and $\sqcap$ is the greater; the divisors are assumed to be non-zero.

$$\begin{aligned}
r \div (p \times q) &= (r \div q) \div p \\
r \div (p \sqcap q) &= (r \div p) \sqcup (r \div q) \\
(r \sqcup s) \div p &= (r \div p) \sqcup (s \div p) \\
p &= (p \times q) \div q \\
(p \div q) \times q &\le p \\
(p \div q) \times (q \div r) &\le p \div r \\
1 &= p \div p
\end{aligned}$$

Another interesting analogy is that between programming operators and logical operators, given in the following table.

$;$	$\wedge$
$/$	$\Rightarrow$
$\sqcup$	$\wedge$
$\sqcap$	$\vee$
$\sqsupseteq$	$\vdash$

The symbol $\vdash$ denotes deduction: $P \vdash Q$ means that Q can be validly deduced from P, and $P \dashv\vdash Q$ means that the reverse deduction is also valid. It is reasonably assumed that

$$X \dashv\vdash X, \qquad \text{for all } X$$

The basic Galois connection of propositional calculus is

$$(P \wedge X) \vdash Y \quad \textbf{iff} \quad X \vdash (P \Rightarrow Y)$$

The consequences of the connection yield many of the familiar proof rules of propositional calculus, including *modus ponens*

$$\begin{array}{rcl} (q \wedge p) \Rightarrow r & \dashv\vdash & p \Rightarrow (q \Rightarrow r) \\ (p \vee q) \Rightarrow r & \dashv\vdash & (p \Rightarrow r) \wedge (q \Rightarrow r) \\ p \Rightarrow (r \wedge s) & \dashv\vdash & (p \Rightarrow r) \wedge (q \Rightarrow s) \\ p & \vdash & q \Rightarrow (p \wedge q) \\ (q \Rightarrow p) \wedge q & \vdash & p \\ (r \Rightarrow q) \wedge (q \Rightarrow p) & \vdash & r \Rightarrow p \\ q & \vdash & (q \Rightarrow p) \Rightarrow p \end{array}$$

The Galois connection between $\wedge$ and $\Rightarrow$ is the basis of an elegant presentation of intuitionistic logic [55]. Linear logic [66] is a variety of logic that distinguishes clearly between the (multiplicative) conjunction that corresponds to ; and the (linear) conjunction that corresponds to $\sqcup$. The surprisingly wide range of application of the Galois connections of a binary operator has aroused interest in a branch of mathematics known as quantale theory [162].

In the stepwise development of a design to meet a specification S, it may be decided to split the task into two parts P and Q, which are specifications or designs for two fragments of program that will be executed sequentially. To check that this design decision is sound, a proof must be provided (preferably before the implementation) that

$$P;Q \ \sqsupseteq \ S$$

As explained in Section 1.5, the design task can be greatly simplified if only one of the designs (say Q) needs to be formulated in detail; the other one (P) should then be obtained purely by calculation from S and Q, with the guarantee that the resulting design will be correct. The calculation should give the weakest allowable specification for P, because that is the one that gives the greatest chance of easy implementation. It is the weakest design of a program to be executed *before* Q in order to achieve S. In other words, it is the weakest prespecification S/Q, and its role in stepwise design is just an intuitive restatement of its defining property (Definition 4.3.1). The weakest postspecification serves a similar purpose if the first component of the sequential composition is designed first.

The weakest prespecification of a design is a design[1]; the only danger is that it may not be a feasible design. Infeasibility occurs when there is no way that a program that ends in Q can achieve the given specification. For example,

$$(\mathbf{true} \vdash n' \text{ is odd})/(n := 2 \times n) \;=\; \top$$

In the rest of this section we introduce Conway's theory of factors [43] which explores all possible ways of implementing a specification S by sequential composition of designs. Consider law **L7**

$$(S/Q);Q \;\sqsupseteq\; S$$

(S/Q) is guaranteed to be the easiest design that will serve its intended purpose in the intended context shown above. But is Q the easiest valid design that will serve for a second component? Perhaps in knowledge of its intended context of use, it could be made weaker, and therefore easier to implement. This question is answered by the weakest postspecification, because by its definition

$$(S/Q);X \;\sqsupseteq\; S \quad \textbf{iff} \quad X \;\sqsupseteq\; (S/Q)\backslash S$$

This means that, in the given context, Q can always validly be replaced by $(S/Q)\backslash S$, which is always a weakening

$$Q \;\sqsupseteq\; (S/Q)\backslash S$$

If Q is already the weakest possible design in the circumstance, it is called a *right factor* of S [43]. A left factor has a similar definition.

Definition 4.3.2 (Right and left factor)

Q is a right factor of S if

$$Q \;=\; (S/Q)\backslash S$$

Q is a left factor of S if $Q = S/(Q\backslash S)$. □

---

[1]Note that this is *not* true of the weakest postspecification.

Any trick that can be played once can be played again, but not perhaps with any useful effect. From the law

$$(S/Q);((S/Q)\backslash S) \sqsupseteq S$$

we can try this time to weaken the first component (S/Q). But there is no point because in fact it is already as weak as possible, as shown by the law

L11 $(S/Q) \;=\; S/((S/Q)\backslash S)$

We explore next the set of right factors of S. This is done with the aid of a linking function which maps each Q onto the strongest right factor of S which is weaker than Q.

Definition 4.3.3 (Link to right factor)

$$L_S(Q) \;=_{df}\; (S/Q)\backslash S$$ □

Theorem 4.3.4

L_S is a retract.

Proof From **L7** and **L11** it follows that L_S is a link. From **L4** and **L5** we conclude that L_S is also monotonic. □

Theorem 4.3.5 (Right factor)

The following conclusions are equivalent.

(1) Q is a right factor of S.

(2) There is an X such that $Q = (X\backslash S)$.

(3) There is a P such that the following laws hold

(a) $X;Q \sqsupseteq S$ **iff** $X \sqsupseteq P$

(b) $P;X \sqsupseteq S$ **iff** $X \sqsupseteq Q$ □

Theorem 4.3.6 (Transitivity)

If Q is a right factor of R and R is a right factor of S, then Q is a right factor of S.

Proof From Theorem 4.3.5 it follows that there exist X and Y such that

$$Q \;=\; X\backslash R \quad \text{and} \quad R \;=\; Y\backslash S$$

It follows that

$$Q \;=\; X\backslash R \;=\; X\backslash(Y\backslash S) \;=\; (Y;X)\backslash S$$ □

4.4* Simulation

In the arithmetic of fractions and reals, reasoning about division is greatly simplified by the existence of reciprocals of non-zero numbers, and similarly in matrix arithmetic, non-singular matrices have exact inverses. Multiplication of a number d by its reciprocal u (in either order) always gives the unit of multiplication

$$d \times u \;=\; 1 \quad \text{and} \quad u \times d \;=\; 1$$

In this section we concentrate on relations that have reciprocals with respect to composition (in place of multiplication), but only in an approximate sense, defined by weakening the above two equations to inequations in opposing directions.

Definition 4.4.1 (Simulation)

Let D and U be designs satisfying

$$(D; U) \sqsupseteq \mathit{II} \quad \text{and} \quad \mathit{II} \sqsupseteq (U; D)$$

In this case, D is called a *simulation* and U is a *co-simulation*; the pair (D, U) is also called a simulation. □

Examples 4.4.2

(1) $(b^{\top}, b_{\perp})$ is a simulation among designs, because

$$(b^{\top}; b_{\perp}) \;=\; b^{\top} \;\sqsupseteq\; \mathit{II} \;\sqsupseteq\; b_{\perp} \;=\; (b_{\perp}; b^{\top})$$

(2) The design $(\mathbf{var}\, x\,;\, x := f(y);\, \mathbf{end}\, y)$ is a co-simulation. Its simulation is a non-deterministic assignment to y of an arbitrary element of $\{m \mid f(m) = x\}$, if this is non-empty, otherwise $\perp$. □

Theorem 4.4.3 (Simulation and Galois connection)

If $(D,\, U)$ is a simulation then

$$(\mathit{pre}_D \circ \mathit{post}_U,\;\; \mathit{pre}_U \circ \mathit{post}_D)$$

is a Galois connection. □

A simulation uniquely determines its co-simulation and vice versa.

Theorem 4.4.4

If $(D_1,\, U_1)$ and $(D_2,\, U_2)$ are simulations then

$$(D_1 \;=\; D_2) \quad \textbf{iff} \quad (U_1 \;=\; U_2)$$ □

To take advantage of this theorem, it is necessary to have an independent test whether a predicate is a co-simulation, and the test should be simpler than formalising its partner in the other direction.

Theorem 4.4.5

U is a co-simulation **iff** $U/U \;=\; U;(\Pi/U)$.

Proof $(\Leftarrow)$ Let $D \;=\; \Pi/U$.

$$\begin{array}{ll} \Pi & \{4.3\mathbf{L9}\} \\ \sqsupseteq\; U/U & \{\text{assumption and def of } D\} \\ =\; U;D & \end{array}$$

The inequality $(D;U) \sqsupseteq \Pi$ follows directly from Definition 4.3.1.

$$\begin{array}{lll} (\Rightarrow) & (Y;U) \sqsupseteq X & \{\Pi \sqsupseteq (U;D)\} \\ & \Rightarrow\; Y \sqsupseteq (X;D) & \{(D;U) \sqsupseteq \Pi\} \\ & \Rightarrow\; (Y;U) \sqsupseteq X & \end{array}$$

which together with the Definition 4.3.1 implies that

$$X/U \;=\; (X;D), \qquad \text{for all } X$$

By taking $X \;=\; \Pi$ we obtain $D \;=\; \Pi/U$ which leads to the conclusion

$$U/U \;=\; U;D \;=\; U;(\Pi/U) \qquad \square$$

Simulations have their most significant application in the concrete representation of abstract data types [87]. An algorithm is often most clearly described as a program operating on variables whose values range over abstract mathematical spaces like sets and functions. But computers do not provide direct methods of storing and operating on such values. Instead, they provide operations on concrete data – bits, bytes, arrays, addresses and files. So before the abstract program can be run, the abstract data must be conceptually translated to the concrete data structure which represents it, and the operations on the abstract data must be transformed to corresponding actions on the concrete data in a completely consistent way. This is done by simulations.

Let the abstract program take the form $F(A_1, A_2, \ldots)$, where the A_i are the collection of all primitive operations which update the abstract data, and F is constructed using the notations of the programming language. In the process of top-down development, we need to find a simulation (D, U), where D is a relation between abstract data values and their concrete representation, whereas U maps the data "upwards" from concrete to abstract. Now the abstract program $F(A_1, A_2, \ldots)$ can be translated to the concrete program

$$D; F((U; A_1; D),\ (U; A_2; D), \ldots); U$$

where the initial D first translates abstract data to concrete, the translated program manipulates the concrete data, and the final U translates its concrete results back up to the abstract data afterwards. The individual operations $U; A_i; D$ are then taken as specifications for optimised programs operating directly by available machine operations on the actually stored concrete data.

Example 4.4.6 (Binary representation)

A natural number n is represented as an array b of bits. The components of the simulation are

$$U \;=\; n := \Sigma_i (b_i \times 2^i)$$

$$D \;=\; \mathbf{true} \vdash \bigwedge_i (b'_i \;=\; (n \div 2^i) mod\ 2)$$

An abstract operation might be

$$A \;=\; (n := n + 1)$$

The corresponding concrete operation $(U; A; D)$ is

$$\mathbf{true} \vdash \wedge_i (b'_i \;=\; ((1 - b_i) \lhd \wedge\{k : k < i : b_k = 1\} \rhd b_i)) \qquad \Box$$

Example 4.4.7 (Machine addresses)

One of the important tasks of a compiler is to replace the identifiers of the symbolic program by the numeric addresses of locations in the machine store. Suppose that Φ is a symbol table that maps each variable name of the symbolic program to the address of the main memory M allocated to hold its value. So $M[\Phi x]$ is the location holding the value of x. Clearly it is necessary to insist that Φ is total and injective. We define U as a sort of symbolic dump; it assigns to each variable the value in the corresponding location.

$$U \;=_{df}\; \mathbf{var}\, x,\, y, \ldots, z\,;\, (x,\, y, \ldots, z \;:=\; M[\Phi x],\, M[\Phi y], \ldots, M[\Phi z])\,;\, \mathbf{end}\, M$$

$$D \;=_{df}\; \mathbf{var}\, M\,;\, (M[\Phi x],\, M[\Phi y], \ldots, M[\Phi z] \;:=\; x,\, y, \ldots, z)\,;\, \mathbf{end}\, x,\, y, \ldots, z$$

It is not difficult to prove that (D, U) is a simulation using the algebraic laws of Chapter 2. $\Box$

Of course, the translation from the abstract to the concrete version of the program must be correct in the sense that it can only improve the result, that is

$$F(A_1, A_2, \ldots) \sqsubseteq (D; F(U; A_1; D,\ U; A_2; D, \ldots); U)$$

Define

$$L =_{df} pre_U \circ post_D$$
$$R =_{df} pre_D \circ post_U$$

Because of the cancellation properties of the Galois connection (L, R) (Theorem 4.4.3), the correctness criterion may be rewritten

$$R(F(A_1, A_2, \ldots)) \sqsubseteq F(R(A_1), R(A_2), \ldots)$$

or more briefly, R is an $F_{\sqsubseteq}$-morphism. Rather than proving this separately for each simulation, we will give a general result that can be applied to all programs.

Since F has been written solely in the notations of the programming language, it is sufficient to prove that R is a $\Sigma_{\sqsubseteq}$-morphism. Recursion is also allowed, by the μ-fusion theorem (Theorem 4.2.12).

Theorem 4.4.8 (Piecewise data refinement)

Let v and w be the program variables used in the abstract and concrete versions of the program respectively. If

$$U =_{df} \textbf{var}\, v := f(w);\ \textbf{end}\, w$$

then U is a co-simulation and the corresponding R is a $\{\sqcap, ;, \lhd b \rhd\}_{\sqsubseteq}$-morphism.

(1) $R(P \sqcap Q) = R(P) \sqcap R(Q)$

(2) $R(P \lhd b(v) \rhd Q) = R(P) \lhd b(f(w)) \rhd R(Q)$

(3) $R(P;Q) \sqsubseteq R(P); R(Q)$ □

Exercise 4.4.9

Prove that if (D, U) is a simulation, then D is a left factor of Π and U is a right factor of Π. □

Chapter 5

The Algebra of Programs

Our study of the theory of programming started in Chapter 2 with a very simple definition within the predicate calculus of the notations of our programming language. Of course, the notations of predicate calculus are much more powerful than those of any implementable programming language – they even include the contradictory predicate **false**. In Chapter 3, a series of healthiness conditions were introduced to characterise more precisely those predicates which are expressible, or at least implementable, in the programming language. Each restriction on the class of predicates was motivated and rewarded by the proof of validity of an additional algebraic law. In this way it was possible to resolve the paradoxes of the first naive attempt at programming language definition.

In this chapter, we adopt a different strategy, which yields an even more precise characterisation of the class of programs and an even more complete collection of properties, including the important concepts of continuity. We start by *defining* a program as a predicate actually expressed (or at least expressible) in the limited notations of the programming language, as summarised in Table 5.0.1. Mathematicians often use similar notational definitions to single out simple classes of functions. For example, the class of polynomials can be defined as functions expressible from just constants and variables, combined by arithmetic operators of addition, subtraction and multiplication.

The next step is to list a collection of laws expressing familiar properties of the chosen operators, and their mutual interactions. These laws can be sufficiently powerful to reduce every expression in the restricted notation to an even more restricted notation, called a *normal form*. For example, it is well known that all polynomials can be reduced to a Horner normal form, whose syntax is defined by a simple recursion

$$< \mathit{HNF} > \ ::= \ < \mathit{constant} > \ | (< \mathit{HNF} >) * < \mathit{variable} > + < \mathit{constant} >$$

Additional properties of polynomials can now be simply deduced by showing them to be valid just for normal forms. Similarly we shall define and use a normal form for programs to prove the validity of the zero laws for our programming language. Once the normal form is established there is no need to look for healthiness conditions that place semantic restrictions on the range of predicates under consideration. These too emerge from analysis of the normal forms. Above all, there is no need to introduce extra variables like *ok* and *ok*′, which can be regarded as artificial coding tricks, and which evoke the philosophical objection that (because of non-termination) they can never be observed to be false.

<program> :: = **true**
  | <variable list> := <expression list>
  | <program> ◁ <Boolean expression> ▷ <program>
  | <program> ; <program>
  | <program> ⊓ <program>
  | <recursive identifier>
  | μ <recursive identifier> • <program>

Table 5.0.1 Syntax

A new objective in this chapter is to bring some order into the large collection of laws about programs that have been proved in previous chapters. The method is to identify a minimum collection of laws from which all the other laws can be deduced by algebraic reasoning. Reduction in the number and complexity of independently postulated laws is one of the primary goals of theoretical investigation in any branch of the natural sciences. Success not only appeals to a sense of intellectual elegance; it also leads to new insight, which unifies understanding, and broadens it to new areas of application. The same goal is sought in the more abstract study of algebra, and for the same reasons. Abstract algebra is clearly the most reusable branch of mathematics, but each time that it is reused, it is necessary to prove that the laws are in fact true in the new application domain. This is much easier if a minimum collection of laws has been identified in advance. Then only these few laws have to be checked, because the rest have already been proved to follow from them. That is why emphasis will constantly return to the question of the completeness of the laws presented.

This chapter starts with a series of increasingly complex and general normal forms, dealing successively with assignment, non-determinism, non-termination and recursion, of which iteration (Section 5.5) is an important special case. In

Sections 5.6 and 5.7 an argument is given for the *computability* of the normal form, and for the completeness of the algebraic presentation of the language as a whole. We derive a denotational semantics from the algebraic in Section 5.8.

5.1 Assignment normal form

The first in our series of normal forms is the total assignment, in which all the variables of the program appear on the left hand side in some standard order

$$x, y, \ldots, z \ := \ e, f, \ldots, g$$

A non-total assignment can be transformed to a total assignment by addition of identity assignments $(z, \ldots \ := \ z, \ldots)$

L1 $(x, y, \ldots \ := \ e, f, \ldots) \ = \ (x, y, \ldots, z \ := \ e, f, \ldots, z)$

The list of variables may be sorted into any desired order, provided that the right hand side is subjected to the same permutation

L2 $(x, \ldots, y, z, \ldots \ := \ e, \ldots, f, g, \ldots) \ = \ (x, \ldots, z, y, \ldots \ := \ e, \ldots, g, f, \ldots)$

As mentioned in Chapter 2, we abbreviate the entire list of variables $(x, y, \ldots, z)$ by the simple vector variable v, and the entire list of expressions by the vector expressions $g(v)$ or $h(v)$; these will usually be abbreviated to g or h. Thus the assignment normal form will be written

$$v \ := \ g \quad \text{or} \quad v \ := \ h(v)$$

The law that eliminates sequential composition between normal forms is

L3 $(v \ := \ g; \ v \ := \ h(v)) \ = \ (v \ := \ h(g))$

The expression $h(g)$ is easily calculated by substituting the expressions in the list g for the corresponding variables in the list v. For example,

$$(x, y \ := \ x+1, y-1 \ ; \ x, y \ := \ y, x) \ = \ (x, y \ := \ y-1, x+1)$$

To deal with the conditional combinator, we now need to assume that our programming language allows conditional expressions on the right hand side of an assignment. Such an expression is defined mathematically

$$\begin{aligned} e \lhd c \rhd f \ &=_{df} \ e \qquad && \text{if } c \\ &=_{df} \ f && \text{if } \neg c \end{aligned}$$

The definition can be extended to lists, for example

$$(e1, e2) \lhd c \rhd (f1, f2) \ =_{df} \ ((e1 \lhd c \rhd f1), (e2 \lhd c \rhd f2))$$

Now the elimination law for conditionals is

L4 $((v \ := \ g) \lhd c \rhd (v \ := \ h)) \ = \ (v := (g \lhd c \rhd h))$

Finally, we need a law that determines when two differently written normal forms are equal. For this, the right hand sides of the two assignments must be equal for all values of the variables that they contain

L5 $(v \ := \ g) \ = \ (v \ := \ h)$ **iff** $[g \ = \ h]$

It is this last law that justifies a claim that the entire collection **L1** to **L5** is *complete*, in the sense that they are sufficient to prove any valid equations between two programs that have been expressed in the programming notations of assignment, sequential composition and conditional. First, the laws **L1** to **L4** are used to reduce both sides of the equations to assignment normal forms, and then **L5** replaces the two normal forms by an equation that contains no programming notations whatsoever. The original equation between programs is valid just if the transformed program-free equation is valid. A proof constructed in this way is called an *algebraic proof*, and any equation (or inequation) that has such a proof is said to be algebraically provable. Of course, if g and h in **L5** are expressions of an incomplete logic, the algebra of programs will be equally incomplete. This means that a kind of relative completeness has to be accepted as the best that can be achieved in a calculus of programming.

Example 5.1.1

$(x := y - x \lhd x \leq y \rhd y := x) \, ; \, (x := x + 3) \ =$

$(y := y \lhd x \leq y \rhd x) \, ; \, (x := (y - x + 3) \lhd x \leq y \rhd (x + 3))$

Proof $\quad LHS$ **{L1, L2}**

$= \ (x, y := y - x, \ y) \lhd x \leq y \rhd (x, \ y := x, \ x) \, ;$

$x, \ y := x + 3, \ y$ **{L4}**

$= \ x, \ y := (y - x \lhd x \leq y \rhd x), \ (y \lhd x \leq y \rhd x) \, ;$

$x, \ y := x + 3, \ y$ **{L3}**

$= \ x, \ y := (y - x \lhd x \leq y \rhd x) + 3, \ (y \lhd x \leq y \rhd x)$

We now reduce the other side to normal form

$$
\begin{aligned}
& RHS && \{\mathbf{L1}, \mathbf{L2}\} \\
= \;& x, y := x, (y \lhd x \leq y \rhd x); \\
& x, y := (y - x + 3 \lhd x \leq y \rhd x + 3), y && \{\mathbf{L3}\} \\
= \;& x, y := (y - x + 3 \lhd x \leq y \rhd x + 3), y \lhd x \leq y \rhd x
\end{aligned}
$$

By **L5** the original equation is equivalent to a statement of the equality of the assigned expressions in these two normal forms, that is

$$
\begin{aligned}
& (y - x \lhd x \leq y \rhd x) + 3, (y \lhd x \leq y \rhd x) \;=\; \\
& (y - x + 3 \lhd x \leq y \rhd x + 3), (y \lhd x \leq y \rhd x)
\end{aligned}
\qquad \square
$$

It is possible to use this kind of algebraic reasoning to prove more useful and more general laws, for example the idempotence law for the conditional

$$P \lhd b \rhd P \;=\; P$$

First, P can be reduced to the assignment normal form, so what needs to be proved is only the special case

$$(v := e) \lhd b \rhd (v := e) \;=\; (v := e)$$

Then law **L4** shows this is equivalent to

$$v := (e \lhd b \rhd e) \;=\; (v := e)$$

Law **L5** requires us to prove

$$[e \lhd b \rhd e \;=\; e]$$

which contains no programming notations, and follows directly from the definition of the conditional expression. Of course, this argument is *schematic*: it is not itself a formal proof, but it shows how a proof is constructed in each particular case.

Reduction of particular programs to normal form is an activity requiring no insight, and so it is more suited for delegation to a machine. For human reasoning and understanding, it is usually better to bypass the normal form, and use a much larger collection of algebraic laws, which have been proved from the minimal set, usually by schematic proof. Minimisation of the number of laws that have to be proved, remembered or implemented on a computer is a good general goal, but it does not obviate the need for a much larger collection of laws in the application of algebra to practical reasoning.

5.2 Non-determinism

Disjunction between two semantically distinct assignments cannot be reduced to a single assignment, which is necessarily deterministic. We therefore move to a more complicated normal form, in which the disjunction operator connects a finite non-empty *set* of total assignments

$$(v := f) \sqcap (v := g) \sqcap \ldots \sqcap (v := h)$$

Let A and B be such sets; we will write the normal form as $\bigsqcap A$ and $\bigsqcap B$. All the previous normal forms can be trivially expressed in the new form as a disjunction over the unit set

$$v := g \;=\; \bigsqcap\{v := g\}$$

The easiest operator to eliminate is disjunction itself; it just forms the union of the two sets

$$(\bigsqcap A) \sqcap (\bigsqcap B) \;=\; \bigsqcap(A \cup B)$$

The other operators are eliminated by distribution laws

L1 $(\bigsqcap A) \lhd b \rhd (\bigsqcap B) \;=\; \bigsqcap\{(P \lhd b \rhd Q) \mid P \in A \wedge Q \in B\}$

L2 $(\bigsqcap A); (\bigsqcap B) \;=\; \bigsqcap\{(P; Q) \mid P \in A \wedge Q \in B\}$

The right hand sides of these equations are disjunctions of terms formed by applying the relevant operator to total assignments P and Q, which have been selected in all possible ways from A and B. Each of these terms can therefore be reduced to a total assignment, using the laws of Section 5.1. Thus the occurrences of ; and $\lhd b \rhd$ in the right hand sides of the laws given above are also eliminable.

The laws which permit comparison of disjunctions are

L3 $(\bigsqcap A) \sqsupseteq R$ **iff** $\forall P : P \in A \bullet (P \sqsupseteq R)$

L4 $(v := f) \sqsupseteq (v := g \sqcap \ldots \sqcap v := h)$ **iff** $[f \in \{g, \ldots, h\}]$

The first law is a tautology; it enables a disjunction in the antecedent to be split into its component assignments, which are then decided individually by the second law.

Exercise 5.2.1

Extend to this more general normal form the schematic proof in the previous section of

$$P \lhd b \rhd P \;=\; P$$

□

5.3 Non-termination

The program constant **true** is not an assignment, and cannot in general be expressed as a finite disjunction of assignments. Its introduction into the language requires a new normal form

$$\textbf{true} \lhd b \rhd P$$

where P is in the previous normal form. It is more convenient to write this as a disjunction

$$b \vee P$$

Any unconditional normal form P can be expressed as

$$\textbf{false} \vee P$$

and the constant **true** as

$$\textbf{true} \vee \mathit{II}$$

where II is $v := v$. The other operators between the new normal forms can be eliminated by the following laws

L1 $(b \vee P) \sqcap (c \vee Q) \;=\; (b \vee c) \vee (P \sqcap Q)$

L2 $(b \vee P) \lhd d \rhd (c \vee Q) \;=\; (b \lhd d \rhd c) \vee (P \lhd d \rhd Q)$

L3 $(b \vee P); (c \vee Q) \;=\; (b \vee (P; c)) \vee (P; Q)$

L4 $(\bigsqcap A); b \;=\; \bigvee \{(P; b) \mid P \in A\}$

L5 $(v := e); b(v) \;=\; b(e)$

As before, the occurrences of each operator on the right hand side can be further reduced by the laws of the previous sections. Laws **L4** and **L5** ensure that the terms $P; c$ and $P; b$ can be reduced to simple conditions.

The laws for testing implication between these new normal forms are

L6 $(b \vee P) \sqsupseteq (c \vee Q)$ **iff** $[b \Rightarrow c]$ and $P \sqsupseteq (c \vee Q)$

L7 $(v := f) \sqsupseteq (c \vee (v := g \sqcap \ldots \sqcap v := h))$ **iff** $[c \vee (f \in \{g, \ldots, h\})]$

Exercises 5.3.1

Prove the following laws if all operands are in the new normal form.

(1) $\textbf{true} \vee (\bigsqcap A) \;=\; \textbf{true} \vee (\bigsqcap B)$

(2) $P; (\textbf{true} \vee (\sqcap A)) \;=\; \textbf{true}$

(3) $(P \lhd b \rhd Q); R \;=\; (P; R) \lhd b \rhd (Q; R)$

(4) $(P \lhd b \rhd (P \lhd c \rhd Q)) \;=\; (P \lhd b \vee c \rhd Q)$

(5) $(P; I\!I) \;=\; P \;=\; (I\!I; P)$ □

5.4 Recursion

The introduction of recursion into the language permits construction of a program whose degree of non-determinism cannot be expressed as a finite disjunction, because it depends on the initial state. For example, let n be a non-negative integer variable in

$$\textbf{while } n \text{ is odd } \textbf{do } (n := n \ominus 1 \sqcap n := n \ominus 2)$$

where $n \ominus k$ abbreviates $0 \lhd k \geq n \rhd n - k$. Informally, the effect of this can be expressed as a disjunction of assignments

$$\begin{array}{rcl} n & := & (n \lhd n \text{ is even} \rhd n - 1) \\ \sqcap\, n & := & (n \lhd n \text{ is even} \rhd n - 3) \\ \vdots & & \\ \sqcap\, n & := & (n \lhd n \text{ is even} \rhd 0) \end{array}$$

But there is no *finite* set of assignments whose disjunction can replace the informal ellipses ($\vdots$) shown above, because the length of the disjunction depends on the initial value of n.

The solution is to represent the behaviour of the program as an *infinite* sequence of expressions

$$S \;=\; \{S_i \mid i \in \mathcal{N}\}$$

Each S_i is a finite normal form, as defined in the previous section; it correctly describes all the possible behaviours of the program, but maybe some impossible ones as well. So we arrange that each S_{i+1} is potentially stronger and therefore a more accurate description than its predecessor S_i

$$(S_{i+1} \sqsupseteq S_i), \qquad \text{for all } i \in \mathcal{N}$$

This is called the descending chain condition. It allows the later members of the sequence to exclude more and more of the impossible behaviours, and in the limit, every impossible behaviour is excluded by some S_i, provided that i is large enough. Thus the exact behaviour of the program is captured by the *least upper bound* of the whole sequence, written $(\bigsqcup_i S_i)$, or more briefly $(\bigsqcup S)$. It is this that will be taken as the normal form for programs that contain recursion.

For the example shown above, we define the infinite sequence S as follows

$$F(X) \;=_{df}\; ((n := n \ominus 1 \sqcap n := n \ominus 2); X) \lhd n \text{ is odd} \rhd I\!I$$

$$\begin{aligned}
S_1 &=_{df} F(\mathbf{true}) && \{5.3\mathbf{L3} \text{ and } 5.3\mathbf{L5}\}\\
&= \mathbf{true} \lhd n \text{ is odd} \rhd I\!I && \{5.3\mathbf{L2}\}\\
&= (n \geq 1 \wedge n \text{ is odd}) \;\vee\; (n := n \lhd n \text{ is even} \rhd n \ominus 1)
\end{aligned}$$

$$\begin{aligned}
S_2 &=_{df} F(S_1) && \{5.3\mathbf{L3}\}\\
&= ((n \geq 3 \wedge n \text{ is odd}) \;\vee\\
&\quad (n := n \ominus 1 \sqcap n := n \ominus 3)) \lhd n \text{ is odd} \rhd I\!I && \{5.3\mathbf{L2}\}\\
&= (n \geq 3 \wedge n \text{ is odd}) \;\vee\\
&\quad ((n := n \lhd n \text{ is even} \rhd n \ominus 1) \;\sqcap\; (n := n \lhd n \text{ is even} \rhd n \ominus 3))
\end{aligned}$$

$$\begin{aligned}
S_{i+1} &=_{df} F(S_i)\\
&= (n \geq 2i + 1 \wedge n \text{ is odd}) \;\vee\\
&\quad \textstyle\bigsqcap_{0 \leq k \leq i} (n := n \lhd n \text{ is even} \rhd n \ominus (2k + 1))
\end{aligned}$$

Each S_i is expressible in finite normal form. It describes exactly the behaviour of the program when n is initially less than $2i$, so that the number of iterations is bounded by i. The least upper bound $\bigsqcup_i S_i$ describes the whole behaviour of the program independent of the initial value of n. This is the insight for Theorem 5.4.1 below, which is used to reduce recursions to normal form.

But first we need to provide the distribution laws that eliminate the other operators of the language. They depend critically on the descending chain condition for S, because that permits distribution of composition through least upper bound.

L1 $(\bigsqcup S) \sqcap P \;=\; \bigsqcup_i (S_i \sqcap P)$

L2 $(\bigsqcup S) \lhd b \rhd P \;=\; \bigsqcup_i (S_i \lhd b \rhd P)$

L3 $P \lhd b \rhd (\bigsqcup S) \;=\; \bigsqcup_i (P \lhd b \rhd S_i)$

L4 $(\bigsqcup S); P \;=\; \bigsqcup_i (S_i; P)$

L5 $P; (\bigsqcup S) \;=\; \bigsqcup_i (P; S_i)$, provided P is a finite normal form

Operators that distribute through least upper bounds of descending chains are called *continuous*. Every combination of continuous operators is also continuous in each of its arguments separately. In fact it is even continuous in all its arguments together. This joint continuity is assured by the descending chain condition

$$S_{i+1} \sqsupseteq S_i, \qquad \text{for all } i \in \mathcal{N}$$

A descending chain of descending chains can be reduced to a single descending chain by diagonalisation

$$\bigsqcup_k (\bigsqcup_l S_{k,l}) = \bigsqcup_i S_{i,i}$$

provided that

$$(S_{k,i+1} \sqsupseteq S_{k,i}) \text{ and } (S_{i+1,l} \sqsupseteq S_{i,l}), \qquad \text{for all } i,\ k \text{ and } l$$

because then $S_{k,l} \sqsubseteq S_{i,i}$, where $i = max(k, l)$. This ensures that a function F, continuous in each of its arguments separately, is also continuous in its arguments as they tend to their limits simultaneously

$$F(\bigsqcup S,\ \bigsqcup T) = \bigsqcup_i F(S_i,\ T_i)$$

In turn, this gives the required elimination laws to compute normal forms for the three operators of the language.

L6 $(\bigsqcup S) \sqcap (\bigsqcup T) = \bigsqcup_i (S_i \sqcap T_i)$

L7 $(\bigsqcup S) \lhd b \rhd (\bigsqcup T) = \bigsqcup_i (S_i \lhd b \rhd T_i)$

L8 $(\bigsqcup S); (\bigsqcup T) = \bigsqcup_i (S_i; T_i)$

The occurrence of the operators $\sqcap$, $\lhd b \rhd$ and ; on the right hand side of these laws can be eliminated by the laws of Section 5.3, since each S_i and T_i is finite.

The continuity laws ensure that descending chains constitute a valid normal form for all the combinators of the language, and the stage is set for treatment of recursion. Consider first an innermost recursive program (containing no other recursions)

$$\mu X \bullet F(X)$$

where $F(X)$ contains X as its only free recursive identifier. The recursive identifier X is certainly not in normal form, and this makes it impossible to express $F(X)$ in normal form. However, all the other components of $F(X)$ are expressible in finite normal form, and all its combinators permit reduction to finite normal form. So, if X were replaced by a normal form (say **true**), $F(\mathbf{true})$ can be reduced to finite normal form, and so can $F(F(\mathbf{true}))$, $F(F(F(\mathbf{true})))$, ... Furthermore, because F is monotonic, this constitutes a descending chain of normal forms. Since F is continuous, by Kleene's famous recursion theorem, the limit of this chain is the least fixed point of F

Theorem 5.4.1 (Kleene)

If F is continuous then

$$\mu X \bullet F(X) \;=\; \bigsqcup_n F^n(\mathbf{true})$$

where $F^0(X) =_{df}$ **true**, and $F^{n+1}(X) =_{df} F(F^n(X))$. $\square$

This reduction can be applied first to replace all the innermost recursions in the program by limits of descending chains. The treatment of the remaining innermost recursions needs a continuity law for recursion, which enables each recursion to be eliminated as soon as it contains no other recursion.

Theorem 5.4.2 (Continuity of μ)

$$\mu X \bullet \bigsqcup_i S_i(X) \;=\; \bigsqcup_i \mu X \bullet S_i(X)$$

provided that $S_i(X)$ contains X as its only free recursive identifier for all i, and that all S_i are continuous and they form a descending chain for all finite normal forms X, that is

$$(S_{i+1}(X) \sqsupseteq S_i(X)), \qquad \text{for all } i \in \mathcal{N}$$

Proof Let $F(X) =_{df} \bigsqcup_i S_i(X)$. We are going to show by induction that for all $n \geq 0$

$$F^n(\mathbf{true}) \;=\; \bigsqcup_i S_i^n(\mathbf{true})$$

For $n = 0$

$$F^0(\mathbf{true}) \;=\; \mathbf{true} \;=\; \bigsqcup_i \mathbf{true} \;=\; \bigsqcup_i S_i^0(\mathbf{true})$$

By induction for any $n > 0$

$$\begin{array}{ll}
F^n(\mathbf{true}) & \{F^{k+1}(X) \;=\; F(F^k(X))\} \\
= \bigsqcup_i S_i(F^{n-1}(\mathbf{true})) & \{\text{induction hypothesis}\} \\
= \bigsqcup_i S_i(\bigsqcup_j S_j^{n-1}(\mathbf{true})) & \{S_i \text{ is continuous}\} \\
= \bigsqcup_i \bigsqcup_j S_i(S_j^{n-1}(\mathbf{true})) & \{\text{diagonalisation}\} \\
= \bigsqcup_i S_i(S_i^{n-1}(\mathbf{true})) & \{\text{def of } S_i^n\} \\
= \bigsqcup_i S_i^n(\mathbf{true}) &
\end{array}$$

The function F is also continuous because all S_i are continuous, and they form a descending chain for all X. By Theorem 5.4.1 we have

$$\mu X \bullet \bigsqcup_i S_i(X) \;=\; \bigsqcup_n F^n(\mathbf{true}) \;=\; \bigsqcup_n \bigsqcup_i S_i^n(\mathbf{true}) \;=\; \bigsqcup_i \mu X \bullet S_i(X) \quad \square$$

Let us now return to the task of eliminating recursions from the program.

Suppose all the innermost recursions have been replaced by limits of descending chains. The remaining innermost recursions now have the form

$$\mu Y \bullet H(\bigsqcup_m \ F^m(\mathbf{true}),\ \bigsqcup_m \ G^m(\mathbf{true}), \ldots, Y)$$

By continuity of H, this transforms to

$$\mu Y \bullet \bigsqcup_m \ H_m(Y)$$

where $H_m(Y) \ =_{df} \ H(F^m(\mathbf{true}),\ G^m(\mathbf{true}), \ldots, Y)$, which is (for fixed Y) a descending chain in m. By Theorem 5.4.2, this equals

$$\bigsqcup_m \ \mu Y \bullet H_m(Y)$$

and by Kleene's theorem

$$\bigsqcup_m \bigsqcup_n \ (H_m^n(\mathbf{true}))$$

Because this is descending in both n and m, we get at last

$$\bigsqcup_n \ H_n^n(\mathbf{true})$$

Thus the next innermost recursions are converted to normal form; by repeating the process, the whole program can be converted to normal form

$$\bigsqcup_n S_n$$

Another way of describing the same conversion is that S_n is the result of replacing *every* recursion $\mu X \bullet F(X)$ in the program by the nth element of its approximating series, that is $F^n(\mathbf{true})$.

The finite normal forms play a role similar to that of rational numbers among the reals. Firstly, there is only a countable number of them. A second similarity is that every real is the limit of a descending chain of rationals. Finally, the rationals are dense in reals, in the sense that any two distinct real numbers can be shown to be so by a rational number which separates them. The application of these insights to computer programs is the contribution of Scott's theory of continuous domains [165, 167].

The definition of a testing criterion for infinite normal forms is postponed to Section 5.6.

Exercises 5.4.3

Prove from the laws of this chapter that

(1) $\mathbf{true}; P \ = \ \mathbf{true}$

(2) If $P \sqsupseteq F(P)$ then $P \sqsupseteq \mu F$. □

5.5 Iteration

Iteration has already been defined in Section 2.6 as a special case of recursion (tail recursion)

$$b * Q \;=_{df}\; \mu X \bullet (Q; X) \lhd b \rhd I\!I$$

On a machine with limited resources it is implemented more economically than general recursion. Furthermore, reasoning about iteration can be simpler than the general case. This section develops the simpler theory of iteration through a series of lemmas that will be useful in later chapters. The proofs will use algebraic reasoning on the basis of the normal form theorem. The theorems are in fact valid for all designs, not just those that can be expressed in normal form.

If condition b is true initially, the iteration $(b * Q)$ executes Q first, and then proceeds like $(b * Q)$. Otherwise it terminates immediately.

L1 $b_\perp; (b * Q) \;=\; b_\perp; Q; (b * Q)$ (loop unfold)

L2 $(\neg b)_\perp; (b * Q) \;=\; (\neg b)_\perp$ (loop elim)

If the execution of Q always establishes the condition b, then $(b * Q)$ behaves like the assertion $(\neg b)_\perp$.

L3 $(b * Q) \;=\; (\neg b)_\perp,$ provided that $(Q; b_\perp) \;=\; Q$ (loop abort)

The next law enables us to transform a tail recursion to an iteration.

L4 $\mu X \bullet (P; X) \lhd b \rhd Q \;=\; (b * P); Q$ (tail recursion)

Proof Define

$$F(X) \;=_{df}\; (P; X) \lhd b \rhd Q$$

$$G(X) \;=_{df}\; (P; X) \lhd b \rhd I\!I$$

We are going to show by induction that

$$F^n(\mathbf{true}) \;=\; G^n(\mathbf{true}); Q$$

When $n = 0$ we have

$$\begin{array}{ll} & F^0(\mathbf{true}) \qquad \{\text{def of } F^0\} \\ = & \mathbf{true} \qquad \{\text{Exercise 5.4.3(1)}\} \\ = & (\mathbf{true}; Q) \qquad \{\text{def of } G^0\} \\ = & G^0(\mathbf{true}); Q \end{array}$$

By induction for any $n \geq 0$ one has

$$\begin{array}{lll} & F^{n+1}(\mathbf{true}) & \{\text{def of } F^{n+1}\} \\ = & (P; F^n(\mathbf{true})) \lhd b \rhd Q & \{\text{induction hypothesis}\} \\ = & (P; G^n(\mathbf{true}); Q) \lhd b \rhd Q & \{\text{Exercises 5.3.1(3) and 5.3.1(5)}\} \\ = & ((P; G^n(\mathbf{true})) \lhd b \rhd I\!I); Q & \{\text{def of } G^{n+1}\} \\ = & G^{n+1}(\mathbf{true}); Q & \end{array}$$

The conclusion then follows from Kleene's theorem and the left continuity of sequential composition. □

Corollary $b * Q \;=\; (b * Q); (\neg b)_\perp$ (loop termination)

The following law allows the combination of loops with the same body.

L5 $(b * Q); (b \vee c) * Q \;=\; (b \vee c) * Q$ (merge of loop)

Proof Define $S(X) \;=_{df}\; (Q; X) \lhd b \rhd (b \vee c) * Q$. From **L4** it follows that

$$LHS \;=\; \mu S$$

so we only need to show $(b \vee c) * Q \;=\; \mu S$.

$$\begin{array}{lll} & (b \vee c) * Q = ((b \vee c) * Q) \lhd b \rhd ((b \vee c) * Q) & \{\mathbf{L1}\} \\ \Rightarrow & (b \vee c) * Q = (Q; (b \vee c) * Q) \lhd b \rhd ((b \vee c) * Q) & \{\text{weakest fixed point}\} \\ \Rightarrow & (b \vee c) * Q \sqsupseteq \mu X \bullet ((Q; X) \lhd b \rhd (b \vee c) * Q) \;=\; \mu S & \end{array}$$

fixed point theorem

$$\begin{array}{lll} \Rightarrow & \mu S = (Q; \mu S) \lhd b \rhd (b \vee c) * Q & \{\text{fixed point}\} \\ \Rightarrow & \mu S = (Q; \mu S) \lhd b \rhd ((Q; (b \vee c) * Q) \lhd b \vee c \rhd I\!I & \{(b \vee c) * Q \sqsupseteq \mu S\} \\ \Rightarrow & \mu S \sqsupseteq (Q; \mu S) \lhd b \rhd ((Q; \mu S) \lhd b \vee c \rhd I\!I) & \{\text{Exercise 5.3.1(4)}\} \\ \Rightarrow & \mu S \sqsupseteq (Q; \mu S) \lhd b \vee c \rhd I\!I & \{\text{weakest fixed point}\} \\ \Rightarrow & \mu S \sqsupseteq \mu X \bullet ((Q; X) \lhd b \vee c \rhd I\!I) \;=\; (b \vee c) * Q & \Box \end{array}$$

Exercises 5.5.1

(1) $b * P \;=\; b * (P; b * P)$

(2) If $c_\perp; P \;=\; c_\perp; P; c_\perp$ then $c_\perp; (b * P) \;=\; c_\perp; (b * P); c_\perp$. □

5.6 Computability

The algebraic laws given in Sections 5.1, 5.2 and 5.3 permit every finite program (one that does not use recursion) to be reduced to finite normal form. The reduction rules are nothing but simple algebraic transformations, of the kind that can be readily mechanised on a computer. The infinite normal form $(\bigsqcup_i S_i)$ of Section 5.4 can never be computed in its entirety; however, for each n, the finite normal form S_n can be readily computed, for example by replacing each internal recursion $(\mu X \bullet F(X))$ by $(F^n(\mathbf{true}))$.

This suggests a highly impractical method of executing a program, starting in a known initial state s, in which Boolean conditions can be evaluated to *true* or *false*. The machine calculates the series S_n of finite normal forms from the program. Each of these is a disjunction $(b_n \vee P_n)$. If $(s; b_n)$ evaluates to *true*, the machine continues to calculate the next S_{n+1}. If *all* the $(s; b_n)$ are *true*, this machine never terminates, but that is the right answer, because in this case the original program, when started in the given initial state s, contains an infinite recursion or loop. But as soon as a false $(s; b_n)$ is encountered, the corresponding P_n is executed, by selecting and executing an arbitrary one of its constituent assignments. We want to prove that the resulting state will be related to the initial state as described by *all* the S_i, when these are interpreted as predicates in accordance with the definitions of Chapter 2.

The validity of this method of execution depends on an additional property of the normal form, that $\{b_n \vee P_n\}$ is a descending chain in a stronger ordering, where comparability requires two terminating programs to be exactly the same in their range of non-determinism

$$(b_n \vee P_n) \equiv (b_n \vee P_{n+k}), \qquad \text{for all } n, k$$

that is once n is high enough for b_n to be false, all the assignments P_m remain the same as P_n, for all m greater than n. Let us therefore define a new ordering relation.

Definition 5.6.1 (Strong ordering)

Let $P =_{df} (v := e_1 \sqcap \ldots \sqcap v := e_m)$ and $Q =_{df} (v := f_1 \sqcap \ldots \sqcap v := f_n)$.
Define

$$(b \vee P) \leq (c \vee Q) =_{df} [c \Rightarrow b] \wedge [\neg b \Rightarrow (\{e_1, \ldots, e_m\} = \{f_1, \ldots, f_n\})] \quad \Box$$

The new ordering is stronger than the familiar implication ordering.

Theorem 5.6.2

If $(b \vee P) \leq (c \vee Q)$ then $(b \vee P) \sqsubseteq (c \vee Q)$. $\Box$

Strong ordering is clearly a preorder, with weakest element **true**. What is more, all the combinators of the programming language are monotonic with respect to $\leq$. If $F(X)$ is a program, it follows that $\{F^n(\mathbf{true}) \mid n \in \mathcal{N}\}$ is a descending chain in this new ordering. This shows that all innermost recursions enjoy the strong descending chain condition. Furthermore, because of continuity, any program combinator preserves this condition. For nested recursions, the proof of the normal form reduction theorem uses the same construction as given at the end of Section 5.4. All the chains involved are descending in the strong ordering as well.

We can use the following laws to compare least upper bounds of strong descending chains.

L1 $(\bigsqcup S) \sqsubseteq (\bigsqcup T)$ **iff** $\forall i : i \in \mathcal{N} \bullet S_i \sqsubseteq (\bigsqcup T)$

L2 Let $T = \{(c_n \vee Q_n) \mid n \in \mathcal{N}\}$ be a descending chain in the strong ordering, and $Q_n = (v := f_1^n \sqcap \ldots \sqcap v := f_{k_n}^n)$ for all $n \in \mathcal{N}$. Then

$(b \vee (v := e_1 \sqcap \ldots \sqcap v := e_m)) \sqsubseteq (\bigsqcup T)$ **iff**

$[(\bigwedge_n c_n) \Rightarrow b]$ and $\forall n : n \in \mathcal{N} \bullet [c_n \vee b \vee (\{f_1^n, \ldots, f_{k_n}^n\} \subseteq \{e_1, \ldots, e_m\})]$

Exercise 5.6.3

Prove that all programming operators are monotonic with respect to $\leq$. □

5.7* Completeness

A reduction to normal form gives a method of testing the truth of any proposed implication between any pair of programs: reduce both of them to normal form, and test whether the inequation satisfies the simpler conditions laid down in 5.6**L1** and 5.6**L2** for implication of normal forms. If so, it holds also between the original programs. This is because the reduction laws only substitute equals for equals, and each of the tests for implication between normal forms has been proved as a theorem. The procedure has been described in detail for the assignment normal form in Section 5.1, but the same idea works just as well for the more general forms introduced in later sections.

For the algebra of programs, the converse conclusion can also be drawn: if the test for implication fails for the normal forms, then the implication does *not* hold between the original programs. The reason is that the tests give both necessary and sufficient conditions for the validity of implication between normal forms. For this reason, the algebraic laws are said to be *complete*. Of course, since the normal form is infinite, there cannot be any general decision procedure; comparison of recursive programs will always require proof.

Theorem 5.7.1 (Completeness)

For all programs P and Q

$$[P \Rightarrow Q] \quad \textbf{iff} \quad P \sqsupseteq Q \text{ has an algebraic proof} \qquad \square$$

Completeness is a significant achievement for a theory of programming. Each of the laws requires a non-trivial proof, involving full expansion of the definitions of all the operators in the formulae, followed by reasoning in the rather weak framework of the predicate calculus. But after a complete set of laws have been proved in this more laborious way, proof of any additional laws can be achieved by purely algebraic reasoning; it will never be necessary again to expand the definitions. For example, we prove the right zero law

$$P\,;\,\mathbf{true} \;=\; \mathbf{true}$$

Since P is a program, it can be reduced to the normal form $\bigsqcup S$.

$$\begin{aligned}
& P; \mathbf{true} \\
= \;& (\textstyle\bigsqcup S); \mathbf{true} && \{\text{for some } P_i,\ b_i\} \\
= \;& \textstyle\bigsqcup_i (b_i \vee P_i); \mathbf{true} && \{5.4\mathbf{L4} \text{ and } 5.3\mathbf{L3}\} \\
= \;& \textstyle\bigsqcup_i ((b_i \vee (P_i; \mathbf{true})) \vee P_i) && \{5.3\mathbf{L4} \text{ and } \mathbf{L5}\} \\
= \;& \textstyle\bigsqcup_i (\mathbf{true} \vee P_i) && \{\text{Exercise } 5.3.1(1)\} \\
= \;& \mathbf{true}
\end{aligned}$$

Apart from the practical advantages, completeness of the laws has an important theoretical consequence in characterising the nature of the programming language. For each semantically distinct program there is a normal form with the same meaning, and this can be calculated by application of the laws. It is therefore possible to regard the normal form itself as a definition of the meaning of the program, and to regard the algebraic laws as a definition of the meaning of the programming language, quite independent of the interpretation of programs as predicates describing observations. This is the philosophy of "initial algebra" semantics for abstract data types [68].

There are many advantages in this purely algebraic approach [16, 117]. It is often quite easy to decide what laws (like the zero laws) are needed or wanted for a programming language, and then it is much easier just to postulate them than to prove them. Furthermore, algebra is the most reusable branch of mathematics. Most algebraic laws are valid for many different programming languages, just as most of conventional schoolroom algebra holds for many different number systems. Even the differences between the number systems are most clearly described and understood by examining the relatively simple differences in their algebraic presentations. That is certainly clearer than the widely differing definitions which they are given in the foundations of mathematics. In the study of the foundations of mathematics, no useful comparison can be made between the classes of sets which define the integers, and the Dedekind cuts which define the reals; only algebra provides the right level of abstraction to compare them effectively and to justify the use of the same symbols to denote the arithmetic operators.

In practical engineering, algebraic laws are widely used in symbolic calculation of parameters and design details, which are derived as consequences of more general structural decisions made by engineering judgement. The algebraic laws neatly encapsulate the engineers' experience and intuition, making them easy to learn, remember and apply. Computer support for algebraic reasoning is far better developed than that for general proof search. In the division of labour between engineers and mathematicians, it is the role of the engineer to calculate and the mathematician to prove, and the proof should establish not only the correctness but also the completeness of the algebra used in calculation.

But there is an alternative approach to the theory of programming, which recognises the greater importance of the laws in the practical application of the theory; it therefore presents the laws by themselves as postulates or axioms; they have to be accepted as self-evident, or at least as an indirect definition of the meaning of the notations involved; they are then used as the basis for all general and particular reasoning about programs. This axiomatic approach is taken in the study of all branches of modern algebra, and has been adopted in the presentation of many versions of programming language semantics [18, 85].

If the algebra is taken as the official starting point for the investigation, the direction of the development of the theory has to be reversed. Instead of deriving a complete set of algebraic laws from the denotational semantics, it is necessary to derive a denotational semantics from the laws. That is the task of the last section of this chapter. It is a matter of personal choice whether the investigation of algebra precedes the search for possible meanings, or the other way round (as in this book). The experienced mathematician probably explores both approaches at the same time. When the task is complete, the practising engineer or programmer has a secure intellectual platform for understanding complex phenomena, and a full set of calculation methods for the reliable design of useful products. That is the ultimate, if not the only, goal of our investigations.

5.8* From algebraic to denotational semantics

In this section, we need to start with a more traditional presentation of a denotational semantics, which explicitly associates with each program the set of observations to which it can give rise, as described in Section 1.2. The set is a relation between the initial and final states of any execution of the program. An observation of the *final* state of a program is coded in the manner described in Section 1.1, as an equation

$$state := k \qquad \text{(defined as the predicate } state' = k\text{)}$$

where k is a list of constants, and *state* consists of variable *ok* and program variables v. Similarly, if j is a list of constants,

$$(state := j); P(state,\ state')$$

describes all possible observations of the final state of an execution of P that starts in *initial* state j. The implication

$$[(state := k) \ \Rightarrow\ ((state := j); P)]$$

means the state k is among the possible final states of a program execution that starts in j. In fact, using the definition of composition, it is exactly equivalent to the result of substitution of constants for all free variables

$$P(j,\ k)$$

Because the only free variables of our predicates are those that describe initial and final states, it is equally trivial to see that one predicate P implies another Q just if its set of initial and final states is a subset of the initial and final states of the other

$$\begin{array}{l} [P \Rightarrow Q] \quad \textbf{iff} \\ [t \Rightarrow (s; P)] \text{ implies } [t \Rightarrow (s; Q)], \quad \text{for all constant assignments } s \text{ and } t \end{array}$$

This is the insight that links our treatment of programs as predicates with a more traditional denotational semantics. The latter is given as a function $\mathcal{R}$ mapping every program onto a relation between its initial and final states

$$\mathcal{R}(P) \ = \ \{(j,\ k) \mid [(state := k) \Rightarrow (state := j; P)]\}$$

From this definition, one can derive a collection of equations relevant to each of the constructions of the programming language.

$$\begin{array}{rcl} \mathcal{R}(v := e(v)) & = & \{((ok,\ v),\ (ok',\ v')) \mid ok \Rightarrow (ok' \wedge v' = e(v))\} \\ \mathcal{R}(P; Q) & = & \{(j,\ k) \mid \exists u \bullet (j,\ u) \in \mathcal{R}(P) \ \wedge\ (u,\ k) \in \mathcal{R}(Q)\} \\ \mathcal{R}(P \sqcap Q) & = & \{(j,\ k) \mid (j,\ k) \in \mathcal{R}(P) \ \vee\ (j,\ k) \in \mathcal{R}(Q)\} \\ \mathcal{R}(P \lhd b \rhd Q) & = & \{(j,\ k) \mid ((state := j); b) = true \ \wedge\ (j,\ k) \in \mathcal{R}(P) \ \vee \\ & & \qquad ((state := j); b) = false \ \wedge\ (j,\ k) \in \mathcal{R}(Q)\} \\ \mathcal{R}(\mu X \bullet F(X)) & = & \{(j,\ k) \mid \forall n : \mathcal{N} \bullet (j,\ k) \in \mathcal{R}(F^n(\mathbf{true}))\} \end{array}$$

A denotational semantics in the traditional sense takes those equations as a *definition* of the function $\mathcal{R}$, which maps each program text to its mathematical meaning as a relation. The equational definition of $\mathcal{R}$ appeals to the principle of structural induction over the texts of programs expressed in the limited notations of the programming language: there is only one function that satisfies all the equations. This principle gives an important proof method: any independently defined function $\mathcal{S}$ which is proved to satisfy these equations is necessarily equal to $\mathcal{R}$.

This insight gives a sufficient basis for deriving a denotational semantics from the algebraic. All that is needed is to use the *algebra* to associate with each program P an appropriate set $\mathcal{S}(P)$ of pairs of constant assignments. The definition uses provability in the algebra to define the appropriate set.

Definition 5.8.1

$$\mathcal{S}(P) \;=_{df}\; \neg d(v) \vdash R(v,\, v')$$

where $d(m) \;=_{df}\; ((v := m; P) \;=\; \mathbf{true})$ is algebraically provable

and $\quad R(m,\, n) \;=_{df}\; ((v := m; P) \sqsubseteq (v := n))$ is algebraically provable. □

Theorem 5.8.2

$\mathcal{S}$ satisfies all the equations used to define $\mathcal{R}$.

Proof Based on structural induction and the following facts that for any program P and any constant assignment $v := m$

either $(v := m; P) \;=\; \mathbf{true}$ is algebraically provable

or there exists a finite set of constant assignments $\{v := n \mid n \in T\}$ such that the following is algebraically provable

$$(v := m; P) \;=\; \bigsqcap \{v := n \,|\, n \in T\}$$ □

Exercise 5.8.3

Fill in the missing clauses $I\!I$ and **true** in the definition of $\mathcal{R}$. □

Chapter 6

Implementation

The main goal of a theory of programming is to help in the design of programs that meet their intended specification. But the whole exercise would be pointless unless there is some effective mechanism for implementing the program once it has been written. And it would be even worse than pointless, perhaps even dangerous, if the implementation itself is not correct. To help in the design of correct implementations is the main goal of this chapter.

Fortunately, we can reuse exactly the same approach to correctness of implementations as we have to correctness of programs. But now it is the program that plays the role of the specification; its implementation is also described by a predicate satisfying even more stringent implementation-oriented constraints, and it is correct if it logically implies the program. The implementation predicate will usually have a different alphabet from that of the program, so that it can describe additional details of the internal working of the implementation. In the case of computers, these will include registers and other storage devices not relevant to an abstract high level programming language. A simulation is often needed to relate the two levels of abstraction, as described in Example 4.4.7.

The construction of an efficient program to meet a general specification is a task that is usually guided by human insight, ingenuity and inventiveness. But the transition between a program and its implementation is much more routine; in fact it can be completely automated. This is done by subjecting the program to a series of transformations, whose validity is put beyond doubt by mathematical proof. The correctness of the implementation is therefore guaranteed by a kind of normal form theorem, which shows that every program can be transformed automatically into an implementation that implies it as a specification.

There are two familiar ways of implementing a program, by compilation or by interpretation. Interpretation executes the text of the program directly, and is described in Section 6.3. Compilation first translates the program into the machine code of some computer, which then executes it more quickly by hardware. All the high level control structures of the language have to be replaced by machine code jumps. The principles of correct compiler design are described in Section 6.2. Both implementation methods split the execution of a program into a large number of steps, and introduce a special control variable to select the action to be performed on each step. This basic idea is described in Section 6.1, where the relevant theory is developed.

The final section of this chapter develops a theory for a language which combines high level structures with explicit jumps that lead directly from one part of the program to a labelled statement in some other part. Provided that there are no jumps into the middle of a structure, the complexity of adding this new feature is not serious, and none of the laws for the original language is invalidated.

6.1 Execution

The execution of a computer program is normally delegated to an automatic device, which splits the task into a collection of atomic actions, and performs them one after another in sequence. The potential for parallel execution will be described in later chapters: in this chapter we will concentrate on programs whose execution can be expressed as a sequential repetition of an individual step. This step is described in the usual way by a predicate relating the values of the variables before each action to the values after that action. The predicate describes the behaviour of an assembled block of machine code instructions. Each instruction too is described by a predicate, and their combined effect is given by an assembly operation on these predicates. Assembly into disjoint regions of machine store is the only form of composition for machine code instructions. In this section we explore its simple mathematical properties. In the next section we will see how it can be used in various ways to implement high level control structures of a programming language.

To define the total behaviour of the executing mechanism, it is necessary also to specify the circumstances under which it terminates. A perfectly general and convenient way of doing this is to introduce into the alphabet of the step a specially named variable (say l), which serves as a *control* variable. Before each repetition of the action, the value of l is tested. As long as it remains within some designated set of values, the execution continues; otherwise it terminates. We will take the set αl of continuation points and the choice of the name l of the control variable as an inseparable and unchangeable part of the description of the implementation; for this reason we include both l and αl as part of the alphabet of the predicate describing the step. This convention greatly simplifies the statement and use of the relevant algebraic laws.

Definition 6.1.1 (Continuations and execution)

Let P be a predicate describing a step, and let a special variable named l in the alphabet of P be reserved to denote the control variable for its execution. Then αlP denotes the set of *continuations* of P. The *execution* of P is defined as a loop, which iterates the step as long as l remains in the continuation set.

$$P^* \;=_{df}\; (l \in \alpha lP) * P \qquad \square$$

The control variable l may be used within the step P in the same way as any other variable in its alphabet. For example, l may be used initially to select which of the many possible actions described by P will be executed on this iteration, and an assignment of a new value to l provides the way in which one action can nominate the action that will be performed on the next iteration of the step.

Example 6.1.2 (Machine code)

Let $P \;=\; (A, l := 27, l+1) \lhd l = 20 \rhd (ram[56],\ l \;:=\; A,\ l+1 \lhd l = 21 \rhd I\!I)$

and $\alpha lP \;=\; \{20,\ 21\}$

This describes the behaviour of a small fragment of a machine code program, consisting of just two instructions stored in locations 20 and 21 of the program store of the machine. The control variable l stands for the program pointer (sequence control register). If its initial value is 20, the first instruction loads a constant value 27 into register A, and adds one to the program pointer, thereby ensuring that the next instruction will be taken from location 21. But if the fragment of program is entered by a jump, the initial value of l may be 21, so only the second instruction is executed. In either case, the second instruction stores the value of A in location 56 of the random access memory *ram*; it also sets l to 22, which is outside αlP, and as a result, execution of the entire fragment of program terminates. The overall effect might be described in a high level language as a simple assignment

$$x := 27 \qquad \square$$

Example 6.1.3 (Algebraic normal form)

In Chapter 5, it was shown how any program can be reduced to the form

$$\textstyle\bigsqcup_l\, (b(l) \vee P(l))$$

where the indexing variable has been selected as the control. As explained in Section 5.6, this normal form can be executed by iteration of the step

$$S \;=_{df}\; ((l := l+1) \lhd b(l) \rhd (P(l); l := -1)) \lhd l \geq 0 \rhd I\!I$$

Execution terminates with $l = -1$; all non-negative integers are continuations

$$\alpha l S \;=\; \mathcal{N}$$

This example shows in principle that every program can be expressed as S^* for some step S. □

Example 6.1.4 (Symbolic interpreter)

In a symbolic interpreter, execution is controlled by the text of the program being interpreted. So it is convenient to arrange that the control variable l ranges over all sequences of program texts expressible in the language. The continuations consist of all sequences of program texts except the empty sequence, which triggers termination of the interpreter. This example is elaborated in Section 6.3. □

What happens if the initial value of l lies outside the continuation set $\alpha l P$? In this case, the effect of the whole execution is to do nothing, as expressed by the idempotence principle

$$P^* \;=\; P^* \lhd l \in \alpha l P \rhd \mathit{I\!I}$$

The same question may be asked about the individual step P. Since P is never even started with l outside its continuation set, it really does not matter what answer is given. However, to simplify the test of equality between predicates describing the step, it is convenient to standardise the behaviour of P even in this impossible case, and for reasons which will soon become apparent, we will choose the behaviour of $\mathit{I\!I}$ as standard. We therefore stipulate that each step must satisfy the same idempotence principle as the whole execution.

Definition 6.1.5 (Step)

A predicate P is a *step* if $l \in \alpha P$ and

$$P \;=\; (P \lhd l \in \alpha l P \rhd \mathit{I\!I})$$

An immediate consequence is

$$(l \notin \alpha l P)_\perp ; P \;=\; (l \notin \alpha l P)_\perp$$ □

In this chapter we will confine attention to programs which satisfy this definition. We shall want to define particular steps using all the operators of our programming language except μ, and for this purpose, we need appropriate definitions of the continuation sets for the result of each operation, and a closure theorem that guarantees that their results still satisfy the defining condition for a step.

Definition 6.1.6 (Continuations of operators)

$$\alpha l(P\, op\, Q) \;=_{df}\; (\alpha lP \,\cup\, \alpha lQ), \qquad \text{where } op \in \{;, \sqcap, \lhd b \rhd\} \qquad \square$$

Theorem 6.1.7 (Step closure)

If P and Q are steps, then

(1) $P;Q$ is a step.

(2) $P \sqcap Q$ and $P \lhd b \rhd Q$ are also steps whenever $\alpha lP = \alpha lQ$.

(3) The set of steps $\{P \mid \alpha lP = L\}$ is a complete lattice.

Proof of (1) Notice that $l \notin \alpha l(P;Q) \Rightarrow (l \notin \alpha lP) \wedge (l \notin \alpha lQ)$.

$$\begin{array}{lll} & P;Q & \{2.1\mathbf{L1}\} \\ = & (P;Q) \lhd l \in \alpha l(P;Q) \rhd (P;Q) & \{(l \notin \alpha lP)_\perp; P = (l \notin \alpha lP)_\perp\} \\ = & (P;Q) \lhd l \in \alpha l(P;Q) \rhd Q & \{(l \notin \alpha lQ)_\perp; Q = (l \notin \alpha lQ)_\perp\} \\ = & (P;Q) \lhd l \in \alpha l(P;Q) \rhd \mathit{II} & \square \end{array}$$

This theorem justifies the use of all familiar programming notations for steps as for complete programs. However, we still have the freedom (and duty) to assign continuation alphabets to the primitive components of a program. This can be done either explicitly or implicitly by a definition which takes the form of the idempotence principle of Definition 6.1.5.

Example 6.1.8

We adopt the definition $\alpha l\mathit{II} =_{df} \{\}$. This convention maintains validity of the unit laws

$$\mathit{II}; P \;=\; P \;=\; P; \mathit{II}$$

Furthermore it ensures that the execution of II also has no effect

$$\mathit{II}^* \;=\; (l \in \{\}) * \mathit{II} \;=\; \mathit{II} \qquad \square$$

Example 6.1.9

$$\begin{array}{rcl} s : \mathtt{jump}\ f & =_{df} & (l := f \lhd l = s \rhd \mathit{II}) \\ \alpha l(s : \mathtt{jump}\ f) & =_{df} & \{s\} \end{array}$$

This notation describes a machine code jump instruction with destination f, which is stored in location s. The classical "tight loop" of machine code is represented

$$(s : \mathtt{jump}\ s)^* \;=\; (l \neq s)_\perp$$

This simple mathematical calculation gives the appropriate warning against allowing control to reach such an instruction. $\square$

The following law is used to peel off the first action of the execution of a step.

Lemma 6.1.10

$P^* \;=\; P; P^*$

Proof

$$\begin{array}{lll} & P^* & \{\text{fixed point}\} \\ = & (P; P^*) \lhd l \in \alpha l P \rhd I\!I & \{2.1\mathbf{L6}\} \\ = & (P; P^*) \lhd l \in \alpha l P \rhd (l \notin \alpha l P)_\perp & \{5.5\mathbf{L2} \text{ and Def. } 6.1.1\} \\ = & (P; P^*) \lhd l \in \alpha l P \rhd P^* & \{2.2\mathbf{L2} \text{ and Def. } 6.1.5\} \\ = & P; P^* & \square \end{array}$$

If a step is guaranteed to assign to l a value outside the continuation set, then the step will be executed exactly once, and this condition is also necessary.

Lemma 6.1.11

$P^* \;=\; P \quad \textbf{iff} \quad P \;=\; P; (l \notin \alpha l P)_\perp$

Proof

$$\begin{array}{lll} & P = P; (l \notin \alpha l P)_\perp & \\ \Rightarrow & P = P; (l \notin \alpha l P)_\perp \;\wedge & \\ & P; P^* = P; (l \notin \alpha l P)_\perp; P^* & \{5.5\mathbf{L2}\} \\ \Rightarrow & P = P; (l \notin \alpha l P)_\perp \;\wedge & \\ & P; P^* = P; (l \notin \alpha l P)_\perp & \{\text{Lemma } 6.1.10\} \\ \Rightarrow & P = P^* & \{\text{Corollary of } 5.5\mathbf{L4}\} \\ \Rightarrow & P = P; (l \notin \alpha l P)_\perp & \square \end{array}$$

From Lemma 6.1.11 and Corollary of 5.5**L4** we establish an idempotence law for execution.

Theorem 6.1.12

$(P^*)^* \;=\; P^*$ □

Two steps are said to be *disjoint* if their execution can never be interleaved, in the sense that neither of them can be started until the other has finished. This can be guaranteed by a simple condition on their alphabets: it ensures that in any circumstance at most one of the two steps can be executed, and the value of l determines which.

Definition 6.1.13 (Disjointness)

Two steps P and Q are *disjoint* if their continuations are disjoint, that is

$$\alpha l P \cap \alpha l Q \;=\; \{\} \qquad \square$$

Two blocks of machine code program which occupy disjoint areas of store will be disjoint in this sense. Two such blocks can be joined together by an assembly operation defined as follows.

Definition 6.1.14 (Assembly)

Let P and Q be disjoint steps. Define

$$\begin{aligned} P\|Q &=_{df} (P \lhd l \in \alpha lP \rhd Q) \lhd (l \in \alpha lP \cup \alpha lQ) \rhd I\!I \\ \alpha l(P\|Q) &=_{df} \alpha lP \cup \alpha lQ \end{aligned}$$ □

Because of disjointness, this operator (when defined) enjoys extra algebraic properties, though for the same reason, it cannot be idempotent.

Theorem 6.1.15 (Algebraic properties of assembly)

$\|$ is associative and commutative and has unit $I\!I$. □

Execution of an assembly consists of an interleaving of the executions of its operands. Because of disjointness, each operand is repeated as many times as possible before the other one can start again.

Theorem 6.1.16 (Execution of an assembly)

$(P\|Q)^* \;=\; (P^*\|Q)^* \;=\; (P^*\|Q^*)^*$

Proof Let $b =_{df} (l \in \alpha lP \cup \alpha lQ)$ and $c =_{df} (l \in \alpha lP)$. Define

$$\begin{aligned} F(X) &=_{df} ((P\|Q); X) \lhd b \rhd I\!I \\ G(X) &=_{df} ((P^*\|Q^*); X) \lhd b \rhd I\!I \end{aligned}$$

So $\mu F \;=\; (P\|Q)^*$ and $\mu G \;=\; (P^*\|Q^*)^*$.

From 5.5**L5** we conclude that

$$\begin{aligned} \mu F &= ((l \in \alpha lP) * (P\|Q)); \mu F \;=\; P^*; \mu F && (\dagger) \\ \mu G &= ((l \in \alpha lP) * (P^*\|Q^*)); \mu G \;=\; (P^*)^*; \mu G \;=\; P^*; \mu G && (\ddagger) \end{aligned}$$

$$\begin{aligned} & \mu F && \{\text{fixed point}\} \\ =\;& F(\mu F) && \{\text{def of } F \text{ and } 2.2\mathbf{L2}\} \\ =\;& (P; \mu F \lhd c \rhd Q; \mu F) \lhd b \rhd I\!I && \{(\dagger)\} \\ =\;& (P; P^*; \mu F \lhd c \rhd Q; Q^*; \mu F) \lhd b \rhd I\!I && \{\text{Lemma } 6.1.10 \text{ and } 2.2\mathbf{L2}\} \\ =\;& G(\mu F) \end{aligned}$$

Using ($\ddagger$) we can show

$$\mu G \;=\; F(\mu G)$$

in a similar way. The conclusion $(P \| Q)^* = (P^* \| Q^*)^*$ follows from the weakest fixed point theorem. Furthermore from Theorem 6.1.12 it follows that

$$(P^* \| Q)^* = ((P^*)^* \| Q^*)^* = (P^* \| Q^*)^* \qquad \square$$

An even stronger disjointness condition on two steps is that one of them cannot be started after the other is terminated.

Definition 6.1.17

If P and Q are disjoint, then Q is said to *inhibit* P if

$$Q = (Q; (l \notin alP)_\perp) \lhd l \in alQ \rhd \mathit{II} \qquad \square$$

Example 6.1.18 (Machine code)

A block of machine code inhibits another if it contains no jumps to any location within the other. $\square$

Lemma 6.1.19

If Q inhibits P, then

$$(l \notin alP)_\perp; Q^* = (l \notin alP)_\perp; Q^*; (l \notin alP \cup alQ)_\perp$$

Proof From Definition 6.1.17 and Exercise 5.5.1(2). $\square$

In the translation of a high level symbolic program to machine code, the only operation available is assembly of larger blocks of code out of smaller. The effect of the various high level program combinators must be achieved by placing constraints on jumps between the blocks, as shown by the following theorem

Theorem 6.1.20 (Sequential assembly)

If Q inhibits P then

$$(P \| Q)^* = P^*; Q^*$$

Proof

$$\begin{aligned}
& (P \| Q)^* && \{5.5\mathbf{L5}\} \\
= \; & (l \in alP) * (P \| Q); \\
& (l \in alQ) * (P \| Q); (P \| Q)^* && \{P \text{ and } Q \text{ are disjoint}\} \\
= \; & P^*; Q^*; (P \| Q)^* && \{\text{Corollary of } 5.5\mathbf{L4}, \text{ Lemma } 6.1.19\} \\
= \; & P^*; Q^*; (l \notin al(P \| Q))_\perp; (P \| Q)^* && \{5.5\mathbf{L2}\} \\
= \; & P^*; Q^* && \square
\end{aligned}$$

Theorem 6.1.21 (Complete disjointness)

If P inhibits Q and Q inhibits P then

$$P^* \| Q^* = (P \| Q)^*$$

Proof Let $b = (l \in \alpha l P \cup \alpha l Q)$.

$$\begin{aligned}
& P^* \| Q^* && \{\text{Def. 6.1.14}\} \\
= \ & (P^* \lhd l \in \alpha l P \rhd Q^*) \lhd b \rhd I\!I && \{P \text{ and } Q \text{ are disjoint}\} \\
= \ & (((l \notin \alpha l Q)_\perp; P^*) \lhd l \in \alpha l P \rhd ((l \notin \alpha l P)_\perp; Q^*)) \\
& \lhd b \rhd I\!I && \{\text{Lemma 6.1.19}\} \\
= \ & ((P^*; (\neg b)_\perp) \lhd l \in \alpha l P \rhd (Q^*; (\neg b)_\perp)) \lhd b \rhd I\!I && \{\text{Def. 6.1.14 and 2.2}\mathbf{L2}\} \\
= \ & (P^* \| Q^*); (\neg b)_\perp
\end{aligned}$$

From Lemma 6.1.11 and Theorem 6.1.16 it follows that

$$P^* \| Q^* = (P^* \| Q^*)^* = (P \| Q)^* \qquad \square$$

The representation of program execution as the repetition of members of a specified set of steps is the basic idea behind the UNITY model of parallel computation [38] and also of action systems [13]. In UNITY, there is an additional fairness constraint that insists that no selectable step is infinitely often rejected in any execution sequence. In the case of disjointness, fairness is automatic, because there is only one selectable step. We will also use disjointness and inhibition to ensure that the single operation of assembly can correctly implement a range of different program structures in Section 6.2.

Exercises 6.1.22

(1) Prove $(l \in \alpha l P) * (P \| Q) = P^*$.

(2) Prove that if both P and Q inhibit R, so does $P \| Q$. □

6.2 Compilation

The efficient execution of a computer program is normally preceded by a preliminary transformation (compilation) of the program into a target program, expressed in the idiosyncratic machine code of the computer that is to execute it. The machine code usually does not include mathematical and program structuring features such as arithmetic expressions, conditionals or iterations. Instead, it provides simple arithmetic operations, and a selection of conditional or unconditional jumps that may be used in combination to achieve the same effect. In this section we explore a range of valid transformation rules whose repeated application will achieve the task of program compilation, without changing the meaning of the program. We shall concentrate on compilation of control structures. Translation of the primitive assignments has been treated in Section 2.9, and translation of symbolic addresses to machine variables has been introduced in Section 4.4.

An obvious obligation on the compiler designer is to know the meaning of all the machine code instructions of the target computer. Fortunately, the effect of each instruction is easily defined using the standard familiar programming notations, particularly assignments and conditionals. The designers of the computer hardware are willing to accept such descriptions as a specification of what is to be implemented on silicon, and the correctness of the hardware implementation is not the responsibility of the designer of a compiler.

Examples 6.2.1

Consider a simple machine with a single register A. An instruction to load the constant n into this register is specified

$$\texttt{LDL}\ n \ =_{df}\ (A,\, l\ :=\ n,\, l+1), \qquad \text{where } 0 \le n < 64$$

This instruction itself occupies one location: so incrementation of l ensures it will point to the next instruction when this one is complete. Similarly a store instruction can be defined

$$\texttt{STO}\ b\ =_{df}\ (ram[b],\, l := A,\, l+1)$$

Arithmetic instructions take the form

$$\texttt{ADD}\ b\ =_{df}\ (A,\, l\ :=\ A + ram[b],\, l+1)$$

A conditional jump instruction skips over the n following locations if A is negative

$$\texttt{cjump}\ n\ =_{df}\ (l\ :=\ (l+n+1 \lhd A < 0 \rhd l+1)) \qquad \Box$$

A single machine code instruction stored in location m of the code store is represented by a step which has the singleton set $\{m\}$ as its continuation set, for example

$$\texttt{LDL}\ 27 \lhd l = m \rhd \mathit{II}$$

We will introduce a special notation for this case.

Definition 6.2.2 (Single instruction)

If INST is a machine code instruction, then

$$m : \texttt{INST}\ =_{df}\ \texttt{INST} \lhd l = m \rhd \mathit{II}$$

is called a single instruction. $\Box$

A block of machine code is defined in terms of its component instructions. For example,

$$(20 : \texttt{LDL } 27 \parallel 21 : \texttt{STO } 56)$$

is a block of two instructions. After expansion of the definitions, it is shown to be the same as Example 6.1.2.

Definition 6.2.3 (Machine code block)

A *machine code block* is a program expressible as an assembly of single instructions

$$S_0 \| S_1 \| \ldots \| S_n \qquad \square$$

A machine code block can in general be entered at any of its constituent continuation points. In practice, it is beneficial to designate one of these as its normal *start point*, and call it by the standard name s. This singles out the instruction that will be activated when control passes sequentially into the code; any other point would have to be entered by a jump. Similarly, we single out the standard *finishing point* (named f) of a block as the value of l when control leaves the block normally, that is not by a jump.

The start point will usually be the first of the locations in which the code is stored, and the finishing point will be the location just following the code. The code will usually be packed into contiguous locations; all its other continuations lie numerically between s and f so that their difference $(f - s)$ gives a count of the length of the code. Our theory will not depend on a contiguous range of addressing for the program store. We will use symbolic values for continuation points, relying only on the reasonable hypothesis that there is an unbounded supply of them.

In any machine code program there will be many blocks which are never entered by a jump instruction, nor do they use a jump instruction to exit. An obligation to terminate normally through the end f is expressed by the assertion $(l = f)_\perp$, and the assumption of normal entry through the beginning s is expressed $(l = s)^\top$. Blocks of code that have these as postcondition and precondition will be called *structured*, by analogy with the recommended programming practice of avoiding explicit jumps.

Definition 6.2.4 (Structured block)

A *structured block* is a program of the form

$$(l = s)^\top; P^*; (l = f)_\perp$$

where P is a machine code block. The value s is called its start point and f is its finishing point. $\square$

Example 6.2.5 (Identity)

There is only one useful structured block for which the start and finish are the same. Since it occupies no storage the only thing that it can do is nothing.

$$(l = s)^{\top}; \Pi^*; (l = s)_{\perp} \;=\; (l = s)^{\top}$$

This can be used to place a label s anywhere within the code. □

Example 6.2.6 (Abort)

$$(l = s)^{\top}; (s : \mathtt{jump}\ s)^*; (l = f)_{\perp} \;=\; (\perp \lhd l = s \rhd \top)$$ □

Example 6.2.7

A step with only one continuation point can never be entered in the middle by a jump. So a block consisting of a single instruction is easy to convert to structured form, for example

$$(l = 20)^{\top}; (20 : \mathtt{LDL}\ 27)^*; (l = 21)_{\perp}$$ □

Example 6.2.8

A block which has been translated from a single assignment will usually be structured. For example, the assignment

$$ram[b] \;:=\; ram[a] + 27$$

could be translated to

$$(l = 20)^{\top}; (20 : \mathtt{LDL}\ 27 \| 21 : \mathtt{ADD}\ a \| 22 : \mathtt{STO}\ b)^*; (l = 23)_{\perp}$$ □

The form of a structured block has been defined to model closely the behaviour of an actual computer executing a block of machine code instructions. The task of a compiler faced with an arbitrary source program P is to compile it to a target program $\hat{P}$ expressed in the machine language of the computer, ensuring that $\hat{P}$ has the same effect as P (or better). The target program has l in its alphabet, but the source does not, so a declaration is needed to match the two sides of the inequation

$$P \;\sqsubseteq\; (\mathbf{var}\ l\,;\ \hat{P}\,;\ \mathbf{end}\ l)$$

We define our target code to match the right hand side of this inequation.

Definition 6.2.9 (Target code)

A program is in *target code* if it is expressed in the form

$$\begin{aligned}\langle s, Q, f\rangle \;&=_{df}\; \textbf{var } l; (l = s)^{\top}; Q^*; (l = f)_{\perp}; \textbf{end } l \\ &=\; \textbf{var } l := s; Q^*; (l = f)_{\perp}; \textbf{end } l\end{aligned}$$

where Q is a machine code block □

The fundamental theorem of compilation states that every program P can be expressed as target code. Its proof is by structural induction on P, based on a series of lemmas which display the transformations used by a compiler. For simplicity, declarations are omitted, and iteration is the only form of recursion.

Theorem 6.2.10 (Compilation)

For each program P expressed in the language of Chapter 5, and for any start point s and for any set L of continuation points (where $s \notin L$), there is a finish point f and a machine code block $\hat{P}$ such that $\alpha l\hat{P}$ is disjoint from L and

$$P \;\sqsubseteq\; \langle s, \hat{P}, f\rangle$$

Proof By structural induction, based on the following lemmas. □

The unit Π can be translated either as an empty segment of code, or as a machine code jump. The jump may be anywhere and lead to anywhere else.

Lemma 6.2.11 (Skip)

$\Pi \;=\; \langle s,\ \Pi,\ s\rangle$

Proof

$$\begin{aligned}&\langle s,\ \Pi,\ s\rangle && \{\text{Lemma 6.1.11}\}\\ =\;& \textbf{var } l := s; \Pi; \textbf{end } l && \{2.9\textbf{L4}, \textbf{L6} \text{ and } \textbf{L8}\}\\ =\;& \Pi && \square\end{aligned}$$

Lemma 6.2.12 (Skip)

If $s \neq f$, then $\Pi \;=\; \langle s,\ (s : \texttt{jump} f),\ f\rangle$

Proof

$$\begin{aligned}&\langle s,\ (s : \texttt{jump } f),\ f\rangle && \{\text{Lemma 6.1.11}\}\\ =\;& \textbf{var } l := s; (s : \texttt{jump } f); (l = f)_{\perp}; \textbf{end } l && \{3.1\textbf{L3} \text{ and } 2.1\textbf{L5}\}\\ =\;& \textbf{var } l := f; (l := f)_{\perp}; \textbf{end } l && \{3.1\textbf{L3},\ 2.9\textbf{L6} \text{ and } \textbf{L8}\}\\ =\;& \Pi && \square\end{aligned}$$

For all reasonable machines, a single assignment can be translated into a sequence of machine code instructions, but the compilation strategy and its proof must depend on details of the machine, so they are omitted.

Lemma 6.2.13 (Assignment)

For every s there is an f and a machine code block $\hat{P}$ such that

$$(v := e) \sqsubseteq \langle s,\ \hat{P},\ f \rangle \qquad \square$$

The compilation of structured statements depends on the fact that the compiler can arrange that the operands can be compiled into disjoint regions of program store with no jumps between them, and that a fresh unused location can be found whenever needed to store an extra compiled instruction. The general strategy is shown by compilation of a non-deterministic choice. Of course in practice no computer has in its repertoire the non-deterministic jump, so a more practical compiler would resolve the non-determinism by selecting and compiling just one of the alternatives.

Lemma 6.2.14 (Non-deterministic choice)

Let $C = s : (l := s_1 \sqcap l := s_2)$ and $s \notin \{s_1, s_2\}$

and P inhibits Q and C and $s_1 \notin \alpha l Q$

and Q inhibits P and C and $s_2 \notin \alpha l P$.

Then $\langle s_1, P, f \rangle \sqcap \langle s_2, Q, f \rangle \;=\; \langle s,\ P \| C \| Q,\ f \rangle$

Proof From Exercise 6.1.22(2) it follows that $P \| Q$ inhibits C.

$$
\begin{array}{lll}
 & \langle s,\ P\|C\|Q,\ f\rangle & \{\text{Theorem 6.1.20}\} \\
= & \mathbf{var}\, l := s; C^*; (P\|Q)^*; (l = f)_\perp; \mathbf{end}\, l & \{\text{Lemma 6.1.11}\} \\
= & \mathbf{var}\, l := s; C; (P\|Q)^*; (l = f)_\perp; \mathbf{end}\, l & \{\text{Theorem 6.1.20}\} \\
= & \mathbf{var}\, l := s_1; (Q^*; P^*); (l = f)_\perp; \mathbf{end}\, l \;\sqcap & \{s_1 \notin \alpha l Q,\ s_2 \notin \alpha l P \\
 & \mathbf{var}\, l := s_2; (P^*; Q^*); (l = f)_\perp; \mathbf{end}\, l & \text{and } 5.5\mathbf{L2}\} \\
= & \langle s_1, P, f\rangle \;\sqcap\; \langle s_2, Q, f\rangle & \square
\end{array}
$$

The treatment of the conditional is similar to that of non-determinism. The two operands must share the same normal exit; this can be readily achieved by planting a jump at the end of one of them.

Lemma 6.2.15 (Conditional)

Let $B = s : (l := s_1 \lhd b \rhd s_2)$ and $s \notin \{s_1, s_2\}$

and P inhibits B and Q and $s_1 \notin \alpha l Q$

and Q inhibits B and P and $s_2 \notin \alpha l P$.

Then $\langle s_1, P, f \rangle \lhd b \rhd \langle s_2, Q, f \rangle \;=\; \langle s,\ P \| B \| Q,\ f \rangle$

Proof Similar to Lemma 6.2.14. $\square$

The compilation of sequential composition requires that the finish point of the first operand must be the same as the normal entry of the second operand. Of course, the operands must be disjoint and the second must not jump back to the first. In this case, the two machine code blocks can be simply assembled, without any extra code to glue them together.

Lemma 6.2.16 (Sequential composition)

If Q inhibits P, then

$$\langle s, P, h\rangle; \langle h, Q, f\rangle \ \sqsubseteq\ \langle s,\ P\|Q,\ f\rangle$$

Proof

$$\begin{array}{lll} & \langle s,\ P\|Q,\ f\rangle & \{\text{Theorem 6.1.20}\} \\ = & \mathbf{var}\, l := s; P^*; Q^*; (l = f)_\perp; \mathbf{end}\, l & \{2.9\mathbf{L7}\} \\ \sqsupseteq & \langle s, P, h\rangle; \langle h, Q, f\rangle & \square \end{array}$$

Iteration is a special case of recursion that is relatively easy to implement in machine code.

Lemma 6.2.17 (Iteration)

Let s, f, s_1 and f_1 be distinct labels and $\alpha l P \cap \{s, f_1, f\} \ = \ \{\}$
and $B = s : (l := s_1 \lhd b \rhd f)$
and $J = f_1 : (l := s)$.
Then $b * \langle s_1,\ P,\ f_1\rangle \ \sqsubseteq\ \langle s,\ B\|P\|J,\ f\rangle$

Proof

$$\begin{array}{lll} & \langle s,\ B\|P\|J,\ f\rangle & \{5.5\mathbf{L5} \text{ and Lemma 6.1.11}\} \\ = & \mathbf{var}\ l := s; B; (B\|P\|J)^*; (l = f)_\perp;\ \mathbf{end}\ l & \{3.1\mathbf{L3},\ 2.9\mathbf{L5} \text{ and } 5.5\mathbf{L2}\} \\ = & (\mathbf{var}\ l := s_1; (B\|P\|J)^*; (l = f)_\perp; \mathbf{end}\ l) & \\ & \lhd b \rhd (\mathbf{var}\ l := f; (l = f)_\perp; \mathbf{end}\ l) & \{5.5\mathbf{L5} \text{ and } J \text{ inhibits } P\} \\ = & (\mathbf{var}\ l := s_1; P^*; J^*; (B\|P\|J)^*; (l = f)_\perp; & \\ & \mathbf{end}\ l) \lhd b \rhd I\!I & \{\text{Lemma 6.1.11 and } 2.9\mathbf{L7}\} \\ \sqsupseteq & ((\langle s_1, P, f_1\rangle; \mathbf{var}\ l := f_1; J; (B\|P\|J)^*; & \\ & (l = f)_\perp; \mathbf{end}\ l) \lhd b \rhd I\!I & \{\text{def of } J\} \\ = & ((\langle s_1,\ P,\ f_1\rangle\ ;\ \langle s,\ B\|P\|J,\ f\rangle) \lhd b \rhd I\!I & \end{array}$$

The conclusion follows from the weakest fixed point theorem. □

Exercise 6.2.18

Prove that Theorem 6.2.17 can be strengthened to an equation. □

6.3 Interpretation

An interpreter is a program that accepts as input the *text* of an arbitrary program expressed in its source language, and then behaves exactly as described by the predicate which the text denotes. Interpretation is in principle slower than direct execution of compiled code; this is in practice tolerable when the interpreter is written in a language which is executed with inherently greater efficiency than the interpreted language. But there is considerable theoretical interest in an interpreter that is written in the *same* language that it interprets. For example, a universal Turing machine is an interpreter capable of simulating all other Turing machines, including itself. Any language which is powerful enough to program all computable functions must be capable of writing its own interpreter. And any method of reasoning about programs should be powerful enough to prove that this interpreter is correct.

The construction and proof of an interpreter requires a clear way of describing and manipulating the texts of a program, quite independent of their meaning. We will use typewriter font variables $\mathtt{P}, \mathtt{Q}, \ldots, \mathtt{b}, \mathtt{e}, \mathtt{v}\ldots$ to stand for program texts, including conditions, expressions and lists of variables. We will use the normal programming operators to stand for the textual operation of combining texts into a larger program text. For example, $\mathtt{P};\mathtt{Q}$ denotes the text obtained by writing the text *denoted* by $\mathtt{P}$ (*not* the letter "$\mathtt{P}$" itself), followed by a semicolon (the symbol ";" itself), followed by the text denoted by $\mathtt{Q}$; the whole result may be enclosed in brackets (if necessary). All these textual operations are independent of the meaning of the text, although they are closely related. If $\mathtt{P}$ denotes a text which has a meaning described by the predicate P, and $\mathtt{Q}$ similarly has meaning Q, then the text $\mathtt{P};\mathtt{Q}$ will clearly have the meaning $(P;Q)$, as defined in Chapter 2. The same applies to all the other symbols of the programming language. In general, we will use an italic font letter to stand for the variable, expression or predicate whose text is denoted by the corresponding typewriter font letter. These rather informal conventions can be formalised by a rigorous separation of syntax from the semantics of the language, and the definition of an explicit function mapping between them. This is the standard practice in the exposition of denotational semantics, but we prefer the lighter notation of just changing the font.

In our interpreter, the control variable l will take as its value a list of texts representing the rest of the program which currently remains to be executed; its initial value is the whole program taken as a unit list, and its final value is empty. Each step of the interpreter analyses the value of l to find the first action to be performed; it also updates the value of l to maintain its record of remaining actions. When no action remains, the interpreter terminates. Apart from l, we assume that the interpreter has exactly the same alphabet of assignable variables as the program that it interprets. Thus the assignment $\mathtt{v} := \mathtt{e}$ has an effect which is described simply by $v := e$.

As in previous sections, the interpreter is designed as an assembly of steps, each of which deals with a particular programming feature. For example, the step which deals assignments is called A, defined by

$$A =_{df} (v, l := e, tail(l)) \lhd l_0 = (\mathtt{v} := \mathtt{e}) \rhd \mathit{II}$$

where l_0 denotes the first member of the list l,

and $tail(l)$ represents the list l after the removal of its first member.

The condition tests whether the first action specified by the current value of l is an assignment. If so, the assignment is performed, and its text is removed from the list. The continuation alphabet of this step is the set of all lists of program texts that begin with an assignment. The condition $l_0 = (\mathtt{v} := \mathtt{e})$ in the clause A is tested by pattern matching; the list of variables v is what is found to match the left hand side $\mathtt{v}$ of the assignment $\mathtt{v} := \mathtt{e}$, and e is similarly determined by $\mathtt{e}$.

The other steps of the interpreter deal with the control structures of the language, and they update only the control variable l. In the following we use $l^\frown m$ to denote the catenation of lists l and m, and $< \mathtt{P} >$ to denote the unit list with just the single element $\mathtt{P}$.

$$B =_{df} ((l :=< \mathtt{P} > {}^\frown tail(l)) \lhd b \rhd (l :=< \mathtt{Q} > {}^\frown tail(l))) \lhd l_0 = (\mathtt{P} \lhd \mathtt{b} \rhd \mathtt{Q}) \rhd \mathit{II}$$

$$C =_{df} ((l :=< \mathtt{P} > {}^\frown tail(l)) \sqcap (l :=< \mathtt{Q} > {}^\frown tail(l))) \lhd l_0 = (\mathtt{P} \sqcap \mathtt{Q}) \rhd \mathit{II}$$

$$J =_{df} (l := tail(l)) \lhd l_0 = \mathit{II} \rhd \mathit{II}$$

$$R =_{df} (l :=< \mathtt{F}(\mu\mathtt{X}.\mathtt{F}(\mathtt{X})) > {}^\frown tail(l)) \lhd l_0 = (\mu\mathtt{X}.\mathtt{F}(\mathtt{X})) \rhd \mathit{II}$$

$$S =_{df} (l :=< \mathtt{P} > {}^\frown < \mathtt{Q} > {}^\frown tail(l)) \lhd l_0 = (\mathtt{P}; \mathtt{Q}) \rhd \mathit{II}$$

$$Z =_{df} \mathit{II} \lhd l_0 = \bot \rhd \mathit{II}$$

The clauses B and C choose which of $\mathtt{P}$ and $\mathtt{Q}$ to execute; J ignores any occurrence of II. S deals with sequential composition by deleting leftmost brackets and adding the two components in front of l. Eventually, this will reveal the first primitive action to be performed. The clause R deals with the case of recursion. It executes $\mu\mathtt{X}.\mathtt{F}(\mathtt{X})$ by executing its body $\mathtt{F}(\mathtt{X})$, but first, all instances of $\mathtt{X}$ in the body have been replaced by the whole of the original recursive construction. These copies will be ready in place when they are needed for further recursive activations. The clause Z is used to deal with abortion by ensuring that the interpreter never terminates.

Each of the steps defined above has its own continuation alphabet; it is the set of all lists which begin with a text of the form displayed in the condition. All of these forms are distinct, and because they are texts, their values are also all different. We can therefore define the interpreter as an assembly of steps with disjoint alphabets

$$INT \ =_{df} \ A \| B \| C \| J \| R \| S \| Z$$

Its alphabet is the union of the alphabets of its constituent steps. It includes all lists of program texts except the empty list. So the interpreter will terminate as soon as it encounters $<>$, which is not dealt with by INT. We therefore define the continuation alphabet of the interpreter to be all lists but $<>$. To make this work, the interpreter assigns the program text as the only member of the list to the variable l before starting to execute it. And, of course, the variable l is declared as a local variable of the interpreter.

Definition 6.3.1 (Interpreter)

$$I(\mathtt{Q}) \ =_{df} \ \langle < \mathtt{Q} >, INT, <> \rangle \qquad \text{(see Definition 6.2.9)} \qquad \square$$

The definitions given above show that it is rather easy to write an interpreter in its own language, especially if pattern matching is used to analyse the program text. It is also rather easy to see that the interpreter does what is expected of it. Nevertheless, it is worthwhile to formulate a theorem expressing what it means for such an interpreter to be correct, and then to see whether the algebraic laws which have been listed and proved in Chapter 5 are adequate to prove its correctness.

Theorem 6.3.2 (Correctness of the interpreter)

Let `Q` be the text of a program described by the predicate Q. Then

$$Q \ = \ I(\mathtt{Q})$$

Proof The proof is by structural induction on the text of the program `Q`, and it is based on the following lemmas. □

As in Section 6.2, each case is proved by algebraic laws justifying symbolic execution. The most difficult case is sequential composition, where it is necessary to show that the interpretation of $l \hat{} m$ passes through an intermediate stage when l has been fully executed, and only m remains. This case needs two lemmas.

Lemma 6.3.3

$$(l \neq <>)_\bot; (l := l\hat{}m); INT \ = \ (l \neq <>)_\bot; INT; (l := l\hat{}m)$$

Proof Based on case analysis on the value of l and the definition of the step function INT. □

Lemma 6.3.4

$$(l := l\hat{}m); ((l \neq <> \wedge l \neq m) * INT) \ = \ INT^*; (l := m)$$

Proof Let $f(X) =_{df} (l := l^\frown m)\ ;\ X$

$g(X) =_{df} (INT; X) \lhd (l \neq <>) \wedge (l \neq m) \rhd II$

$h(X) =_{df} (INT; X) \lhd l \neq <> \rhd (l := m)$

$$\begin{array}{lr} \text{Lemma 6.3.3} & \{\text{def of } f,\ g \text{ and } h\} \\ \Rightarrow\ f \circ g = h \circ f & \{\text{Theorem 4.2.12}\} \\ \Rightarrow\ f(\mu g) = \mu h & \{5.5\mathbf{L4}\} \\ \Rightarrow\ LHS = RHS & \square \end{array}$$

Lemma 6.3.5 (Sequential composition)

$I(\mathtt{P};\mathtt{Q}) = I(\mathtt{P}); I(\mathtt{Q})$

Proof Let $b =_{df} (l \neq <>) \wedge (l \neq < \mathtt{Q} >)$.

$$\begin{array}{llr} & I(\mathtt{P};\mathtt{Q}) & \{\text{def of } INT \text{ and } 5.5\mathbf{L1}\} \\ = & \mathbf{var}\, l := < \mathtt{P} > ^\frown < \mathtt{Q} >; INT^*; (l = <>)_\perp; \mathbf{end}\, l & \{5.1\mathbf{L3} \text{ and } 5.5\mathbf{L5}\} \\ = & \mathbf{var}\, l := < \mathtt{P} >;\ l := l^\frown < \mathtt{Q} >;\ (b * INT); & \\ & INT^*; (l = <>)_\perp; \mathbf{end}\, l & \{\text{let } m = < \mathtt{Q} > \text{ in Lemma 6.3.4}\} \\ = & \mathbf{var}\, l := < \mathtt{P} >; INT^*; (l := < \mathtt{Q} >); INT^*; (l = <>)_\perp; \mathbf{end}\, l & \{5.5\mathbf{L3}\} \\ = & \mathbf{var}\, l := < \mathtt{P} >; INT^*; (l = <>)_\perp; & \\ & (l := < \mathtt{Q} >); INT^*; (l = <>)_\perp; \mathbf{end}\, l & \{2.9\mathbf{L7}\} \\ = & I(\mathtt{P}); I(\mathtt{Q}) & \square \end{array}$$

The only other significant case is recursion.

Lemma 6.3.6 (Recursion)

$I(\mu\mathtt{X}.\mathtt{F}(\mathtt{X})) = \mu X.\, F(X)$

Proof

$$\begin{array}{llr} & I(\mu\mathtt{X}.\mathtt{F}(\mathtt{X})) & \{5.5\mathbf{L1}\} \\ = & \mathbf{var}\ l := < \mathtt{F}(\mu\mathtt{X}.\mathtt{F}(\mathtt{X})) >; INT^*; (l = <>)_\perp; \mathbf{end}\ l & \{\text{induction}\} \\ = & F(I(\mu\mathtt{X}.\mathtt{F}(\mathtt{X}))) & \end{array}$$

which implies that $I(\mu\mathtt{X}.\mathtt{F}(\mathtt{X})) \sqsupseteq \mu X.\, F(X)$.

To show correctness of the interpreter I, this inequation is sufficient. To establish the inequation in the other direction, we construct a more abstract interpreter T as an infinite assembly of clauses, each of which interprets a whole sequence of programs in a single step

$$T =_{df} (\exists \mathtt{Q1}, \ldots, \mathtt{Qn} \bullet ((l = < \mathtt{Q1}, \ldots, \mathtt{Qn} >)^\top; Q1; \ldots; Qn) \lhd l \neq <> \rhd II); \mathbf{end}\, l$$

T is not a program, but it is reasonable to regard it as a predicate, and for purposes of proof that is good enough. In the case of a unit sequence, we have

$$(\mathbf{var}\, l := < \mathtt{Q} >;\, T) \;=\; Q \qquad (\dagger)$$

Furthermore

$$\begin{aligned} & T && \{2.1\mathbf{L1}\} \\ = \;& T \lhd l \in \alpha l INT \rhd T && \{\text{def of } INT\} \\ = \;& (INT; T) \lhd l \in \alpha l INT \rhd \mathbf{end}\, l \end{aligned}$$

from which and 5.5**L4** it follows that

$$T \;\sqsupseteq\; \mu X \bullet ((INT; X) \lhd l \in \alpha l INT \rhd \mathbf{end}\ l) \;=\; (INT^*;\, \mathbf{end}\, l) \qquad (\ddagger)$$

and

$$\begin{aligned} & \mu X.\, F(X) && \{(\dagger)\} \\ = \;& \mathbf{var}\, l := < \mu\mathtt{X.F(X)} >; T && \{(\ddagger)\} \\ \sqsupseteq \;& \mathbf{var}\, l := < \mu\mathtt{X.F(X)} >; (INT^*); \mathbf{end}\, l && \{\text{def of } I\} \\ \sqsupseteq \;& I((\mu\mathtt{X.F(X)})) && \square \end{aligned}$$

These lemmas show the main clauses of the proof of the correctness of the interpreter I.

6.4* Jumps and labels

The process of compilation described in Section 6.2 translates a language with high level control structures like conditionals, compositions and iterations into a language which replaces all such structures by conditional and unconditional jumps to labels placed elsewhere in the program. Many of the older programming languages provide jumps and labels in addition to more abstract program structures. Such a mixture of levels of abstraction is not always recommended in programming practice, but it provides a good exercise for the extensibility of our theory. Our goal is to preserve the validity of all the laws relating to structures, and just to add the laws needed for reasoning about the additional unstructured features. Our method is to concentrate mainly on *forward* jumps, and *backward* jumps are treated separately, because they can give rise to iteration.

To reason about the structure of a program P in a language with jumps, it is necessary to keep an account of all the *exit* points of P, that is all the labels that may be destinations outside P of jumps which originate inside P. This is nothing but the set of expected final values of the control variable l, and it will be denoted $\alpha l'P$. The set plays the same role as the single finishing point f of Section 6.2.

Similarly, we single out the complementary set $\alpha l_0 P$, containing the permissible set of initial values of l before execution of P. It denotes the subset of $\alpha l P$ that contains the intended entry points of P; it will contain the labels placed internally within P, but exclude labels which are intended only as destinations for jumps which are also internal to P. It plays the same role as the single start point s of Section 6.2.

We will also single out a special value $\mathbf{n}$, which is the value that l takes when P is entered normally through the beginning, and not by a jump. This is the value that l will also take on normal exit from P, which occurs not by a jump but by falling through the end. It is convenient to exclude $\mathbf{n}$ from both $\alpha l_0 P$ and $\alpha l' P$; it will *never* be used for a backward jump.

The structure and control flow of a program with jumps and labels can often be made instantly obvious to the eye by means of a flow chart. This is a pictorial representation in which the program text is written in boxes, and the label values are written on arrows drawn between pairs of boxes, and on arrows connecting a box to the outside.

$$\alpha l_0 P = \{s_1,, s_2, \ldots, s_m\}$$

$$s_m = f_n$$

$$\alpha l' P = \{f_1, f_2, \ldots, f_n\}$$

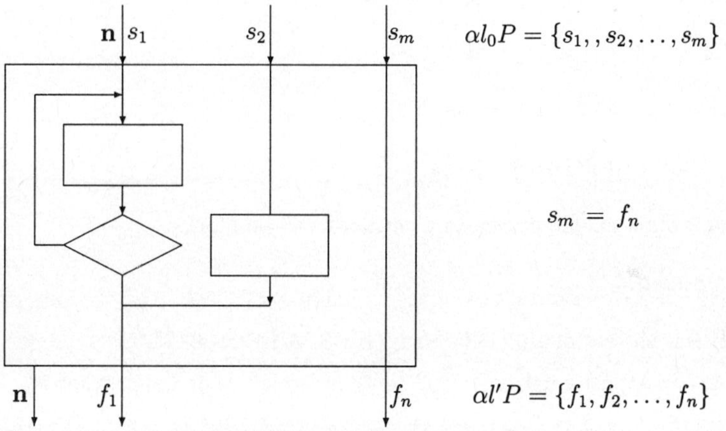

Figure 6.4.1 Flow chart

$\alpha l_0 P$ is the set of labels (other than $\mathbf{n}$) on arrows leading into the box surrounding P, $\alpha l' P$ is the set of labels on arrows leading out. We allow structuring, that is flow charts may be drawn within the boxes of a flow chart, as shown in Figure 6.4.1.   □

Suppose k is an internal label inside P. If k occurs as a label *after* all the jumps to k within P, then k will not be an exit label of P. It may or may not be in

$\alpha l_0 P$, depending on whether an external jump to that label is also to be allowed. If, however, a jump to k occurs *after* the label k, then k is definitely in $\alpha l' P$. If the jump is intended to lead back to the label k, then k must also be among the entries of P. In this case, the execution P^* will model explicitly the iterations that result from executing backward jumps; they will be detected by the fact that their labels are in the intersection $\alpha l_0 P \cap \alpha l' P$. If there are only forward jumps, the entry labels will be disjoint from the exit labels, and we will single out this special case as easier to reason about.

The expectation that the initial value of l will lie in $\alpha l_0 P \cup \{\mathbf{n}\}$ is encoded in the same way as for steps (Definition 6.1.5) by making the action of P vacuous otherwise. The obligation for l to terminate in the set $\alpha l' P \cup \{\mathbf{n}\}$ is encoded as in Definition 6.2.4 (structured block) by an appropriately placed assertion.

Definition 6.4.2 (Blocks and proper blocks)

Let S and F be sets of labels, and $\mathbf{n} \notin S$ and $\mathbf{n} \notin F$.

$$(P : S \Rightarrow F) \;=_{df}\; (P \;=\; (P; (l \in (F \cup \{\mathbf{n}\})_\perp) \lhd l \in (S \cup \{\mathbf{n}\}) \rhd \mathit{II})$$

A program P is a *block* if it satisfies

$$(P : \alpha l_0 P \Rightarrow \alpha l' P)$$

A block P is called a *proper* block if

$$\alpha l_0 P \cap \alpha l' P \;=\; \{\}$$

In this section all the programs mentioned will be blocks. □

Examples 6.4.3

(1) If L is the set of all labels, then $(P : L \Rightarrow L)$ for all P.

(2) At the opposite extreme, if P contains no labels or jumps, that is

$$\alpha l_0 P \;=\; \alpha l' P \;=\; \{\}$$

then it is a proper block. It is entered only at the beginning (with $l = \mathbf{n}$) and exits only at the end (with l again equal to $\mathbf{n}$). □

A label s is placed within a program by the construction **label** s, at the point intended as the destination of any jump to s. It may be entered either normally or by a jump, but it always exits normally. A jump plays a complementary role. It is entered normally but it always exits by means of a jump. Neither of them has any effect on anything except l.

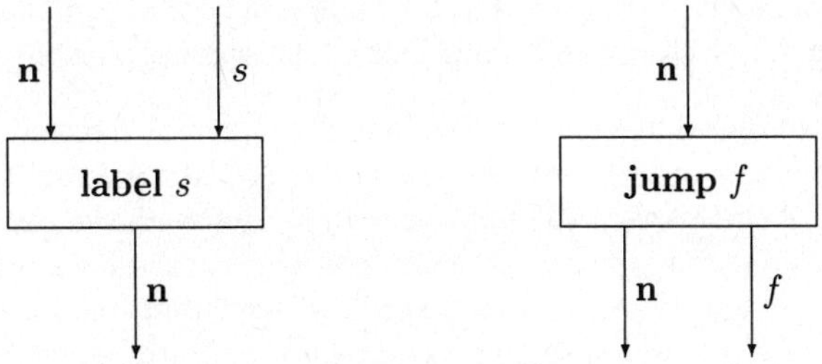

Figure 6.4.4 **label** s and **jump** f

Definition 6.4.5 (Labels and jumps)

$$\begin{array}{lll}
\textbf{label } s & =_{df} & (l := \mathbf{n}) \lhd l \in \{s, \mathbf{n}\} \rhd \mathit{\Pi} \\
\alpha l_0 \, \textbf{label } s & =_{df} & \{s\} \\
\alpha l' \, \textbf{label } s & =_{df} & \{\} \\
\textbf{jump } f & =_{df} & (l := f) \lhd l = \mathbf{n} \rhd \mathit{\Pi} \\
\alpha l_0 \, \textbf{jump } f & =_{df} & \{\} \\
\alpha l' \, \textbf{jump } f & =_{df} & \{f\}
\end{array}$$

□

The following laws show how a forward jump can be executed by omitting the code that follows it.

Theorem 6.4.6

L1 If $P : \{\} \Rightarrow \{\}$, then $(\textbf{jump } f\,;\, P) \;=\; \textbf{jump } f$

L2 $(\textbf{jump } s\,;\, \textbf{jump } f) \;=\; \textbf{jump } s$

L3 $(\textbf{label } s\,;\, \textbf{label } f) \;=\; (\textbf{label } f; \textbf{label } s)$

L4 $(\textbf{label } s\,;\, \textbf{label } s) \;=\; \textbf{label } s$

Proof of L2

$$\begin{array}{lll}
& \textbf{jump } s; \textbf{jump } f & \{\text{Def. 6.4.5 and 2.2}\mathbf{L2}\} \\
= & (l := s; \textbf{jump } f) \lhd l = \mathbf{n} \rhd \mathit{\Pi} & \{\text{Def. 6.4.5 and 2.3}\mathbf{L4}\} \\
= & ((l := s; l := f) \lhd \mathit{false} \rhd l := s) & \\
& \lhd l = \mathbf{n} \rhd \mathit{\Pi} & \{\text{Def. 6.4.5 and 2.1}\mathbf{L5}\} \\
= & \textbf{jump } s &
\end{array}$$

□

Our goal is to apply to blocks all the structuring notations of our programming language. For blocks with the same alphabet of entry and exit points, the permitted operators are defined by the following theorem.

Theorem 6.4.7 (Block closure)

The set of blocks $\{P \mid P : S \Rightarrow F\}$ is a complete lattice, and closed with respect to non-deterministic choice and conditional. The same applies to proper blocks. □

The main omission from this theorem is sequential composition. This is because the alphabets of the two operands of composition are usually different, and the alphabet of the result is different yet again. However, the result alphabet can be defined as a function of the operand alphabets in such a way that the relevant closure theorem can be proved. In general, a sequential composition may be entered at any entry point of either of its operands, and it may exit by a jump out of either of its operands. However, any label by which the first operand jumps into the second now becomes an internal forward jump, and will not lead to an exit from the sequential composition.

Definition 6.4.8 (Alphabets for sequential composition)

$$\begin{aligned} \alpha l_0(P;Q) &=_{df} \alpha l_0 P \cup \alpha l_0 Q \\ \alpha l'(P;Q) &=_{df} (\alpha l' P \setminus \alpha l_0 Q) \cup \alpha l' Q \end{aligned}$$ □

This definition is essentially restated by the following theorem.

Theorem 6.4.9 (Composition closure)

If $P : S \Rightarrow F$ and $Q : T \Rightarrow G$, then

$$(P;Q) : (S \cup T) \Rightarrow ((F \setminus T) \cup G)$$ □

To reason effectively about labelled programs, we need a method of abstracting from internal label values which are never intended to be seen or used from outside. In the interests of modularity, the hiding should be selective; as soon as an assembly P has been built up to include all jumps to an internal label value, that value can be hidden, while all the other labels are still visible. Labels that are used only for entry or only for exit are easy to hide, by just removing them from the alphabet. But a label in both alphabets can only be hidden by making explicit the internal iteration. This case must be dealt with first.

A backward jump (**jump** f) executed in a program P is one that leads to a label f in $\alpha l' P \cap \alpha l_0 P$. It also gives rise to a repetition of P whenever l takes f as its final value. On completion of the repetitions, the label can no longer be a final value of l; it is therefore removed from $\alpha l' P$. Let H be a set of labels which are used as destinations of backward jumps in P. We define $P^{\setminus H}$ to represent the desired effect of the iteration; in addition the labels of H are hidden by exclusion from the *exit* alphabet. This operation can be used to turn any block P into a proper block, by hiding all labels in $\alpha l_0 P \cap \alpha l' P$. Once backward jumps have been dealt with, all remaining jumps are forward, and all remaining blocks are proper.

H is usually a subset of both the exit and the entry alphabets: any extraneous elements are irrelevant; they are ignored in the following definitions.

Definition 6.4.10 (Hiding exits)

$$\begin{aligned} P^{\backslash H} &=_{df} P; (l \in H \cap al_0P) * P \\ al_0\, P^{\backslash H} &=_{df} al_0P \\ al'\, P^{\backslash H} &=_{df} al'P \setminus (al_0P \cap H) \end{aligned} \qquad \square$$

The theorem effectively shows that the definition has its intended effect.

Theorem 6.4.11 (Hiding exits)

If $P : S \Rightarrow F$, then $P^{\backslash H} : S \Rightarrow (F \setminus (S \cap H))$. $\square$

The hiding of exits has all the expected properties of a hiding operator. Hiding what is not there has no effect; the order of hiding different labels is irrelevant, and if hiding is irrelevant for one operand of a composition, it distributes to the other.

Theorem 6.4.12

L5 $P^{\backslash H} = P$ whenever $H \cap al'P = \{\}$

L6 $(P^{\backslash H})^{\backslash G} = P^{(H \cup G)}$

L7 $(P;Q)^{\backslash H} = P;(Q^{\backslash H})$ whenever $H \cap al_0P = \{\}$

L8 $(P;Q)^{\backslash H} = (P^{\backslash H});Q$ whenever $H \cap (al_0Q \cup al'Q) = \{\}$

Proof of **L7** Let $A = al_0P \cup al_0Q$.

$$\begin{aligned} & (l \in H \cap A) * (P;Q) && \{5.5\mathbf{L1}\} \\ = \ & (l \in H \cap A) * ((l \in H \cap A)_\perp; P; Q) && \{\text{Def. } 6.4.2\} \\ = \ & (l \in H \cap A) * ((l \in H \cap A)_\perp; && \{b_\perp; c_\perp = (b \wedge c)_\perp \\ & (P; Q \lhd l \in al_0P \cup \{\mathbf{n}\} \rhd Q)) && \text{and } H \cap al_0P = \{\}\} \\ = \ & (l \in H \cap A) * ((l \in H \cap A)_\perp; Q) && \{5.5\mathbf{L1}\} \\ = \ & (l \in H \cap A) * Q && \{H \cap al_0P = \{\}\} \\ = \ & (l \in H \cap al_0Q) * Q \end{aligned}$$

which implies

$$LHS = P;Q;((l \in H \cap A) * (P;Q)) = P;Q;((l \in H \cap al_0Q) * Q) = RHS \ \square$$

Hiding of an entry label is simpler than hiding an exit label. It is applied to a label in P which is intended only as the destination of a forward jump that is also within P, and from nowhere else. Indeed, the correctness of the program may depend on observance of this restriction. Such a restriction can be enforced syntactically by removing the label from the alphabet of permitted entry points of the block.

Definition 6.4.13 (Hiding entries)

Let H be a set of labels to be removed from the entry points of P.

$$\begin{aligned} {}^{H/}P &=_{df} \ I\!I \lhd l \in H \rhd P \\ \alpha l_0\, {}^{H/}P &=_{df} \ \alpha l_0 P \setminus H \\ \alpha l'\, {}^{H/}P &=_{df} \ \alpha l' P \end{aligned} \qquad \square$$

This definition also has the properties expected of any hiding operator.

Theorem 6.4.14 (Hiding entries)

If $P : S \Rightarrow F$, then ${}^{H/}P : (S \setminus H) \Rightarrow F$. $\square$

Theorem 6.4.15

L9 ${}^{H/}P \ = \ P$ whenever $H \cap \alpha l_0 P \ = \ \{\}$

L10 ${}^{H/}({}^{G/}P) \ = \ {}^{(H \cup G)/}P$

L11 ${}^{H/}(P;Q) \ = \ ({}^{H/}P);Q$ whenever $H \cap \alpha l_0 Q \ = \ \{\}$

L12 ${}^{H/}(P;Q) \ = \ P;({}^{H/}Q)$ whenever $H \cap (\alpha l_0 P \cup \alpha l' P) \ = \ \{\}$

Proof of **L12** Let $B \ = \ \alpha l_0 P \cup \{\mathbf{n}\}$.

$$\begin{aligned} & P;({}^{H/}Q) && \{\text{Def. 6.4.2 and 2.2}\mathbf{L2}\} \\ = \ & (P;(l \in \alpha l' P)_\perp;({}^{H/}Q)) \lhd l \in B \rhd ({}^{H/}Q) && \{2.1\mathbf{L5} \text{ and } H \cap \alpha l' P = \{\}\} \\ = \ & (P;Q) \lhd l \in B \rhd ({}^{H/}Q) && \{\text{Def. 6.4.13 and 2.1}\mathbf{L2}\} \\ = \ & (I\!I \lhd l \in H \rhd Q) \lhd l \notin B \rhd (P;Q) && \{2.1\mathbf{L3} \text{ and } H \cap B = \{\}\} \\ = \ & I\!I \lhd l \in H \rhd (Q \lhd l \notin B \rhd (P;Q)) && \{\text{Def. 6.4.2 and 2.2}\mathbf{L2}\} \\ = \ & I\!I \lhd l \in H \rhd (P;Q) && \{\text{Def. 6.4.13}\} \\ = \ & {}^{H/}(P;Q) && \square \end{aligned}$$

Our theory of labels and jumps is powerful enough to treat *exception handling* as a special case. An exception is just a specially restricted kind of label e that can never appear in an entry alphabet, and can never be the destination of a backward jump. To raise the exception within P, an ordinary forward jump can be used. If Q is the handler designed to catch exception e within P, their combined effect can be defined

$$P;((l := \mathbf{n}; Q) \lhd l = e \rhd I\!I)$$

This is a block with $\alpha l_0\, P \cup \{e\}$ as its entry label set, and $(\alpha l'\, P \setminus \{e\}) \cup \alpha l'\, Q$ as its exit label set. If Q raises the same or a different exception, it will automatically be directed forward to a more global handler.

It is now possible to hide *all* the labels and jumps within a block P, and thereby obtain a module of program that can be treated as though it were expressed in a language without any jumps and labels at all. This is in fact recommended practice: jumps should be confined in range to a self-contained unit of program, for example the body of a subroutine. We therefore define an *encapsulation* operator which hides all labels, and even conceals the control variable l.

Definition 6.4.16 (Encapsulation)

If $P : S \Rightarrow F$ then

$$\langle P \rangle \;=_{df}\; \mathbf{var}\ l; (l := \mathbf{n});\ {}^{S/}(P^{\setminus F}); \mathbf{end}\ l \qquad \square$$

Theorems 6.4.7 and 6.4.9 give the constraints under which structured notations can be mixed with jumps and labels. In the case of recursion, the entry and exit alphabets of the recursive call must exactly match those of the whole body, and if there are any labels local to the body, the alphabet of the recursive call must be extended to accept and ignore any of these labels (Exercise 6.4.17). Extension may also be used to equalise the alphabets of the two components of a conditional. But the effect may be rather different from what is expected. Our theory requires that if a conditional is entered by a jump, the condition still has to be tested to determine whether to go to the label in the first operand or the label in the second operand. Implementors of structured programming languages have not been prepared to take this trouble. They have therefore forbidden jumps into a conditional, effectively requiring the input alphabet to be empty.

Exercise 6.4.17

The converse operation to hiding is alphabet extension. Under reasonable conditions, define this operation and prove that it has the required properties. $\square$

Chapter 7

Concurrency

The reduced cost of microprocessor chips has made it economic to obtain yet higher computational performance by harnessing many processors to execute different parts of the same program concurrently. A program component intended for concurrent execution with other such components is called a *process*, and its composition with other processes is known as *parallel* composition, in analogy with the familiar *sequential* composition, which reuses a single processor to execute both components. There are two main classes of concurrent programming paradigm, based on different ways of connecting the hardware processing elements. In a *distributed* architecture, each processor has its private local memory, and communicates with other processors, usually by means of a common bus (often a ring) or by dedicated wires which connect them in pairs. In the *shared*-memory architecture, the processors each have access to the same global memory, which interleaves service requests from all of them in a fair and efficient manner. It is the second kind of paradigm that will be treated in this chapter.

The shared-memory paradigm permits considerable variation in the implementing architecture. For example, it is possible (and often desirable) for a single processing element to share its attention among several processes of a single program using interrupts to switch between them at unpredictable points. This is known as multiprogramming or time-slicing, and is common on conventional single-processor machines. A good theory must be sufficiently abstract that it permits an implementation of concurrency in this way too.

Other possible architectural variations include the provision of multiple memory banks, capable of concurrent service of many access requests. Some (or even all) of these banks may be primarily devoted to service of requests from a single processor; in particular, each processor has exclusive access to its own local bank of special hardware registers intimately connected to its arithmetic unit. It often also has its own local memory cache, providing rapid access to more or less up-to-date copies of information held in the slower global memory.

Most of the complexity of such a memory hierarchy is concealed from the programmer by the hardware, which provides a simulation of a global virtual memory, and a single homogeneous addressing range. Valiant and even expensive measures are taken in hardware design to achieve a defined level of predictability. Nevertheless, non-determinism is an almost inevitable consequence of executing programs on such an architecture. It arises because there is no way of predicting or controlling the order in which the memory will service requests from the many processing elements. Further non-determinism may arise from an unknown delay between changing the value of the local cached copy of a global variable and the transmission of the new value to the global memory, from which it can be read by the other processors. Finally, an optimising compiler or a hardware instruction pipeline may (within certain, maybe not obvious, limits) change the order of execution of assignments within a single process, in a manner which varies from one computer supplier to another, or even from one version of the same product to the next.

The goal of a theory of concurrency is to provide an effective method of reasoning to avoid or to control all such complexity and non-determinism, from whatever source it arises. In this chapter we take the simplest measures to achieve this goal. We maintain a level of abstraction that requires no consideration of the values of variables at any time except at the start and termination of the process. As a result, all finite programs using parallelism can be translated into programs that are purely sequential, and infinite programs can be reduced to the same sequential normal form. Systems which allow intermediate observations after initiation but before termination will be treated in the next chapter.

The simplest cases of parallelism are those that forbid the possibility of sharing store. Each process is allocated a disjoint region, ensuring that it never reads or writes in any region of store except its own. These restrictions are usually enforced by special hardware in a multiprogrammed computer. In our theory, the regions can be defined by partitioning the alphabet between the processes, and the observance of the restrictions can be enforced by a syntactic check. This case is described in Section 7.1.

Section 7.2 relaxes the disjointness condition to allow processes to share one or more variables. This case can be reduced to the disjoint case as follows. Each process is first executed on its *private* version of the shared variables independently. When all have terminated, their updates on the shared variables are *merged* and written back to the *global* version of the shared variables. The parallel by merge can be used to model a variety of shared-variable concurrency paradigms, such as *interleaving* and *synchronisation*; and it also obeys algebraic laws similar to those for disjoint parallelism. We also investigate the conditions on the merge relation which ensure that familiar healthiness conditions can be preserved by parallel composition.

The method described above for implementing the updates on a shared variable has been introduced primarily for reasoning about the overall effect of concurrent execution of two or more processes. In practice, only one copy of the shared variable is kept, and it is updated by interleaving the atomic actions invoked by the processes which share it. The consistency of these two implementation methods must be established by proof of the relevant algebraic laws. Systematic application of these laws can even transform a parallel program into an equivalent sequential one. This often results in massive expansion to make all the non-determinism explicit. Section 7.3 establishes a range of expansion laws applicable to various kinds of merge operation.

Section 7.4 discusses the case where a large global array is shared by parallel processes. The processes are allocated disjoint regions of indices in the array, and each may change array elements in its own region and no other. The rest of the array, which is not allocated for updating by any process, may be freely read by all of them. When these rules are observed, all updates and accesses on the array will commute with each other, and this completely avoids non-determinism and its associated risks.

The disjointness conditions on shared variables deliberately prevent their use for communication between processes. The combined effect of all the updates becomes accessible only after the processes have terminated. To make safe access to intermediate results, it is essential that the processes have the capability to synchronise with each other. Synchronisation is treated in Section 7.5 in its simplest form as a global action in which all processes must engage simultaneously [123, 183].

The final section introduces the logic programming paradigm in a concurrent form. The disjunction operator is implementable by concurrent execution and interleaving as an alternative to the backtracking which characterises ordinary sequential logic programming.

7.1 Disjoint processes

The basic idea of concurrency has been described in Chapter 1, where it was explained by simple conjunction of predicates describing the concurrently operating components. This explanation works just as well for specifications as for implementations. Suppose a customer's needs are described by two separate predicates S and T, each describing a separate physical object, say a shirt and a shoe. The combination of the needs of the customer is therefore described by the conjunction $S \wedge T$. To avoid confusion, it is necessary that each variable in S (describing a property of the shirt) should be distinguishable from each variable in T (describing a property of the shoe).

Definition 7.1.1 (Disjointness)

Two predicates S and T are disjoint if their alphabets have no variables in common

$$\alpha S \cap \alpha T \;=\; \{\} \qquad \square$$

When a specification $(S \wedge T)$ is expressed as a conjunction of disjoint predicates, it is usually easiest to satisfy the specification by designing and delivering two separate products (call them P and Q), each of which satisfies just one part of the specification

$$\alpha P \;=\; \alpha S \;\text{ and }\; [P \Rightarrow S]$$
$$\alpha Q \;=\; \alpha T \;\text{ and }\; [Q \Rightarrow T]$$

The two products will usually be entirely disconnected and independent, and could be delivered at different times to different places; after delivery, they may be used separately or together, one after another, or in overlapping periods of time. That is what justifies the claim made in Chapter 1, that in the case of disjoint predicates the concurrent behaviour of many processes is accurately described by the conjunction of the predicates describing their individual behaviours.

In describing two objects of different kinds, it is reasonable to assume (because it is easy to ensure) that the alphabets are disjoint. But the customer may want two disjoint objects of the *same* kind, say two shirts. This requirement cannot be described by the conjunction of two copies of the same predicate $(S \wedge S)$: firstly, this is identical to the description of just a single object S; and secondly, it violates the rule that the alphabets of concurrent processes must be disjoint. Both of these problems are solved by assigning a different name or serial number (say 0 or 1) to each of the two objects. Then each observation x of the object with name 0 is denoted by prefixing the serial number to the observation name, to give a new double-barrelled or *qualified* observation name $0.x$, and $1.x$ denotes a distinct but similar kind of observation of the other object. In general, if m is a different serial number from n, then we assume $m.x$ is a name distinct from $n.x$; it denotes a similar kind of observation made of a different instance of the same kind of product. Product naming or numbering gives a homogeneous way of forcing the alphabets of predicates to be disjoint. It is important in practical applications, but its role in the development of theory is mainly to demonstrate that the constraint of disjointness is one that can easily be met whenever needed.

Definition 7.1.2 (Labelling)

Let p be a value used as a process name. Then

$$p.P(v) \;=_{df}\; P(p.v)$$

where $P(p.v)$ is the result of replacing every occurrence of an observation variable

x in P by an occurrence of the qualified name $p.x$. Accordingly

$$\alpha(p.P) \;=_{df}\; \{p.x \mid x \in \alpha P\}$$

It is assumed that $p.x$ is a different variable from $q.x$ whenever $p \neq q$. □

This definition permits a conjunction of any number of distinct and disjoint instances of S, whether finite or infinite, for example

$$(1.S) \;\wedge\; (2.S)$$

$$\bigwedge \{p.S \mid p \in \mathbf{PID}\}, \quad \text{where } \mathbf{PID} \text{ is a set of process names}$$

As explained above, to model concurrency by conjunction permits each process to start and finish completely independently of the other. But in parallel programming, we often want to start the processes at the same time, and allow them to operate on disjoint areas of a store that has been initialised as a whole on completion of some previous part of the program. Equally often, we want the two processes to terminate together, so that the entire store becomes available again for further processing by the following part of the program. This kind of synchronised initiation and termination of processes can be treated only in a theory which already models these phenomena, for example by the variables ok and ok'. We will therefore confine attention to predicates that are designs (Definition 3.1.1). These have distinguishable input and output alphabets, referring to the initial state before execution and the final state afterwards. If P and Q are disjoint relations, the undashed variables of their conjunction $P \wedge Q$ describe a simultaneous observation of the initial state of P and of the initial state of Q, and similarly, the final state of $P \wedge Q$ is given by simultaneous observation of the values of the dashed variables contributed by both processes. This means that execution of a concurrent composition should start with the start of *both* the processes, and similarly, its execution terminates with the termination of *both* of them. This kind of structured concurrency was introduced by Dijkstra with the notation **cobegin** ... **coend** [49]. It is different from the concurrent use of shirts and shoes which may be purchased, worn and discarded without any synchronisation.

There is one unfortunate consequence of the requirement of simultaneous termination: if one of the processes fails to terminate, then so does its composition with any other process whatsoever. As a result, it is not possible to observe the final values, even of variables updated by a process that by itself would have terminated. So in practice, abortion of a component causes abortion of the whole program. But this is not what is predicted by a theory which defines parallel composition as conjunction, because obviously

$$\mathbf{true} \wedge Q \;=\; Q \qquad \text{rather than} \qquad \mathbf{true} \wedge Q \;=\; \mathbf{true}$$

The same problem arose in the original treatment of sequential composition, which failed to satisfy the necessary zero laws, and we solve it for concurrency in a similar way. This is another reason for restricting attention to *designs*, in which the precondition for termination is made explicit. Since parallel execution involves starting *both* the processes, it is necessary to ensure that *both* their preconditions are valid to start with. Thus the precondition for successful execution of the parallel composition is the *conjunction* of their separate preconditions rather than their disjunction. The corresponding new definition of concurrency will be denoted by parallel bars $\|$.

Definition 7.1.3 (Parallel composition)

Let P and Q have disjoint alphabets, and let $P = P_0 \vdash P_1$ and $Q = Q_0 \vdash Q_1$.

$$\begin{aligned} P\|Q &=_{df} (P_0 \wedge Q_0) \vdash (P_1 \wedge Q_1) \\ \alpha(P\|Q) &=_{df} \alpha P \cup \alpha Q \end{aligned} \qquad \square$$

Example 7.1.4 (Parallel assignment)

Let x and y be distinct variables. The parallel assignment

$$(x := f(x))\|(y := g(y))$$

has the same effect as the multiple assignment

$$\begin{aligned} & (x := f(x)) \,\|\, (y := g(y)) && \{\text{def of assignment}\} \\ = \ & (\mathbf{true} \vdash x' = f(x))\|(\mathbf{true} \vdash (y' = g(y))) && \{\text{Def. 7.1.3}\} \\ = \ & (\mathbf{true} \vdash ((x' = f(x)) \wedge (y' = g(y)))) && \{\text{def of assignment}\} \\ = \ & x, y := f(x), g(y) && \square \end{aligned}$$

In a strict interpretation of output disjointness, Definition 7.1.3 is invalid, because the variables *ok* and *ok'* are in the alphabet of both the component processes. The relaxation of the restriction is justified as follows. The implementation is required to start execution of the parallel composition by starting execution of both the components. Even if one or both components start with an initial delay, we do not need or want to contemplate or observe a time when one of the two processes has started but not the other. That is why only one variable *ok* is needed to record the synchronised start of both of them, which is the same as the start of the parallel composition. Similar reasoning based on synchronised termination applies to the output variable *ok'*. The reasoning will later be generalised to other synchronised events like input and output between communicating processes.

Definition 7.1.5 (Disjointness of designs)

Two designs P and Q are disjoint if

$$\alpha P \cap \alpha Q \;=\; \{ok,\, ok'\} \qquad \square$$

In Chapter 3, designs were classified according to their degree of healthiness, and all the operators of the language were shown to conserve the healthiness properties of their operands. Fortunately, the new definition of parallelism is equally conservative; the disjointness condition is what makes it so.

Theorem 7.1.6

If P and Q both satisfy **H3** or both satisfy **H4**, then $P \| Q$ has the same property.

Proof Direct from Definition 7.1.3. □

Although the new definition of parallelism is more complicated than conjunction, it obeys nearly all the same algebraic laws, except idempotence, which is excluded by the disjointness condition on the alphabets. In stating the laws, we will implicitly assume that all the obviously intended disjointness constraints are satisfied.

L1 $P \| Q \;=\; Q \| P$ $\qquad$ ($\|$ comm)

L2 $P \| (Q \| R) \;=\; (P \| Q) \| R$ $\qquad$ ($\|$ assoc)

L3 $I\!I_X \| I\!I_Y \;=\; I\!I_{X \cup Y}$ $\qquad$ ($\|$-unit)

L4 $\mathbf{true} \| P \;=\; \mathbf{true}$ $\qquad$ ($\|$-zero)

It is well known that simple forms of parallel composition can be implemented by (or even transformed into) sequential composition by simply interleaving execution of atomic actions from the participating processes. That is the message of the following distribution laws.

L5 $(P \lhd b \rhd Q) \| R \;=\; (P \| R) \lhd b \rhd (Q \| R)$

L6 $(P \sqcap Q) \| R \;=\; (P \| R) \sqcap (Q \| R)$

L7 $(\bigsqcup S) \| R \;=\; \bigsqcup_n (S_n \| R)$, for any descending chain $S = \{S_n \mid n \in \mathcal{N}\}$

L8 $(x := e; P) \| Q \;=\; (x := e); (P \| Q)$

Proof of L8

$$
\begin{aligned}
& (x := e); (P \| Q) && \{\text{Def. 7.1.3}\} \\
= \;& (x := e); ((P_0 \wedge Q_0) \vdash (P_1 \wedge Q_1)) && \{x \notin \alpha Q\} \\
= \;& (P_0[e/x] \wedge Q_0) \vdash (P_1[e/x] \wedge Q_1) && \{\text{Def. 7.1.3}\} \\
= \;& (P_0[e/x] \vdash P_1[e/x]) \| (Q_0 \vdash Q_1) && \{\text{Theorem 3.1.4}\} \\
= \;& (x := e; P) \| Q && \Box
\end{aligned}
$$

The final proof that parallelism introduces nothing new into the language is achieved by showing that parallel programs have the same normal form as shown for sequential programs in Chapter 5.

Theorem 7.1.7 (Normal form of disjoint parallel programs)

Let $S = \{S_n \mid n \in \mathcal{N}\}$ and $T = \{T_n \mid n \in \mathcal{N}\}$ be descending chains of finite normal forms. Then

$$(\bigsqcup S) \| (\bigsqcup T) \;=\; \bigsqcup_n (S_n \| T_n)$$

and each $(S_i \| T_i)$ can be reduced to a finite normal form.

Proof

$$\begin{array}{lll} & \bigsqcup_n (S_n \| T_n) & \{(S_i \| T_j) \sqsubseteq (S_{i+j} \| T_{i+j})\} \\ = & \bigsqcup_{i,j} (S_i \| T_j) & \{\mathbf{L7}\} \\ = & (\bigsqcup S) \| (\bigsqcup T) & \end{array}$$

Let $P = ((\bigsqcap_i x := e_i) \lhd b \rhd \mathbf{true})$ and $Q = ((\bigsqcap_j y := f_j) \lhd c \rhd \mathbf{true})$.
We are going to show how to convert $P\|Q$ into a finite normal form.

$$\begin{array}{lll} & P \| Q & \{\mathbf{L4} \text{ and } \mathbf{L5}\} \\ = & ((\bigsqcap_i x := e_i) \| (\bigsqcap_j y := f_j)) \lhd b \wedge c \rhd \mathbf{true} & \{\mathbf{L6}\} \\ = & (\bigsqcap_{i,j} (x := e_i \| y := f_j)) \lhd b \wedge c \rhd \mathbf{true} & \{\mathbf{L3} \text{ and } \mathbf{L8}\} \\ = & (\bigsqcap_{i,j} x := e_i; y := f_j) \lhd b \wedge c \rhd \mathbf{true} & \{5.1\mathbf{L3}\} \\ = & (\bigsqcap_{i,j} x, y := e_i, f_j) \lhd b \wedge c \rhd \mathbf{true} & \square \end{array}$$

The disjointness condition is designed to prevent any process from reading any variable which is subject to update by any concurrent process. The disjointness condition can therefore be relaxed to allow the input alphabets to share variables that are never updated at all. In fact, it is even possible to share initial values of variables that are updated by just one of the two processes and excluded from the output alphabet of the other. But this places upon an implementation the obligation to make a separate copy of the initial value for the benefit of the process that does not change it. Any update by the other process is therefore invisible: disjointness is effectively preserved, and so is determinacy. The main problem is the expense of making a fresh copy of the initial values.

Exercises 7.1.8

Prove that for disjoint processes

(1) If both P and Q satisfy **H3** and **H4** then $P\|Q \;=\; (P;Q) \;=\; (Q;P)$.

(2) If both P and Q satisfy **H4** then $(P;R)\|(Q;S) \;=\; (P\|Q);(R\|S)$.

(3) $(P; x := e)\|(Q; y := f) \;=\; (P\|Q); (x := e \| y := f)$ $\square$

7.2 Parallel by merge

The reason why disjoint parallelism is so simple to implement, and so obviously obeys all the stated laws, is that all the actions of each process commute with all the actions of any process disjoint from it. A parallel implementation can execute disjoint processes by arbitrary interleaving of their actions, or even by sequential execution of the entire processes in either order (Exercise 7.1.10(1)). In spite of this range of implementations, commutativity ensures that there is no increase in non-determinism. Furthermore, disjointness is subject to a syntactic check. In this section we first extend the treatment of parallelism to allow the processes to update a shared variable in various ways, some of them commuting and some not.

Initially, we will deal with a single shared variable at a time. Our plan is to reduce the sharing case of parallelism to the disjoint case. This will ensure that the more complex kind of parallelism obeys the same algebraic laws, and preserves the same healthiness properties. Disjointness is achieved by replacing the shared variables m' in each process by new labelled variables $0.m'$ and $1.m'$. Of course, we assume throughout that these labelled variables are not already in the alphabets of the processes involved. Otherwise we would have used different labels. Under this proviso, the undashed variables can be left unlabelled. Once the shared variables are differentiated by labelling, the processes are disjoint, and they may each produce different results in the variables $0.m'$ and $1.m'$. The final effect of parallel execution is then defined by a *merging* operation, which shows how the real final value of m is computed from these two results, and from the initial value of m. Different kinds of parallelism will use different merging operations, as illustrated by a series of simple canonical examples.

Example 7.2.1 (Shared resource)

Consider an integer variable r (short for *resource*) used to count the total utilisation of some resource, say machine time. Each process updates the value of r by assignments

$$r := r + e \qquad \text{or} \qquad r := r + f$$

where e and f are expressions containing only local variables of the updating process. In the concurrent execution of the processes, the updates contributed by each of them are arbitrarily interleaved. Let us suppose that neither process needs to access any of the intermediate values of r. Then the same effect can be achieved by a disjointly parallel execution, in which each process updates its own private copy $0.r$ or $1.r$ of the variable r by assignments like

$$0.r := 0.r + e \qquad \text{or} \qquad 1.r := 1.r + f$$

where $0.r$ and $1.r$ are initialised to r. The actual final value of r is the same as if it were computed from $0.r$ and $1.r$ afterwards by an assignment that merges their values

$$r := 0.r + 1.r - r$$

Here subtraction of the initial value r is needed to counteract the initial value assigned to both $0.r$ and $1.r$. □

Example 7.2.2 (Shared log)

In this example, we relax the constraint that all operations on shared variables must commute, and accept that the interleaving of actions by parallel processes can lead to a vast explosion in non-determinism. A particularly common example of sharing is by interleaving of output messages on a display or file, used as a system log. We will represent the log by a specially named variable *out*, which holds as its value the sequence of messages output so far. Each output operation appends to the sequence a new message, with value defined by an expression e

$$out := out^\frown < e >$$

The sharing of an output stream by interleaving is modelled in the same way as in Example 7.2.1. Firstly, separate streams $0.out$ and $1.out$ are declared for use by each process, and they have the global stream as their initial values. Each process then appends messages to its own output stream. When both processes have terminated, the final value of *out* will be found to contain its initial value followed by an interleaving of the sequences of messages output by the separate processes. The final action of parallel composition computes this result from the final values of $0.out$ and $1.out$, contributed by the two processes. The merging operation is therefore

$$\mathbf{true} \vdash (out' - out) \in (0.out - out)|||(1.out - out)$$

where $s - t$ is the result of moving an initial copy of t from s, and $s|||t$ is the set of all interleavings of s and t. If either s or t is empty, this is easy to define. Otherwise, one of them must contribute the first element of the result, and the rest of the result is obtained recursively

$$\begin{aligned} <>|||t \;=\; t|||<> &=_{df} t \\ (< x >^\frown s)|||(< y >^\frown t) &=_{df} \{< z >^\frown u \mid z = x \wedge u \in (s|||(< y >^\frown t)) \vee \\ &\qquad z = y \wedge u \in ((< x >^\frown s)|||t)\} \end{aligned}$$ □

Example 7.2.3 (Shared clock)

In discrete event simulation on a computer, multiple processes of the program are used to model the concurrent activities of people and objects in the real world, and then synchronisation in the program represents an action (like shaking hands) in which all the processes involved are engaged simultaneously. For an example of global synchronisation, consider the passage of simulated time, which always has the same (or negligibly different) value accessible to all the processes of the system. We represent this by a shared variable called *clock*, recording the value of the current simulated time, in some convenient unit. The responsibility of each process is to carry out all the actions that are supposed to take place at this current moment of time, and then to wait until the clock moves on to the next moment of time. The tick of the clock is represented within each process by the synchronised action

$$clock := clock + 1$$

In order to use disjoint parallelism, we provide each process with its own private clock $0.clock$ and $1.clock$ (initially synchronised to the public clock), which can be incremented apparently in an independent fashion. When both processes are finished, the public clock is set to the larger of the two private clocks. This represents the fact that the process that terminates earlier no longer has the obligation to update its private clock.

$$clock := max(0.clock,\ 1.clock) \qquad \square$$

Example 7.2.4 (Synchronised input)

In certain kinds of real-time application, input data are presented to the computer at regular intervals, say 30 times per second. To a first approximation, we assume that there is enough computing power to deal with input at this rate; indeed, the main purpose of parallelism is to ensure exactly this. The successive values that are input are represented by a sequence-valued input variable in, where in_c is the value that is input on the occasion that the clock has value c. On each occasion, the input is assigned to a fixed shared-memory location m; this kind of memory-mapped input is often implemented in hardware. The effect is modelled abstractly in each process by a simultaneous assignment on (labelled versions of) the variables m and c

$$m,\ c := in_c,\ c + 1$$

As in the case of the clock, these assignments are executed simultaneously in all processes, and they all assign the same value to the shared variables m and c. There is no need to merge the values of m and c at the end, provided that all processes engage in all inputs, and so terminate at the same time. This is an obligation placed upon the programmer by an assertion at the end of parallel execution

$$(0.c = 1.c)_\perp\ ;\ c := 0.c \qquad \square$$

Example 7.2.5 (Synchronised output)

Synchronised output is treated like synchronised input, with the aid of a counter c and an output sequence *out*. On each tick of the clock, the value assigned to out_c is defined by a local expression e of the outputting process

$$out_c,\ c := e,\ c+1$$

The values of the expressions assigned to out_c by different processes will be different, and the actual output to the environment of both processes will be a combination of the information contributed by each process. The notation $x|y$, denoting the desired combination of the value of x and y, is taken from the Synchronous Calculus of Concurrent Systems (SCCS) [125]; it is assumed to be associative and commutative. The operator is applied to every element of the output sequence. The final values of *out* and c are then defined by the merge

$$(0.c = 1.c)_\perp \ ;$$
$$\mathbf{true} \vdash (\forall i : i < 0.c \bullet out_i' = out_i \lhd i < c \rhd (0.out_i | 1.out_i)) \ \wedge \ (c' = 0.c)$$

This states that messages output before the processes start will remain unchanged, and those output after the start will be the combination of messages output at the same time by the two processes. □

In all these examples, the intended interpretation of the observation of the shared variable is what determines the choice of the appropriate merging operation. It also determines the range of possible actions that are permitted to be performed upon the shared variable. For example, the variable *clock* does not stand for a variable in the store of the computer; it stands for the global time recorded (say) by a caesium clock and transmitted by a radio signal. The intended implementation of the assignment $clock := clock + 1$ is to wait until the next tick of this clock. Such an implementation is certainly permitted, because on completion of the action, the final reading of the clock is one greater than the initial reading. But no such implementation would be possible for any assignment that *decreases* the value of *clock*. For reasons of realism, it is necessary to keep close control over the atomic actions which are allowed on each of the shared variables. We will therefore introduce the letter $\mathcal{A}$ to stand for the set of permitted actions.

A general definition of parallel composition $(P \| Q)$ requires first a definition of the transformation that is made to each of the two processes; each assignment $m := f(m)$ to the shared variable m must be replaced by the corresponding assignment to one of the two private variables

$$0.m := f(0.m) \ \text{ in } P \qquad \text{or} \qquad 1.m := f(1.m) \ \text{ in } Q$$

These modified processes (say P_0 and Q_1) must be preceded by declaration and initialisation of the private variables. The overall effect of the parallel execution is then described

$$\mathbf{var}\ 0.m,\ 1.m := m,\ m\,;(P_0 \| Q_1)\,;\ M$$

where M is the appropriate operation for merging the values of $0.m$ and $1.m$.

The description given above ensures the processes P and Q are presented textually as programs in which textual changes can be made to the component assignments. But in the top-down design of programs, we need to apply parallel composition at an earlier stage in the design progression, that is to the predicates $P(m, m')$ and $Q(m, m')$ which specify the individual processes. Fortunately, all that is needed is to substitute m' by $0.m'$ or $1.m'$ in each predicate, giving $P(m, 0.m')$ and $Q(m, 1.m')$. The same substitution must be made in the alphabets of the two processes. It is convenient to define the required effect by a pair of simulations $U0$ and $U1$.

Definition 7.2.6 (Separating simulations)

$$\begin{aligned} U0(m) &=_{df} \ \mathbf{var}\ 0.m := m\,;\ \mathbf{end}\ m \\ \alpha U0(m) &=_{df} \ \{m,\ 0.m'\} \end{aligned}$$

$U1(m)$ and $U2(m)$ may be given a similar definition. □

We will conventionally use the letter M to stand for the predicate that merges the final values $0.m$ and $1.m$ produced by the two processes. The examples show that its input alphabet also needs to include the initial value of the shared variable m. Its output alphabet is just m'; in this way M contains an implicit end to the declarations of $0.m$ and $1.m$ which were introduced by $U0$ and $U1$.

Definition 7.2.7 (Parallel merge)

Let m be the shared variables of programs P and Q

$$\{m\} \ = \ out\alpha P \cap out\alpha Q$$

Let M be a predicate with the alphabet $\alpha P \cup \alpha Q \cup \{0.m,\ 1.m\}$.

Let $A \ = \ out\alpha P \setminus \{m\}$ and $B \ = \ out\alpha \setminus \{m\}$.

$$P \|_M Q \ =_{df} \ ((P; U0(m)_{+A}) \| (Q; U1(m)_{+B}))_{+m}\,;\ M$$ □

Exercise 7.2.8

Show that for healthy predicates P and Q, Definition 7.1.3 is just a special case of Definition 7.2.7, where the shared variable is just *ok*. □

In order to satisfy 7.1**L1** to **L8**, the merge predicate M needs to be *valid* in the sense defined below.

Definition 7.2.9 (Valid merge)

A merge predicate $M(ok,\ m,\ 0.m,\ 1.m,\ m',\ ok')$ is *valid* if it is a design satisfying the following properties

(1) M is *symmetric* in its input $0.m$ and $1.m$

$$(0.m,\ 1.m := 1.m,\ 0.m); M \ = \ M$$

(2) M is *associative*

$$(0.m,\ 1.m,\ 2.m \ := \ 1.m,\ 2.m,\ 0.m); M3 \ = \ M3$$

where $M3$ is a three-way merge relation generated by M

$$M3 \ =_{df} \ \exists x, t \bullet M(ok,\ m,\ 0.m,\ 1.m,\ x,\ t) \wedge M(t,\ m,\ x,\ 2.m,\ m',\ ok')$$

(3) $(\mathbf{var}\ 0.m,\ 1.m \ := \ m,\ m\ ;\ M) \ = \ I\!I$ □

The purpose of the definition of validity is to prove the familiar laws of disjoint parallelism.

Theorem 7.2.10 (Parallel by valid merge)

If M is valid then $\|_M$ satisfies 7.1**L1** to **L8**, where **L8** needs to include a proviso

L8 $(x := e; P)\|_M Q \ = \ (x := e); (P\|_M Q),$ if $x := e$ does not mention m

Proof of **L2**

$$\begin{array}{lll}
 & (P\|_M Q)\|_M R & \{\text{Def. 7.2.7}\} \\
= & (((P\|_M Q); U0)\|(R; U1))_{+m}\ ;\ M & \{\text{def of ;}\} \\
= & ((((P; U0)\|(Q; U1))_{+m}; M; U0) & \\
 & \|(R; U2))_{+m}; M[2.m/1.m] & \{\text{Exercise 7.1.8(2)}\} \\
= & (((P; U0)\|(Q; U1))\|(R; U2))_{+m}; & \\
 & (M; U0)_{+\{m,\,2.m\}}; M[2.m/1.m] & \{\text{7.1}\mathbf{L2}\text{ and def of }M3\} \\
= & ((P; U0)\|(Q; U1)\|(R; U2))_{+m}; M3 & \{\text{Def. 7.2.9(2)}\} \\
= & ((P; U0)\|(Q; U1)\|(R; U2))_{+m}; & \\
 & (0.m, 1.m, 2.m := 1.m, 2.m, 0.m); M3 & \{\text{def of ;}\} \\
= & ((P; U2)\|(Q; U0)\|(R; U1))_{+m}; M3 & \{\text{7.1}\mathbf{L2}\} \\
= & ((Q; U0)\|(R; U1)\|(P; U2))_{+m}; M3 & \{\text{similar argument}\} \\
= & (Q\|_M R)\|_M P & \{\mathbf{L1}\} \\
= & P\|_M(Q\|_M R) & \square
\end{array}$$

Examples 7.2.11 (Valid merge)

The merge operations of Examples 7.2.1 to 7.2.5 are valid. □

Examples 7.2.1 to 7.2.3 introduced three separate shared variables, and defined separate merging operators for each of them. Examples 7.2.4 and 7.2.5 each introduced a group of variables, which were updated and merged by the appropriate multiple assignments. The general definition of parallelism is formulated to apply equally well to single variables as to groups of variables. The same theory therefore applies to a language which shares all the variables treated in the examples, and maybe more. Of course, a merge operation for a long list of variables is in general more complicated than one for shorter lists. Fortunately, the complexity can often be avoided. If separate merge operations are already defined for each variable (or small group) individually, the appropriate merge operation for the group containing all the variables is just the (necessarily disjoint) parallel composition of all the separate merge operations. The validity of this result is guaranteed by the following theorem.

Theorem 7.2.12 (Composition of valid merge)

If M and N are valid merges of distinct variables m and n respectively, then $M \| N$ is also valid. □

Although this is a simple way of decomposing the complexity of sharing many variables, the effect may be somewhat unexpected. For example, here is a simple parallel program which shares both a clock and an output log

$$(out := out^\frown < 0 >; clock := clock + 1) \| (clock := clock + 1; out := out^\frown < 1 >)$$

One of them appears to output before the tick of the clock and one of them after. But in our theory, each process is simply a multiple assignment to disjoint variables, and there is no obligation to perform the assignments in any particular order. The overall effect of the parallel composition is calculated as

$$\begin{aligned} & (out,\, clock := out^\frown < 0 >,\, clock + 1) \| (out,\, clock := out^\frown < 1 >,\, clock + 1) \\ = \ & clock := clock + 1; (out := out^\frown < 0, 1 > \sqcap out := out^\frown < 1, 0 >) \end{aligned}$$

The second of the non-deterministic alternatives may be unexpected. If synchronisation were the guaranteed implementation method for the clock, the possibility of the message coming out in the wrong order $< 1, 0 >$ would be ruled out. This would also prohibit an implementation of the log by separate buffers associated with each process. If it is desired to enforce a stricter synchronisation, one method would be to record the clock time in each output message, and redefine interleaving in a way that preserves an ascending sequence of clock times. In general, synchronisation is an atomic action involving all shared variables of the system simultaneously, as described in Section 7.5.

In the following we show the healthiness conditions defined in Chapter 3 are preserved by parallel composition with sharing.

Theorem 7.2.13 (Healthiness conditions of parallel merge)

(1) $\|_M$ preserves **H1** if M satisfies **H1**.

(2) $\|_M$ preserves **H2** if M satisfies **H2**.

(3) $\|_M$ preserves **H3** if $(\mathit{II}_{\{0.m\}} \| \mathit{II}_{\{1.m\}}); M \ = \ M; \mathit{II}_{\{m\}}$.

(4) $\|_M$ preserves **H4** if M satisfies **H4**.

Proof of (3)

$$
\begin{array}{lll}
 & (P\|_M Q); \mathit{II}_{\{m\}} & \{\text{Def. 7.2.7}\} \\
= & ((P; U0)\|(Q; U1))_{+m}; M; \mathit{II}_{\{m\}} & \{\text{assumption of } M\} \\
= & ((P; U0)\|(Q; U1))_{+m}; & \\
 & (\mathit{II}_{\{0.m\}} \| \mathit{II}_{\{1.m\}}); M & \{\text{Exercise 7.1.8(3)}\} \\
= & ((P; U0; \mathit{II}_{\{0.m\}})\| & \\
 & (Q; U1; \mathit{II}_{\{1.m\}}))_{+m}; M & \{U0; \mathit{II}_{\{0.m\}} \ = \ \mathit{II}_{\{m\}}; U0\} \\
= & ((P; \mathit{II}_{\{m\}}; U0) & \\
 & \|(Q; \mathit{II}_{\{m\}}; U1))_{+m}; M & \{P \text{ and } Q \text{ satisfy } \mathbf{H3}\} \\
= & P\|_M Q & \Box
\end{array}
$$

7.3 The spreadsheet principle

The discussion of the previous sections has suggested two rather different approaches to the implementation of parallelism. The one that more closely follows the theoretical definition requires that separate copies are taken of the initial values of any shared variable, one for each process, and each process updates its own copy. This is the method used for *forking* in the UNIX operating system. Nevertheless, for larger shared variables like arrays, copying could be expensive, and it is clearly impossible for most of the objects in the real world, including the world itself and each of its inhabitants.

A more generally practical method of implementation is to maintain just a single copy of the shared variable, and allow it to be updated by synchronisation or interleaving of the actions of the sharing processes. Care will be needed to prevent interference between interleaved actions; they must be executed serially without risk of overlap. For example, when one action has been started, any attempt by another process to initiate another update of the same variable must be delayed until the first action is complete. This property of actions is called *atomicity*; it is implemented by mutual exclusion of critical regions, but details of the mechanism need not concern us here. Sometimes, atomic actions must be executed in strict synchronisation, but we will also postpone details of the treatment of synchronisation to the next section and the next chapter.

The main purpose of this section is to demonstrate the compatibility of the theoretical and the practical method of implementing parallelism. An implementation may even use a dynamically varying mixture of the methods to achieve the highest efficiency. To justify this we prove a collection of algebraic laws which permit an atomic action to be moved from the start of the parallel processes to the start of the whole program. These laws have the shape

$$(op; P)\|Q \sqsubseteq op;\ (P\|Q)$$

or

$$(op1; P)\|(op2; Q) \sqsubseteq (op1\|op2);\ (P\|Q)$$

where *op* is called an *asynchronous* atomic action and ($op1$, $op2$) is called a *synchronising pair.* (In an operational semantics of parallelism, the $\sqsubseteq$ is usually written as $\rightarrow$.) Each such law describes just one of the ways of implementing the parallelism. A collection of laws offers a non-deterministic choice of implementations, which can be made explicit in a single, more complicated derived law, for example

$$(op1; P)\|(op2; Q) \sqsubseteq op1; (P\|(op2; Q)) \sqcap op2; ((op1; P)\|Q)$$

But this law cannot be used to prove correctness of the left hand side of the inequation. For that, the right hand side needs to enumerate *all* permitted implementation methods, so that the inequality can validly be replaced by an equation. For obvious reasons, such equations are known as *expansion* laws. Their systematic application to finite programs can eliminate the parallel combinator in favour of a non-deterministic choice of sequential programs. In an algebraic semantics, the expansion laws would be taken as a definition of parallelism, and the theorems of this section would be an approach to a proof of the consistency of the algebra with our more abstract view of program specification and correctness. The corresponding completeness property is akin to the *full abstraction* of recent models of the typed lambda calculus [5].

To carry through this task, we will need to analyse more carefully the nature of the atomic operations, the way in which they update the shared variable, and the interaction between the update and the merge used to define parallel composition. We will introduce the theory in its simplest form by an analogy with a spreadsheet, laid out as a two-dimensional array containing at the bottom a row of column sums and on the right a column of row sums, and an overall total in the bottom right corner. The total may be computed identically in two different ways. One way is to get separate processes to compute the column sums, and when they have done so, the total is computed from these. This corresponds to the abstract definition of parallel composition by a final merge. The other method is to compute the row sums serially in the order written, and keep a running total on the right hand side. That is the method of calculation suggested by the expansion law. The equality of the results of these two methods of calculation may be called the *spreadsheet* principle.

Example 7.3.1 (Spreadsheet)

9	7	16
4	3	7
13	10	23

Generalising to a matrix of symbolic variables, consider

p	q	$p+q$
r	s	$r+s$
$p+r$	$q+s$	

The spreadsheet principle can now be expressed algebraically as an equation between the two ways of filling the missing square

$$(p+q)+(r+s) \quad = \quad (p+r)+(q+s)$$

This is an immediate consequence of associativity and commutativity of $+$. □

Modern spreadsheets are not confined to addition. They allow the rightmost column to be computed by an arbitrary operator specified by the user; for our purpose, we choose $\|$. The operator used to compute the column results on the bottom row may be chosen independently; let this be sequential composition.

p	q	$p\|q$
r	s	$r\|s$
$p;r$	$q;s$	

The spreadsheet property states the uniqueness of the value for the checksquare

$$(p\|q)\,;\,(r\|s) \quad = \quad (p;r)\,\|\,(q;s) \qquad (*)$$

This is just the exchange law of category theory, which we met in Exercise 2.1.12. In practical use, spreadsheets are certainly not confined to four entries: they may have any number of rows and columns. How can we be sure that these larger tables still have the spreadsheet property? It is sufficient to require that both the composition operators are associative. This means that any pair of adjacent columns in a spreadsheet (excluding the rightmost) may be replaced by their horizontal composition without affecting the correctness of the spreadsheet, and similarly with vertical composition of adjacent rows. Thus any larger matrix can be reduced to a matrix with just four elements.

In its general form, the spreadsheet principle is far too strong. It is violated by many definitions of $\|_M$ which we have given so far. We therefore need to investigate the various conditions under which restricted forms of the principle are valid for particular definitions of $\|_M$. Theories of parallel programming may then be classified according to the restrictions that are needed to ensure a complete reconciliation with their more practical methods of implementation.

The first and most important restriction is to confine attention to programs that can be expressed solely by means of the set $\mathcal{A}$ of allowed actions on the shared variables. Formally, it is the smallest set which contains $\mathcal{A}$ and is closed with respect to all the operators of the programming language. Because of the normal form theorem (Theorem 7.1.7), it is sufficient to characterise the closure by the single assignments to the shared variable that are possible in the normal form. The set of such assignments will be called $\mathcal{A}^+$.

Example 7.3.2 (Resource)

For the shared resource (Example 7.2.1), the atomic actions all have the form

$$\mathcal{A} \;=\; \{r := r + e \mid e \text{ does not mention } r\}$$

The set $\mathcal{A}^+$ is exactly equal to $\mathcal{A}$, as may be proved by the reductions

$$\begin{aligned}
(r := r + e); (r := r + f) &= r := r + (e + f)\\
(r := r + e) \lhd b \rhd (r := r + f) &= r := r + (e \lhd b \rhd f)\\
(r := r + e) \| (r := r + f) &= r := r + (e + f)
\end{aligned}$$

In the case of the conditional, we need to take advantage of the general restriction that a condition must not mention a shared variable. The shared resource is the simplest of examples, because it satisfies the spreadsheet principle in the greatest generality. All that is needed is to restrict the variables in the law $(*)$ to the members of $\mathcal{A}^+$

$$\begin{aligned}
&(r := r + e\,;\, r := r + f) \| (r := r + g\,;\, r := r + h)\\
=\;& r := r + e + f + g + h\\
=\;& (r := r + e \| r := r + g)\,;\, (r := r + f \| r := r + h)
\end{aligned}$$

This simple proof extends automatically to all programs, because it holds between normal forms. □

Example 7.3.3 (Clock)

For the clock (Example 7.2.3), the atomic actions are more restricted than for the resource, consisting just of

$$\mathit{clock} := \mathit{clock} + 1$$

The closure $\mathcal{A}^+$ is similar to that for the resource, except that the expression added to the clock must be strictly positive. As a result the unit $I\!I$ is not a member of $\mathcal{A}^+$, and a special law is necessary to guide implementation in this case

$$P \| I\!I \;=\; P, \qquad \text{for all } P \in \mathcal{A}^+$$

Furthermore, the spreadsheet principle is severely restricted to the case where the first two operands are equal

$$(P;Q)\|(P;S) \;=\; (P\|P);(Q\|S), \qquad \text{for } P \in \mathcal{A}^+$$

Implementation of equal actions in parallel takes advantage of idempotence

$$P\|P \;=\; P$$ □

Example 7.3.4 (Shared log)

Atomic updates on the shared log (see Example 7.2.2) have the form

$$out \;:=\; out^\frown < e >$$

and their closure has the form

$$out \;:=\; out^\frown s$$

where s is a sequence-valued expression not containing *out*. In this case the spreadsheet principle can simply be weakened to an inequation, indicating that parallel composition is less deterministic than sequential

$$(P;Q)\|(R;S) \;\sqsubseteq\; (P\|R)\,;\,(Q\|S)$$

To obtain an equation, the non-determinism must be made explicit, and the first two actions must be restricted to atomic actions

$$(p;Q)\|(r;S) \;=\; p;(Q\|(r;S)) \sqcap r;((p;Q)\|S)$$

provided that p and r are atomic actions. Since $I\!I$ is not in the closure, we need also the unit law

$$P\|I\!I \;=\; P$$ □

Exercise 7.3.5

Define $\mathcal{A}$ and $\mathcal{A}^+$ for Examples 7.2.4 and 7.2.5. Formulate and prove the relevant expansion laws. □

7.4 Shared array

Preservation of the principle of commutativity is an obligation that must sometimes be passed to the programmer. Consider for example a common requirement in an engineering and scientific calculation, which updates some large global array A. In each phase of the calculation, it may be possible to define certain disjoint regions within the array which need updating, and allocate each region to a separate process. Each process may change array elements in its own region and no other. The rest of the array, which is not allocated for updating to any process, may be freely read by all of them. If these rules are observed, all atomic actions on the array and all accesses to it from different processes will commute with each other.

Definition 7.4.1 (Disjoint regions)

Let W and R be subsets of the index set of the array A. The pair $r =_{df} (W, R)$ is called a *region* of A.
Regions $r0 = (W0, R0)$ and $r1 = (W1, R1)$ are *disjoint* if

$$W0 \cap (W1 \cup R1) \;=\; \{\} \quad \text{and} \quad W1 \cap (W0 \cup R0) \;=\; \{\} \qquad \square$$

In the examples of Section 7.2, the restriction to commuting operations is checkable by a scan of the processes involved. But in the case of a shared array, it is the programmer who has to discharge all the obligations of disjointness which are needed to validate our relatively simple theory of concurrency. There is no way that any general kind of static analysis could check the disjointness of the run-time values of the indices used to access the elements of the array.

In a language which permits disjoint sharing of arrays among parallel processes, we have to introduce a slight complexity into the declaration of an array, and into the definition of access and assignment to a subscripted variable. The declaration of an array with index range I and values of type T may be written

$$\textbf{array}\, A : I \to T$$

This is interpreted as introducing two additional variables $A.W$ and $A.R$, which range over subsets of I; they are initialised to the whole set

$$\textbf{var}\ A.W,\ A.R := I,\ I$$

In a parallel process, the values of the private copies of these variables will be reduced to the actual region allocated and accessible to the process. Any attempt to access A outside $A.R$ will fail, as ensured by the definition

$$\mathcal{D}(A[i]) \;=_{df}\; (i \in A.R)$$

Similar failure occurs on an attempt to assign to a subscripted variable with an index outside $A.W$

$$(A[i] := e) \;=_{df}\; (i \in A.W)_\perp \,;\, A := (A \oplus \{i \mapsto e\})$$

The parallel composition operator ${}_r\|_s$ is now decorated with two subscripts, indicating the regions in which the two processes operate. The merge operation uses the two write regions to indicate which updates have to be written back into the final value of the array.

$$\begin{aligned} M \;=_{df}\; & (A := A \oplus (r_0 \lhd 0.A) \oplus (s_0 \lhd 1.A))\,; \\ & \mathbf{end}\, 0.A,\ 1.A \end{aligned}$$

where r_0 and s_0 are the W components of the pairs r and s, and $X \lhd A$ represents the subarray of A with its domain restricted to indices in X, and $\oplus$ is the overriding operator on functions.

The full definition of parallel composition has to adjust the value of $A.R$ and $A.W$ in the obvious way before executing each of the processes. But their global values remain unchanged.

Definition 7.4.2 (Shared array with disjoint regions)

Let r and s be disjoint regions and let M be as defined above.

$$\begin{aligned} P\,{}_r\|_s Q \;=_{df}\; & (A.W,\ A.R := r_0 \cap A.W,\ r_1 \cap A.R\,;\ P) \\ & \|_M\, (A.W,\ A.R := s_0 \cap A.W,\ s_1 \cap A.R\,;\ Q) \end{aligned}$$ □

Theorem 7.4.3

The parallel composition of shared array with disjoint regions satisfies 7.2**L2** to **L8**, and the adapted commutative law

L1a $P\,{}_r\|_s Q \;=\; Q\,{}_s\|_r P$

It also obeys the following expansion law for commuting updates

L9 $(op; P)\,{}_r\|_s Q \;=\; \hat{op}\,;\ (P\,{}_r\|_s Q)$

where

$$\hat{op} \;=_{df}\; (\exists AW',\ AR' \bullet op[A.W \cap r_0,\ A.R \cap r_1 / A.W,\ A.R])_{+\{A.W,\,A.R\}}$$ □

7.5 Synchronisation

In this section, we transfer attention from interleaving to synchronisation, which we introduce in its purest form as a single action

sync

By definition, this can take place only with simultaneous participation by all active processes. If there are no variables shared between the synchronising processes, their synchronisation is vacuous. The only purpose of synchronisation is to force a merge of the values of all the shared variables, and so to make sure that the same result is accessible to all the processes of the system. This gets round the deficiency of all the interleaving models considered so far: that no process can ever reliably access any result produced by any other concurrent process. Synchronisation is surely a necessary condition of reliable communication. Otherwise there is the grave risk of accessing a necessary result before it has actually been computed.

The intended effect of synchronisation is most clearly explained by an algebraic law. Let M be the merge operation for *all* the shared variables m of the system. Let P describe the behaviour of one process up to its first **sync** action, and let Q be the initial non-synchronising behaviour of the other process. Then the **sync** action invokes the merge operation M to consolidate the results of P and Q in their global store, so that results computed separately in m by each of them are available subsequently to both of them. The synchronisation action is retained to deal with the possibility that there are three or more processes involved. This informal account is summarised in the following expansion law

L9 $(P; \mathbf{sync}; R) \|_{\widetilde{M}} (Q; \mathbf{sync}; S) \quad = \quad (P \|_M Q); \mathbf{sync}; (R \|_{\widetilde{M}} S)$

provided that P and Q do not contain **sync**

Here the tilde over the M is meant to indicate that M is executed not just once at the end of parallel execution but also at all the intermediate synchronisation points. The main goal of this section is to define a meaning for the tilde and the **sync**, so as to ensure validity of this law. But first some examples:

Example 7.5.1 (Clocked hardware)

In the synchronous paradigm of hardware design, a clock signal is distributed regularly to all storage elements (registers). Between clock signals, the combinational circuitry performs its intended calculation with maximal concurrency. But the results of the calculation are not stored back into the registers until the clock signal arrives. The stored results become available to all combinational circuits only at the beginning of the next cycle. The length of the cycle is adjusted to ensure there is time for all the combinational circuits to stabilise before the next clock signal.□

Example 7.5.2 (BSP)

Section 7.4 describes how an array may be updated in parallel by splitting it into disjoint regions. In a scientific simulation, it is usually necessary to iterate a series of such updates, and use a different split into regions on each update. This is what permits information to propagate (perhaps more slowly than one would like) from one region of the array to other more remote regions. The treatment of regions in Section 7.4 requires all processes to terminate before any reallocation can be made. But in this section it becomes possible to perform the reallocation on each occasion of global synchronisation. This pattern of parallel programming is known as the Bulk Synchronous Paradigm (BSP) [183, 123], and it offers two advantages in high performance computing.

1. It is relatively easy to predict and optimise the performance of the system as a whole.
2. The effectiveness of the optimisation is relatively independent of the details of the implementing configuration and architecture. □

Example 7.5.3 (Cache memories)

In a modern microprocessor, there is a fast cache memory interposed between the arithmetic unit and the slower external main store. Any value read from a location in main store is held in the cache for a while, so that any later read operation from the same location may be satisfied more rapidly than by repeated access to main store. Any value written to memory is also held in the cache until the main store is ready to accept it. An operation is provided in the machine code that causes the processor to wait until all cached writes are written back through to main store. Only then is it known that the contents of the cache are in complete agreement with the main store.

When a single main store is shared among many processors, its workload increases proportionally. To balance the increase, each processor needs its own large and independent cache. The exact timings of reading from and writing to the shared main store become even more unpredictable. To achieve reliable communication between the processors, the waiting operation must act like **sync**. It must be obeyed simultaneously by all the processors, and it must also empty all the caches. This certainly ensures that the cache is up-to-date with the main store: it is the only reasonable way of doing so. It is only after the synchronisation that changes made by other processes can be reliably accessed from the shared main store. □

The formal definition of parallelism by synchronisation uses a combination of the techniques of Examples 7.2.4 and 7.2.5, though the input and output involved is purely conceptual. A sequence variable *out* is used by each process to record the value of its own copy of the shared variable m on each occasion of synchronisation. These values are combined by the merge operator M, playing the role of the SCCS | [125]. The merged result is recorded in the input sequence *in*, and so made available to all the contributing processes simultaneously. As before, a count is maintained of the serial number of the synchronisation.

Definition 7.5.4 (Sharing with synchronisation)

The atomic operation **sync** is defined as a simultaneous memory-mapped input and output

$$\mathbf{sync} \;=_{df}\; (c,\ out_c,\ m\ :=\ c+1,\ m,\ in_c)$$

The final merge $\widetilde{M}$ simply applies M to every element of the output sequences. Assuming M is feasible, the final merge is also implementable.

$$\begin{aligned}\widetilde{M} =_{df}\; & ((0.c = 1.c)_\perp\,;\ (c := 0.c)\\ & \|\ M(m,\ 0.m,\ 1.m,\ m')\\ & \|\ \{M((m \lhd i = c \rhd in_{i-1}),\ 0.out_i,\ 1.out_i,\ out_i') \mid c \le i < 0.c\}\\ & \|\ \{\Pi_{\{out_i\}} \mid i < c\})\ ;\\ & \mathbf{end}\ 0.c,\ 1.c,\ 0.out,\ 1.out\end{aligned}$$

Here $\|\,\{P_i \mid l \le i < n\}$ stands for the parallel program $(P_l \| P_{l+1} \| \ldots \| P_{n-1})$. □

The first line of this definition of $\widetilde{M}$ deals with the clock in the usual way. The second line says that the final value of the shared variable m is computed by the merge operation M. The third line states that on each occurrence of **sync**, the value of *output* is computed on the assumption that m had the value input on the previous **sync** (if any).

Theorem 7.5.5

If M is valid so is $\widetilde{M}$, and $\|_{\widetilde{M}}$ satisfies **L9**, and 7.1**L1** to **L8**.

Proof of **L9** Consider the case where

$$P \;=_{df}\; (m := e_0(m))$$

$$Q \;=_{df}\; (m := f_0(m))$$

and

$$R \;=_{df}\; m,\ out,\ c\ :=\ e_1(m),\ out\frown s,\ c+i$$

$$S \;=_{df}\; m,\ out,\ c\ :=\ f_1(m),\ out\frown t,\ c+j$$

Then we have

$$(P;\mathbf{sync};R) = (m,\ out,\ c\ :=\ e_1(in_c),\ out\frown <e_0(m)>\frown s,\ c+i+1) \qquad (\dagger)$$
$$(Q;\mathbf{sync};S) = (m,\ out,\ c\ :=\ f_1(in_c),\ out\frown <f_0(m)>\frown t,\ c+j+1) \qquad (\ddagger)$$

$$
\begin{array}{lll}
 & (P\|_M Q); \mathbf{sync}; (R\|_{\widetilde{M}} S) & \{\text{def of } P,\ Q \text{ and } \|_{\widetilde{M}}\} \\
= & M(m,\ e_0(m),\ f_0(m),\ m')\,;\ \mathbf{sync}; & \\
 & \widetilde{M}((c,\ out,\ m),\ (c+i,\ out^\frown s,\ e_1(m)), & \\
 & (c+j,\ out^\frown t,\ f_1(m)),\ (c',\ out',\ m')) & \{\text{def of } \widetilde{M} \text{ and } \mathbf{sync}\} \\
= & \widetilde{M}((c,\ out,\ m), & \\
 & (c+i+1,\ out^\frown < e_0(m) > {}^\frown s,\ e_1(in_c)), & \\
 & (c+j+1,\ out^\frown < f_0(m) > {}^\frown t,\ f_1(in_c)), & \\
 & (c',\ out',\ m')) & \{(\dagger) \text{ and } (\ddagger)\} \\
= & (P; \mathbf{sync}; R)\|_{\widetilde{M}}(Q; \mathbf{sync}; S) & \square
\end{array}
$$

All the definitions given so far would be entirely applicable to a system like those of Examples 7.2.4 and 7.2.5, which engages in real input and real output with the external environment. The only extra constraint is that input and output take place simultaneously. In particular, the values from the sequence *in* are completely unconstrained. But for our present proposes we want all the communication and synchronisation to be internal to the system itself. This is done by declaring the clock c and the sequences *out* and *in* to be local variables of the program which uses them. They are declared implicitly, together with a declaration of the variable m, whose sharing is achieved by synchronisation. But most important of all, we want the values of the input messages not just to be arbitrary values plucked from the environment; instead, they must be exactly the same messages that have been jointly output by all the synchronising processes on exactly the same cycle! This apparently instantaneous feedback is characteristic of hardware description languages (e.g. Esterel [24, 25], Signal [72]). It is easily specified: the initial value of the *in* stream must be the same as the final value of the *out* stream. The implementation would be easy too, if it were able to guess magically in advance what the final value of the output stream was going to be.

Definition 7.5.6

$$
\begin{array}{rl}
(\mathbf{shared}\ m;\ P;\ \mathbf{end}\ m) =_{df} & \mathbf{var}\ in,\ out,\ c\,;\ (out,\ c :=<>,\ 0); \\
 & (P \wedge (in = out'));\mathbf{end}\ in,\ out,\ c \qquad \square
\end{array}
$$

To show how this works, consider the following example where P is used to compute the maximal delay.

Example 7.5.7

$$
\begin{array}{rl}
\text{Let } P = & (time := time + r1\,;\ \mathbf{sync}\,;\ time := time + r2)\|_{\widetilde{M}} \\
 & (time := time + s1\,;\ \mathbf{sync}\,;\ time := time + s2)
\end{array}
$$

where $M =_{df} time := max(0.time,\ 1.time)$.

We are going to show that this has the expected effect

$$\textbf{shared } time;\, P;\, \textbf{end } time \;=\; time := time + max(r1,\, s1) + max(r2,\, s2)$$

$$\begin{aligned}
& P && \{\text{def of } \textbf{sync} \text{ and } 3.1\textbf{L2}\}\\
= \;& (c,\, out_c,\, time := c+1,\, time + r1,\, in_c + r2) \|_{\widetilde{M}} \\
& (c,\, out_c,\, time := c+1,\, time + s1,\, in_c + s2) && \{\text{Def. } 7.5.4\}\\
= \;& c,\, out_c,\, time := \\
& c+1,\, time + max(r1,\, s1),\, in_c + max(r2,\, s2) && (\dagger)
\end{aligned}$$

The assumption that $in_c = out_c$ ensures that the variable *time* gets the expected final value. Everything else is then hidden.

$$\begin{aligned}
& \textbf{shared } time;\; P;\; \textbf{end } time && \{\text{Def. } 7.5.6\}\\
= \;& \textbf{var } in,\, out,\, c;\; (out,\, c := <>,\, 0);\\
& ((in = out') \wedge P);\, \textbf{end } in,\, out,\, c && \{(\dagger) \text{ and } 3.1\textbf{L2}\}\\
= \;& \textbf{var } in,\, out,\, c;\\
& ((in_0 = time + max(r1,\, s1)) \;\wedge\\
& (c,\, out_0,\, time := 1,\, time + max(r1,\, s1),\, in_0\\
& +max(r2,\, s2)));\, \textbf{end } in,\, out,\, c && \{\text{def of assignment}\}\\
= \;& \textbf{var } in,\, out,\, c;\\
& c,\, out_0,\, time := 1, m + max(r1,\, s1),\, time + max(r1,\, s1)\\
& +max(r2,\, s2);\, \textbf{end } in,\, out,\, c && \{2.9\textbf{L6} \text{ and } 2.9\textbf{L8}\}\\
= \;& time := time + max(r1,\, s1) + max(r2,\, s2) && \square
\end{aligned}$$

Exercise 7.5.8

Prove that if P is a program that does not contain **sync** then

$$\textbf{shared } m;\; P; \textbf{sync}; Q\,;\, \textbf{end } m \;=\; P\,;\, \textbf{shared}\, m;\; Q;\; \textbf{end } m \qquad \square$$

7.6* Concurrent logic programming

The conventional logic programming paradigm is one which allows the program to give not just a single result of a computation, but rather a whole sequence of results, depending on how many are wanted on each occasion. So the desired behaviour can be specified as a relation L with alphabet $\{q, a'\}$, where q stands for the initial observation (usually called a question), and a' stands for the resulting sequence of answers. We use J, K and L to range over predicates with such an alphabet. Note that these are non-homogeneous relations: the input and output variables have different types and different names. As a result, sequential composition cannot be used directly between logic programs, though with care it can be used in reasoning about them.

The simplest logic program is the one that always gives an empty sequence of answers. This is used to indicate that the question is in face unanswerable; it is therefore used to represent the answer **no**.

Definition 7.6.1 (**no**)

$$\mathbf{no} \ =_{df} \ a :=<> \qquad \square$$

The opposite answer is **yes**; it is given to a question that is so simple that it serves as its own answer.

Definition 7.6.2 (**yes**)

$$\mathbf{yes} \ =_{df} \ a :=< q > \qquad \square$$

Any homogeneous relation $Q(q,\ q')$ can easily be transformed to a logic program $LQ(q,\ a')$ which gives q' as its only answer. This is done by composition with **yes**

$$LQ(q, < q' >) \ =_{df} \ Q; \mathbf{yes}$$

Other primitive operations of a logic programming language can be defined in this simple way, provided that they give just a single answer to any question.

In order to construct longer lists of answers, a concurrent logic language uses the interleaving operator $|||$, which merges the lists of answers given by its two operands.

Definition 7.6.3 (Parallel or)

Let K and L be logic programs. Define

$$K|||L \ =_{df} \ K \ \underset{Por}{\|} \ L$$

where

$$Por \ =_{df} \ \mathbf{true} \vdash a' \in (0.a|||1.a)$$

Because $|||$ permits a concurrent implementation, the language is said to be or-parallel. $\square$

This operation is known as disjunction, and it shares many of the algebraic properties of the logical operator with the same name (except idempotence).

Theorem 7.6.4

$|||$ is commutative, associative, and has **no** as its unit. It is also disjunctive and has **true** as its zero. □

A sequential logic programming language like PROLOG has a version of disjunction which can be defined as an extreme special case of interleaving. This is obtained by simple concatenation, where all the answers produced by the first operand come before any produced by the second. This reduces the benefit of concurrent implementation, because if the second operand produces answers before the first, they have to be saved up until after the first has finished.

Definition 7.6.5 (Sequential or)

$$K \textbf{ or } L \;=_{df}\; K \underset{Sor}{\|} L$$

where the merge operation Sor is defined by

$$Sor \;=_{df}\; \textbf{true} \vdash a' = 0.a \frown 1.a \qquad \square$$

This operator enjoys all the properties of parallel or except that it is no longer commutative. It also differs slightly from the true PROLOG disjunction, because it has **true** as its right zero. In PROLOG this is not so. As a result, PROLOG allows infinite sequences of answers. For example, the PROLOG program

$$(\mu X \bullet \textbf{yes or } X)$$

will give as its answers an infinite sequence of copies of its question. The above definition gives a much worse response, namely abortion.

Example 7.6.6 (Factorisation)

Questions and answers are just positive integers. $F0$ is defined to respond to a question by giving one of its proper factors (say the largest one that does not exceed the square root), and $F1$ gives the other proper factor. If the number is prime, both $F0$ and $F1$ say no. Then $(F0|||F1)$ also gives a no answer to a prime; otherwise it gives two answers whose product equals the original question. The order of the answers is arbitrary. For example,

$$(q := 13; F0) \;=\; \textbf{no}$$

$$(q := 14; F0) \;=\; a := \langle 2 \rangle$$

$$(q := 14; F1) \;=\; a :=< 7 >$$

$$(q := 14; (F0 ||| F1)) \;=\; (a :=< 2,7 >) \sqcap (a :=< 7,2 >) \qquad \square$$

Any logic program $L(q, a')$ can be converted to a homogeneous relation $L^*(a, a')$ on sequences of answers. This is done by applying L to each of the questions in the input sequence a, and concatenating the sequences of all the answers that result.

Definition 7.6.7 (Star)

$$L^* \;=_{df}\; \mu X \bullet \mathbf{no} \lhd a =<> \rhd (q := head(a); L) \;\mathbf{or}\; (a := tail(a); X) \qquad \square$$

In fact L^* is the unique fixed point of the above equation. The recursion conceals the simplicity of the idea, which is revealed better in the following algebraic laws.

Theorem 7.6.8

L1 $\mathbf{yes}^* \;=\; \mathit{II}_{\{a\}}$

L2 $\mathbf{no}^* \;=\; (a :=<>)$

L3 $\mathbf{true}^* \;=\; (a =<>)_\perp$

L4 $\mathbf{no}\,;\, L^* \;=\; \mathbf{no}$

L5 $\mathbf{yes}\,;\, L^* \;=\; L$

L6 $a := (a_0 {}^\frown a_1)\,;\, L^* \;=\; (a := a_0\,;\, L^*) \;\mathbf{or}\; (a := a_1\,;\, L^*)$

L7 $(K; L^*)^* \;=\; K^*\,;\, L^*$

Proof of L7

$$\begin{aligned}
& K^*\,;\, L^* && \{\text{Def. 7.6.7}\}\\
=\;& (\mathbf{no} \lhd a =<> \rhd ((q := head(a); K) \\
& \qquad \mathbf{or}\; (a := tail(a); K^*)));\, L^* && \{2.2\mathbf{L2}\}\\
=\;& (\mathbf{no}; L^*) \lhd a =<> \rhd (((q := head(a); K) \\
& \qquad \mathbf{or}\; (a := tail(a); K^*)); L^*) && \{\mathbf{L4} \text{ and } \mathbf{L6}\}\\
=\;& (\mathbf{no} \lhd a =<> \rhd ((q := head(a); K; L^*) \\
& \qquad \mathbf{or}\; (a := tail(a); K^*; L^*)) && \{\mathbf{L6}\}
\end{aligned}$$

which together with the uniqueness of the fixed point of the defining equation of the star operator implies **L7**. $\square$

The star helps in defining the other main operator of logic programming, which is called conjunction (**and**). This is akin to sequential composition, in that the answers produced by the first operand are fed as questions to the second operand. The final result is a concatenation of all the sequences of answers produced by the second operand.

Definition 7.6.9 (Conjunction)

$$K \,\mathbf{and}\, L \;=_{df}\; K; L^* \qquad \square$$

The algebraic properties of this operator reveal its close similarity with sequential composition between homogeneous relations.

Theorem 7.6.10

and is associative and has **yes** as its unit. As left zeros it has both **true** and **no**. It distributes leftward through sequential or. □

But **true** is not a right zero of **and**, because when the first operand gives an empty answer the second operand is never started

$$\mathbf{no}\,;\,\mathbf{true}^* \;=\; \mathbf{no}$$

Conjunction **and** does not distribute rightward through **or**, because the right operand may have to be executed many times, once for each of the answers produced by the left operand.

The following distribution laws are useful in computing the result of a logic program.

Theorem 7.6.11

L8 $q := e; (K|||L) \;=\; (q := e; K)|||(q := e; L)$

L9 $q := e; (K \,\mathbf{or}\, L) \;=\; (q := e; K) \,\mathbf{or}\, (q := e; L)$

L10 $Q; (K \,\mathbf{and}\, L) \;=\; (Q; K) \,\mathbf{and}\, L$ □

Example 7.6.12 (Complete factorisation)

Using conjunction and recursion, it is now possible to write the program FAC, producing a complete list of prime factors of its question. $F0$ and $F1$ do the real work, together with a primality test to terminate the recursion.

$$FAC \;=_{df}\; \mu X \bullet \mathbf{yes} \;\lhd prime(q) \rhd ((F0|||F1) \;\mathbf{and}\; X)$$

An example of a simple calculation shows how this works

$$\begin{array}{lll} & q := 182 \;;\; FAC & \{\text{def of } FAC\} \\ = & q := 182 \;;\; ((F0|||F1) \,\mathbf{and}\, FAC) & \{\mathbf{L8} \text{ and } \mathbf{L10}\} \\ = & ((q := 182 \;;\; F0)|||(q := 182 \;;\; F1)) \,\mathbf{and}\, FAC & \{\text{def of } F0, F1\} \\ = & (a := <13> \;|||\; a := <14>) \,\mathbf{and}\, FAC & \{\text{Def. 7.6.3}\} \\ = & (a := <13, 14> \sqcap a := <14, 13>) \;\mathbf{and}\; FAC & \{2.4\mathbf{L6}\} \end{array}$$

$$\begin{aligned} &= (a :=< 13, 14 > \textbf{ and } FAC) \sqcap \\ &\quad (a :=< 14, 13 > \textbf{ and } FAC) && \{\mathbf{L6}\} \\ &= (a :=< 13 >; FAC^* \textbf{ or } a :=< 14 >; FAC^*) \sqcap \\ &\quad (a :=< 14 >; FAC^* \textbf{ or } a :=< 13 >; FAC^*) && \{\text{def of } FAC\} \\ &= a :=< 13, 2, 7 > \ \sqcap \ a :=< 13, 7, 2 > \sqcap \\ &\quad a :=< 2, 7, 13 > \ \sqcap \ a :=< 7, 2, 13 > && \square \end{aligned}$$

On occasion, it is known that no more than one answer will ever be required for a question. Clearly it is a waste of time to compute unwanted answers, so PROLOG provides a *cut* operation to guide a more efficient implementation. The cut has often been criticised as illogical or worse. However, it presents no difficulty in our theory. It is a deterministic homogeneous relation on sequences of answers.

Definition 7.6.13 (Cut)

$$! \ =_{df} \ a := (< head(a) > \lhd a \neq <> \rhd <>) \qquad \square$$

Theorem 7.6.14

L11 $\textbf{no}\,;! \ = \ \textbf{no} \qquad \textbf{yes}\,;! \ = \ \textbf{yes}$

L12 $!;! \ = \ !$

L13 $(K \textbf{ or } L);! \ = \ ((K;!) \textbf{ or } (L;!));!$

L14 $(K \textbf{ and } L);! \ = \ (K \textbf{ and } (L;!));!$

L15 $(K|||L);! \ = \ ((K;!)|||(L;!));!$

Proof of L13 Define

$$\begin{aligned} 0.! &=_{df} 0.a := (< head(0.a) > \lhd 0.a \neq <> \rhd <>) \\ 1.! &=_{df} 1.a := (< head(1.a) > \lhd 1.a \neq <> \rhd <>) \\ e &=_{df} (< head(0.a), head(1.a) > \lhd 1.a \neq <> \rhd < head(0.a) >) \\ &\quad \lhd 0.a \neq <> \rhd (< head(1.a) > \lhd 1.a \neq <> \rhd <>) \end{aligned}$$

$$\begin{aligned} &\quad Sor;! && \{\text{Def. 7.6.5}\} \\ &= (a := 0.a ^\frown 1.a);! && \{\text{Def. 7.6.13 and 3.1}\mathbf{L2}\} \\ &= a := head(0.a) \lhd 0.a \neq <> \rhd \\ &\quad (head(1.a) \lhd 1.a \neq <> \rhd <>) && \{\text{def of } e \text{ and 3.1}\mathbf{L2}\} \\ &= a := e;! && \{\text{def } 0.!,\ 1.! \text{ and 3.1}\mathbf{L2}\} \\ &= (0.!\|1.!); Sor;! \end{aligned}$$

which implies

$$
\begin{aligned}
& (K\ \mathbf{or}\ L);! && \{\text{Def. 7.6.5}\}\\
= \ & ((K; U0(a))\|(L; U1(a))); Sor;! && \{Sor;! \ = \ (0.!\|1.!); Sor;!\}\\
= \ & ((K; U0(a))\|(L; U1(a))); (0.!\|1.!); Sor;! && \{\text{Exercise 7.1.8(2)}\}\\
= \ & ((K; U0(a); 0.!)\|(L; U1(a); 1.!)); Sor;! && \{U0(a); 0.! \ = \ !; U0(a)\}\\
= \ & ((K;!)\ \mathbf{or}\ (L;!));! && \square
\end{aligned}
$$

The last three distributive laws are useful in optimising execution by inhibiting answers that can never be used.

The most controversial of all PROLOG operators is negation. It turns an empty list of answers into **yes** and any non-empty list into **no**.

Definition 7.6.15 (Negation)

$$\neg L \ =_{df} \ L;\ (\mathbf{yes} \lhd a = <> \rhd \mathbf{no}) \qquad \square$$

$\neg$ is disjunctive and distributes through conditional. It also has fixed point **true**.

Theorem 7.6.16

L16 $\neg\mathbf{yes} \ = \ \mathbf{no} \qquad \neg\mathbf{no} \ = \ \mathbf{yes} \qquad \neg\mathbf{true} \ = \ \mathbf{true}$

L17 $\neg\neg\neg L \ = \ \neg L$

L18 $\neg(K \lhd b \rhd L) \ = \ (\neg K) \lhd b \rhd (\neg L)$

L19 $\neg(L;!) \ = \ (\neg L) \ = \ (\neg L);!$

L20 $\neg(K|||L) \ = \ (\neg K)\ \mathbf{and}\ (\neg L),$ provided that $L;\top \ = \ \top$ $\square$

Negation provides a means of replacing the conditional. For example, $\neg F0$ gives the answer **yes** to any prime, so the factorising program could be rewritten

$$\mu X :: \neg F0|||((F0|||F1)\ \mathbf{and}\ X)$$

The termination of this recursion depends crucially on **L4**: $\mathbf{no\ and}\ L \ = \ \mathbf{no}$.

In this section, most of the operators of the logic programming language have been defined in terms of operators which are known to reduce to the normal form of Chapter 5. The only exception is negation, for which we must prove

Theorem 7.6.17

Let $S \ = \ \{S_n \mid n \in \mathcal{N}\}$ be a descending chain of finite normal forms. Then

$$\neg(\bigsqcup S) \ = \ \bigsqcup_n (\neg S_n)$$

where $\neg S_n$ can be converted into a finite normal form.

Proof $\quad \neg(\bigsqcup S)$ $\qquad$ {; is continuous and Def. 7.6.15}

$= \ \bigsqcup_n \neg S_n$

In the following we show how to convert $\neg S_n$ into a finite normal form.

$$\begin{array}{lll} & \neg(\sqcap_i a := f_i(q) \lhd b \rhd \mathbf{true}) & \{\mathbf{L18}\} \\ = & (\neg \sqcap_i a := f_i(q)) \lhd b \rhd \neg\mathbf{true} & \{\neg \text{ is disjunctive}\} \\ = & \sqcap_i(\neg a := f_i(q)) \lhd b \rhd \neg\mathbf{true} & \{\text{Def. 7.6.15}\} \\ = & (\sqcap_i a := (<> \lhd f_i(q) \neq <> \rhd < q >)) \lhd b \rhd \mathbf{true} & \square \end{array}$$

There is nothing in the theory which prevents combined use of the parallel and the sequential form of disjunction. The advantage of the sequential form is that it gives closer control over the order of evaluation, which is very important if the later answers are going to be cut. Indeed, successful use of parallel or sequential searches may depend on the programmer giving hints about the sensible degree of priority allocated to the two branches. The disadvantage of the parallel **or** is that it introduces a high degree of non-determinism. This can be very easily eliminated by regarding the results of the program as a *bag* (or even as a set) rather than a sequence. Then the interleaving in the definition of disjunction is replaced by the deterministic operation of bag union. All the non-determinism is now concentrated in the cut operation, which selects an arbitrary member of the bag. Even this can be eliminated if the programmer promises never to apply cut except to a bag with only one member. This promise can be enforced by redefining cut to result in abortion when the promise fails

$$! \;=_{df}\; (\# a \leq 1)_\perp$$

This treatment of logic programming completely ignores one of the most delightful features of PROLOG: that it makes no fixed distinction between its input and output variables. For example, the same predicate

$$a \;=\; b \frown c$$

can be used to test the truth of the equation, to compute a by concatenation of b and c, to compute b from a and c, or c from a and b, or even to compute from a the list of all pairs (b, c) satisfying the equation.

Exercise 7.6.18

Write a specification of each of the four modes of use of the PROLOG program for catenation described above. Using the notations of this section, write a program that implements the fourth of them. □

Chapter 8

Communication

The fundamental property of a sequential process is that its behaviour can be adequately described by observations made on just two occasions, at the moment of its initiation and at the moment of its termination. The basic distinguishing property of a *reactive* process is that it also admits intermediate observations on suitable occasions between initiation and termination. Additional variables and naming conventions are introduced to denote the results of these observations.

We take a view similar to that of modern quantum physics, that an observation is always an interaction between a process and one or more observers in its neighbouring environment. The role of observer will often be played by other processes, and the subsequent behaviour of all the processes involved will usually be affected by the interaction. In any case, the occurrence of interaction is always regarded as an atomic event, without duration in time. If P is a process, we let $\mathcal{A}P$ denote the set of all actions which are physically and logically possible for the process (even in the case of one that never actually performs them). This is taken to be an unchangeable part of the process alphabet.

A common kind of interaction is a communication between processes; this can be analysed in greater detail as the input or output of a message m along some channel with name c; the event is then denoted by the pair $c.m$, and the set of all such pairs is included in $\mathcal{A}$. The names of the channels which connect a process to its environment are therefore part of its alphabet: they are classified as input channels or as output channels to indicate the direction of transmission. But for many purposes it is simpler to ignore this analysis, and regard a communication as no different from every other atomic event in $\mathcal{A}$. That is the view taken in the early sections of this chapter.

A process may engage many successive interactions, and we assume that they can be recorded sequentially in the order in which they occur. Simultaneous actions are allowed, but the recording conventions require that they are written down in some particular order, maybe arbitrary. The sequence of interactions recorded up to some given moment in time is called a *trace*; this is abbreviated to tr and is included in the alphabet of every reactive process. The variable tr represents the sequence of actions which takes place before the process is started, and the variable tr' stands for the sequence of all actions which have been recorded so far, up to the moment of observation. The values of tr and tr' range over all finite sequences of events, that is the Kleene closure $\mathcal{A}^*$ of the alphabet $\mathcal{A}$. Since the execution of a process can never *undo* any action performed previously, the trace can only get longer. The current value of tr must therefore always be an extension of its initial value. The predicate P which describes a reactive process behaviour must therefore imply this fact. So it satisfies the healthiness condition

R1 $P \;=\; P \wedge (tr \leq tr')$

Note that the sequence $tr' - tr$ represents the trace of events in which the process itself has engaged from the moment that it starts to the moment of observation.

The purpose of the undashed variable tr is to permit reuse in the theory of reactive processes of the same definition of sequential composition as in a sequential language. In fact this variable plays no other significant role. In particular it has no influence on the behaviour of the process. So a reactive process also satisfies a second healthiness condition

R2 $P(tr, tr') \;=\; \sqcap_s P(s, s^\frown(tr' - tr))$

This means that the initial value of tr may be replaced by an arbitrary s, and the events in which the process itself engages remain the same.

We assume that the occurrence of an event and its observation by the environment are always exactly simultaneous. In fact they are recorded in the trace as the same event. If there is some delay in communication along a channel, we model this by including in $\mathcal{A}$ the separate events of sending the message to the channel and receiving the message from it. When the environment is actually another process, simultaneity requires an implementation to ensure that each event occurs only when both the process and its environment are ready, willing and waiting for it. So occurrence of an event is often preceded by a wait on the part of one (or more) of the processes involved.

Because of the requirement for synchronisation, an active process will usually engage in alternate periods of internal activity (computation) and periods of quiescence or stability, while it is waiting for reaction or acknowledgement from its environment. We therefore introduce into the alphabet of a reactive process a variable *wait'*, which is true just during these quiescent periods. Its main purpose is to distinguish intermediate observations from the observations made on termination. If *wait'* is true, then all the other dashed variables also stand for intermediate observations rather than final ones.

The introduction of intermediate waiting states has implications for sequential composition: all the intermediate observations of P are of course also intermediate observations of $P;Q$. Control can pass from P to Q only when P is in a final state, distinguished by the fact that $wait'$ is false. Rather than change the definition of sequential composition, we enforce these rules by means of a healthiness condition. If the process Q is asked to start in a waiting state of its predecessor, it leaves the state unchanged

R3 $Q \;=\; I\!I \lhd wait \rhd Q$

where the predicate $I\!I$ adopts the following new meaning in this chapter

$$I\!I \;=_{df}\; \neg ok \wedge (tr \le tr') \;\;\vee\;\; ok' \wedge (tr' = tr) \wedge \ldots \wedge (wait' = wait)$$

A process reaches a waiting state when it can make no further internal progress until after the occurrence of some event that requires participation from its environment. In fact, we allow a process to wait simultaneously for more than one kind of event, in a way that permits the environment to select which of these events will actually occur. For example, an inputting process may wait for any of the possible messages that can be transmitted along some subset of its input channels, and the outputting environment selects which one. An efficient implementation will ensure that the first event which actually becomes possible will occur immediately. The occurrence of the event is observed by the environment and recorded in the trace. The subsequent behaviour of the process is therefore as predictable as before the event. Waiting for the first of a selection of events does not itself introduce non-determinism. Non-determinism only becomes a risk if the event is concealed from the observer.

Another grave risk incurred by reactive systems is that of deadlock. This occurs when the environment continuously refuses to participate in any of the events which the process is waiting for; the usual cause is that the process itself is also refusing to participate in any of the events in which the environment is ready to engage. To avoid such risk, we need to model it by keeping track of the set of events which are refused by a process in each of its waiting states. The variable ref' is introduced to denote this set.

The following definition summarises the discussion so far.

Definition 8.0.1 (Reactive process)

A reactive process is one which satisfies the healthiness conditions **R1**, **R2** and **R3**, and has an alphabet consisting of the following:

- $\mathcal{A}$, the set of events in which it can potentially engage.
- $tr : \mathcal{A}^*$, the sequence of events which have happened up to the time of observation.

- *wait* : *Boolean*, which distinguishes its waiting states from its terminated states.
- *ref* : $\mathcal{PA}$, the set of events refused by the process during its wait. □

As a subtheory, reactive processes can be defined by a monotonic idempotent. Here and elsewhere, we will use the same name for the healthiness condition and its associated embedding.

Theorem 8.0.2

P is a reactive process **iff** it is a fixed point of $\mathbf{R} =_{df} \mathbf{R3} \circ \mathbf{R2} \circ \mathbf{R1}$ where

$$\begin{aligned} \mathbf{R1}(X) &=_{df} X \wedge (tr \leq tr') \\ \mathbf{R2}(X(tr,\, tr')) &=_{df} \bigsqcap_s X(s,\; s^\frown(tr' - tr)) \\ \mathbf{R3}(X) &=_{df} I\!I \lhd wait \rhd X \end{aligned}$$

Proof It is evident that a process P satisfies the healthiness condition $\mathbf{R}i$ iff it is a fixed point of the monotonic mapping $\mathbf{R}i$ defined above. The conclusion follows from the commutativity of the idempotents $\mathbf{R}i$ and Theorem 4.1.7. □

Corollary

Reactive processes form a complete lattice. □

Theorem 8.0.3 (Closure of reactive processes)

The set of reactive processes is a $\{\wedge,\, \vee,\, \lhd tr' = tr \rhd,\, ;\}$-closure. □

The theory of reactive processes with synchronisation has been a prolific topic of research, and many systems and notations have been proposed. In this chapter, we select just three of them for unified treatment on the basis of the observable properties listed above. Ignoring notational trivialities, the theories are differentiated mainly by a different selection of healthiness conditions. The three theories are the Algebra of Communicating Processes (ACP) [23], Communicating Sequential Processes (CSP) [88], and Data Flow (Kahn–McQueen networks) [106, 107].

The simplest model is that of ACP. Its simplicity derives from three related design decisions.

1. It does not include a unit for sequential composition. In fact, every terminating process satisfies a healthiness condition that it must engage in at least one event before termination.
2. It does not include any divergent process. Partly because of 1, it is possible to avoid divergence by restricting recursion to cases in which there is known to be an unique fixed point.

3. There is no explicit refinement ordering between processes. Non-determinism is present, but there is no separate symbol for it.

The well-known Calculus of Communicating Systems (CCS) [125, 126] is very similar to ACP, and the main minor differences will be pointed out in passing. The absence from CCS of a primitive combinator for sequential composition can be easily remedied by a construction. One valuable objective of CCS was to define the common properties of a whole family of process algebras. It therefore preserves a number of more subtle distinctions between processes, which cannot be represented in our limited alphabet of observations. For example, significance is attached to the order in which non-deterministic choices are made. A full explicit model for CCS is therefore beyond the scope of this chapter [46, 81, 83].

In ACP and CCS, internal communications between components of a system are identified by a special event name τ, which is recorded in the trace. It is interpreted as a silent or invisible transition, and its occurrence never needs to be synchronised with the environment. One good motive for its retention in the trace is to preserve the uniqueness of fixed points. Nevertheless, τ presents a noticeable inconvenience in specification and design. The main distinguishing feature of CSP is to define a hiding operator that succeeds in total concealment of internal events. But it is necessary to recognise the danger that a system will engage in an *infinite* sequence of internal actions, and never again reach a stable state in which it is ready to interact with its environment – a phenomenon known as *livelock*. CSP models this danger by divergence, so that its avoidance can be proved.

Our last example paradigm is data flow. This was the first paradigm to be modelled mathematically, and achieved early implementation as the pipe of UNIX. The characteristic property of data flow is that its communication channels are all buffered, so that they can accept an output message at any time, storing it until the process at the other end of the channel is ready to input it. Consequently, a process never has to wait to perform output. The reduction in wait times is paid for in the overhead of buffering and the risk of buffer overflow.

The first theories of data flow were deterministic, in that the output messages had to be functions of earlier input, or otherwise paradoxical results would emerge. By recording the sequence of all events in a single trace, our treatment of non-determinism avoids the classical paradoxes. Data flow is still one of the most elegant of process paradigms, and it can be modelled simply by traces, without any need for explicit waiting states or refusals [33, 34]. The purpose of the data flow paradigm is to replace control flow by data flow. So sequential composition has no role; it is replaced by a chaining operator, which hides the data that are output by one process and transmitted for input by the other.

Both synchronous and asynchronous models of communication have found application in industry.

Example 8.0.4 (LOTOS)

The international standard formal language LOTOS [98] (ISO 8807) is defined for mathematical analysis of networked, distributed and concurrent systems. It uses synchronised communication, and has been beneficially influenced by the process algebras described in this chapter. □

Example 8.0.5 (SDL)

The specification and description language SDL has been standardised internationally (CCITT Z.100, 1993). It is based on an asynchronous model of communication, as in data flow. □

8.1 Algebra of Communicating Processes (ACP)

ACP [23] is an algebra that includes both sequential and concurrent composition. For purposes of unification, we want to use exactly the same definition for sequential composition as in all the theories described so far. This means that we must include in the alphabet both dashed and undashed versions of all variables, for example tr as well as tr'. Because an ACP process never diverges, there is no need for the variables ok and ok'. Whenever it is not waiting it has terminated.

In ACP there is a slightly unexpected healthiness condition that no ACP process can terminate before performing at least one atomic action.

ACP1 $[(P \wedge (tr' = tr)) \;\Rightarrow\; wait']$

Definition 8.1.1 (ACP processes)

A reactive process is an ACP process if it satisfies **ACP1**. □

Example 8.1.2 (Deadlock)

The process δ never terminates and never performs a proper action. It is the representation of deadlock, which waits forever

$$\delta \;=_{df}\; \mathbf{R3}(tr' = tr \;\wedge\; wait')$$ □

Theorem 8.1.3 (Closure of ACP processes)

ACP processes form a complete lattice, which is closed under $\lhd \delta \rhd$ and sequential composition.

Proof From Theorem 4.1.7 and Definition 8.1.1 it follows that P is an ACP process **iff** it is a fixed point of the monotonic idempotent

$$\Phi \;=_{df}\; \mathbf{R} \circ and_B \;=\; and_B \circ \mathbf{R}$$

where

$$B =_{df} ((tr' = tr) \wedge wait' \vee (tr < tr'))$$

and **R** was defined in Theorem 8.0.2. That is why ACP processes form a complete lattice. We are going to show that **ACP1** is preserved by composition.

$$\begin{array}{lll} & (X;Y) \wedge (tr' = tr) & \{\mathbf{R1}\} \\ \Rightarrow & \exists s \bullet (X[s/tr'] \wedge tr = s)\,;\,(Y[s/tr] \wedge tr' = s) & \{\mathbf{ACP1}\} \\ \Rightarrow & \exists s \bullet (wait'; wait') & \{\text{def of ;}\} \\ = & wait' & \square \end{array}$$

Example 8.1.4 (Communication)

Let $a \in \mathcal{A}$. The process $do_{\mathcal{A}}(a)$ cannot refuse to perform an a-action at the very beginning. After performing that action, it terminates successfully. It therefore has exactly two stable states, denoted by

$$do_{\mathcal{A}}(a) \;=_{df}\; \Phi(a \notin ref' \lhd wait' \rhd tr' \;=\; tr^\frown < a >)$$

Because Φ (see Theorem 8.1.3) is idempotent and $do_{\mathcal{A}}(a)$ lies in its range, so $do_{\mathcal{A}}(a)$ is an ACP process. In future we will write just a instead of $do_{\mathcal{A}}(a)$. $\square$

The deadlock process δ is a left zero of sequential composition.

L1 $\delta; P \;=\; \delta$

Proof

$$\begin{array}{lll} & \delta; P & \{\text{Theorem 8.0.3 and } \mathbf{R3}\} \\ = & II \lhd wait \rhd (\delta; P) & \{\text{def of } \delta\} \\ = & II \lhd wait \rhd ((\delta \wedge wait'); P) & \{P \text{ meets } \mathbf{R3}\} \\ = & II \lhd wait \rhd ((\delta \wedge wait'); II) & \{\text{def of } \delta \text{ and } \mathbf{R3}\} \\ = & \delta & \square \end{array}$$

Let P and Q be ACP processes. The notation $P+Q$ describes a process that may behave like P or like Q. It is distinguished from the disjunction $P \vee Q$ by the fact that the selection is made after the first event has happened rather than before. If the first event is one in which P cannot engage, then it must be one in which Q has engaged, and the rest of the behaviour of $P+Q$ is described by Q. Similarly, P can be selected by occurrence of an event possible for P but not for Q. Finally, if the first event is possible for both P and Q, then selection between them is fully non-deterministic. Since the choice of first event can be made by some other process running in parallel with both P and Q, $+$ is often called *external* choice, whereas $\sqcap$ denotes a choice made *internally*, as it were by the process itself.

The distinctive feature of $+$ is that initially, when tr' is still equal to tr, the process $P + Q$ cannot refuse a set of actions unless it is refused by *both* P and by Q. That explains its very simple truth functional definition, which permits the properties of $+$ to be proved in propositional calculus.

Definition 8.1.5 (Alternative composition)

$$P + Q \;=_{df}\; (P \wedge Q) \lhd \delta \rhd (P \vee Q) \qquad \square$$

Example 8.1.6

$$
\begin{array}{lll}
 & a + b & \{\text{Def. } 8.1.5\} \\
= & (a \wedge b) \lhd \delta \rhd (a \vee b) & \{\text{Theorem } 8.0.3\} \\
= & \mathbf{R3}(a \wedge b) \lhd \delta \rhd \mathbf{R3}(a \vee b) & \{2.1\mathbf{L3}\} \\
= & \mathbf{R3}((a \wedge b) \lhd \delta \rhd (a \vee b)) & \{\text{Example } 8.1.4\} \\
= & \mathbf{R3}((ref' \cap \{a, b\}) = \{\} \lhd wait' \rhd (tr' - tr) \in \{< a >, < b >\}) & \square
\end{array}
$$

Alternative composition is idempotent, commutative and associative.

L2 $P + P \;=\; P$

L3 $P + Q \;=\; Q + P$

L4 $(P + Q) + R \;=\; P + (Q + R)$

The deadlock process δ is unable to perform an action; thus it can never be chosen to be executed by alternative composition.

L5 $\delta + Q \;=\; Q$

An alternative composition makes its choice in accordance with the first events which its alternatives are offering to perform. Since no ACP process can terminate before executing an action, the successor of alternative composition cannot affect that choice. Hence the distributive law

L6 $(P + Q); R \;=\; (P; R) + (Q; R)$

This law is not valid if P is the unit $I\!I$, and this is perhaps one reason why $I\!I$ is omitted from ACP.

The CCS $+$ operator is essentially the same as that of ACP, and the CCS NIL process plays the same role as δ. They obey all the algebraic laws quoted above. However, in CCS sequential composition is restricted to the case when the first component is a single action. Furthermore, this is the only context in which a single action may be written. Finally, dot is used instead of semicolon

$$a.P \qquad b.NIL \qquad a.(b.(c.NIL))$$

The laws **L2** to **L5** justify introduction of the notation

$$\Sigma_{i \in I} P_i$$

to represent the alternative composition of a family of i-indexed processes

$$\{P_i \mid i \in I\}$$

We also adopt the convention that

$$\delta \;=\; \Sigma_{i \in \{\}} P_i$$

This notation will be used to define a normal form for ACP processes.

Definition 8.1.7 (Normal form)

An ACP process

$$\Sigma_{i \in I} (a_i; P_i) \;+\; \Sigma_{j \in J} b_j$$

is said to be in *head normal form.* If all the P_i and their descendants are similarly expressed, the process is in *normal form* (which may therefore be infinite). □

The interleaving of ACP processes is defined in a manner similar to the interleaving of Example 7.2.2. Each action of the system $P|||Q$ is an action of exactly one of its components. If one of the processes cannot engage in the action, then it must be the other one, but if both processes could have engaged in the same action, the choice between them is non-deterministic. Conversely, $P|||Q$ can refuse an action only when it is refused by both the operands, and it terminates when both its operands have terminated.

Definition 8.1.8 (Interleaving)

$$P|||Q \;=_{df}\; P\|_{M_{ACP}}Q$$

where the merge relation M_{ACP} is defined

$$\begin{aligned} M_{ACP} \;=_{df}\; & (wait' \;=\; 0.wait \lor 1.wait) \land \\ & (ref' \;=\; 0.ref \cap 1.ref) \land \\ & (tr' - tr) \in (0.tr \;-\; tr)|||(1.tr \;-\; tr) \end{aligned}$$ □

Since the merge relation M_{ACP} is valid, from Theorem 7.2.11 it follows that the ACP interleaving operator $|||$ is commutative and associative (it cannot have a unit, because there isn't one in ACP). The following expansion law shows how to transform an interleaving composition into normal form.

L7 Let $P \;=\; (\Sigma_i (a_i; P_i) \;+\; \Sigma_j b_j)$ and $Q \;=\; (\Sigma_l (c_l; Q_l) \;+\; \Sigma_m d_m)$.

Then $P|||Q \;=\; \Sigma_i (a_i; (P_i|||Q)) \;+ \Sigma_j (b_j; Q) + \; \Sigma_l (c_l; (P|||Q_l)) \;+\; \Sigma_m (d_m; P)$

The interleaving composition $P|||Q$ does not allow communication between processes P and Q, because their behaviour is completely independent. A different operator $||$ is therefore needed to allow processes to interact by synchronisation. Communication is accomplished when one of the two processes selects an alternative offered by a + operator in the other.

In ACP, synchronisation is defined in considerable generality. For example, suppose a and b are two actions that can occur simultaneously, but when they do so, they actually result in some different action c. ACP postulates a partial function $(a|b)$ which maps pairs of synchronisable actions to the action that results from successful synchronisation. As in Example 7.2.5, it is postulated to be commutative and associative. When $(a, b) \notin dom(|)$, this indicates that no synchronisation between actions a and b is expected or intended. Let S and T be subsets of $\mathcal{A}$; we will adopt the following convention

$$S|T =_{df} \{(a|b) \mid (a, b) \in dom(|) \wedge a \in S \wedge b \in T\}$$

Definition 8.1.9 (Parallel composition)

The parallel composition $P||_{ACP}Q$ may at any time perform an independent action of P or an independent action of Q. Alternatively, it may perform an action synchronised between P and Q, whenever such a synchronisation is defined. It then behaves as the parallel composition of the remainders of P and Q

$$P||_{ACP}Q =_{df} P||_N Q$$

where

$$\begin{aligned} N =_{df}\ & (wait' = 0.wait \vee 1.wait) \wedge \\ & (tr' - tr) \in (0.tr - tr) \mid\mid (1.tr - tr) \wedge \\ & ref' \subseteq 0.ref \cap 1.ref - ((\mathcal{A} \setminus 0.ref)|(\mathcal{A} \setminus 1.ref)) \end{aligned}$$

and the trace merge operator $||$ is defined by

$$\begin{aligned} u|| <> &=_{df} \{u\} \\ <> ||u &=_{df} \{u\} \\ (< a >^\frown u)||(< b >^\frown v) &=_{df} < a >^\frown (u||(< b >^\frown v)) \cup < b >^\frown ((< a >^\frown u)||v) \cup \\ & \quad < a|b >^\frown ((u||v) \lhd (a, b) \in dom(|) \rhd \{\}) \end{aligned}$$ □

The three disjuncts in the last definition represent the three possibilities that a or b may occur independently without mutual synchronisation, or that they may occur simultaneously (provided that they are synchronisable).

This parallel composition of ACP is a generalisation of the parallel composition | of CCS, where events are classified into

(1) passive events a, b, c, ...

(2) active events, which have the same name as passive events, but are written with an overbar $\bar{a}$, $\bar{b}$, $\bar{c}$, ...

(3) a special event τ, which is supposed to occur silently and invisibly, and without synchronisation with any other event.

Synchronisation occurs only between a passive event and an active event with the same name, and the resulting event is always silent. So the CCS definition of parallelism may be obtained from the ACP definition by a special choice of synchronising function

$$(x|\bar{x}) = \tau, \qquad \text{for all } x$$

Like the interleaving operator, the ACP parallel operator is commutative and associative. The following complicated expansion law enables us to convert a parallel composition into a head normal form.

L8 Let $P = (\Sigma_i\,(a_i; P_i) + \Sigma_j\, b_j)$ and $Q = \Sigma_l\,(c_l; Q_l) + \Sigma_m\, d_m$,

and let P_i and Q_l be head normal forms.

$$\begin{aligned}\text{Then } P||_{ACP}Q \;=\; & \Sigma_i\,(a_i; (P_i||_{ACP}Q)) + \Sigma_j\,(b_j; Q) + \\ & \Sigma_l\,(c_l; (P||_{ACP}Q_l)) + \Sigma_m\,(d_m; P) + \\ & \Sigma_{i,l}\,((a_i|c_l); (P_i||_{ACP}Q_l)) + \Sigma_{i,m}\,((a_i|d_m); P_i) + \\ & \Sigma_{j,l}\,((b_j|c_l); Q_l) + \Sigma_{j,m}\,(b_j|d_m)\end{aligned}$$

The expansion law shows that whenever a synchronisation $(a|b)$ is possible, the separate actions a and b are also possible. These often represent an unsuccessful attempt to synchronise, which may be successful when additional parallel processes are added to the system. But after all the processes have been included, these unsuccessful attempts cannot now occur. Their removal is achieved by an encapsulation operator, which prevents them from happening: they are replaced by deadlock in those cases when all the actions have been prevented.

Definition 8.1.10 (Encapsulation)

Let $E \subseteq \mathcal{A}$. The process $\varrho_E(P)$ behaves like P, except that it always refuses to perform any action of E, and all traces containing them are simply omitted.

$$\varrho_E(P(ref')) =_{df} \mathbf{R3}((tr' - tr) \downarrow E = \langle\rangle \wedge \exists X \bullet P(X) \wedge (ref' \subseteq X \cup E))$$

where $s \downarrow E$ stands for the subsequence of s consisting only of elements of E. □

The following law permits symbolic execution of the encapsulation operator by distributing it through a head normal form

L9 $\varrho_E(\Sigma_i\,(a_i; P_i) + \Sigma_j\, b_j) = \Sigma_{a_i \notin E}\,(a_i; \varrho_E(P_i)) + \Sigma_{b_j \notin E}\, b_j$

Theorem 8.1.11 (Closure of ACP processes)

ACP processes are closed under $+$, ϱ_E, $|||$ and $\|$.

Proof From Theorem 8.1.3 it follows that the set of ACP processes is closed under $\vee$, $\wedge$ and $\lhd\delta\rhd$. The conclusion that ACP processes are closed under $+$ follows directly from Definition 8.1.5. For the encapsulation operator one has

$$
\begin{array}{lll}
& \Phi(\varrho_E(P)) & \{\text{def of } \Phi \text{ and } B \text{ in Theorem 8.1.3}\} \\
= & (\mathbf{R3} \circ \mathbf{R2} \circ and_B)(\varrho_E(P)) & \{\wedge - \vee \text{ distributivity}\} \\
= & (\mathbf{R3} \circ \mathbf{R2})(\varrho_E(and_B(P))) & \{\text{Theorem 8.1.3 and idemp of } and_B\} \\
= & (\mathbf{R3} \circ \mathbf{R2})(\varrho_E(P)) & \{\varrho_E \text{ is disjunctive}\} \\
= & \mathbf{R3}(\varrho_E(\mathbf{R2}(P))) & \{\text{Theorem 8.1.3 and idemp of } \mathbf{R2}\} \\
= & \mathbf{R3}(\varrho_E(P)) & \{\text{idemp of } \mathbf{R3}\} \\
= & \varrho_E(P) &
\end{array}
$$

The interleaving operator $|||$ preserves the conditions **R2** and **R3** because

$$
\begin{array}{lll}
& \mathbf{R3}(\mathbf{R2}(P|||Q)) & \{||| \text{ is disjunctive}\} \\
= & \mathbf{R3}(\mathbf{R2}(P)|||\mathbf{R2}(Q)) & \{P \text{ and } Q \text{ satisfy } \mathbf{R2}\} \\
= & \mathbf{R3}(P|||Q) & \{\text{def of } \mathbf{R3}\} \\
= & \Pi \lhd wait \rhd (P|||Q) & \{\Pi|||\Pi \; = \; \Pi\} \\
= & (\Pi|||\Pi) \lhd wait \rhd (P|||Q) & \{P \text{ and } Q \text{ satisfy } \mathbf{R3}\} \\
= & (P|||Q) \lhd wait \rhd (P|||Q) & \{2.1\mathbf{L1}\} \\
= & P|||Q &
\end{array}
$$

From the fact that $(tr \leq tr')|||(tr \leq tr') \; = \; (tr \leq tr')$ we conclude that $|||$ also preserves **R1**.

In a similar way we can prove $\|$ preserves the healthiness conditions. □

ACP does not model non-determinism directly, and does not include disjunction as an operator. Furthermore, there is no concept of an ordering defined between processes. Thus it is not possible to define recursion by means of a strongest or a weakest fixed point. Instead, ACP restricts the use of recursion to cases when it is known that there exists exactly one fixed point of the defining equation. The technique is to ensure by a textual check that a process always engages in a visible action before invoking a recursion. Thus no empty sequence of actions is possible. Every other trace has a finite length n, so it is always possible to tell whether that trace is possible for a recursively defined process by unfolding the recursion just n times.

Definition 8.1.12 (Guarded recursion)

Let X be a process variable, and let $P(X)$ be a process expression. $P(X)$ is *guarded* if it is a head normal form. Then the notation $\mu X_{\mathbf{Rea}} \bullet P(X)$ stands for the weakest reactive process satisfying the recursive equation

$$X \;=\; P(X) \qquad \Box$$

Theorem 8.1.13 (Unique fixed point of guarded recursion)

If $P(X)$ is guarded then $\mu X_{\mathbf{Rea}} \bullet P(X) \;=\; \nu X_{\mathbf{Rea}} \bullet P(X)$.

Proof Define for $n \geq 0$

$$E_n =_{df} \; (tr \leq tr') \wedge (\#tr' < \#tr + n)$$

Clearly $E = \{E_n \mid n \geq 0\}$ is an approximation chain (Definition 2.7.3) for

$$C = (tr \leq tr')$$

Because P is guarded we have

$$P(X) \wedge E_{n+1} = P(X \wedge E_n) \wedge E_{n+1}$$

for all X and n. From Theorem 2.7.6 it follows that

$$C \wedge \mu X_{\mathbf{Rea}} \bullet P(X) = C \wedge \nu X_{\mathbf{Rea}} \bullet P(X)$$

The conclusion follows directly from the healthiness condition (**R1**). $\Box$

Corollary

If $P(X)$ is guarded then $\mu X_{\mathbf{Rea}} \bullet P(X) \;= \Phi(\mu X_{\mathbf{Rea}} \bullet P(X))$.

Proof From the fact that **ACP** $\subseteq$ **Rea** it follows that

$$\nu X_{\mathbf{Rea}} \bullet P \sqsupseteq \nu_{\mathbf{ACP}}\, X \bullet P \sqsupseteq \mu_{\mathbf{ACP}}\, X \bullet P \sqsupseteq \mu X_{\mathbf{Rea}} \bullet P \;=\; \nu X_{\mathbf{Rea}} \bullet P \qquad \Box$$

Example 8.1.14 (Bag)

The guarded recursive equation

$$BAG \;=\; in.0; (out.0 ||_{ACP} BAG) \;+\; in.1; (out.1 ||_{ACP} BAG)$$

describes the process behaviour of a bag that may contain finitely many instances of data 0 and 1. The actions $in.0$ and $out.0$ are putting a 0 into the bag and getting a 0 from the bag respectively, and likewise for $in.1$ and $out.1$. $\Box$

Example 8.1.15 (Queue)

Let T be a finite set of data. The alphabet consists of read actions $r.d$ and write actions $w.d$ for $d \in T$. Consider the following family of guarded recursive equations

$$Q_{<>} = \Sigma_{d \in T}\,(r.d\,;\,Q_{<d>})$$

$$Q_{<d>^\frown u} = w.d\,;\,Q_u + \Sigma_{e \in T}\,(r.e\,;\,Q_{<d>^\frown u^\frown <e>})$$

They specify the process behaviour of an unbounded buffer which reads and writes the data of the set T. What it writes is always an initial segment of what it reads; the balance is stored in a queue for later output on demand. □

Finally, we show how to convert a finite ACP process into normal form.

Theorem 8.1.16 (Normal form reduction)

Every finite ACP process can be transformed into head normal form algebraically.

Proof Let P and Q be normal forms. From Definition 8.1.8 it is clear that $P+Q$ is also in normal form. $P;Q$ can be transformed into normal form by using **L6**. Applying **L7** and **L8** allows us to convert $(P|||Q)$ and $(P||_{ACP}Q)$ into normal form respectively. **L9** indicates that $\varrho_E(P)$ can be rewritten as a normal form. □

8.2 Communicating Sequential Processes (CSP)

The theory of CSP [32, 78, 88] was developed to reason about the behaviour of a network of microprocessors, communicating along the wires which connect them. In addition, each microprocessor is capable of executing one or more normal sequential programs, with internal parallelism simulated by timesharing, and internal communication simulated by copying between storage locations. It was very important that the theory should maintain a level of abstraction at which the same program could be executed interchangeably on single processors or on multiple processors, without any discernible change to its logical behaviour. Only this makes it safe to improve performance of a correct program by adjusting the architecture, the number of processors, and the network of interconnections.

In order to accommodate sequential programs as part of a system of communicating processes, it was essential that CSP should allow a process that engages only on internal computations, even if it never engages in communication. The simplest example is $SKIP$, the unit of sequential composition. Such a process violates the healthiness condition **ACP1** of ACP. In addition, unification with the sequential language requires the addition of ok and ok', to the alphabet, as well as the $wait$ and $wait'$ of ACP. But ok' and $wait'$ can be both false, indicating that the process never reaches a stable state. This is what happens on divergence.

Since sequential programs can diverge, there is no reason to exclude this possibility for communicating processes. Indeed, it is no longer possible to rely on guarded recursions to ensure uniqueness of fixed points, and the general theory of weakest fixed points must be used. As a result, CSP is able to model the possibility of livelock, which occurs when a process expends an unlimited amount of resource on internal concealed communication, without ever making externally perceived progress, or ever reaching a stable or terminated state.

These are the main differences between CSP and ACP. But their similarities are much more significant. A process in CSP certainly conforms to the healthiness conditions **R1** to **R3** for reactive processes. Furthermore, it also conforms to the basic healthiness conditions **H1** and **H2** of sequential processes given in Section 3.2, that it makes no prediction about a process that has not started, and it is also monotonic in the variable ok'.

CSP1 $P \;=\; or_Q(P)$, where

$$Q \;=_{df}\; \neg ok \wedge (tr \leq tr')$$

CSP2 $P \;=\; post_J(P)$, where

$$J \;=_{df}\; (ok \Rightarrow ok') \wedge (v' = v) \wedge (tr' = tr) \wedge (wait' = wait) \wedge (ref' = ref)$$

Definition 8.2.1 (CSP process)

A reactive process P is a CSP process if it satisfies **CSP1** and **CSP2**. □

Theorem 8.2.2 (Closure of CSP processes)

CSP processes form a complete lattice, which is closed under sequential composition. It also contains $\mathbf{R}(x := e)$ where x is any list of stored program variables, and **R** has been defined in Theorem 8.0.2.

Proof The first conclusion follows from the fact that P is a CSP process **iff**

$$P \;=\; \mathbf{R}(\neg P[false/wait,\, false/ok'] \vdash P[false/wait,\, true/ok'])$$

The second conclusion can be proved in a similar way to Theorem 8.1.3. □

Examples 8.2.3

(1) The deadlock process $STOP$ is incapable of communicating with its environment, and always stays in a waiting state

$$STOP \;=_{df}\; \mathbf{CSP1}(ok' \wedge \delta) \;=\; \mathbf{R}(wait := true)$$

(2) The process $a \to SKIP$ waits to perform a communication event a at the very beginning. After engaging in that event it terminates successfully.

$$a \to SKIP \;=_{df}\; \mathbf{CSP1}(ok' \wedge do_{\mathcal{A}}(a))$$

where $do_{\mathcal{A}}(a)$ was defined in Example 8.1.4.

(3) The process $SKIP$ refuses to engage in any communication event, but terminates immediately.

$$SKIP \;=_{df}\; \mathbf{R}(\exists ref \bullet I\!I)$$

Existential quantification indicates that the initial value of ref is entirely irrelevant, as discussed again in Definition 8.2.16.

(4) Defined as the weakest fixed point of the monotonic mapping $\mathbf{R}$, $CHAOS$ is the worst CSP process.

$$CHAOS \;=_{df}\; \mathbf{R}(\mathbf{true})$$

Note that this is strictly stronger than **true**. Not even $CHAOS$ is allowed to undo events that have already happened. For this reason $CHAOS$ is not a right zero of sequential composition. □

Exercise 8.2.4

Prove that $\lhd STOP \rhd$ preserves **CSP1** but not **CSP2**. □

Both $CHAOS$ and $STOP$ are left zeros of sequential composition of CSP processes.

L1 $CHAOS; P \;=\; CHAOS$

L2 $STOP; P \;=\; STOP$

The CSP prefix operator is defined in the same way as in ACP. The process $a \to P$ is willing to engage in the event a at the very beginning. After performing that event it behaves like P.

Definition 8.2.5 (Prefix)

Let $a \in \mathcal{A}P$.

$$a \to P \;=_{df}\; (a \to SKIP); P$$

$$\mathcal{A}(a \to P) \;=_{df}\; \mathcal{A}P$$ □

CSP is closed under the prefix operator $a \to$ because it is closed under sequential composition. Clearly, the prefix operator is disjunctive.

Example 8.2.6 (Clock)

Consider a perpetual clock which never does anything but tick

$$\mathcal{A}(CLOCK) \ =_{df} \ \{tick\}$$

Consider next a process that behaves exactly like the clock, except that it first emits a single tick

$$tick \rightarrow CLOCK$$

The behaviour of this process is indistinguishable from that of the original clock. This reasoning leads to the following definition of $CLOCK$

$$CLOCK \ = \ \mu X_{\mathbf{CSP}} \bullet (tick \rightarrow X) \qquad \square$$

The external choice operator of CSP is denoted by $[\!]$. In order to deal with $SKIP$ and $CHAOS$, its definition is slightly more complicated than that of ACP. In particular, if either operand is $CHAOS$, so is the result, and if either of them is $SKIP$, the result may non-deterministically be $SKIP$. These effects are achieved simply by applying the relevant healthiness condition.

Definition 8.2.7 (External choice)

Let $\mathcal{A}P \ = \ \mathcal{A}Q$. Then

$$P[\!]Q \ =_{df} \ \mathbf{CSP2}((P \wedge Q) \lhd STOP \rhd (P \vee Q)) \qquad \square$$

Theorem 8.2.8

The set of CSP processes is closed under the external choice operator $[\!]$.

Proof From the idempotency of the embedding **CSP2** and Exercise 8.2.4. $\square$

The external choice operator $[\!]$ enjoys almost the same algebraic laws as the ACP + operator: it is idempotent, commutative and associative, and has the deadlock process $STOP$ as its unit. Furthermore, it distributes over $\sqcap$ and the other way round.

L3 $(P \sqcap Q)[\!]R \ = \ (P[\!]R) \sqcap (Q[\!]R)$

L4 $P \sqcap (Q[\!]R) \ = \ (P \sqcap Q)[\!](P \sqcap R)$

If one component can terminate at the very beginning, then the alternative composition may terminate immediately.

L5 $P[\!]SKIP \ \sqsubseteq \ SKIP$

Let $E = \{a_1, \ldots, a_n\}$ be a set of events. We use the notation

$$x : E \to P(x)$$

to denote *guarded choice*

$$(a_1 \to P(a_1)) \,[\!]\, (a_2 \to P(a_2)) \,[\!]\, \ldots \,[\!]\, (a_n \to P(a_n))$$

Sequential composition distributes over guarded choice.

L6 $(x : E \to P(x)); Q \;=\; x : E \to (P(x); Q)$

However, sequential composition does not in general distribute backward through the external choice operator in CSP, because one of its components may be $SKIP$, which by **L5** may occur non-deterministically. The relevant law is

$$((a \to SKIP) \,[\!]\, SKIP); (b \to Q) \;=\; ((a \to b \to Q) \,[\!]\, (b \to Q)) \sqcap (b \to Q)$$

If the environment refuses a, the only possibility is $(b \to Q)$. Otherwise, the event a may happen, but it does not have to; $(b \to Q)$ may be chosen instead, which will result in deadlock if the environment refuses b.

Example 8.2.9

A copying process engages in the following events

in.0	input of zero on its input channel
in.1	input of one on its input channel
out.0	output of zero on its output channel
out.1	output of one on its output channel

Its behaviour consists of a repetition of pairs of events. On each cycle, it inputs a bit and outputs the same bit

$$COPYBIT \;=_{df}\; \mu X_{\mathbf{CSP}} \bullet (in.0 \to out.0 \to X \,[\!]\, in.1 \to out.1 \to X)$$

Note how this process allows its environment to choose which value should be input, but no choice is offered in the case of output. This distinction between input and output will be developed in Section 8.3. □

The CSP interleaving operator is defined in the same way as its ACP counterpart: it joins processes with the same alphabet to be executed concurrently without interacting or synchronisation. In this case, each action of the system is an action of exactly one process. An interleaving composition enters a divergent state when one of its components becomes chaotic. In that case, the only sure fact is that initial value of the trace cannot be shortened.

Definition 8.2.10 (Interleaving)

Let $\mathcal{A}P = \mathcal{A}Q$. Define

$$\mathcal{A}(P|||Q) =_{df} \mathcal{A}P = \mathcal{A}Q$$
$$P|||Q =_{df} (P\|_M Q)$$

where the merge operation M is defined by

$$M =_{df} (M_{ACP} \wedge ok' = (0.ok \wedge 1.ok)); SKIP$$

where M_{ACP} was defined in Definition 8.1.8. □

Theorem 8.2.11

The set of CSP processes is closed under the interleaving operator $|||$.

Proof $\quad P|||Q$ {Def. 8.2.10}

$= P \|_M Q$ {P and Q satisfy **CSP1**}

$= \mathbf{R}(ok \Rightarrow P) \|_M \mathbf{R}(ok \Rightarrow Q)$ {7.1**L5**–**L6**}

$= \mathbf{R}(\mathbf{R1}(ok \Rightarrow P)\|_M \mathbf{R1}(ok \Rightarrow Q))$ {$\|_M$ is disjunctive}

$= \mathbf{R}((\mathbf{R1}(\neg ok)|||\mathbf{R1}(\neg ok)) \vee (P|||Q))$ {Def. 8.2.10}

$= \mathbf{R}(\mathbf{R1}(\neg ok) \vee (P|||Q))$ {**R1** is idemp, **R** is disj}

$= \mathbf{R}(ok \Rightarrow (P|||Q))$ □

Interleaving composition is commutative and disjunctive, and has the following expansion law

L7 Let $P = (x : A \rightarrow P(x))$ and $Q = (y : B \rightarrow Q(y))$.

Then $P|||Q = (x : A \rightarrow (P(x)|||Q)) \,[\!]\, (y : B \rightarrow (P|||Q(y)))$

CSP parallel composition is used to model interaction and synchronisation between concurrent processes. The parallel system $P\|_{CSP}Q$ executes P and Q in such a way that actions in the alphabet of both components require simultaneous participation of them both, whereas the remaining events of the system occur in an arbitrary interleaving. The system terminates after both P and Q have terminated successfully, and it becomes divergent after either one of its components does so.

Definition 8.2.12 (Parallel composition)

$$\mathcal{A}(P\|_{CSP}Q) =_{df} \mathcal{A}P \cup \mathcal{A}Q$$
$$P\|_{CSP}Q =_{df} P\|_N Q$$

where

$$\begin{aligned} N =_{df} \ & (ok' = (0.ok \wedge 1.ok) \wedge \\ & wait' = (0.wait \vee 1.wait) \wedge \\ & ref' = (0.ref \cup 1.ref) \wedge \\ & \exists u \bullet (u \downarrow \mathcal{A}P = (0.tr - tr) \ \wedge \ u \downarrow \mathcal{A}Q = (1.tr - tr) \wedge \\ & \qquad u \downarrow \mathcal{A}(P \| Q) = u \ \wedge \ tr' = tr ^\frown u)) \ ; \\ & SKIP \end{aligned}$$ □

Like the interleaving operator, the CSP parallel operator is commutative and disjunctive.

Theorem 8.2.13

The set of CSP processes is closed under the parallel operator $\|_{CSP}$.

Proof Similar to Theorem 8.2.11. □

Let E be a set of events which are regarded as internal events of a process P; for example, they may be interactions between component processes from which P is composed. We want the events of E to occur silently and automatically whenever they can, without the participation or even the knowledge of the environment of P. We use

$$P \backslash E$$

to denote the resultant process. $P\backslash E$ can reach a stable state only when P is stable and unable to perform any event of E; if any internal event can happen, P is obviously unstable until after it does. $P\backslash E$ becomes divergent when P does, and it terminates when P has terminated successfully.

Definition 8.2.14 (Hiding)

$$\mathcal{A}(P\backslash E) =_{df} \mathcal{A}P - E$$

$$P(tr', ref')\backslash E =_{df} \mathbf{R}(\exists s \bullet P(s, E \cup ref') \wedge L); \ SKIP$$

where $L =_{df} (tr' - tr) = (s - tr) \downarrow (\mathcal{A}P - E)$ □

Like the abstraction operator in ACP, the CSP hiding operator is associative and disjunctive. Furthermore, it does not affect the behaviour of $SKIP$ and $CHAOS$, and it distributes over prefixing.

L8 $(a \to Q)\backslash E \ = \ a \to (Q\backslash E), \quad$ if $a \notin E$

Examples 8.2.15

(1) $(\mu X_{\mathbf{CSP}}(a \to X))\backslash\{a\} \ = \ CHAOS$

(2) $(\bigsqcap_n P_n)\backslash\{a\} \ = \ STOP$, where $P_0 = STOP$ and $P_{n+1} = a \to P_n$. □

In the proof of Example 8.2.15(1) we need to allow tr to range over infinite traces as well as finite. The infinite trace consisting of all the a is not ruled out by the weakest fixed point $\mu X \bullet (a \to X)$, but the value $ok' = false$ is also not ruled out. This possibility of divergence is turned into the actual $CHAOS$ by the $SKIP$ which is included in Definition 8.2.14.

Theorem 8.2.16

The set of CSP processes is closed under the hiding operator $\backslash E$.

Proof From Definition 8.2.14 it follows that the hiding operator preserves the healthiness condition **CSP2**.

$$
\begin{array}{lll}
& P(tr', ref')\backslash E & \{\text{Def. 8.2.14}\} \\
= & \mathbf{R}(\exists s \bullet P(s,\ E \cup ref') \wedge L); SKIP & \{P \text{ satisfies } \mathbf{CSP1}\} \\
= & \mathbf{R}(\exists s \bullet \mathbf{R}(ok \Rightarrow P)(s,\ E \cup ref') \wedge L); SKIP & \{\mathbf{R1},\ \mathbf{R3} \text{ are idemp and disj}\} \\
= & \mathbf{R}(\exists s \bullet \mathbf{R2}(ok \Rightarrow P)(s,\ E \cup ref') \wedge L); SKIP & \{\neg ok \text{ and } P \text{ satisfy } \mathbf{R2}\} \\
= & \mathbf{R}(\exists s \bullet (ok \Rightarrow P)(s,\ E \cup ref') \wedge L); SKIP & \{\text{Theorem 8.0.3 and def of } L\} \\
= & \mathbf{R}((\neg ok); SKIP \vee P(tr', ref')\backslash E) & \{(\neg ok); SKIP \ = \ \neg ok\} \\
= & \mathbf{CSP1}(P(tr', ref')\backslash E) & \square
\end{array}
$$

In spite of all the healthiness conditions introduced above for CSP, there are still many laws of the standard theory of CSP that cannot be proved when the operands are general predicates rather than programmable processes. In the remainder of this section we will present many of the additional healthiness conditions that are required. Adopting the technique of Chapter 3 used in describing healthiness conditions of the sequential programming language, we will introduce a set of monotonic weakening idempotent mappings, each of which embeds CSP processes into a complete lattice of processes with a given healthiness condition. We will also show how each individual healthiness condition can be characterised by a specific algebraic law.

Definition 8.2.17

A CSP process P is **CSP3** if its behaviour does not depend on the initial value of ref, that is it satisfies

$$\mathbf{CSP3} \quad \neg wait \ \Rightarrow \ (P \ = \ \exists ref \bullet P)$$

The antecedent $\neg wait$ is necessary for the same reason as the healthiness condition (**R3**). $\square$

Examples 8.2.18

$SKIP$, $STOP$, $CHAOS$ and $a \rightarrow P$ are **CSP3**. □

Theorem 8.2.19

P is **CSP3** **iff** it satisfies the left unit law

L9 $SKIP; P \ = \ P$ □

CSP3 is not only a desirable condition in itself; it is also needed to prove the important expansion law for $||$, and other obvious distribution laws for hiding.

Theorem 8.2.20 (Algebraic properties of **CSP3** processes)

Let $P(x)$ and $Q(y)$ and U be **CSP3**, for all x and y.

Let $P \ = \ (x : A \rightarrow P(x))$ and $Q \ = \ (y : B \rightarrow Q(y))$. Then

L10 $$P||_{CSP}Q = (x : (A - B) \rightarrow (P(x)||_{CSP}Q)) \,[\!]\, (y : (B - A) \rightarrow (P||_{CSP}Q(y))) \,[\!]\, (z : (A \cap B) \rightarrow (P(z)||_{CSP}Q(z)))$$

L11 $(a \rightarrow U)\backslash E \ = \ U\backslash E, \quad \text{if } a \in E$

L12 Let $A \cap E \ = \ \{\}$ and $B \ \subseteq \ E$ and $S \ = \ \sqcap_{y \in B} (Q(y)\backslash E)$.

Then $(P[\!]Q)\backslash E \ = \ ((x : A \rightarrow (P(x)\backslash E))[\!]S) \sqcap S$

As described before (under **L6**), the environment cannot force the occurrence of an event a in A, unless it is acceptable to S as well. In that case, choice between S and $P(x)$ is non-deterministic. □

Definition 8.2.21 (Right unit)

P is **CSP4** if it satisfies the right unit law

CSP4 $P; SKIP = P$ □

Example 8.2.22

$STOP$, $SKIP$, $CHAOS$ and $a \rightarrow SKIP$ are **CSP4**. □

Theorem 8.2.23 (Algebraic properties of **CSP4** processes)

Let P be **CSP4**, and let S and T be **CSP3** and **CSP4**. Then

L13 $P\backslash\{\} \ = \ P$

L14 $(S; T)\backslash E \ = \ (S\backslash E); (T\backslash E)$ □

The next healthiness condition says that if a process is deadlocked, and refusing some set of events offered by its environment, then it would clearly still be deadlocked in an environment which offers even fewer events.

Definition 8.2.24 (Refusal subset-closed)

P is **CSP5** if it satisfies the unit law of interleaving

CSP5 $P|||SKIP \;=\; P$ □

Exercise 8.2.25

Show that P satisfies **CSP5** **iff** it is a fixed point of the mapping $\mathbf{R3} \circ post_K$, where

$$K \;=_{df}\; \mathbf{R1}((\mathbf{true} \vdash (ref' \subseteq ref))_{+\{v,\,tr,\,wait\}})$$ □

Theorem 8.2.26 (Closure of healthy processes)

Processes of **CSPi** (for $\mathbf{i} = 3, 4, 5$) form a complete lattice, and all CSP operators preserve these healthiness conditions.

Proof The first conclusion comes from the fact that the mappings

$$\mathbf{CSP3} \;=_{df}\; pre_{SKIP}$$

$$\mathbf{CSP4} \;=_{df}\; post_{SKIP}$$

$$\mathbf{CSP5} \;=_{df}\; \mathbf{R3} \circ post_K$$

(which are used to characterise the healthiness conditions) are monotonic.

It is clear from the definitions of **CSP3**, **CSP4** and **CSP5** that sequential composition respects the healthiness conditions **CSP3** to **CSP5**.

The healthiness condition **CSP3** is preserved by $[\!]$, $|||$, $\|_{CSP}$ and $\backslash E$ because they are disjunctive.

Notice that

$$((ok \Rightarrow ok') \;\wedge\; (v' = v)); SKIP \;=\; SKIP; ((ok \Rightarrow ok') \;\wedge\; (v' = v)) \quad (\dagger)$$

$$\begin{array}{lll} & (P[\!]Q); SKIP & \{(\dagger)\} \\ = & \mathbf{CSP2}((P \wedge Q \lhd STOP \rhd P \vee Q) \,;\, SKIP) & \{STOP; SKIP \;=\; STOP\} \\ = & \mathbf{CSP2}((P \wedge Q) \lhd STOP \rhd ((P \vee Q); SKIP)) & \{P \text{ and } Q \text{ satisfy } \mathbf{CSP4}\} \\ = & \mathbf{CSP2}((P \wedge Q) \lhd STOP \rhd (P \vee Q)) & \{\text{Def. } 8.2.6\} \\ = & P[\!]Q & \end{array}$$

From the fact $SKIP; SKIP = SKIP$ it follows that $|||$, $\|$ and $\backslash E$ also preserve **CSP4**.

Assume that P and Q satisfy **CSP5**. From the definition of N we can show

$$N; K \;=\; (0.K \| 1.K); N \qquad (\ddagger)$$

$$\begin{aligned}
& \mathbf{R3}((P \|_{CSP} Q); K) && \{\text{Def. } 8.2.12\} \\
= \;& \mathbf{R3}((P \|_N Q); K) && \{(\ddagger)\} \\
= \;& \mathbf{R3}(((P; U0; 0.K) \| (Q; U1; 1.K)); N) && \{U0; 0.K = K; U0\} \\
= \;& \mathbf{R3}((P; K) \|_N (Q; K)) && \{P,\ Q \text{ satisfy } \mathbf{CSP5}\} \\
= \;& \mathbf{R3}(P \|_N Q) && \{\text{Theorem } 8.2.13\} \\
= \;& (P \|_{CSP} Q)
\end{aligned}$$

In a similar way we can also show the other finite CSP operators respect **CSP5**.

From the above proof we conclude that **CSP3**, **CSP4** and **CSP5** are all $\Sigma_{\sqsupseteq}$ links. From Theorem 4.1.15 it follows that the recursion also preserves the healthiness conditions **CSP3** to **CSP5**. □

We have omitted a number of important healthiness conditions, including the most familiar of all: that the set of traces of a process is *non-empty* and *prefix-closed*. For a full treatment see [160].

8.3* Data flow

A data flow network is one in which the channels along which the processes communicate are capable of buffering an arbitrary number of messages between the time that they are output and the time that they are needed for input. As a result, a network as a whole, when in a stable state, can never refuse to accept input (because all its components are waiting for input), nor will it ever wait to perform output (because its output channels are all buffered). Since we want to compose larger networks from smaller ones, we require all subnetworks, right down to the individual processes, to share the same properties. Among other benefits, this convention allows a distributed implementation to store the buffered messages either in the outputting processor or in the inputting processor, or partly in both.

The simplest possible example of a data flow process is a buffer $BUF_{\{a:c\}}$ with an input channel a and an output channel c. The buffer is at all times ready to accept a message from its input channel a, and (whenever possible) is ready to deliver to its output channel c the earliest message which has been input but not yet output. When there is no message left for output, the process $BUF_{\{a:c\}}$ enters a stable state in which it remains inactive unless it receives more input. In fact, each channel of a data flow network behaves just like this, so the only point of a buffer is to connect processes which use different names a and c for the channel along which they communicate. A more interesting process is one that applies some useful function to each message before sending it on (see Example 8.3.1(3)).

In previous sections we have introduced a general concept of an event as an action without duration, whose occurrences may require simultaneous participation by more than one independently described process. In this section we will concentrate on a special class of event known as a communication. A communication is an event that is described by a pair

$$c.m$$

where c is the name of channel on which the communication takes place and m is the value of the message which passes. The set of all messages which P can communicate on channel c is defined

$$\mathcal{A}_c(P) \;=_{df}\; \{m \mid c.m \in \mathcal{A}P\}$$

We also define functions which extract channel and message components of a communication

$$channel(c.m) = c \qquad\qquad message(c.m) = m$$

We will use the notation $inchan(P)$ to denote the set of channels used for input by P, and the notation $outchan(P)$ for the set of channels used for output by P respectively. Any channel can only be used in a single process either for input or for output, but not for both

$$inchan(P) \cap outchan(P) \;=\; \{\}$$

Example 8.3.1 (Output and input)

(1) Let $m \in \mathcal{A}_c(P)$. A process which first outputs m on the channel c and then behaves like P is defined

$$c!m \rightarrow P \;=_{df}\; c.m \rightarrow P$$

(2) A process which is initially prepared to input any value x communicable on the channel c, and then behaves like $P(x)$, is defined

$$c?x \rightarrow P(x) \;=_{df}\; (y : \{y | channel(y) = c\} \rightarrow P(message(y)))$$

(3) Inc applies the function $\lambda x \bullet (x+1)$ to each input message from channel d before outputting it to channel a. It behaves chaotically if the environment sends it two consecutive messages before it has completed the treatment of the first one.

$$Inc \;=\; \mu X_{\mathbf{CSP}} \bullet (d?x \rightarrow ((a!(x+1) \rightarrow X) [\!] (d?x \rightarrow CHAOS)))$$

This example models a communication channel (like a simple wire in hardware) which is incapable of buffering more than one message. The designer has to take the responsibility for avoiding buffer overflow. This general model has been developed as a theory for asynchronous circuit design [105, 181]. □

Let P and Q be CSP processes, and let c be a channel used for output by P and for input by Q. When these processes are composed concurrently in the system $P \|_{CSP} Q$, a communication $c.m$ can occur only when both processes engage simultaneously in that event, that is whenever P outputs a value m on the channel c, and Q simultaneously inputs the same value. An inputting process is prepared to accept any communicable value, so it is the outputting process that determines which actual message value is transmitted on each occasion, as in Example 8.2.9. Thus output may be regarded as a specialised case of the prefix operator, and input is a special case of choice; this leads to the law

L1 $(c!m \to Q) \|_{CSP} (c?x \to P(x)) \quad = \quad c!m \to (Q \|_{CSP} P(v))$

Note that $c!m$ remains on the right hand side of this equation as an observable action in the behaviour of the system. It is available for input by another process added to the system later. Multiple synchronised input of a single output is an occasionally useful feature of CSP. But when no more inputting processes are needed, such a communication event can be concealed by applying the hiding operator described in Section 8.2. Obviously, this can be done only outside the parallel composition of the two processes which communicate on the same channel. The effect is shown by the law

L2 $((c!m \to Q) \|_{CSP} (c?x \to P(x))) \backslash C \quad = \quad (Q \|_{CSP} P(m)) \backslash C$
where $C =_{df} \{c.m \mid m \in \mathcal{A}_c\}$

Example 8.3.2 (Buffer)

$BUF_{\{a:c\}}$ is at all times ready to input a message on the channel a, and to output on the channel c the first message which it has input but not yet output

$$\begin{aligned} inchan(BUF_{\{a:c\}}) &=_{df} \{a\} \\ outchan(BUF_{\{a:c\}}) &=_{df} \{c\} \\ BUF_{\{a:c\}} &=_{df} BUF_{\{a:c\}}(<>) \end{aligned}$$

where

$$\begin{aligned} BUF_{\{a:c\}}(<>) &= a?x \to BUF_{\{a:c\}}(< x >) \\ BUF_{\{a:c\}}(< x >\,\hat{}\,s) &= a?y \to BUF_{\{a:c\}}(< x >\,\hat{}\,s\,\hat{}\,< y >) \\ &\quad\ \| \ c!x \to BUF_{\{a:c\}}(s) \end{aligned}$$

The subscript of the buffer will be dropped if it is clear from the context. □

We now define a restricted form of parallel composition, in which data can flow only from the left operand to the right. Let P and Q be processes satisfying the following three conditions

(1) none of the output channels of Q is used for input by P, that is

$$outchan(Q) \cap inchan(P) \;=\; \{\}$$

(2) there is no input channel shared by P and Q

$$inchan(P) \cap inchan(Q) \;=\; \{\}$$

(3) no channel is used for output by both P and Q

$$outchan(P) \cap outchan(Q) \;=\; \{\}$$

The processes P and Q can be joined together so that the output channels of P are connected to the like-named input channels of Q, and the messages output by P and input by Q on these internal channels are concealed from the environment. The result of the connection is denoted

$$P \gg Q$$

and may be pictured as the series shown in Figure 8.3.3.

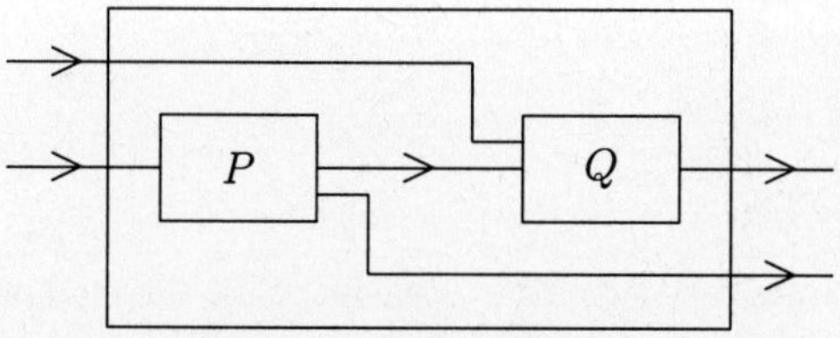

Figure 8.3.3 $P \gg Q$

Definition 8.3.4 (Chain)

$$\begin{aligned} inchan(P \gg Q) \;&=_{df}\; inchan(P) \cup (inchan(Q) \setminus outchan(P)) \\ outchan(P \gg Q) \;&=_{df}\; outchan(Q) \cup (outchan(P) \setminus inchan(Q)) \\ P \gg Q \;&=_{df}\; (P \|_{CSP} Q)\backslash C \end{aligned}$$

where $C \;=_{df}\; \bigcup\{c.m \mid m \in \mathcal{A}_c \,\wedge\, c \in outchan(P) \cap inchan(Q)\}$ □

Like sequential composition, the chaining operator is associative and disjunctive.

L3 $(P \gg Q) \gg R \;=\; P \gg (Q \gg R)$

L4a $(P_1 \sqcap P_2) \gg Q \;=\; (P_1 \gg Q) \sqcap (P_2 \gg Q)$

L4b $P \gg (Q_1 \sqcap Q_2) \;=\; (P \gg Q_1) \sqcap (P \gg Q_2)$

The following laws are useful in deriving further properties of BUF and the chaining operator.

L5 If any two of P, Q, $P \gg Q$ are buffers, then so is the third.

L6 If $P_s \gg Q_s$ is a buffer with an input channel a and an output channel c for all $s \in S$, then for any function $g : \mathcal{A}_a \rightarrow S$ the process

$$a?x \rightarrow (P_{g(x)} \gg (c!x \rightarrow Q_{g(x)}))$$

is a buffer.

If a buffer holds a message, then either an input from the input channel or the output of the stored message may happen first.

L7 $BUF(< x >) \;=\; BUF \gg (c!x \rightarrow BUF)$

Proof

$$\begin{aligned} & a?x \rightarrow BUF(< x >) && \{\text{def of } BUF\} \\ = \;& BUF && \{\textbf{L5} \text{ and } \textbf{L6}\} \\ = \;& a?x \rightarrow (BUF \gg (c!x \rightarrow BUF)) && \square \end{aligned}$$

If P is a CSP process, a buffer can be attached to each of its input and output channels, giving a result which is a data flow process. The buffer ensures that it is willing to receive input at any time, and its output channels can buffer an arbitrary number of outgoing messages. Using such a buffer interface we are able to model data flow processes as a simple closed class of CSP processes.

Definition 8.3.5 (Data flow)

A CSP process P is a data flow process if it satisfies the defining equation $P = [P]$, where

$$[P] =_{df} IN \gg P' \gg OUT$$

where IN and OUT are families of buffers attached to channels of P

$$\begin{aligned} IN &=_{df} \|_{CSP}\{BUF_{\{a:a'\}} \mid a \in inchan(P)\} \\ OUT &=_{df} \|_{CSP}\{BUF_{\{c':c\}} \mid c \in outchan(P)\} \end{aligned}$$

and the process P' behaves the same as P except that all channel names are decorated with a dash. We adopt the convention $(c')' = c$, so $(P')' = P$.

The defining equation is known as the Foam Rubber Wrapper postulate when used to characterise delay-insensitive circuits [105, 181]. For convenience the decoration $'$ in the defining equation will be dropped in the later discussion. $\square$

Because all input channels are buffered, a data flow process can never refuse an input. However, a stable process with an empty output buffer will refuse an output on that channel. When all its output buffers are empty, we say that a stable process is *quiescent*. A process reaches a quiescent state when it has finished all the tasks that are currently required of it; it will do no more until it has input some new task. For example, a buffer is quiescent just when it is empty, because then it has output everything that it has input. A process can be conveniently specified by just describing its quiescent states. We regard a process that never reaches a quiescent state to be like one that is livelocked or divergent.

Example 8.3.6

(1) The process $BUF(<m>)$ (which behaves like $BUF_{\{a:c\}}$ after receipt of a message m from input channel a) is a data flow process because

$$\begin{array}{lll} & BUF(<m>) & \{\mathbf{L5}\text{ and }\mathbf{L7}\} \\ = & BUF \gg BUF(<m>) & \{\mathbf{L2}\text{ and }\mathbf{L5}\} \\ = & BUF \gg (!m \to BUF) \gg BUF & \{\mathbf{L5}\text{ and }\mathbf{L7}\} \\ = & BUF \gg BUF(<m>) \gg BUF & \end{array}$$

(2) The process $SINK$ never performs any output (but of course must always accept input). It is always quiescent, and represents the deadlocked data flow process

$$SINK \ =_{df} \ IN \gg STOP \qquad \square$$

Theorem 8.3.7 (Closure of data flow processes)

Data flow processes form a complete lattice, which is closed under sequential composition, $\gg$ and $\backslash$.

Proof Here we are going to show that data flow machines are closed under $\gg$. Let $X =_{df} outchan(P) - inchan(Q)$ and $Y =_{df} inchan(Q) - outchan(P)$.

$$\begin{array}{lll} & IN \gg (P \gg Q) \gg OUT & \{\text{Def. } 8.3.5\} \\ = & (\|_{CSP}\{BUF_{\{a:a'\}} \mid a \in inchan(P)\}) \gg P & \\ & \gg (\|_{CSP}\{BUF_{\{c':c\}} \mid c \in X\}) \gg (\|_{CSP}\{BUF_{\{a:a'\}} \mid a \in Y\}) & \\ & \gg Q \gg (\|_{CSP}\{BUF_{\{c':c\}} \mid c \in outchan(Q)\}) & \{\mathbf{L5}\} \\ = & P \gg Q & \square \end{array}$$

Note that $SKIP$ is not a data flow process. The problem cannot be solved by closure, because

$$[SKIP] \ = \ SINK$$

and so every terminated program would behave like $SINK$. Furthermore, sequential composition becomes void since for all data flow processes P and Q

$$P;Q \ = \ P$$

Data flow processes are not even closed under input or output (Example 8.3.1). This is because in CSP all communications are synchronised, whereas in data flow outputs can occur instantaneously. This effect is modelled in the following definition by reclosure after prefixing. From now on, we will use the word process simply to mean a data flow process.

Definition 8.3.8 (Output prefix)

Let P be a process and let $c \in outchan(P)$. The process $c!m \rightsquigarrow P$ behaves like P, but with one more message m inserted in front of the output buffer on channel c. It is not quiescent, and will not become so until that message has been accepted by the environment.

$$c!m \rightsquigarrow P \;=_{df}\; (c!m \rightarrow P) \gg OUT$$

Here we use a curly arrow notation $\rightsquigarrow$ to distinguish buffered communication from the fully synchronised type. □

The order in which a process transmits messages on distinct channels is not significant, because it does not determine the order in which the messages are received by the environment.

L8 $c!m \rightsquigarrow (d!n \rightsquigarrow P) \;=\; d!n \rightsquigarrow (c!m \rightsquigarrow P), \qquad \text{if } c \neq d$

As in CSP, output prefix is distributive.

L9 $c!m \rightsquigarrow (P \sqcap Q) \;=\; (c!m \rightsquigarrow P) \sqcap (c!m \rightsquigarrow Q)$

We have defined output prefix in a way that allows a process that is capable of diverging to corrupt any value buffered by its output channel, before the environment has received it. As a result, output prefix is strict

L10 $c!m \rightsquigarrow CHAOS \;=\; CHAOS$

Examples 8.3.9

(1) The process $c!0 \rightsquigarrow SINK$ outputs 0 once on channel c, and then deadlocks.

(2) The process $\mu X \bullet (c!0 \rightsquigarrow X)$ is equivalent to $CHAOS$. This gives a clear warning of the danger that the process can overflow any finite amount of buffering that it may be given. □

Example 8.3.9(2) illustrates an obligation placed upon the programmer to fix a bound on the amount of data that needs to be stored in the buffer before quiescence. So a process that inputs only a finite number of times must not output infinitely often. Alternative models of data flow incorporate a concept of fairness, which places the obligation to avoid infinite buffer filling upon the implementor [?]. But it is not easy to combine this kind of infinite fairness with non-determinism, and we shall not do it.

The definition of input is similar to that for output. However, it starts in a quiescent state, and will remain so until it accepts a message on channel c. Messages on other channels will be accepted, but they will be simply buffered for later consumption. That is why closure is needed in the following definition.

Definition 8.3.10 (Input prefix)

Let $a \in inchan(Q(m))$ for all m. The process $a?x \leadsto Q(x)$ will wait until its environment sends a message (say m) on channel a, and then it will behave like the process $Q(m)$

$$a?x \leadsto Q(x) \;=_{df}\; IN \gg (a?x \rightarrow Q(x)) \qquad \square$$

If a process must wait for input on two different channels before it can continue, it does not matter which of the two channels it waits on first. This means that internal choice is not so often explicitly needed in data flow.

L11 $a?x \leadsto (b?y \leadsto P(x,\, y)) \;=\; b?y \leadsto (a?x \leadsto P(x,\, y)), \qquad \text{if } a \neq b$

The following distributive law suggests that a non-deterministic choice can be made before or after receipt of an input.

L12 $(a?x \leadsto P(x)) \sqcap (a?x \leadsto Q(x)) \;=\; a?x \leadsto (P(x) \sqcap Q(x))$

A process that waits for input on channel a and then deadlocks cannot be distinguished from the process $SINK$, since the latter is always waiting for input on any channel. Thus input prefix has $SINK$ as its zero

L13 $(a?x \leadsto SINK) \;=\; SINK$

Examples 8.3.11

(1) The process *Copy* copies data from input channel c to output channel d

$$Copy \;=_{df}\; \mu X \bullet (c?x \leadsto (d!x \leadsto X))$$

As a data flow process, it behaves the same as $BUF_{\{c:d\}}$.

(2) A *Delay* element in hardware is one that outputs on each step the same message on channel d that it has input on the previous step from channel c

$$Delay \;=_{df}\; c?x \leadsto Delay(x)$$

$$Delay(x) \;=_{df}\; c?y \leadsto (d!x \leadsto Delay(y))$$

(3) The *Fork* process receives each input item on channel a and outputs it to both channels c and d

$$Fork_{\{a:c,d\}} \;=_{df}\; \mu X \bullet (a?x \leadsto (c!x \leadsto d!x \leadsto X)) \qquad \square$$

Examples 8.3.12

(1) Processes $Copy_1$ and $Copy_2$ have input channel c and output channel d. Both processes produce exactly two items x and y as output along c provided they have received x and y as inputs. But $Copy_1$ will produce its first output as soon as it receives its first input, while $Copy_2$ will not produce any output until it has received two input values.

$$Copy_1 \;=_{df}\; c?x \rightsquigarrow d!x \rightsquigarrow c?y \rightsquigarrow d!y \rightsquigarrow SINK$$

$$Copy_2 \;=_{df}\; c?x \rightsquigarrow c?y \rightsquigarrow d!x \rightsquigarrow d!y \rightsquigarrow SINK$$

$Copy_2$ (but not $Copy_1$) has a quiescent state after $< c.x >$, whereas $Copy_1$ is quiescent after $< c.x, d.x >$, which is not even a trace of $Copy_2$. The distinction between $Copy_1$ and $Copy_2$ cannot be made except by observing the relative order of communications on channel c and channel d.

(2) The process $Merge$ combines sequences of items received on two input channels a and b into a single output sequence on channel c. The output sequence produced in any quiescent state is always an interleaving of the two sequences that have been input so far. Note that this merge is fair, in the sense that it offers an external choice of which channel supplies its input. Furthermore, it never reaches a quiescent state until it has fully output all the messages from both its input channels. For most practical purposes, this is an adequate definition of fairness, with the possible advantage that it does not rely on reasoning about infinite behaviours.

$$Merge \;=_{df}\; [a?x \rightsquigarrow (c!x \rightsquigarrow Merge) \,\|\, b?y \rightsquigarrow (c!y \rightsquigarrow Merge)] \qquad \square$$

Let P and Q be CSP processes. For notational simplicity in later discussions we define their composite choice

$$P \oslash Q$$

as a mixture of external choice and internal choice. It describes a process that may either engage in an event acceptable to P and then behave like P, or make internal progress and then behave like Q. As shown in 8.2**L5** and 8.2**L12**, such a behaviour can result from concealment of some but not all of the actions in which a process is ready to engage.

Definition 8.3.13 (Composite choice)

$$P \oslash Q \;=_{df}\; (P \,\|\, Q) \sqcap Q \qquad \square$$

The following theorem states that the function [ ] distributes through prefixing and composite choice.

Theorem 8.3.14 (Distributivity of [ ])

(1) $[c!m \to Q] = [c!m \to [Q]] \;=\; c!m \leadsto [Q]$

(2) $[a?x \to P(x)] = [a?x \to [P(x)]] \;=\; a?x \leadsto [P(x)]$

(3) $[(\|a_i?x \to P(x)) \oslash Q] \;=\; [(\|a_i?x \to [P(x)]) \oslash [Q]]$

Proof of (1) Define

$$OUT(<c.m>) \;=_{df}\; BUF_{\{c':c\}}(<m>) \| (\|_{d \in outchan-\{c\}} BUF_{\{d':d\}})$$

$$\begin{aligned}
& [c!m \to Q] && \{\text{Def. 8.3.5}\} \\
= \; & IN \gg (c!m \to Q) \gg OUT && \{\mathbf{L2}\} \\
= \; & IN \gg Q \gg OUT(<c.m>) && \{\mathbf{L5} \text{ and } \mathbf{L7}\} \\
= \; & IN \gg [Q] \gg OUT(<c.m>) && \{\mathbf{L2}\} \\
= \; & IN \gg (c!m \to [Q]) \gg OUT && \{\text{Def. 8.3.5}\} \\
= \; & [c!m \to [Q]] && \{\text{Def. 8.3.8 and } \mathbf{L5}\} \\
= \; & c!m \leadsto [Q] && \square
\end{aligned}$$

It is often convenient to define the cyclic behaviour of a process before deciding at what point in its cycle it should start. The following definition gives a means of getting a process into its desired initial state: it provides an operator which is the inverse of input prefixing; it thereby also assists in reasoning about processes.

Definition 8.3.15 (After)

The process $P/a.m$ behaves like P behaves after it has accepted m on input channel a. The value m remains buffered by the channel until P is ready to use it.

$$P/a.m \;=_{df}\; BUF_{a,\hat{a}}(<m>) \gg P[\hat{a}/a]$$

where $P[\hat{a}/a]$ behaves the same as P except that channel a is renamed as $\hat{a}$. For notational simplicity we adopt the convention that

$$P/a.m \;=\; P$$

whenever $a \notin chan(P)$. $\square$

Theorem 8.3.16 (Well-definedness of the after operator)

$P/a.m$ is a data flow process.

Proof From Theorem 8.3.7 and the fact that $BUF_{\{a:\hat{a}\}}(<m>)$ is a data flow process. $\square$

The after operator is distributive and has both $CHAOS$ and $SINK$ as zeros.

L14 $CHAOS/a.m \;=\; CHAOS$

L15 $SINK/a.m \;=\; SINK$

Because distinct channels buffer their data independently of each other

L16 $(P/a.m)/b.n \;=\; (P/b.n)/a.m, \qquad \text{if } a \neq b$

The value made available to a process which starts with input on channel a is just the one buffered by the after operation

L17 $(a?x \rightsquigarrow P(x))/a.m \;=\; P(m)$

The after operator on a distributes through prefixing on channels other than a

L18 $(b?x \rightsquigarrow P(x))/a.m \;=\; b?x \rightsquigarrow (P(x)/a.m), \qquad \text{if } a \neq b$

L19 $(c!n \rightsquigarrow Q)/a.m \;=\; c!n \rightsquigarrow (Q/a.m), \qquad \text{if } a \neq c$

After also distributes over $\oslash$.

L20 $P/b.m \;=\; [(\|_{a \in A \setminus \{b\}}\, a?x \rightarrow (P_a(x)/b.m)) \;\oslash\; S]$

$$
\begin{aligned}
\text{where} \qquad P &=_{df} [(\|_{a \in A}\, a?x \rightarrow P_a(x)) \oslash Q] \\
S &=_{df} (Q/b.m) \sqcap P_b(m), && \text{if } b \in A \\
&=_{df} Q/b.m, && \text{if } b \notin A
\end{aligned}
$$

The chaining operator acts for data flow in the same way that sequential composition acts for control flow. They are both restricted to flow in a single direction. But more interesting programs can be written with the aid of a facility for constructing loops. In the case of data flow, this is done by a parallel combinator similar to that for CSP. The main difference is that multiple inputs of the same output require an explicit forking for desynchronisation.

Let P and Q be processes with disjoint output channels. The notation

$$P \|_{DF} Q$$

represents a network with nodes P and Q, where the like-named channels of P and Q are connected. If P and Q share an input channel a, then both P and Q will input all messages sent to the network on the channel a. Input by P and Q on a does not have to be synchronised; an implementation should copy all messages sent on a into two buffers, so that they can be consumed at different rates by P and Q (or it can achieve the same effect by two pointers, one for each inputting process). Furthermore, the components P and Q may communicate with each other along any channel c which is an output channel of one and an input channel of the other. In $P\|_{DF}Q$, the output on c is retained so that c may be connected to yet further input channels. Again, extra buffers are needed for desynchronisation. Thus the output alphabet of the network $P\|_{DF}Q$ is the union of its components' output channels

$$outchan(P\|_{DF}Q) \;=_{df}\; outchan(P) \cup outchan(Q)$$

The input alphabet of the network is

$$inchan(P\|_{DF}Q) \;=_{df}\; (inchan(P) \cup inchan(Q)) \setminus outchan(P\|_{DF}Q)$$

Clearly the network $P\|_{DF}Q$ may refuse to output whenever both P and Q so refuse. As a result, $P\|_{DF}Q$ reaches a quiescent state only when both P and Q become inactive and do not produce any more output.

Definition 8.3.17 (Parallel composition)

Let $A \;=\; inchan(P) \cap inchan(Q)$ be the set of shared input channels.

Let $outchan(P) \cap outchan(Q) \;=\; \{\}$.

$$P\|_{DF}Q \;=_{df}\; (\|_{CSP}\{Fork_{\{a:0.a,\,1.a\}} \mid a \in A\}) \gg (0.P\|_{CSP}1.Q) \gg OUT$$

where $0.P$ behaves like P except the input channel names of A are decorated with label 0, and $1.Q$ is defined in a similar way. □

Theorem 8.3.18 (Well-definedness of the parallel operator)

$P\|_{DF}Q$ is a data flow process. □

Parallel composition is commutative, associative and distributive, and has $CHAOS$ as its zero. The expansion laws for data flow parallelism are given in **L21** to **L26**. The first law states that it is immaterial whether two processes in parallel wait independently or together for input to become available on a shared channel

L21 $(a?x \leadsto P(x))\,\|_{DF}\,(a?y \leadsto Q(y)) \;=\; a?z \leadsto (P(z)\,\|_{DF}\,Q(z))$

Let $a \neq b$, and $P \;=\; (a?x \leadsto P(x))$ and $Q \;=\; (b?y \leadsto Q(y))$. If both processes are waiting for input from the external world on different channels a and b, either input may take place. Subsequently, the corresponding process uses the input value, while the other one saves it up for later use.

L22 If $a \notin outchan(Q)$ and $b \notin outchan(P)$

then $P\,\|_{DF}\,Q \;=\; [(a?x \leadsto (P(x)\,\|_{DF}\,(Q/a.x)))\;[\!]\;(b?y \leadsto (P/b.y\,\|_{DF}\,Q(y)))]$

If one process is waiting for input from the environment on channel a and the other one is waiting for input from its partner on channel c, then only input on a may take place.

L23 If $a \notin outchan(Q)$ and $b \in outchan(P)$
then $P \|_{DF} Q \;=\; a?x \rightsquigarrow (P(x) \|_{DF} (Q/a.x))$

If each process is waiting for input from the other, we have deadlock.

L24 If $a \in outchan(Q)$ and $b \in outchan(P)$
then $P \|_{DF} Q \;=\; SINK$

If one of the processes is prepared to output, this may happen straight away. The message is buffered by the other process for future consumption if relevant, and is ignored otherwise.

L25 $(c!m \rightsquigarrow P) \|_{DF} Q \;=\; c!m \rightsquigarrow (P \|_{DF} (Q/c.m))$

The final complicated expansion law shows how to convert a network of alternative compositions into a single composition.

L26 $P \|_{DF} Q \;=\; [(S \oslash T)]$

where
$$\begin{aligned}
P &=_{df} [(\|_{a \in A} a?x \to P_a(x)) \;\oslash\; U] \\
Q &=_{df} [(\|_{b \in B} b?y \to Q_b(y)) \;\oslash\; V] \\
S &=_{df} (\|_{a \in A \setminus outchan(Q)}\, a?x \to (P_a(x) \|_{DF} (Q/a.x))) \;\| \\
&\qquad (\|_{b \in B \setminus outchan(P)}\, b?y \to ((P/b.y) \|_{DF} Q_b(y))) \\
T &=_{df} (U \|_{DF} Q) \sqcap (P \|_{DF} V)
\end{aligned}$$

Concealment of an internal channel of an assembly requires systematic concealment of all possible values passing along the channel. It is convenient just to use the channel name for this, so we introduce the convention that

$$P \setminus \{c\} \quad \text{means} \quad P \setminus \{c.m \mid m \in \mathcal{A}_c(P)\}$$

and similarly for hiding a set C of channels. A hidden channel is used for output by (exactly) one of the component processes, and by definition of $\|_{DF}$ it is an output channel of the whole assembly. In fact we insist that only output channels are hidden, thus avoiding problems of massive non-determinism. Hiding as defined in CSP fortunately preserves the data flow process property. The algebraic properties of hiding in data flow are the ones already familiar from CSP.

L27 $(c!m \rightsquigarrow P) \setminus C \;=\; P \setminus C, \qquad \text{if } c \in C$

L28 $(d!m \rightsquigarrow P) \setminus C \;=\; d!m \rightsquigarrow (P \setminus C), \qquad \text{if } d \tilde{\in} C$

L29 $[(\|_{a\in A} a?x \to P_a(x)) \oslash Q]\backslash C \;=\; [(\|_{a\in A} a?x \to P_a(x)\backslash C) \oslash (Q\backslash C)]$

The hiding operator in data flow would have a much simpler definition if the single observable trace of our process model were split into a collection of traces, one for each channel of the alphabet. It is attractive to use the channel name itself to denote the sequence of values that have passed along it up to the time of the observation. Such a channel could then be hidden by simple existential quantification

$$P\backslash c \;=\; (\exists c, c' \bullet c = \langle\rangle \;\wedge\; P)$$

Specification could also be simpler: the copying process (Example 8.3.11(1)) is described just by the predicate, stating that the output is a prefix of the input

$$d \le c$$

Of course, it becomes impossible to describe the difference between $Copy_1$ and $Copy_2$ (Example 8.3.12(1)). Nevertheless, the simpler model works well for deterministic data flow; it fails only on introduction of external choice, as shown by the following example [31].

Example 8.3.19 (Brock–Ackerman anomaly)

Let $P_i = (Merge/b.5/b.5\|_{DF} Copy_i)\backslash\{c\}$, for $i = 1, 2$.

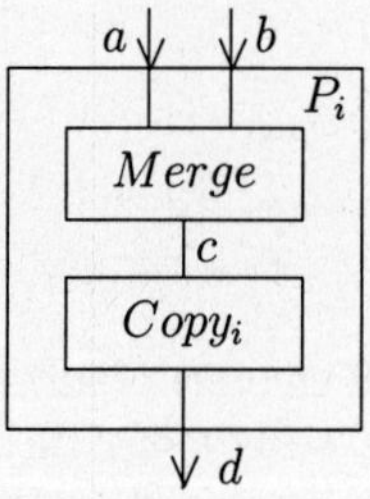

Figure 8.3.20 Data flow processes P_i

Using the algebraic laws we can show

$$\begin{aligned} P_1 \;&=\; [a?x \to d!x \rightsquigarrow [a?y \to (d!y \rightsquigarrow SINK) \oslash (d!5 \rightsquigarrow SINK)] \\ &\quad \oslash d!5 \rightsquigarrow [a?y \to (d!y \rightsquigarrow SINK) \oslash (d!5 \rightsquigarrow SINK)]] \end{aligned}$$

$$\begin{aligned} P_2 \;&=\; [a?x \to [(a?y \to d!x \rightsquigarrow d!y \rightsquigarrow SINK) \\ &\quad \oslash (d!x \rightsquigarrow d!5 \rightsquigarrow SINK \sqcap d!5 \rightsquigarrow d!x \rightsquigarrow SINK)] \\ &\quad \oslash d!5 \rightsquigarrow d!5 \rightsquigarrow SINK] \end{aligned}$$

It is evident that P_2 is strictly more deterministic than P_1, even though the processes have identical input–output histories when recorded in separate variables for each channel a and d. But the two processes *can* be distinguished in the environment which incorporates feedback on channel a as shown below

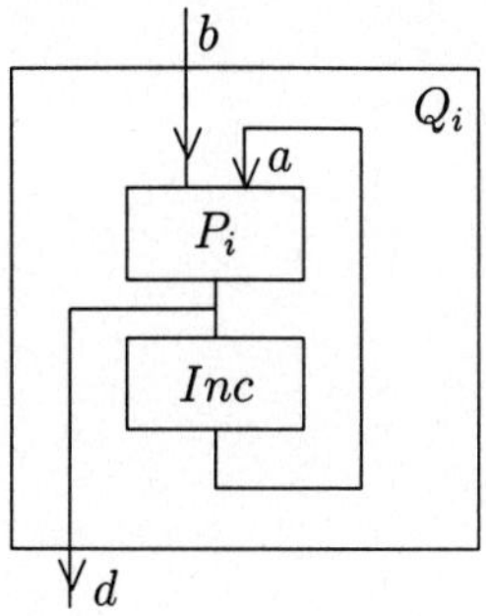

Figure 8.3.21 Data flow processes Q_i

where *Inc* was defined in Example 8.3.1(3). After some calculation we have

$$Q_1 = (d!5 \rightsquigarrow d!6 \rightsquigarrow SINK) \sqcap (d!5 \rightsquigarrow d!5 \rightsquigarrow SINK)$$
$$Q_2 = d!5 \rightsquigarrow d!5 \rightsquigarrow SINK$$

In a practical implementation, the extra non-determinism of Q_1 can hardly be avoided. That is why we need a more complex theory for non-deterministic data flow, one which describes relative ordering of input on different channels. □

In this section, the set of data flow processes has been shown to be a subset of CSP processes. But this embedding is of significant complexity: it is no more and no less than an implementation of data flow within CSP. Unfortunately, the complexity conceals much of the extra value that the theory of data flow offers to the system designer. The value consists in the greater abstraction that the data flow paradigm offers in the specification: only the quiescent states need to be described. Furthermore, no mention need be made of refusals, because no process can ever refuse to input; nor can it refuse to output except in a quiescent state, and then it refuses *all* outputs. The transition between two levels of abstraction is a major step, similar to the step made several times in hardware design, for example between logic design and switching circuit design.

Chapter 9

High Order Programming

First-order programming uses variables of a type whose values are simple entities like Booleans, integers, and finite structures containing such values. Consequently, each type has at most a countable range of values, and a test of the equality of two such values will always terminate. In high order programs, these constraints are relaxed; program variables are themselves allowed to hold programs. In principle, the number of different programs is non-denumerable, and there is no computable test which ever tests whether two variables have an equal value. A stored program is commonly called a *procedure*.

The only operation permitted on a procedure is to invoke its execution. No test is allowed of its properties. The method by which it was constructed and the method by which it computes its result are totally concealed. An implementation may store a textual or binary representation of the code of a procedure. However, all reasoning about the program should assume that the variable actually stores an abstract specification of the procedure as its value. Furthermore, any assignment that improves the value of a procedure-valued variable also improves the value of the whole program. Finally, the inclusion of high order variables does not increase the power of the language. Every program that contains a local high order variable can be transformed to the same kind of normal form as one that does not. This reproduces a result originally due to Kleene [110]. We limit our exploration of high order programming to languages which satisfy this criterion.

The introduction of procedures into a programming language can involve considerable complexity, particularly in their parameter passing mechanisms [70, 86, 119, 155, 176]. We therefore take care to introduce the complexities gradually. To begin with, in Section 9.1 there is no parameter, and all interactions are through global variables. Section 9.2 introduces a single parameter at a time, and describes value and result parameters as special cases of name parameters [149]. Certain care with the alphabet is necessary to prevent interference between parameters and global variables. Section 9.3 considers a language in which there is a single variable (out') in the output alphabet. Further restriction to the deterministic case then gives a functional programming language.

Declarative programming, as described in Section 9.4, uses high order procedure variables to specify the desired properties of a program. If the expression of the properties is restricted to the notations of a programming language (usually functional or logical), it is possible to interpret the text directly, so as to implement a program that meets the given specification. Declarative programming is a first step towards an ideal of the abolition of programming, and its replacement by direct execution of specifications.

In this chapter we assume that all declarations are properly nested with the end of their scopes, and that all predicates are at least designs, if not programs. As always, the relationship between designs and programming notations is a central issue for study.

9.1 Procedures without parameters

In this section, we introduce a new type of variable, the *procedure* variable, whose values range over predicates, or rather some subset of predicates (or programs) with a given alphabet A. Such variables may be declared, assigned and ended in the same way as variables ranging over familiar data types such as integers or characters. The purpose of procedure assignment is to determine the effect of a later call of that procedure by its variable name. If the predicate assigned to the variable is expressed wholly in the notations of the same programming language, the call can be easily implemented by execution of that program text, or (in practice) by running its machine code translation.

A procedure variable is declared

$$\mathbf{var}\ p : proc_A$$

where A determines the alphabet of the predicate that may be assigned to p. It will usually be the same as (or at most a subset of) the alphabet current at the place of the declaration; it will always exclude p itself. We will see that strict accounting of the types and alphabets of procedures is even more necessary than for variables of first-order type.

Since the alphabet of a procedure may contain procedure variables with different alphabets, the type structure has the general form of a tree, defined by the following recursion

$$\begin{array}{rcl} <\mathit{alphabet}> & ::= & \text{list of } (<\mathit{variable}>:<\mathit{type}>) \\ <\mathit{type}> & ::= & <\mathit{procedure\ type}> \mid <\mathit{other\ type}> \\ <\mathit{procedure\ type}> & ::= & \mathit{proc}(<\mathit{alphabet}>) \end{array}$$

However, we do not want a type to contain a cycle, that is a component variable with the same alphabet as the whole program. This is one reason why the procedure variable is forbidden to appear in its own alphabet. Another reason is to simplify reasoning about procedure calls. A consequence is that we must continue to use the fixed point notation to define recursive procedures.

As with other data types, we need a way of denoting procedure values by constants, like numerals and strings. Clearly, the most direct way of denoting a procedure constant is just to write the intended predicate or program in the normal way. But this risks confusion with predicates describing the rest of the program. To distinguish what is to be stored from what is to be executed, we enclose procedure constants in brackets, for example

$$\{\![x := x + 1]\!\}$$

The brackets here have no semantic significance; they are simply omitted when the procedure is executed.

In a high order programming language, assignment of a value to a procedure variable will be written in the usual way

$$p := \{\![P]\!\}$$

where P itself is a design or a program text (called the *body* of the procedure). It has to have exactly the same alphabet as that declared for the variable p. This will deliberately exclude all variables declared later than p but earlier than the assignment to p. The restriction is needed to prevent what is known as the *dangling reference* problem [155]. On termination of the program

$$\mathbf{var}\ p : proc_A;\ \ \mathbf{var}\ x;\ \ p := \{\![x := x + 1]\!\};\ \ \mathbf{end}\ x; \ldots$$

the value of p is a program which updates a variable x that no longer exists, because its scope has been ended. The alphabet constraint prevents this by disallowing the occurrence of x on the right hand side of the assignment to p. In many languages, the restriction is implicit in an even stronger restriction: that the only assignment allowed to a procedure variable is one that is written at the point of its declaration. For this case we will use the notation

$$\mathbf{proc}\ p := \{\![P]\!\}$$

A text written in brackets like this is always a constant; it is not subject to substitutions for the variables that it contains. For example,

$$(x := x + 1)\,;\,(p := \{\![y := x]\!\}) \quad = \quad (p := \{\![y := x]\!\})\,;\,(x := x + 1)$$

It is certainly *not* equal to

$$(p := \{\![y := x + 1]\!\})\,;\,(x := x + 1)$$

Assignment of constants is just a special case of assignment of expressions. A procedure-valued expression may be built from constants and variables combined with the notations of the programming language, for example

$$p := (\{\![x := x + 1]\!\}; q)$$

assigns to p a value similar to the value of q, except that its execution will be preceded by incrementation of x. Note again that a procedure value is an abstract object of mathematics, and not just a text. For example,

$$\{\![x := x + 1]\!\}; \{\![x := x + 3]\!\} \;=\; \{\![x := x + 4]\!\}$$

This is in exact analogy to the equation between numeric constants

$$1 + 3 \;=\; 4$$

The ability of programs to write programs is called *metaprogramming*, and there is hope that its wider application will lead to software that is easier to adapt to varying needs and changing environments.

To invoke the procedure which is the current value of the procedure p, we just write the variable as an executable statement of the program. The effect is clearly shown in the algebraic law

$$(p := \{\![Q]\!\})\,; p \;=\; (p := \{\![Q]\!\})\,; Q$$

Since p is not allowed in the alphabet of Q, this is also equal to

$$Q\,; (p := \{\![Q]\!\})$$

In an implementable programming language, a procedure value must obviously be written as a program, most usually in the same implemented language. But in reasoning about program design, we want to use the design of a program in place of the program text that has not yet been written. The later substitution of the program itself for the design should be justified by the usual appeal to monotonicity, as described for stepwise refinement in Section 2.4. This means that procedure assignment should be monotonic in the assigned value

$$P \sqsubseteq Q \;\Rightarrow\; (p := \{\![P]\!\}) \sqsubseteq (p := \{\![Q]\!\})$$

Unfortunately, this law would be invalid for the standard definition of assignment which equates the final value of the variable with the assigned value

$$p' \;=\; Q$$

The solution is to redefine assignment to allow an implementation to replace the assigned value by any value that is actually stronger than it; the effect is described by weakening the previous equation to an inequation

$$p' \sqsupseteq Q$$

In fact, every assignment can be defined by an inequation in this same way. In the case of first-order data, two values are comparable only if they are equal

$$v' \sqsupseteq v \quad \textbf{iff} \quad v' = v$$

The replacement of equality by an ordering in the definition of assignment also helps in reasoning about the use of computer resources (Example 7.2.1). One of the main objectives of such reasoning is to ensure that an implementation may validly replace a program by one that consistently uses less resources. But the present theory of assignment dictates that programs which assign different values to the resource variable r will be totally incomparable. The solution is to use numerical ordering in the definition of assignment to r

$$r := r + e \ =_{df} \ \textbf{true} \vdash r' \leq r + e \land y' = y \land \ldots$$

As a result, we can use normal implication ordering to validate replacement of any program by a more efficient one, for example

$$r := r + 4 \ \sqsubseteq \ r := r + 3$$

Because equality is a special case of an ordering, the following definitions are entirely consistent with the previous definitions used up to this point. The definition of alphabet extension needs the same kind of generalisation to allow procedure values to improve instead of staying the same.

Definition 9.1.1 (Procedure assignment)

Let $\alpha p \ = \ \alpha Q$

$$p := \{\!\![Q]\!\!\} \ =_{df} \ (\textbf{true} \vdash (p' \sqsupseteq Q) \ \land \ (v' \sqsupseteq v))$$

where $\quad \alpha(p := \{\!\![Q]\!\!\}) \ = \ \{p, p', v, v'\}$ □

Examples 9.1.2

(1) The declaration **proc** *double* $:= \{\!\![x := 2 \times x]\!\!\}$ expands to

$$\textbf{true} \vdash (v' \sqsupseteq v) \land (double' \sqsupseteq x := 2 \times x)$$

(2) Assignment $inc := \{\!\![x := x + 1]\!\!\}$ is described by

$$\textbf{true} \vdash (v' \sqsupseteq v) \land (inc' \sqsupseteq x := x + 1)$$

(3) Execution of $(inc := \{\!\![x := x + 1]\!\!\})$; $(p := (\{\!\![x := x + 2]\!\!\}; inc))$ has the following effect

$$\textbf{true} \vdash (p' \sqsupseteq x := x + 3) \land (inc' \sqsupseteq x := x + 1) \land (v' \sqsupseteq v)$$ □

Definition 9.1.3 (Alphabet extension)

Let $p \notin \alpha P$

$$P_{+\{p\}} \;=_{df}\; P \| (\mathbf{true} \vdash (p' \sqsupseteq p)) \qquad \square$$

Alphabet extension will frequently be needed to extend the alphabet of a procedure call to that of its context. For example,

$$\begin{aligned}&(\mathbf{proc}\ p := \{\!\![Q]\!\!\});\ \mathbf{var}\ x := x+1;\ p\\ =\ &(\mathbf{proc}\ p := \{\!\![Q]\!\!\});\ \mathbf{var}\ x := x+1;\ Q_{+\{p,x\}}\end{aligned}$$

In many languages a problem arises if the variable name x is already in the alphabet of the procedure p and is declared again local to the call, for example

$$(inc := \{\!\![x := x+1]\!\!\});\ \mathbf{var}\ x := 1;\ inc; \ldots; \mathbf{end}\ x$$

Here it would be wrong to replace the call by its meaning

$$(inc := \{\!\![x := x+1]\!\!\});\ \mathbf{var}\ x := 1;\ x := x+1; \ldots; \mathbf{end}\ x$$

The reason is that the x in the alphabet of inc is a different variable from the more recently declared x at the place where inc is called. The problem is one of collision of local (bound) and global (free) variables. This problem cannot occur in our programming language because local variables must have different names from global ones (see Section 2.9).

As a result of the change in our basic definitions, the meaning of $\mathit{I\!I}$ also changes

$$\mathit{I\!I} \;=_{df}\; (\mathbf{true} \vdash v' \sqsupseteq v)$$

We therefore need new healthiness conditions to ensure that this new identity is still a left unit and a right unit of composition.

Definition 9.1.4 (Healthiness conditions of procedure variables)

A predicate Q is said to be **P1** if it satisfies the following left unit law

P1 $\mathit{I\!I}\,; Q \;=\; Q$

It is said to be **P2** if it obeys the following right unit law

P2 $Q; \mathit{I\!I} \;=\; Q$ $\square$

Theorem 9.1.5 (Closure of healthy predicates)

Predicates satisfying the healthiness conditions **P1** and **P2** form a complete lattice which is closed under ;, $\sqcap$, $\lhd b \rhd$ and μ.

Proof From the facts that $\Pi \sqsubseteq (v' = v)$ and $\Pi;\Pi = \Pi$ it follows that

$$L =_{df} \lambda X \bullet (\Pi; X; \Pi)$$

is a $\{;, \sqcap, \lhd b \rhd\}_{\sqsupseteq}$-link. The conclusion that **P1** and **P2** are preserved by all programming operators comes from Theorems 4.1.15 and 4.1.19. □

In spite of the changed definitions of this section, all the laws given in Chapter 5 are still valid. As a result every finite program which has no procedure variables in its alphabet can be reduced to finite normal form, using additional laws given below. Local procedure declarations are removed by normalisation. The normalisation procedure is to move all procedure declarations rightward in the text of the program, replacing all its calls by the current value.

L1 $\mathbf{var}\, p : proc_A\, ; (v := e) \; = \; (v := e)\, ; \mathbf{var}\; p : proc_A$

L2 $\mathbf{var}\; p : proc_A\, ; p \; = \; \mathbf{true}$

L3 $(p := \{\!\![Q]\!\!\})\, ; p \; = \; Q_{+\{p\}}\, ; (p := \{\!\![Q]\!\!\})$

9.2 Parameter mechanism

In the previous section, procedure variables took values ranging over programs, or (more generally) predicates which describe program behaviour. In this section, we introduce variables whose values are not themselves predicates but rather functions from some other domain to predicates. The application of such a function to a particular parameter value from that domain will yield a predicate which describes the behaviour of a procedure call. Thus the parameter passing mechanism in the programming language is given the same meaning that it has in the realm of mathematics: just the application of a function. The intention, as always, is to provide the maximum assistance in reasoning about the design of programs from their specifications.

Programming convenience is the main reason for introducing parameters into a programming language. The alphabet constraints imposed in the previous section on procedure variables, assignments and call are both strict and burdensome. To get a procedure to operate on some desired initial values, these have to be copied before the call to certain fixed global locations. To get the results of the procedure into the place where they will be used afterwards, they have to be copied after the call out of fixed global variables . These variables, and all other global resources used by the call, are fixed at the time of declaration of the procedure variable. Such inconvenience is accepted in machine code programming, but it is greatly eased in high order programming language by including a facility for passing the *name* of a variable (even a local variable) as a parameter to a procedure. These name parameters are often efficiently implemented by passing the address of the machine location allocated to store the variable. Within the machine code of the body of the procedure, the variable is accessed by indirect addressing.

Let p be a procedure variable, and let x be a variable of type T in the alphabet of p which has been selected as a name parameter. An assignment of the procedure will be written

$$p := \{\!\![\lambda x : var(T) \bullet P]\!\!\}$$

The procedure p needs to have the appropriate type, which is a function from a variable y of type T to predicates with alphabet

$$\alpha P - \{x, x'\} \cup \{y, y'\}$$

Note that the alphabet of the result of applying the function depends on the choice of parameter. Functions whose type is dependent on the argument of each call are called *polymorphic* [128]. A procedure with two or more parameters can be defined by successive lambda abstraction

$$\lambda x, y : var(T) \bullet P \;=\; \lambda x : var(T) \bullet (\lambda y : var(T) \bullet P)$$

In principle, such a procedure is a function of the single parameter x, whose result is itself a function of the single parameter y. When (and only when) both parameters have been supplied, the result is a predicate which can be called in the same way as in the previous section.

A call of a parameterised procedure is written in the usual way as $p(y)$, where y must be a variable of type T, and one which is *not* in the alphabet of p. This restriction applies to all the arguments of a procedure: not only must they be disjoint from the alphabet of the procedure body, they must also be distinct from each other. The reason for this restriction will soon be abundantly clear.

A variable x in a program is represented in the corresponding predicate as two observational variables x and x'. The notation $\lambda x : var(T)$ in a programming language is therefore represented in the language of predicates by lambda abstraction $\lambda x, x'$ over both the corresponding observational variables. With this interpretation, the meaning of λ is exactly the same as that familiar in mathematics. The value of the function applied to particular parameters y and y' is the predicate obtained on replacing x by y and x' by y' in the body of the procedure. But there is an extra constraint: the second parameter must be the dashed variant of the first.

Example 9.2.1

$$\begin{aligned}
& \{\!\![\lambda x : var(T) \bullet \mathbf{true} \vdash (x' = x + 3 \wedge z' = z + 4)]\!\!\}(y) \\
= \; & \{\!\![\lambda x, x' \bullet \mathbf{true} \vdash (x' = x + 3 \wedge z' = z + 4)]\!\!\}(y, y') \\
= \; & \mathbf{true} \vdash (y' = y + 3 \wedge z' = z + 4)
\end{aligned}$$

□

The rule that prohibits sharing between the argument and the body of the procedure is essential to avoid contradiction, as shown below.

Counterexample 9.2.2

$$\begin{aligned} & \{\!\![\lambda x : var(T) \bullet \mathbf{true} \vdash (x' = x + 3 \wedge z' = z + 4)]\!\!\}(z) \\ = \; & \mathbf{true} \vdash (z' = z + 3 \wedge z' = z + 4) \\ = \; & \mathbf{true} \vdash \mathbf{false} \end{aligned}$$

□

Many programming languages have a variety of parameter passing mechanisms to meet various needs. For example, a *result* parameter is one that is used solely to determine where to store a result of the procedure call: the initial value of the corresponding argument is irrelevant. Furthermore, it is safe to relax the disjointness constraint on result arguments. A suitable notation might be

$$\{\!\![\lambda x : res(T) \bullet P]\!\!\}$$

An advantage of a result parameter is a potential increase in efficiency of implementation, by avoiding the use of indirect addressing. Another advantage is the calculation of the effect of a procedure call by the following law

$$\{\!\![\lambda x : res(T) \bullet P]\!\!\}(y) \quad = \quad \mathbf{var}\ x; P; y := x; \mathbf{end}\ x$$

A definition that gives us this law also gives a strong hint on an efficient method of implementation.

Definition 9.2.3 (Result parameter)

$$\lambda x : res(T) \bullet P \;\; =_{df} \;\; \lambda y : var(T) \bullet (\mathbf{var}\, x; P; y := x; \mathbf{end}\ x)$$

where y is a fresh variable. □

A similar treatment can be given to the *value* parameter; the corresponding argument specifies where to find an initial value for the call, and the procedure body is not allowed to change the argument. A suitable notation might be

$$\{\!\![\lambda x : val(T) \bullet P(x)]\!\!\}$$

In this case it is usual to allow the argument to be an arbitrary expression of type T, without any extra restriction. The meaning is explained by the law

$$\{\!\![\lambda x : val(T) \bullet P]\!\!\}(e) \quad = \quad \mathbf{var}\ x := e; P; \mathbf{end}\ x$$

A definition that gives us this law is as follows.

Definition 9.2.4 (Value parameter)

$$\lambda x : val(T) \bullet P \;\; =_{df} \;\; \lambda y : T \bullet (\mathbf{var}\, x := y; P; \mathbf{end}\ x)$$

where y is a fresh variable. Note that in this case it ranges over *values* of type T rather than over *variables*. That is what allows the actual argument to be an expression. □

For purposes of direct implementation, it is essential that the body of a called procedure be expressed as a program, using only the notations of the programming language, and these certainly do not include dashed variables. For procedure bodies that are already programs, we need to ensure that the result of parameter substitution is still a program that can be directly executed. In fact, the simplest way of obtaining that program is to substitute the undashed argument variable for all occurrences of the parameter in the program itself, even those on the left of an assignment. If the resulting program is expressed as a predicate, this predicate is the *same* as if the dashed and undashed versions of the variable had been substituted into the corresponding predicate.

Example 9.2.5

$$\begin{array}{lll} & \{[\lambda x : var(T) \bullet (x := x+3;\ z := z+4)]\}(y) & \{\text{substitution in the program}\} \\ = & (y := y+3;\ z := z+4) & \{\text{def of assignment and composition}\} \\ = & \mathbf{true} \vdash (y' = y+3 \ \wedge\ z' = z+4) & \{\text{substitution in the predicate}\} \\ = & (\mathbf{true} \vdash (x' = x+3 \ \wedge\ z' = z+4))[y,\ y'/x,\ x'] & \{\text{function application}\} \\ = & \{[\lambda x,\ x' \bullet \mathbf{true} \vdash (x' = x+3) \wedge (z' = z+4)]\}(y,\ y') & \Box \end{array}$$

Coincidence of meaning of two methods of substitution (in the program and in the predicate) depends on the restriction that the actual argument should be outside the alphabet of the procedure.

Counterexample 9.2.6

$$\begin{array}{ll} & \{[\lambda x : var(T) \bullet (x := x+3;\ z := z+4)]\}(z) \\ = & (z := z+3;\ z := z+4) \\ \neq & \mathbf{true} \vdash \mathbf{false} \\ = & \{[\lambda x,\ x' \bullet \mathbf{true} \vdash (x' = x+3) \wedge (z' = z+4)]\}(z,\ z') \qquad \Box \end{array}$$

This counterexample shows the need for a proof that the result of substitution of names in correctly written programs is exactly the same as in correctly written predicates. That is the topic of the following theorem. It shows (e.g. in Cases 1, 4 and 5) that name substitution in a program requires substitution to be applied even in procedure alphabets and procedure bodies.

Theorem 9.2.7 (Substitution)

Let `P(x)` be a program text using **x** as a variable name. Let $\lceil \mathtt{P(x)} \rceil$ be its meaning. Let **ax** be a variable name. Suppose that

(A1) **ax** does not occur in `P(x)`, and

(A2) none of the global variable names of `P(x)` is used as a local variable.

Then $\quad \lceil \mathtt{P(ax)} \rceil \;=\; \lceil \mathtt{P(x)} \rceil [ax,\, ax'/x,\, x']$

Proof Define

$$R(X) \;=_{df}\; (\mathbf{true} \vdash (ax = x'));\, X;\, (\mathbf{true} \vdash (x = ax'))$$

From Theorem 3.1.4 it follows that for all predicates $P(x,\, x')$ satisfying the healthiness conditions **H1** to **H3**

$$R(P(x,\, x')) \;=\; P(ax,\, ax') \;=\; P(x,\, x')[ax,\, ax'/x,\, x']$$

The following proof is based on structural induction on the program text `P(x)`.

Case 1 $\mathtt{P(x)} \;=\; (\mathtt{x},\, \mathtt{y}, \ldots := \mathtt{e(x)},\, \mathtt{f(x)}, \ldots)$.

$$
\begin{array}{lll}
 & \lceil \mathtt{P(ax)} \rceil & \{\text{def of } \mathtt{P}\} \\
= & \lceil (\mathtt{ax},\, \mathtt{y}, \ldots := \mathtt{e(ax)},\, \mathtt{f(ax)}, \ldots) \rceil & \{\text{def of assignment}\} \\
= & \mathbf{true} \vdash (ax' = e(ax)) \wedge (y' = f(ax)) \wedge \ldots & \{\text{assumption (A2)}\} \\
= & R(\mathbf{true} \vdash (x' = e(x)) \wedge (y' = f(x)) \wedge \ldots) & \{\text{def of assignment}\} \\
= & R(\lceil \mathtt{P(x)} \rceil) &
\end{array}
$$

Case 2 $\mathtt{P(x)} \;=\; \mathtt{P1(x)} \lhd \mathtt{b(x)} \rhd \mathtt{P2(x)}$.

$$
\begin{array}{lll}
 & \lceil \mathtt{P(ax)} \rceil & \{\text{def of } \mathtt{P}\} \\
= & \lceil \mathtt{P1(ax)} \lhd \mathtt{b(ax)} \rhd \mathtt{P2(ax)} \rceil & \{\text{def of conditional}\} \\
= & \lceil \mathtt{P1(ax)} \rceil \lhd b(ax) \rhd \lceil \mathtt{P2(ax)} \rceil & \{\text{inductive hypothesis}\} \\
= & R(\lceil \mathtt{P1(x)} \rceil) \lhd b(ax) \rhd R(\lceil \mathtt{P2(x)} \rceil) & \{\text{Theorem 4.4.8}\} \\
= & R(\lceil \mathtt{P1(x)} \rceil \lhd b(x) \rhd \lceil \mathtt{P2(x)} \rceil) & \{\text{def of conditional}\} \\
= & R(\lceil \mathtt{P(x)} \rceil) &
\end{array}
$$

Case 3 $\mathtt{P(x)} \;=\; \mathbf{var}\, \mathtt{lv};\, \mathtt{Q(lv,\, x)};\, \mathbf{end}\, \mathtt{lv}$.

$$
\begin{array}{lll}
 & \lceil \mathtt{P(ax)} \rceil & \{\text{def of } \mathtt{P} \text{ and assumption (A2)}\} \\
= & \lceil \mathbf{var}\, \mathtt{lv};\, \mathtt{Q(lv,\, ax)};\, \mathbf{end}\, \mathtt{lv} \rceil & \{\text{def of declaration}\} \\
= & \exists lv,\, lv' \bullet \lceil \mathtt{Q(lv,\, ax)} \rceil & \{\text{inductive hypothesis}\}
\end{array}
$$

$$= \exists lv, lv' \bullet R(\lceil \mathtt{Q(lv, x)} \rceil) \qquad \{(A1) \text{ and } (A2)\}$$
$$= R(\exists lv, lv' \bullet \lceil \mathtt{Q(lv, x)} \rceil) \qquad \{\text{def of declaration}\}$$
$$= R(\lceil \mathtt{P(x)} \rceil)$$

Case 4 $\mathtt{P(x)} = \textbf{proc}\ (\mathtt{p} := \mathtt{Q(x)});\ \mathtt{p};\ \textbf{end}\,\mathtt{p}.$

$$\lceil \mathtt{P(ax)} \rceil \qquad \{\text{def of } \mathtt{P} \text{ and assumption (A2)}\}$$
$$= \lceil \textbf{proc}\ \mathtt{p} := \mathtt{Q(ax)};\ \mathtt{p};\ \textbf{end}\,\mathtt{p} \rceil \qquad \{\text{def of procedure call}\}$$
$$= \lceil \mathtt{Q(ax)} \rceil \qquad \{\text{inductive hypothesis}\}$$
$$= R(\lceil \mathtt{Q(x)} \rceil) \qquad \{\text{def of procedure call}\}$$
$$= R(\lceil \textbf{proc}\ \mathtt{p} := \mathtt{Q(x)};\ \mathtt{p};\ \textbf{end}\,\mathtt{p} \rceil) \qquad \{\text{def of } \mathtt{P}\}$$
$$= R(\lceil \mathtt{P(x)} \rceil)$$

Case 5 $\mathtt{P(x)} = \textbf{proc}\ \mathtt{p} := (\lambda \mathtt{f} : \mathtt{var(T)} \bullet \mathtt{Q(f, y)});\ \mathtt{p(x)};\ \textbf{end}\ \mathtt{p}.$

From procedure alphabet constraints it follows that $\mathtt{x} \notin \alpha\mathtt{Q}$.

$$\lceil \mathtt{P(ax)} \rceil \qquad \{\mathtt{x} \notin \alpha\mathtt{Q}\}$$
$$= \lceil \textbf{proc}\,\mathtt{p} := \lambda \mathtt{f} : \mathtt{var(T)} \bullet \mathtt{Q(f, y)};$$
$$\mathtt{p(ax)};\textbf{end}\,\mathtt{p} \rceil \qquad \{\text{def of procedure call}\}$$
$$= \lceil \mathtt{Q(f, y)} \rceil [ax, ax'/f, f'] \qquad \{(A2) \text{ and inductive hypothesis}\}$$
$$= \lceil \mathtt{Q(ax, y)} \rceil \qquad \{\text{inductive hypothesis}\}$$
$$= R(\lceil \mathtt{Q(x, y)} \rceil) \qquad \{\text{inductive hypothesis}\}$$
$$= R(\lceil \mathtt{Q(f, y)} \rceil [x, x'/f, f']) \qquad \{\text{def of procedure call}\}$$
$$= R(\lceil \mathtt{P(x)} \rceil)$$

Case 6 $\mathtt{P(x)} = \textbf{proc}\ (\mathtt{p} := \lambda \mathtt{f} : \mathtt{var(T)} \bullet \mathtt{Q(x, f)});\ \mathtt{p(y)};\ \textbf{end}\,\mathtt{p}.$

Similar to **Case 5**.

Case 7 $\mathtt{P(x)} = \mathtt{P1(x)}\,\mathrm{op}\,\mathtt{P2(x)}$ where $\mathrm{op} \in \{\sqcap, ;\}$.

Similar to **Case 2**.

Case 8 $\mathtt{P(x)} = \textbf{proc}\ (\mathtt{p} := \mathtt{Q(x)});\ \mathtt{S(x)};\ \mathtt{p};\ \mathtt{T(x)};\ \textbf{end}\,\mathtt{p},$

where $\mathtt{S(x)}$ does not mention p.

The conclusion follows from **Case 7** and the fact that

$$\lceil \mathtt{P(ax)} \rceil = \lceil \mathtt{S(ax)}; (\textbf{proc}\,(\mathtt{p} := \mathtt{Q(ax)}); \mathtt{p}; \textbf{end}\,\mathtt{p}); (\textbf{proc}\,(\mathtt{p} := \mathtt{Q(ax)}); \mathtt{T(ax)}; \textbf{end}\,\mathtt{p}) \rceil$$

Case 9 $\mathtt{P(x)} = \mu\mathtt{X} \bullet \mathtt{F(b(x), Q(x), X)},$

where F is wholly composed by operators ;, $\sqcap$ and $\lhd\ \rhd$.

$$\begin{array}{lll} & \lceil \mathtt{P(ax)} \rceil & \{(\text{A1}) \text{ and } (\text{A2})\} \\ = & \lceil \mu \mathtt{X} \bullet \mathtt{F(b(ax),\ Q(ax),\ X)} \rceil & \{\text{def of } \mu\} \\ = & \mu X \bullet F(b(ax),\ \lceil \mathtt{Q(ax)} \rceil,\ X) & \{\text{inductive hypothesis}\} \\ = & \mu X \bullet F(b(ax),\ R(\lceil \mathtt{Q(x)} \rceil),\ X) & \{\text{Theorem 4.2.12}\} \\ = & R(\mu X \bullet F(b(x),\ \lceil \mathtt{Q(x)} \rceil,\ X)) & \{\text{def of } \mu\} \\ = & R(\mathtt{P(x)}) & \square \end{array}$$

This is a long and arduous proof, but the result is very important in establishing the mathematical coherence of the programming notation: that it is appropriately independent of the choice of the names of local variables. The details of the proof are essential to check the need for all the alphabet restrictions imposed on parameter passing. Similar proofs will be needed by the implementors of any tool which processes program texts or their proofs.

9.3 Functions

A function in a programming language is often introduced as a special case of a procedure, one that delivers just a single value as its only result. A call of such a procedure is written as an operand in an expression; during evaluation of the expression, the procedure is called, and the result that it delivers is used in further calculation of the value of the whole expression. In this way, a function defined by the programmer is no different from the functions and operators (e.g. plus and minus) which are built into the programming language.

The simplest way of defining the result of a function call is by a body consisting just of an expression e that delivers the required value. The expression will usually depend on the value of some parameter, occurring as a variable in e (say x of type T). The function is written in the usual lambda notation

$$\lambda x : T \bullet e$$

The actual argument of the function must be an expression (say f) of type T, and the result of the call can be calculated by systematic substitution of this expression for the parameter in the body of the function. The substituted body is evaluated in the normal way.

$$(\lambda x : T \bullet e(x))(f) \;=\; e(f)$$

This familiar rule of the lambda calculus is called beta-reduction. In languages which do not exclude meaningless expressions (say 1/0), its consequences may be rather surprising. Consider the constant function of real numbers

$$K2 =_{df} \lambda x : real \bullet 2$$

Since the defining expression 2 does not contain x, substitution of $1/0$ for x makes no difference, so we get

$$K2(1/0) \;=\; 2$$

The result of the call is well defined as 2, even though the argument is not. This minor paradox is similar to that encountered in Section 2.5, and it can be resolved in the same two ways.

The more elegant resolution is to adopt a method of implementation that conforms to the principle of beta-substitution. This is known as *lazy* evaluation, because it attempts to postpone evaluation of the argument of a function until it can be no longer avoided; that is when the value is known to be needed for computation of the overall result of the program. The computed value of the argument is then stored, so that it can be used again without recalculation. In the case of the constant function described above, the argument value is never needed, because the answer can be given straight away. In other cases, the need to evaluate the argument will depend on the values of the other arguments and global variables in the body of the function.

Lazy evaluation is quite standard in a purely functional language, but unusual in an imperative language, because of its inefficiency. It is generally more efficient to evaluate all arguments fully before calling the function. This *strict* implementation is the same as that for the value argument, introduced for procedures in the previous section. We might as well use the same notation

$$\lambda x : val(T) \bullet e$$

The result of applying this function to an actual argument f is defined by substitution in exactly the same way as in the lazy case. The difference between the two parameter mechanisms lies solely in the definition of the $\mathcal{D}$ operator (see Section 3.1), which gives the weakest precondition under which the expression is sure to deliver a value. In the strict case, the argument is required to be defined as well as the body of the function.

Definition 9.3.1 ($\mathcal{D}$ for lazy and strict functions)

$$\begin{aligned} \mathcal{D}((\lambda x : T \bullet e)(f)) &=_{df} \mathcal{D}(e[f/x]) \\ \mathcal{D}((\lambda x : val(T) \bullet e)(f)) &=_{df} \mathcal{D}(f) \wedge \mathcal{D}(e[f/x]) \end{aligned} \qquad \square$$

Note that if functions are definable in the language by recursion, it is no longer possible to ensure that $\mathcal{D}(e)$ will itself always be computable. The only way a computer can test its truth is to attempt to evaluate e. If this terminates, then $\mathcal{D}(e)$ is true. If it does not terminate, the computer will never find out that $\mathcal{D}(e)$ is false. Like most mathematical notations, the fact that a computer cannot compute it is of no concern. Quite the reverse: introduction of the notation is even more necessary, for assistance in reasoning about avoidance of exactly these failures in a program.

Many programming languages permit the result of a function to be computed by a block of imperative program, which assigns the intended function value to some local variable of the body, say *res*. Such a program block is turned into an expression by the operator τ, which declares the name of the variable from which the result will be taken.

$$(\tau\, res : T \bullet P) \qquad\qquad \text{(the } res \text{ such that } P\text{)}$$

This construction may appear anywhere as a component in a larger expression, for example

$$x := (\tau\, t : T \bullet Q) + (\tau\, s : S \bullet R) \times 3$$

Such result blocks are often useful as bodies of functions, and they assist in explaining the intention of value parameters, as shown in the law

$$(\lambda x : val(S) \bullet (\tau\, res : T \bullet P))(e) \;=\; \tau\, res : T \bullet (\mathbf{var}\ x := e; P; \mathbf{end}\ x)$$

The inclusion of programs inside expressions is a facility which faces the language designer with the question of *side-effect*. What happens if the body of the function makes an assignment to some global variable of the program? In many programming languages, the effect is explained by the manner of its implementation, which is quite simple if parameter passing is treated strictly. All function calls in an expression can be converted into procedure calls with a result parameter. These calls are executed before evaluating the expression, and the results are used whenever the corresponding function calls appear within the expression. To reason successfully about the program, the programmer has to make the same transformation in exactly the same way as the implementor. But if this has to be done by both programmer and implementor, there was no good reason to use functional notation in the first place. There are many good reasons not to. Hidden side-effects in function calls are a potent source of program misunderstanding and error. They can readily be banned by a syntactically checkable restriction, which enforces the rule that the variable that holds the result must be the only one in the output alphabet of the function body. In the formalisation and use of a theory of programming, this is the restriction that we recommend.

In a language which permits non-determinism, a more serious question arises. What happens if there is more than one value of *res* that satisfies P? An early answer was given by Russell's theory of descriptions. But we adopt the version given by Church, who introduced the choice operator as the basic method of quantification in higher order logic [39, 69]; Church's answer was taken over in the logic of the specification language Z [171]. Consider the set of possible answers

$$\{res' : T \mid P(res')\}$$

The operator τ acts like a choice function, selecting a member of this set. If the set is non-empty, its result is definitely a member of the set. We don't know which member it is, but every time a selection is made from the same set, the same member is selected. τ is a genuine function, so these properties of τ are encapsulated in the axiom

$$(\exists res' \bullet P(res')) \;\Rightarrow\; P(\tau\ res : T \bullet P)$$

Unfortunately, it is practically impossible for a non-deterministic programming language implementation to match the logical properties of Church's choice function. The only reasonable way of implementing non-determinism is by selecting an arbitrary one of the possible results. But suppose the same possible set of values crops up again later in the execution of the program. Church's axioms require the implementor to detect this fact and always deliver the same value on the later occasion as the earlier. The inefficiency is unthinkable. But if a different choice is made non-deterministically on the two occasions, there is virtually no hope of reasoning successfully about the results: one cannot even rely on the most elementary property of all mathematics, namely that

$$e = e$$

There is only one case in which the problem is avoided – the case in which the implemented choice function is guaranteed to agree with Tarski's choice: that is, when the set has only one member anyway. We must therefore prohibit the application of τ to programs that are non-deterministic in their results. The obligation to avoid non-determinism can be placed upon the programmer by a suitable definition of the $\mathcal{D}$ operator applied to expressions that contain programs.

Definition 9.3.2 ($\mathcal{D}$ for design blocks)

$$\mathcal{D}(\tau\ res : T \bullet (p \vdash P)) \;=_{df}\; p \wedge \text{there is at most one } res' \text{ such that } P \qquad \square$$

Another very strong motive for this harsh definition is given by the lemma

Lemma 9.3.3 τ is monotonic. $\square$

At the other end of the scale, what happens if τ is applied to an empty set? Church's logic then selects a particular value of the intended type of the result. In Z, this may be a non-standard value. We do not know which value it is, *but it is always the same value.* This logic is frequently implemented for built-in functions by computer hardware: for example, if the result of a calculation cannot be represented as a floating point number, it is given as a bitpattern called a *nan* (not a number). In fact this solution is not needed for programmer-defined functions, because the feasibility conditions for program blocks guarantee that the set of possible results is non-empty.

The introduction of $\mathcal{D}$ into reasoning about expressions that may be undefined is closely analogous to the introduction of ok, ok' (or $\vdash$) into reasoning about programs that may fail to terminate, and $\mathcal{D}$ obeys a very similar collection of healthiness conditions. In exploring these properties, we abandon the rule that $\mathcal{D}x$ is always true for a variable x. In fact, if x is a lazy parameter, it will be false whenever the corresponding argument is undefined. Note that $\mathcal{D}x$ is *not* a function of the value of x. It is a separate Boolean variable associated with the variable x; like all logical variables, it admits quantification and substitution.

The first healthiness condition guarantees that when the operands of an expression become more defined, the result cannot become less defined.

D1 $\mathcal{D}(e)$ is monotonic in $\mathcal{D}x$.

The second healthiness condition deals with the case when the value of an expression e is defined, even though the value of one of its operands x is undefined. This can only happen if the value of e is genuinely independent of the value of x. These conditions are formalised in the law

D2 $\mathcal{D}e \wedge \neg\mathcal{D}x \;\Rightarrow\; \forall x, \forall\mathcal{D}x \bullet \mathcal{D}e$

It is reasonable to insist that $\mathcal{D}e$ is always defined, that is

D3 $\mathcal{D}(\mathcal{D}e) \;=\; true$

Exercise 9.3.4

Here is a structural definition of $\mathcal{D}$ over a simple language of expressions

$$\begin{aligned}
\mathcal{D}(x+y) &= \mathcal{D}x \wedge \mathcal{D}y \\
\mathcal{D}(x\times y) &= \mathcal{D}x \wedge (x\neq 0 \Rightarrow \mathcal{D}y) \\
\mathcal{D}(x\vee y) &= (x\wedge\mathcal{D}x) \vee (y\wedge\mathcal{D}y) \vee (\mathcal{D}x\wedge\mathcal{D}y)
\end{aligned}$$

(1) Extend the definition of $\mathcal{D}$ to conditional expressions.

(2) Prove that all the definitions are healthy. □

The definition of $\mathcal{D}$ for disjunction in this exercise would cause a serious problem for implementation. It decrees that the only method of evaluating $(x \vee y)$ is to embark on the evaluation of both x and y; if either evaluation terminates with the answer *true*, that is the right answer, and evaluation of the other operand can be discontinued. If one evaluation terminates with *false*, evaluation of the other operand continues and eventually gives the right answer. If neither evaluation terminates, that is the right answer too. This method of implementation is called *non-sequential*, because the two evaluations must in principle be undertaken concurrently, or by some simulation of concurrency such as interleaving. The implementation overhead for non-sequential calculations is severe, but what is worse is the wasted effort on evaluation of alternatives that are never used. Non-sequentiality is usually avoided in programming language design. For example, the definition of $\mathcal{D}(x \vee y)$ is often given as

$$\mathcal{D}x \ \wedge \ (x \ \vee \ \mathcal{D}y)$$

which specifies that evaluation of y must be *short circuited* if the value of x is found to be true. This definition is sequential, because every reference to an operand x is protected by a positive occurrence of $\mathcal{D}x$. But it does introduce an unwelcome asymmetry into the normally symmetric meaning of disjunction.

Exercise 9.3.5

Define a syntactic normal form for expressions in x, $\mathcal{D}x$, y, $\mathcal{D}y$, ... which guarantees sequentiality, for example every occurrence of x is protected by $\mathcal{D}x$. Define an ordering which permits the limit of infinite chains of such normal forms. Prove that if $\mathcal{D}e$ is in normal form, then

$$\mathcal{D}(e[f/x]) \ = \ \mathcal{D}e[f, \mathcal{D}f/x, \mathcal{D}x] \qquad \square$$

9.4* Declarative programming

A purely functional programming language like Haskell [95] is one in which all programs are defined as functions, and there are no assignments, jumps or side-effects. Such programs are commonly defined by a set of equations which describe the results of the function in all the relevant special cases.

Example 9.4.1 (Factorial)

A factorial function is defined by a pair of equations

$$\begin{aligned} fac(0) &= 1 \\ fac(n) &= n \times fac(n-1), \qquad \text{if } n > 0 \end{aligned} \qquad \square$$

If the equations specifying the function are expressed within the rules of the programming language, an implementation can undertake the evaluation of any call of the function; it does so by repeatedly replacing each call of a function by the corresponding right hand side of the relevant equation, with appropriate substitutions of arguments for parameters, and calculation of any operations with operands which are now constants. This is called the *procedural* interpretation of the equations. If there exists a unique function that satisfies all the equations of the program, *and* if the above implementation terminates, then the result given by the implementation will be the correct value of the intended function.

In the case of the factorial, the successive steps in the evaluation of $fac(2)$ might be

$$\begin{aligned} fac(2) &= 2 \times fac(2-1) && \{\text{since } 2 > 0\} \\ &= 2 \times fac(1) && \{\text{since } 1 > 0\} \\ &= 2 \times 1 \times fac(1-1) && \{\text{calculation}\} \\ &= 2 \times fac(0) && \{\text{substitution}\} \\ &= 2 \times 1 && \{\text{calculation}\} \\ &= 2 \end{aligned}$$

But the promise of functional programming is that the programmer need not be concerned with the execution details, and can check each equation separately as a true statement of a property of the function in question. In this view, the set of simultaneous equations shown in Example 9.4.1 is regarded not as a definition of the factorial, but rather as true and provable facts about a function already known to mathematics – in this case it is the one defined as the product of all numbers up to n. This view of programming is known as *declarative*. Its use is not confined to functional programs: logic programming and even imperative programming can share the same benefit. This section investigates the circumstances in which programs can be successfully specified in the declarative style as the solutions of simultaneous equations. It highlights the problem of mismatch of declarative and procedural interpretations, and works towards their reconciliation.

In standard mathematics, a set of simultaneous equations contains n equations for n unknowns, and each unknown occurs (by itself) on the left hand side of exactly one equation. Of course, any unknown may also occur any number of times on the right hand side of any number of the equations. Fortunately, all the important ideas can be illustrated on an example with only two unknowns and only two equations

$$\begin{aligned} X &= P(X, Y) \\ Y &= Q(X, Y) \end{aligned}$$

In an imperative programming language, such a set of equations defines X and Y by *mutual* recursion, because each of the programs X and Y is called from within the body of the other. We will use Tarski's analysis [175] to show the existence of a weakest solution to such mutual recursions.

As always, we start with the assumption that each variable (X, Y) ranges over a complete lattice, and that all the functions involved are monotonic in all their operands. The main theorem that we need is

Theorem 9.4.2 (Product of complete lattices)

If A and B are complete lattices, so is their Cartesian product $A \times B$. The ordering is defined

$$(X1, Y1) \sqsubseteq_{A\times B} (X2, Y2) \quad \textbf{iff} \quad X1 \sqsubseteq_A X2 \textbf{ and } Y1 \sqsubseteq_B Y2 \qquad \square$$

In the Cartesian product space, the pair of equations can be expressed as a single equation

$$(X, Y) \;=\; (P(X, Y), Q(X, Y))$$

Furthermore the right hand side is monotonic in X and Y, because both P and Q are. It therefore has a weakest fixed point, which is also a pair. The pair consists of values of X and Y respectively which solve the original simultaneous equations. The same construction works for any number of equations; it also gives the same answer if the equations are replaced by inequations, for example

$$X \;\sqsupseteq\; P(X, Y)$$

$$Y \;\sqsupseteq\; Q(X, Y)$$

Programming in the declarative style does not necessarily restrict itself to n equations for n unknowns. The example of the factorial already uses two equations for a single unknown. In general, a greater number of equations leads to an *over-determined* or *inconsistent* system, for which there is *no* solution, not even in a complete lattice. Solubility can be restored by the trick suggested above: replace all the equations by inequations

$$X \;\sqsupseteq\; P(X, Y)$$

$$X \;\sqsupseteq\; Q(X, Y)$$

By the definition of the least upper bound in a lattice, two equations like this can always be amalgamated into the single equation

$$X \sqsupseteq P(X, Y) \sqcup Q(X, Y)$$

Thus the number of inequations can be reduced to the number of unknowns, which guarantees their consistency and solubility. This treatment of over-determinacy is the one that is most consistent with the declarative interpretation of programs.

But the price of consistency is that the top of the lattice has to be acceptable as a valid solution. For example, the inequation

$$X \sqsupseteq (x := 3) \sqcup (x := 4)$$

has the miracle $\top$ as its weakest solution. Although the theory has shown the existence of a solution within the complete lattice, this solution does not satisfy the healthiness conditions that are necessary for implementability. Any attempt to base an implementation on the given inequations must (sometimes at least) give an answer that does not satisfy them. This is an explanation of the notorious gap between the declarative semantics and the procedural semantics of many implemented declarative programming languages.

Exercise 9.4.3

Explore the consequence of turning the inequations the other way, and of taking the *strongest* fixed point of the inequations

$$X \sqsubseteq P(X, Y)$$

$$Y \sqsubseteq Q(X, Y)$$

Under what circumstances is the result an unimplementable program? □

In many cases of individual programs, the problem of implementability does not arise. For example, consider the pair of inequations

$$X \sqsupseteq (b \Rightarrow P) \qquad\qquad X \sqsupseteq (\neg b \Rightarrow Q)$$

The declarative and the procedural semantics of these inequations are the same, because when they are combined into a single equation, the result is the perfectly implementable

$$X \sqsupseteq (P \lhd b \rhd Q)$$

Many higher level declarative languages introduce compile-time checkable syntactic constraints which reconcile procedural and declarative semantics in a similar way. But we will take the complementary approach of giving a realistic abstract semantics to the procedural interpretation of the program. This will enable the programmer to prove of a particular program that the procedural and the declarative interpretations coincide, or at least that the executed program anyway meets some independently formulated specification.

The main problem in matching a procedural reading with a declarative reading of a set of equations is surprisingly simple. According to the declarative reading, the inequation

$$X \sqsupseteq X$$

is always true, so its addition to or removal from any set of inequations makes absolutely no difference. But for an implementation, the effect of adding this vacuous equation in general would be disastrous. The computer would loop forever, replacing one side of the inequation (X) by the other (X). If we want to reason about the actual effect of executing a program that is specified by general inequations, we are forced to move at least a short way from the purely declarative ideal.

The central assumption of the declarative reading is that all the inequations of the program, like all the requirements in a specification, are connected simply by conjunction. But $X \sqsupseteq X$ is a unit of conjunction, and all our problems arise from that. They are the same problems as those of Section 7.1, where a solution was given in the form of a strict parallel combinator to replace the non-strict conjunction. In this section we adopt the same solution. To begin with, we need to write dashes on all the variables on the left hand sides of the inequations, for example

$$X' \sqsupseteq P(X, Y)$$

$$Y' \sqsupseteq Q(X, Y)$$

$$X' \sqsupseteq R(X, Y) \qquad \text{etc.}$$

Each inequation thereby takes the form of an assignment, as defined in Section 9.1. The conjunction of all the inequations is therefore a simultaneous assignment to all the variables. The programs specified by the set of inequations are just the weakest ones that are unchanged by execution of the assignment.

If each identifier occurs exactly once on the left hand side of an assignment, nothing has been gained (or lost) by the more elaborate construction. But if the the same dashed variable appears in two or more inequations, we have a potential conflict. As in the case of concurrency, this must be resolved by applying an associative merging operator $\oplus$ on the values contributed by two assignments. To deal with the original problem of $X' \sqsupseteq X$, $\oplus$ must be strict. It must also be idempotent: repetition of an equation has no effect. In a language which assigns no significance to the ordering between clauses, $\oplus$ will be commutative, but we will also show how to deal with languages that give some sort of precedence to the earlier clauses.

The final important property of $\oplus$ is that it should have a unit – at least a left unit. This is introduced to deal with the case that a dashed variable never appears on the left hand side of any of the inequations. On executing the inequations, an implementation can clearly detect this case, and report it to the user or programmer, maybe with a request for further instructions. This phenomenon is known as *finite* failure, to distinguish it from the infinite failure which results from an ill-designed recursion, and which can never be detected by the computer itself. We have already encountered finite failure which results from parallelism; in a reactive system it takes the form of deadlock. We will therefore represent it by the familiar *STOP*

$$STOP \;=_{df}\; wait := true$$

This involves introducing the variable *wait* into the alphabet, together with the healthiness conditions

W1 $P \;=\; \mathit{I\!I} \lhd wait \rhd P$

W2 $P \;=\; P \vee (P \wedge wait' \wedge v' \neq v); \mathbf{true}$

where the healthiness condition **W2** ensures that the program variables remain unchanged when P stops. However, there is no need for ref or tr. And we will forbid $STOP$ to appear explicitly in any program: its only use is in the context of Definition 9.4.4 below.

A first candidate for selection as the merge operator is the non-deterministic choice $\sqcap$. This has all the required algebraic properties. But it has to be rejected because its unit is the unimplementable $\top$. The closest available alternative is the $\|$ operator defined in Section 8.2; its unit is the perfectly implementable $STOP$. This gives us an excellent procedural interpretation of the conditional equations which feature so strongly in declarative programming.

Definition 9.4.4 (Conditional equation)

$$(X \;=\; P \text{ if } b) \;=_{df}\; X' \sqsupseteq (P \lhd b \rhd STOP) \qquad \square$$

The assembly of many such clauses is denoted by $||$.

Definition 9.4.5 (Assembly)

$$P||Q \;=_{df}\; P||_M Q$$

where $$M \;=_{df}\; X' \sqsupseteq (0.X\|1.X) \;\wedge\; Y' \sqsupseteq (0.Y\|1.Y) \;\wedge\; \ldots. \qquad \square$$

This encoding appears to solve all remaining semantic problems, as shown in the following examples, where P and Q are programs free of finite failures, that is they do not contain $STOP$.

Example 9.4.6 (Non-determinism)

$$(X' \sqsupseteq P \;||\; X' \sqsupseteq Q) \;=\; (X' \sqsupseteq (P\|Q)) \;=\; (X' \sqsupseteq (P \sqcap Q))$$

Unconditional equations lead to a non-deterministic choice. $\square$

Example 9.4.7 (Determinism)

$$(X \;=\; P \text{ if } b) \,||\, (X \;=\; Q \text{ if } \neg b) \;=\; (X' \sqsupseteq (P \lhd b \rhd Q))$$

Conditional equations give the power to avoid non-determinism. $\square$

Example 9.4.8 (A mixture)

$$\begin{aligned} &(X \;=\; P \text{ if } b) \,||\, (X \;=\; Q \text{ if } c) \\ &= (X' \sqsupseteq (P \sqcap Q) \lhd b \wedge c \rhd (P \lhd b \rhd (Q \lhd c \rhd STOP))) \end{aligned}$$

If b (or c) is false, it inhibits selection of P (or Q). If they are both true, the choice between them is non-deterministic. In logic programming, this is *committed* non-determinism. Once the choice is made, it cannot be reversed by backtracking. □

Example 9.4.9 (Divergence)

$$(X' \sqsupseteq X \parallel X' \sqsupseteq x := 3) \;=\; (X' \sqsupseteq (X \,\|\, x := 3))$$

The weakest fixed point of any set of disjoint inequations containing this one will assign the bottom value **true** to X. □

In a functional programming language, the intrusion of non-determinism leads to the severe logical problems discussed in Section 9.3. The solution suggested there places responsibility for avoiding non-determinism upon the programmer. But the simplest way of avoiding a risk is to avoid all notations which entail that risk, and obviously the merging operator $\|$ must be avoided too. For this reason, many functional programming languages give significance to the ordering between the clauses of a program. If several of the conditions of different clauses are all true, the first of the clauses is always selected. The relevant merging operator is similar to the overriding operator of Z, which extends the domain of a function, and we denote it by $^{\bullet}\|$. We require it to obey the algebraic law

$$(P \lhd b \rhd STOP)\,^{\bullet}\|\,(Q \lhd c \rhd STOP) \;=\; P \lhd b \rhd (Q \lhd c \rhd STOP)$$

provided that P is free of finite failure.

The idea of the definition of $P\,^{\bullet}\|\,Q$ is that the $STOP$ of P is treated as a jump to Q, which is otherwise not executed.

Definition 9.4.10

$$P\,^{\bullet}\|\,Q \;=_{df}\; I\!I \lhd wait \rhd (P;\, ((wait := false;\, Q) \lhd wait \rhd I\!I)) \qquad \square$$

This definition uses the healthiness condition **W2** to ensure that the initial values of program variables will pass to program Q after P gets deadlocked.

Exercise 9.4.11

Prove that $^{\bullet}\|$ enjoys the following algebraic laws.

L1 $P\,^{\bullet}\|\,P \;=\; P$

L2 $(P\,^{\bullet}\|\,Q)\,^{\bullet}\|\,R \;=\; P\,^{\bullet}\|(Q\,^{\bullet}\|\,R)$

L3 $STOP\,^{\bullet}\|\,P \;=\; P \;=\; P\,^{\bullet}\|\,STOP$

L4 $CHAOS\,^{\bullet}\|\,P \;=\; CHAOS$

L5 $P\,^{\bullet}\|\,Q \;=\; P,$ whenever P is free of finite failure

L6 $P \| Q \;=\; (P\,^{\bullet}\|\,Q) \sqcap (Q\,^{\bullet}\|\,P)$ □

Exercise 9.4.12

The asymmetry of $^{\bullet}\|$ is displeasing to declarative programmers. Define an alternative operator that punishes non-determinism by abortion, and prove its algebraic properties. Hint: Define a function that leaves a wholly deterministic predicate unchanged, but maps every other predicate to $\perp$. □

Most declarative programming languages offer considerable flexibility in writing the left hand sides of the equations. For example, the single high order variable can be followed by a list of formal parameters, as in

$$X(n) \quad = \quad n \times X(g(n))$$

As a declaration, this equation is intended to be true of all n. Consequently, it is just another way of writing

$$X \quad = \quad \lambda n : val(\mathcal{N}) \bullet n \times X(g(n))$$

Certain kinds of function are often allowed in the formal parameter list, for example

$$X(f(n)) \quad = \quad (n+1) \times X(n)$$

Here again, restrictions are imposed to ensure implementability. The function f must have an easily testable image and an easily computable inverse. In that case, the equation given above is equivalent to

$$X \quad = \quad \lambda n : val(\mathcal{N}) \bullet (f^{-1}(n)+1) \times X(f^{-1}(n)), \qquad \text{if } n \in image(f)$$

These restrictions in many languages require f to be a constructor for some data type, perhaps one defined by the programmer.

The original idea of declarative programming is that programs can serve as their own specifications, so that doubts about program correctness are logically inconceivable. Programming languages designed in pursuit of this ideal tend to be clear and simple and easy to use. Particular attention is given to rigorous compile-time checking of data types, often defined by recursion and implemented by automatic storage allocation and deallocation. Even if the original idea of declarative programming is not achieved, it certainly eases the task of programming. It does this by splitting the design process into clearly defined stages. The first is to construct a set of inequations which, in their declarative interpretation, correctly describe the intended function. The second stage is to prove that the procedural interpretation of the same program text gives the same meaning as the declarative. At either stage, the program may be made more efficient, though perhaps less clear, by correctness-preserving transformations. The current section has given an unusually abstract and general treatment of the procedural semantics, which facilitates proof of the relevant algebraic laws. An alternative treatment can be based on an operational semantics, which treats each equation of the program as defining a step in its execution, whereby an appropriate chosen instance of the left hand side of the equation is replaced by an appropriate modified copy of the right hand side. Clearly, this operational semantics must correspond correctly to the other models of semantic presentation; that is the topic of the next chapter.

Chapter 10

Operational Semantics

An *operational* semantics of a programming language is one that defines not the observable overall effect of a program but rather suggests a complete set of possible individual steps which may be taken in its execution. The observable effect can then be obtained by embedding the steps into an iterative loop, like that of the interpreter described in Section 6.3. Different programs which always give the same overall result under interpretation are thereby shown to be the same. Similarly, different presentations of operational semantics which always agree in the result they give to the same program are thereby shown to define the same meaning for the language.

The individual steps of an operational semantics are usually written in a special notation SOS (Structured Operational Semantics), which is due to Plotkin [151]. It is well suited to its purpose, and has been used to define many different languages [73, 126, 127]. It consists of a collection of transition rules of the form

$$m \rightarrow m'$$

where m is a pattern describing the state of an executing mechanism before a typical step, and m' describes the state immediately after. Frequently the interpreter is required to take some action a whenever it makes the transition; this is written above the arrow

$$m \xrightarrow{a} m'$$

There are many advantages in a purely operational definition of the semantics of a programming language. Firstly, it does not require advanced mathematics to formalise the programmer's intuitive understanding of the way in which a computer executes a program. This understanding is essential when using run-time tracing and symbolic dumps for detecting errors in a program written carelessly, perhaps by someone else. The transition rules abstract nicely from the details of a particular implementing mechanisation, but they are sufficiently faithful to guide the design of a practical implementation of the language. A detailed count of the number of steps executed is immediately available as a basis for the optimisation of algorithms and the study of their complexity. Finally, an operational semantics gives an in-built guarantee of the computability of the language defined. With so many advantages for the programmer, the debugger, the implementor and the complexity theorist, it is not surprising that operational semantics has been given as the presentation of the semantics of a great many programming languages, and sometimes it is the only available presentation.

But it can never be a complete presentation, because it does not specify the circumstances under which two differently written programs are to be regarded as equal, or one of them as better than the other. Furthermore it does not specify the way in which a selection is made between alternative steps, when more than one is possible. For example, is the choice made in advance? Or at run time? Or is it made according to the first transition in the list? Or is it necessary to explore both alternatives, with or without a later selection? Even the concept of repetition is left vague: perhaps the strongest fixed point may be used rather than the weakest. This lack of precision has been turned to advantage by theorists, who delight in exploring a wide variety of possible dialects of the same language, where the sameness is defined as sharing the same operational semantics. This kind of bottom-up classification is complementary to the top-down classification of languages, which share the same or similar alphabets, signatures and laws.

10.1 Derivation of the step relation

It is the purpose of an operational semantics to define the relationship between a program and its possible executions by machine. For this we need a concept of execution and a design of machine which are sufficiently abstract for application to the hardware of a variety of real computers. In the most abstract view, a computation consists of a sequence of individual *steps*. Each step takes the machine from one state m to a closely similar one m'. Each step is drawn from a very limited repertoire, within the capabilities of a simple machine. A definition of the set of all possible single steps simultaneously defines the machine and all possible execution sequences that it can give rise to in the execution of a program.

The step can be defined as a relation between the machine state before the step and the machine state after. In the case of a stored program computer, the states are identified as pairs (`s`, `P`), where

- `s` is a *text*, defining the data state as an assignment of constants to all variables of the alphabet, as described in Section 5.8.
- `P` is a *program text*, representing the rest of the program that remains to be executed. When this is `II`, there is no more program to be executed; the

state (s, Π) is the last state of any execution sequence that contains it, and s defines the final values of the variables.

As in Section 6.3, we have to make the vital distinction between two natures of a program: *syntactic* (its textual representation) and *semantic* (its meaning as a predicate). In the rest of this chapter, we use typewriter font to distinguish text from meaning: P is the text of a program whose meaning is the predicate P and s is the text of the assignment s. The important point is that the step relation $\rightarrow$ is defined between the texts, rather than the meanings.

Suppose that $(s; P) \sqsubseteq t$, where s and t range over data states as represented above. As described in Section 5.8, this means that t is a possible final observation of the final data state of an execution of program P that has started in data state s. As a practical consequence, an implementation which is required to execute P in the initial state s is permitted instead to execute the much shorter program t, and this immediately defines the final state t. Similarly, $(s; P) \sqsubseteq (t; Q)$ means that an implementation of the program (s; P) is permitted instead to execute (t; Q), and the result can only be an improvement of the original. This suggests a criterion for valid stepwise execution of a program. Each step merely replaces the current machine state (s, P) with a new machine state (t, Q), which is known to be an improvement of it. This account does not yet give a fully sufficient condition for total correctness of execution, but it explains the preliminary definition of the step relation given below.

Definition 10.1.1 (Step relation)

$$(\mathtt{s},\ \mathtt{P}) \rightarrow (\mathtt{t},\ \mathtt{Q}) \quad =_{df} \quad (s; P) \sqsubseteq (t; Q) \qquad \square$$

This definition allows the following transition rules numbered (1) to (7) to be derived as theorems, rather than being presented as postulates or definitions; they are easily proved from the algebraic laws of the programming language.

The effect of a total assignment v := e starting on an initial state s is to end in a final state in which the variables of the program have constant values (s; e), by which we mean the result of evaluating the list of expressions e with all variables in it replaced by their initial values in the data state s. Here we recall the simplifying assumption that expressions are everywhere defined, and state the law

(1) (s, v := e) $\rightarrow$ (v := (s; e), Π)

Proof From 3.1**L4** (Π-; left unit) and 3.1**L2** (combine assignments). $\square$

A Π in front of a program Q is immediately discarded.

(2) (s, Π; Q) $\rightarrow$ (s, Q)

Proof From 3.1**L4** (Π-; left unit). $\square$

The first step of the sequential composition (P; R) is the same as the first step of P, with R saved up for execution (by the preceding rule) when P has terminated.

(3) (s, P; R) $\rightarrow$ (t, Q; R), whenever (s, P) $\rightarrow$ (t, Q)

Proof From 2.2**L1** (; assoc) and 2.4**L6** (;-$\sqcap$ left distr). $\square$

The first step of the non-deterministic choice (P $\sqcap$ Q) is to discard either one of the components P or Q. The criterion for making the choice is completely undetermined.

(4) (s, P $\sqcap$ Q) $\rightarrow$ (s, P)

(s, P $\sqcap$ Q) $\rightarrow$ (s, Q)

Proof From 2.4**L7** (;-$\sqcap$ right distr). $\square$

The first step of the conditional (P $\lhd$ b $\rhd$ Q) is also a choice, but unlike in the previous rule, the choice is made in accordance with the truth or falsity of (s; b); that is, the result of evaluating b with all free variables replaced by their initial values in the data state s.

(5) (s, P $\lhd$ b $\rhd$ Q) $\rightarrow$ (s, P), whenever $s; b$

(s, P $\lhd$ b $\rhd$ Q) $\rightarrow$ (s, Q), whenever $s; \neg b$

Proof From 3.1**L3** (:=-; right distr) and 2.1**L5** (cond unit). $\square$

Recall that s and t are total assignments of constants, so $(s; b)$ effectively reduces to *true* or *false* and $(s; \neg b)$ to *false* or *true* accordingly.

Recursion is implemented by the copy rule, whereby each recursive call within the procedure body is replaced by the whole recursive procedure.

(6) (s, μX $\bullet$ P(X)) $\rightarrow$ (s, P(μX $\bullet$ P(X)))

Proof From 2.6**L2** (fixed point). $\square$

The worst program **true** engages in an infinite repetition of vacuous steps.

(7) (s, **true**) $\rightarrow$ (s, **true**)

Proof $\sqsubseteq$ is reflexive. $\square$

The correctness of each of these transition rules has been proved simply and separately from the algebraic laws. But the main motive for formulating and proving these particular laws was to give a complete recipe for executing an arbitrary program expressed in the programming language, and for reasoning about such executions. In effect, the laws constitute an operational semantics whose step is *defined* as the *least* relation satisfying the transition rules (1) to (7). As so often in mathematics, the theorems of one branch have become the axioms or the definitions of some apparently distinct branch. Henceforth in this chapter, we will adopt the operational approach. Accordingly, we will regard (1) to (7) as a *definition* of the step relation between machine states. The proof outlined above is regarded as a demonstration of the *soundness* of the operational semantics with respect to the denotational semantics for the programming language, in the sense that every final state of an execution satisfies the predicate associated with the program. This is certainly a necessary condition for correctness. But it is not a sufficient condition. There are two kinds of error that it does not guard against:

1. There may be too few transitions (or even none at all). An omitted transition would introduce a new and unintended class of terminal state. A more subtle error would be omission of the second of the two rules (4) for $(\mathtt{P} \sqcap \mathtt{Q})$, thereby eliminating non-determinism from the language.
2. There may be too many transitions. For example, the transition

   $$(\mathtt{s},\ \mathtt{P}) \rightarrow (\mathtt{s},\ \mathtt{P})$$

   is entirely consistent since it just expresses reflexivity of $\sqsubseteq$. But its inclusion in the operational definition of the language means that every execution of every program could result in an infinite repetition of such vacuous transitions. Such infinite sequences are inevitable in the case of non-terminating iterations which results from rule (7) and sometimes from rule (6), but these should be the only cases.

The definition of the meaning of correctness for an operational semantics is therefore open to question. An adequate answer to the question should show how to derive the algebraic or denotational semantics back again from the operational. This is the topic of the next two sections.

10.2 Bisimulation

The operational semantics uses the actual text of programs to control the progress of the computation; as a consequence, two programs are equal if they are written in exactly the same way, so there cannot be any non-trivial algebraic equations. Instead, we have to define and use some reasonable *equivalence* relation (conventionally denoted $\sim$) between program texts. In fact, it is customary to define this relation first between complete machine states, including the data part. Two programs P and Q will then be regarded as equivalent if they are equivalent whenever they are paired with the same data state

$$\mathtt{P} \sim \mathtt{Q} \ =_{df}\ \forall \mathtt{s} \bullet\ (\mathtt{s},\ \mathtt{P}) \sim (\mathtt{s},\ \mathtt{Q})$$

Now the basic question is: What is meant by a *reasonable* equivalence between states? The weakest equivalence is the universal relation, and the strongest is textual equality; clearly we need something between these two extremes. There are a great many possible answers to these questions, but we shall concentrate on two of the first and most influential of them, which are due to Milner and Park [125, 144].

To exclude the universal relation, it is sufficient to impose an obligation on a proposed equivalence relation $\sim$ that it should preserve the distinctness of a certain minimum of "obviously" distinguishable states. For example, the terminal states of each computation are intended to be recognisable as such, and their data parts are intended to be directly observable. We define the terminal states as those that do not lead to any other state

$$(\mathtt{s},\ \mathtt{P}) \not\to \quad =_{df} \quad \neg\exists(\mathtt{t},\ \mathtt{Q}) \bullet (\mathtt{s},\ \mathtt{P}) \to (\mathtt{t},\ \mathtt{Q})$$

The first requirement on our equivalence is that it respects terminal states

(i) If $(\mathtt{s},\ \mathtt{P}) \sim (\mathtt{t},\ \mathtt{Q})$ and $(\mathtt{t},\ \mathtt{Q}) \not\to$, then $\mathtt{s} = \mathtt{t}$ and $(\mathtt{s},\ \mathtt{P}) \not\to$.

The second condition on a reasonable equivalence relation between states is that it should respect the transition rules of the operational semantics, or more formally

(ii) If $(\mathtt{s},\ \mathtt{P}) \sim (\mathtt{t},\ \mathtt{Q})$ and $(\mathtt{t},\ \mathtt{Q}) \to (\mathtt{v},\ \mathtt{S})$, then there is a state $(\mathtt{u},\ \mathtt{R})$ such that

$$(\mathtt{s},\ \mathtt{P}) \to (\mathtt{u},\ \mathtt{R}) \text{ and } (\mathtt{u},\ \mathtt{R}) \sim (\mathtt{v},\ \mathtt{S})$$

(iii) Since $\sim$ is an equivalence relation, the same must hold for the converse of $\sim$.

The condition **(ii)** may be contracted to a simple inequation in the calculus of relations between machine states

$$(\sim;\to) \ \subseteq\ (\to;\sim)$$

or it may be expanded to a weak commuting diagram

$$\begin{array}{ccc} (\mathtt{u},\ \mathtt{R}) & \sim & (\mathtt{v},\ \mathtt{S}) \\ \uparrow & \supseteq & \uparrow \\ (\mathtt{s},\ \mathtt{P}) & \sim & (\mathtt{t},\ \mathtt{Q}) \end{array}$$

A relation $\sim$ which satisfies these three reasonable conditions is called a *strong bisimulation.* Two states are defined to be strongly *bisimilar* if there exists *any* strong bisimulation between them. So the bisimilarity $\sim_s$ is a relation defined as the union of *all* strong bisimulations. Fortunately, distribution of relational composition through such a union means that bisimilarity $\sim_s$ is itself a strong bisimulation, in fact the weakest relation satisfying the three reasonable conditions listed above.

As an example of the use of bisimulation, we will prove the commutative law of $\sqcap$.

Lemma 10.2.1

$\mathtt{P} \sqcap \mathtt{Q} \;\sim_s\; \mathtt{Q} \sqcap \mathtt{P}$

Proof The trick is to define a relation $\sim$ which makes the law true, and then prove that it has the properties of a strong bisimulation. So let us define a reflexive relation $\sim$ that relates every state of the form $(\mathtt{s},\ \mathtt{P} \sqcap \mathtt{Q})$ with itself and with the state $(\mathtt{s},\ \mathtt{Q} \sqcap \mathtt{P})$, and relates every other state to itself. This is clearly an equivalence relation. It vacuously satisfies bisimilarity condition (**i**). Further, if $(\mathtt{s},\ \mathtt{P} \sqcap \mathtt{Q}) \to (\mathtt{t},\ \mathtt{X})$ then inspection of the two transitions for $\sqcap$ reveals that $\mathtt{t} = \mathtt{s}$ and $\mathtt{X}$ is either $\mathtt{P}$ or $\mathtt{Q}$. In either case, inspection of step (4) shows that $(\mathtt{s},\ \mathtt{Q} \sqcap \mathtt{P}) \to (\mathtt{t},\ \mathtt{X})$. The mere existence of this bisimulation proves the bisimilarity of $\mathtt{P} \sqcap \mathtt{Q}$ with $\mathtt{Q} \sqcap \mathtt{P}$. □

An additional most important property of an equivalence relation is that it should be respected by all the operators of the programming language, for example

$$\text{If } \mathtt{P} \sim \mathtt{R} \text{ and } \mathtt{Q} \sim \mathtt{S} \text{ then } \;(\mathtt{P};\mathtt{Q}) \sim (\mathtt{R};\mathtt{S})$$

An equivalence relation with this property is called a *congruence*. It justifies the principle of substitution which underlies all algebraic calculation and reasoning: without it, the algebraic laws would be quite useless. Fortunately, the bisimularity relation $\sim_s$ happens to be a congruence for all operators mentioned in our operational semantics.

Theorem 10.2.2

If $\mathtt{P} \sim_s \mathtt{Q}$, then $\mathtt{F(P)} \sim_s \mathtt{F(Q)}$ for any programming combinator $\mathtt{F}$.

Proof We define a relation $\sim$ that is clearly weaker than $\sim_s$, and which trivially satisfies $F(P) \sim F(Q)$ whenever $P \sim_s Q$. We then prove that $\sim$ is a bisimulation, and therefore *equal* to the weakest one $\sim_s$.

$$\begin{aligned} \sim \;\; =_{df} \;\; \sim_s \;&\cup\; \{(\mathtt{s},\ \mathtt{F(X)}),\ (\mathtt{s},\ \mathtt{F(Y)}) \mid \mathtt{X} \sim_s \mathtt{Y}\} \\ &\cup\; \{(\mathtt{s},\ \mathtt{X};\mathtt{R}),\ (\mathtt{t},\ \mathtt{Y};\mathtt{R}) \mid (\mathtt{s},\ \mathtt{X}) \sim_s (\mathtt{t},\ \mathtt{Y})\} \end{aligned}$$

(**i**) is trivially satisfied, because $(\mathtt{s},\ \mathtt{F(X)})$ is never a terminal state. Since $\sim$ is symmetric, we only need to concentrate on (**ii**). The proof proceeds by case analysis.

Case 1 $\mathtt{F(X)} = (\mathtt{X} \sqcap \mathtt{R})$.

The antecedent of (**ii**)

$$(\mathtt{s},\ \mathtt{P} \sqcap \mathtt{R}) \sim (\mathtt{t},\ \mathtt{Q} \sqcap \mathtt{R}) \;\text{ and }\; (\mathtt{t},\ \mathtt{Q} \sqcap \mathtt{R}) \to (\mathtt{v},\ \mathtt{S})$$

by step (4) implies that $\mathtt{t} = \mathtt{v}$ and $\mathtt{S}$ is either $\mathtt{Q}$ or $\mathtt{R}$. By the definition of $\sim$ it follows that either $\mathtt{P} \sqcap \mathtt{R} \sim_s \mathtt{Q} \sqcap \mathtt{R}$ (which completes the proof) or $\mathtt{s} = \mathtt{t}$.

Case 1a $S = Q$.

$$(s, P \sqcap R) \sim (s, Q \sqcap R) \ \wedge \ (s, Q \sqcap R) \to (s, Q) \qquad \{\text{step } (4)\}$$
$$\Rightarrow (s, P \sqcap R) \to (s, P) \ \wedge \ (s, P) \sim_s (s, Q) \qquad \{\text{def of } \sim\}$$
$$\Rightarrow (s, P \sqcap R) \to (s, P) \ \wedge \ (s, P) \sim (s, Q)$$

Case 1b $S = R$.

$$(s, P \sqcap R) \sim (s, Q \sqcap R) \ \wedge \ (s, Q \sqcap R) \to (s, R) \qquad \{\text{step } (4) \text{ and } \sim_s \subseteq \sim\}$$
$$\Rightarrow (s, P \sqcap R) \to (s, R) \wedge (s, R) \sim (s, R)$$

Case 2 $F(X) = (X \lhd b \rhd R)$.

Similar to **Case 1**.

Case 3 $F(X) = (X; R)$.

First consider the case when $Q \neq \text{II}$.

def $\sim$ and step (3)

$$\Rightarrow (s, P; R) \sim (s, Q; R) \ \wedge \ (s, Q; R) \to (v, Q'; R) \qquad \{\text{step } (3)\}$$
$$\Rightarrow (s, Q) \to (v, Q') \qquad \{P \sim_s Q\}$$
$$\Rightarrow (s, P) \to (u, P') \ \wedge \ (u, P') \sim_s (v, Q') \qquad \{\text{def } \sim, \text{ step } (3)\}$$
$$\Rightarrow (s, P; R) \to (u, P'; R) \ \wedge \ (u, P'; R) \sim (v, Q'; R)$$

If $Q = \text{II}$, from condition (**i**) of a strong bisimulation it follows that $P = \text{II}$.

Case 4 $F(X) = (R; X)$.

Similar to **Case 3**.

Case 5 $F(X) = \mu Y \bullet G(X, Y)$.

def $\sim$ and step (6)

$$\Rightarrow (s, \mu Y \bullet G(P, Y)) \sim (s, \mu Y \bullet G(Q, Y))$$
$$\wedge\ (s, \mu Y \bullet G(Q, Y)) \to (s, G(Q, \mu Y \bullet G(Q, Y))) \qquad \{\text{def of } \sim \text{ and step } (6)\}$$
$$\Rightarrow (s, \mu Y \bullet G(P, Y)) \to (s, G(P, \mu Y \bullet G(P, Y)))$$
$$\wedge\ (s, G(P, \mu Y \bullet G(P, Y))) \sim (s, G(Q, \mu Y \bullet G(Q, Y)))$$

From the above analysis we conclude that $\sim$ is a strong bisimulation. □

But there is no strong bisimulation that would enable one to prove the idempotence law for $\sqcap$. For example, let $\sim$ be a relation such that

$$(s, \text{II}) \sim (s, \text{II} \sqcap \text{II})$$

Clearly $(\mathtt{s}, \mathtt{II} \sqcap \mathtt{II}) \rightarrow (\mathtt{s}, \mathtt{II})$. However, the operational semantics deliberately excludes any $(\mathtt{t}, \mathtt{X})$ such that $(\mathtt{s}, \mathtt{II}) \rightarrow (\mathtt{t}, \mathtt{X})$; condition **(ii)** for bisimulation is therefore violated. In fact, this condition is so strong that it requires any two bisimilar programs to terminate in exactly the same number of steps. Since one of the main motives for exploring equivalence of programs is to replace a program by one that can be executed in fewer steps, strong bisimilarity is far too strong a relation for this purpose.

Milner's solution to this problem is to define a weak form of bisimilarity (which we denote $\approx$) for which the first two conditions are weakened to

(i) if $(\mathtt{s}, \mathtt{P}) \approx (\mathtt{t}, \mathtt{Q})$ and $(\mathtt{t}, \mathtt{Q}) \not\rightarrow$

then there is a state $(\mathtt{t}, \mathtt{R})$ such that

$$(\mathtt{s}, \mathtt{P}) \xrightarrow{*} (\mathtt{t}, \mathtt{R}) \quad \text{and} \quad (\mathtt{t}, \mathtt{R}) \not\rightarrow$$

where $\xrightarrow{*}$ is defined formally in the next section as the *reflexive transitive closure* of the relation $\rightarrow$.

(ii) $(\approx; \rightarrow) \subseteq (\xrightarrow{*}; \approx)$

Condition **(ii)** is very similar to the confluence condition used in the proof of the Church–Rosser property of a set of algebraic transformations. Weak bisimilarity $\approx_w$ is defined from weak bisimulation in the same way as for strong bisimilarity, and it is also a congruence.

Theorem 10.2.3

If $\mathtt{P} \approx_w \mathtt{Q}$ then $\mathtt{F}(\mathtt{P}) \approx_w \mathtt{F}(\mathtt{Q})$ for all programming combinators $\mathtt{F}$.

Proof Analogous to Theorem 10.2.2. □

Using the weak bisimilarity we can prove disjunction is idempotent.

Lemma 10.2.4

$\mathtt{P} \sqcap \mathtt{P} \approx_w \mathtt{P}$

Proof Let $\approx$ relate every $(\mathtt{s}, \mathtt{P})$ just to itself and to $(\mathtt{s}, \mathtt{P} \sqcap \mathtt{P})$ and vice versa. In the operational semantics $(\mathtt{s}, \mathtt{P} \sqcap \mathtt{P})$ is related by $\rightarrow$ only to $(\mathtt{s}, \mathtt{P})$; fortunately $(\mathtt{s}, \mathtt{P}) \xrightarrow{*} (\mathtt{s}, \mathtt{P})$ since $\xrightarrow{*}$ is reflexive. Conversely, whenever $(\mathtt{s}, \mathtt{P}) \rightarrow (\mathtt{s}', \mathtt{P}')$ then $(\mathtt{s}, \mathtt{P} \sqcap \mathtt{P}) \rightarrow (\mathtt{s}, \mathtt{P}) \rightarrow (\mathtt{s}', \mathtt{P}')$, so equality is restored after two steps. This therefore is the bisimulation that shows the weak bisimilarity

$$(\mathtt{P} \sqcap \mathtt{P}) \approx_w \mathtt{P}$$ □

Unfortunately, we still cannot prove the associative law for disjunction. The three simple states $(\mathtt{s}, \mathtt{x} := 1), (\mathtt{s}, \mathtt{x} := 2)$ and $(\mathtt{s}, \mathtt{x} := 3)$ end in three distinct final states, and by condition (i), none of them is bisimilar to any other. The state (s, (x := 1 ⊓ x := 2)) and (s, (x := 2 ⊓ x := 3)) are also distinct, because each of them has a transition to a state (i.e. (s, x := 1) and (s, x := 3) respectively) which cannot be reached in any number of steps by the other. For the same reason (s, (x := 1 ⊓ x := 2) ⊓ x := 3) is necessarily distinct from (s, x := 1 ⊓ (x := 2 ⊓ x := 3)). The associative law for disjunction is thereby violated.

In fact, there is a perfectly reasonable sense in which it is possible to observe the operational distinctness between the two sides of an associative equation

$$(P \sqcap Q) \sqcap R \quad = \quad P \sqcap (Q \sqcap R)$$

Let us suppose that at any time it is possible to split the machine state into two identical copies, and examine the behaviour of each member of the pair independently (some card games offer a similar option). The left hand side of the associative equation may follow any of the paths of the tree of Figure 10.2.5 (where the data state is unchanged, and therefore omitted).

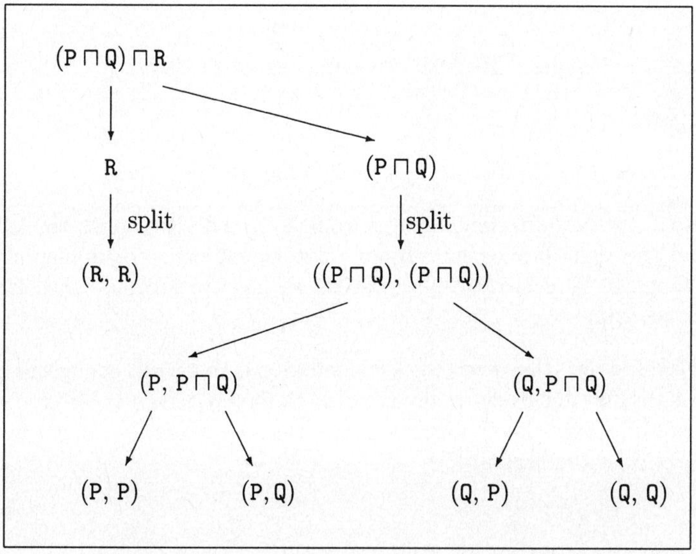

Figure 10.2.5 The game tree of (P ⊓ Q) ⊓ R

The leaves of this tree are the pairs of games

(R, R), (P, P), (P, Q), (Q, P) and (Q, Q)

A similar tree for the bracketing P ⊓ (Q ⊓ R) is given in Figure 10.2.6.

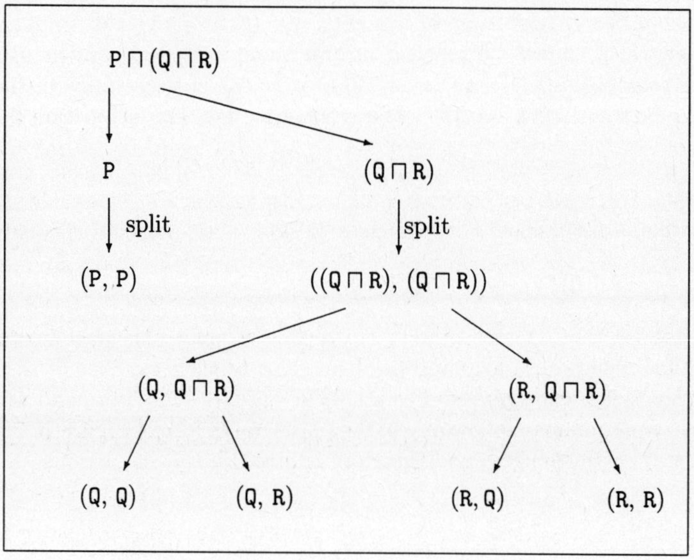

Figure 10.2.6 The game tree of P ⊓ (Q ⊓ R)

It has the leaves

(P, P), (Q, Q), (Q, R), (R, Q) and (R, R)

Observation of a pair of terminal states from (P, Q) will distinguish the left bracketing from the right bracketing. If we want to explore a theory applicable to systems that can be arbitrarily duplicated, we have to abandon associativity of non-determinism.

We have shown that even weak bisimilarity is not weak enough to give one of the laws that we quite reasonably require. Unfortunately, it is also too weak for our purposes: it gives rise to algebraic laws that we definitely do *not* want. For example, consider the program

μX • (II ⊓ X)

This could lead to an infinite computation (if the second disjunct X is always selected), or it could terminate (if the first disjunct II is ever selected, even only once). Weak bisimilarity ignores the non-terminating case, and equates the program to II. However, in our theory it is equated to **true**, the weakest fixed point of the equation

$$X = II \sqcap X$$

Our weaker interpretation **true** permits a wider range of implementations: for example, the "wrong" choice may be infinitely often selected at run time; indeed, the "right" choice can even be eliminated at compile time! For a theory based on bisimilarity, neither of these implementations is allowed. A non-deterministic construction $(\mathtt{P} \sqcap \mathtt{Q})$ is expected to be implemented *fairly*: in any infinite sequence of choices, each alternative must be chosen infinitely often. Weak bisimilarity is a very neat way of imposing this obligation, which at one time was thought essential to the successful use of non-determinism.

Unfortunately, the requirement of fairness violates the basic principle of monotonicity, on which so much of engineering design depends. The program $(\mathtt{X} \sqcap \mathtt{II})$ is necessarily less deterministic than $\mathtt{X}$, so $(\mu\mathtt{X} \bullet \mathtt{X} \sqcap \mathtt{II})$ should (by monotonicity) be less deterministic than $(\mu\mathtt{X} \bullet \mathtt{X})$, which is the worst program of all. However, weak bisimulation identifies it with the completely deterministic program $\mathtt{II}$. It would therefore be unwise to base a calculus of design on weak bisimulation.

But that was never the intention; bisimulation was originally proposed by Milner as the strongest equivalence that can reasonably be postulated between programs, and one that could be efficiently tested by computer, without any consideration of any possible meaning of the texts being manipulated. It was used primarily to explore the algebra of communication and concurrency. It was not intended for application to a non-deterministic sequential programming language, and the problems discussed in this section suggest it would be a mistake to do so. A great many alternative definitions of program equivalence based on operational semantics have been explored by subsequent research. The one that serves our purposes best is described in the next section.

10.3 From operations to algebra

In this section we will define a concept of simulation which succeeds in reconstructing the algebraic semantics of the programming language on the basis of its operational semantics. Firstly, we define $\stackrel{*}{\rightarrow}$ as the reflexive transitive closure of $\rightarrow$

$$\stackrel{*}{\rightarrow} \;=_{df}\; \nu X \bullet (id \vee (\rightarrow; X))$$

where *id* stands for the identity relation on machine states.

Secondly, we define the concept of *divergence*, being a state that can lead to an infinite execution

$$(\mathtt{s},\,\mathtt{P})\uparrow \;=_{df}\; \forall n, \exists \mathtt{t}, \mathtt{Q} \bullet (\mathtt{s},\,\mathtt{P}) \rightarrow^{n} (\mathtt{t},\,\mathtt{Q})$$

where $\quad \rightarrow^{1} \;=_{df}\; \rightarrow$

and $\quad \rightarrow^{n+1} \;=_{df}\; \rightarrow^{1}; \rightarrow^{n}$

Now, we define an ordering relation $\sqsubseteq$ between states. One state is *better* in this ordering than another if any result given by the better state is also possibly given by the worse and, furthermore, a state that can fail to terminate is worse than any other

$$(\mathtt{s},\ \mathtt{P}) \sqsubseteq (\mathtt{t},\ \mathtt{Q}) \ =_{df}\ \neg(\mathtt{s},\ \mathtt{P}) \uparrow$$
$$\Rightarrow\ (\neg(\mathtt{t},\ \mathtt{Q}) \uparrow\ \wedge\ (\forall \mathtt{u} \bullet (\mathtt{t},\ \mathtt{Q}) \stackrel{*}{\rightarrow} (\mathtt{u},\ \Pi) \Rightarrow (\mathtt{s},\ \mathtt{P}) \stackrel{*}{\rightarrow} (\mathtt{u},\ \Pi)))$$

One program is better than another if it is better in all data states

$$\mathtt{P} \sqsubseteq \mathtt{Q} \quad \textbf{iff} \quad \forall \mathtt{s} \bullet (\mathtt{s},\ \mathtt{P}) \sqsubseteq (\mathtt{s},\ \mathtt{Q})$$

Our task in this section is to show that the $\sqsubseteq$ relation defined between machine states by the operational semantics corresponds exactly with the refinement ordering relation of the algebraic semantics, which is already in correspondence with implication between predicates of the denotational semantics (see Section 5.10).

Theorem 10.3.1

The syntactically defined $\sqsubseteq$ relation is a preorder. □

The following theorem states that the operational semantics *faithfully* implements the algebraic semantics in the following sense:

- a state $(\mathtt{s},\ \mathtt{P})$ is divergent **iff** the algebra agrees that P when started in the initial state s fails to terminate, and
- a state $(\mathtt{s},\ \mathtt{P})$ can lead to a termination state $(\mathtt{t},\ \Pi)$ **iff** the algebra agrees that P when started in the initial state s may deliver t as the final state.

Theorem 10.3.2

(1) $(\mathtt{s},\ \mathtt{P}) \uparrow$ **iff** $(s; P) = \mathbf{true}$ is algebraically provable.

(2) $(\mathtt{s},\ \mathtt{P}) \uparrow$ or $(\mathtt{s},\ \mathtt{P}) \stackrel{*}{\rightarrow} (\mathtt{t},\ \Pi)$ **iff** $(s; P) \sqsubseteq t$ is algebraically provable.

Proof We prove the conclusion by structural induction on P.

Case 1 $\mathtt{P} = \mathbf{true}$.

The conclusion follows from 5.3**L5** and the fact that $(\mathtt{s},\ \mathbf{true}) \uparrow$.

Case 2 $\mathtt{P} = (\mathtt{v} := \mathtt{e})$.

The conclusion follows from 5.1**L3** and step (1)

$$(\mathtt{s},\ \mathtt{v} := \mathtt{e}) \rightarrow (\mathtt{v} := (\mathtt{s}; \mathtt{e}),\ \Pi)$$

Case 3 $\mathtt{P} = (\mathtt{P1} \sqcap \mathtt{P2})$.

The proof is based on the fact that all results from a disjunction, whether terminating or not, must arise from one of the disjuncts.

$(\sqcap - 1)$ $(\mathtt{s}, \mathtt{P1} \sqcap \mathtt{P2}) \uparrow$ **iff** $(\mathtt{s}, \mathtt{P1}) \uparrow$ or $(\mathtt{s}, \mathtt{P2}) \uparrow$

$(\sqcap - 2)$ $(\mathtt{s}, \mathtt{P1} \sqcap \mathtt{P2}) \overset{*}{\rightarrow} (\mathtt{t}, \Pi)$ **iff** $(\mathtt{s}, \mathtt{P1}) \overset{*}{\rightarrow} (\mathtt{t}, \Pi)$ or $(\mathtt{s}, \mathtt{P2}) \overset{*}{\rightarrow} (\mathtt{t}, \Pi)$

$$
\begin{array}{lll}
 & (\mathtt{s}, \mathtt{P}) \uparrow & \{(\sqcap - 1)\} \\
\equiv & (\mathtt{s}, \mathtt{P1}) \uparrow \ \lor \ (\mathtt{s}, \mathtt{P2}) \uparrow & \{\text{induction hypothesis}\} \\
\equiv & (s; P1 \ = \ \mathbf{true}) \lor (s; P_2 \ = \ \mathbf{true}) & \{(s; b1) \lor (s; b2) \ = \ \mathbf{true\ iff} \\
 & & s; b1 = \mathbf{true} \text{ or } s; b2 = \mathbf{true}\} \\
\equiv & s; (P1 \sqcap P2) \ = \ \mathbf{true} &
\end{array}
$$

Case 4 $\mathtt{P} \ = \ (\mathtt{P1} \lhd b \rhd \mathtt{P2})$.

Similar to **Case 1**.

Case 5 $\mathtt{X} \ = \ \mathtt{P1};\mathtt{P2}$.

In the proof we will use the fact that the second component of sequential composition can start its execution only after termination of the first one.

$(; -1)$ $(\mathtt{s}, \mathtt{P1};\mathtt{P2}) \uparrow$ **iff** $(\mathtt{s}, \mathtt{P1}) \uparrow$ or $\exists \mathtt{u} \bullet ((\mathtt{s}, \mathtt{P1}) \overset{*}{\rightarrow} (\mathtt{u}, \Pi) \ \land \ (\mathtt{u}, \mathtt{P2}) \uparrow)$

$(; -2)$ $(\mathtt{s}, (\mathtt{P1};\mathtt{P2})) \overset{*}{\rightarrow} (\mathtt{u}, \Pi)$ **iff** $\exists \mathtt{t} \bullet ((\mathtt{s}, \mathtt{P1}) \overset{*}{\rightarrow} (\mathtt{t}, \Pi)$ and $(\mathtt{t}, \mathtt{P2}) \overset{*}{\rightarrow} (\mathtt{u}, \Pi))$

$$
\begin{array}{lll}
 & (\mathtt{s}, \mathtt{P}) \uparrow \ \lor \ (\mathtt{s}, \mathtt{P}) \overset{*}{\rightarrow} (\mathtt{t}, \Pi) & \{(; -1) \text{ and } (; -2)\} \\
\equiv & (\mathtt{s}, \mathtt{P1}) \uparrow \ \lor & \\
 & \exists \mathtt{u} \bullet ((\mathtt{s}, \mathtt{P1}) \overset{*}{\rightarrow} (\mathtt{u}, \Pi) \ \land \ (\mathtt{u}, \mathtt{P2})) \uparrow \ \lor & \\
 & \exists \mathtt{u} \bullet ((\mathtt{s}, \mathtt{P1}) \overset{*}{\rightarrow} (\mathtt{u}, \Pi) \ \land \ (\mathtt{u}, \mathtt{P2}) \overset{*}{\rightarrow} (\mathtt{t}, \Pi)) & \{\text{simplification}\} \\
\equiv & (\mathtt{s}, \mathtt{P1}) \uparrow \ \lor & \\
 & \exists \mathtt{u} \bullet ((\mathtt{s}, \mathtt{P1}) \overset{*}{\rightarrow} (\mathtt{u}, \Pi) \ \land & \\
 & (\mathtt{u}, \mathtt{P2}) \uparrow \ \lor \ (\mathtt{u}, \mathtt{P2}) \overset{*}{\rightarrow} (\mathtt{t}, \Pi)) & \{\text{induction hypothesis}\} \\
\equiv & \exists \mathtt{u} \bullet \ ((s; P1) \sqsubseteq u) \ \land \ ((u; P2) \sqsubseteq t) & \{5.3\mathbf{L3} \text{ and } 5.3\mathbf{L4}\} \\
\equiv & (s; P1; P2) \sqsubseteq t &
\end{array}
$$

Case 6 $\mathtt{P} \ = \ \mu \mathtt{X} \bullet \mathtt{F}(\mathtt{X})$.

The proof is based on the following facts:

$(\mu - 1)$ $(\mathtt{s}, \mu \mathtt{X} \bullet \mathtt{F}(\mathtt{X})) \uparrow$ **iff** $\forall n \bullet (\mathtt{s}, \mathtt{F}^{(n)}(\mathbf{true})) \uparrow$

$(\mu - 2)$ $\neg(\mathtt{s}, \mathtt{F}^n(\mathbf{true})) \uparrow \ \Rightarrow \ ((\mathtt{s}, \mathtt{F}^n(\mathbf{true})) \overset{*}{\rightarrow} (\mathtt{t}, \Pi) \equiv (\mathtt{s}, \mu \mathtt{X} \bullet \mathtt{F}(\mathtt{X})) \overset{*}{\rightarrow} (\mathtt{t}, \Pi))$

$$
\begin{array}{ll}
\quad (\texttt{s, P})\uparrow \ \lor\ (\texttt{s, P}) \xrightarrow{*} (\texttt{t, }\Pi) & \{(\mu-1) \text{ and } (\mu-2)\} \\
\equiv\ \forall n \bullet\ (\texttt{s, F}^n(\textbf{true}))\uparrow\ \lor & \\
\quad \exists n \bullet \neg(\texttt{s, F}^n(\textbf{true}))\uparrow\ \land & \\
\quad (\texttt{s, F}^n(\textbf{true})) \xrightarrow{*} (\texttt{t, }\Pi) & \{\text{induction hypothesis}\} \\
\equiv\ \forall n \bullet (s; F^n(\textbf{true})\ =\ \textbf{true}) \lor & \\
\quad \exists n \bullet (s; F^n(\textbf{true}) \neq \textbf{true}) \land & \{\text{Theorem 5.4.1 and} \\
\qquad (s; F^n(\textbf{true}) \sqsubseteq t) & \text{strong ordering of Section 5.6}\} \\
\equiv\ (s; P\ =\ \textbf{true})\ \lor\ ((s;P) \sqsubseteq t) & \{\textbf{true} \sqsubseteq t\} \\
\equiv\ (s;P) \sqsubseteq t & \square
\end{array}
$$

We have now proved a close correspondence between the syntactic ordering defined operationally between program texts and the semantic ordering relation used in an algebraic presentation. The correspondence can be strengthened by a standard construction to operational equivalence and algebraic equality

$$\texttt{P} \sim \texttt{Q} =_{df} (\texttt{P} \sqsubseteq \texttt{Q}) \land (\texttt{Q} \sqsubseteq \texttt{P})$$

Because $\sqsubseteq$ is a preorder, the relation $\sim$ is an equivalence. The algebraic semantics is isomorphic to the operational, when abstracted by this particular notion of bisimulation.

Theorem 10.3.3

$\texttt{P} \sim \texttt{Q}$ **iff** $P = Q$ is algebraically provable.

Proof From Theorem 10.3.2 and the fact that

$$
\begin{array}{ll}
 & P\ =\ Q \quad \text{is algebraically provable} \\
\textbf{iff} & \forall \texttt{s} \bullet (s; P = \textbf{true})\ \equiv\ (s; Q = \textbf{true})\ \land\ \forall \texttt{s, t} \bullet\ ((s;P) \sqsubseteq t)\ \equiv\ ((s;Q) \sqsubseteq t) \\
\textbf{iff} & \forall \texttt{s} \bullet (\texttt{s, P})\uparrow\ \equiv\ (\texttt{s, Q})\uparrow \\
 & \land\ \forall \texttt{s, t} \bullet (\texttt{s, P})\uparrow \lor (\texttt{s, P} \xrightarrow{*} (\texttt{t, }\Pi))\ \equiv\ (\texttt{s, Q})\uparrow \lor (\texttt{s, Q} \xrightarrow{*} (\texttt{t, }\Pi)) \\
\textbf{iff} & \texttt{P} \sim \texttt{Q} \qquad \square
\end{array}
$$

10.4* From operational to denotational semantics

In Chapter 5 we derived a complete algebraic presentation of the theory of programming from a denotational definition of the semantics of the programming language. In Section 5.8, we showed how to reverse the direction of derivation, and obtain a denotational semantics from the algebraic laws. It is encouraging that the same theory is obtained in all cases. In this section we will make a similar reversal of direction. Having derived an operational semantics from an algebraic, we complete the cycle by showing how to derive a denotational semantics from an operational.

The technique is the same as that of Section 5.8. We define a function $\mathcal{O}$ which maps any program text to a relation, and then prove that $\mathcal{O}$ satisfies the equations (given in Section 5.8) which defines the denotational semantics $\mathcal{R}$. Of course $\mathcal{O}$ must be defined wholly in terms of the step relation $\rightarrow$, which is given as the primitive in the operational presentation.

Definition 10.4.1 (denotation from operations)

$$\mathcal{O}(\mathtt{P}) =_{df} pre(v) \vdash post(v, v')$$

where

$$pre(v_0) =_{df} \neg((\mathtt{v} := \mathtt{v}_0,\ \mathtt{P}) \uparrow)$$

$$post(v_0, v_1) =_{df} (\mathtt{v} := \mathtt{v}_0,\ \mathtt{P}) \uparrow \ \vee\ (\mathtt{v} := \mathtt{v}_0,\ \mathtt{P}) \xrightarrow{*} (\mathtt{v} := \mathtt{v}_1,\ \mathtt{II})$$ □

Exercise 10.4.2

Prove that $\mathcal{O}$ satisfies the equations defining $\mathcal{R}$. □

10.5* Operational semantics of CSP

This section illustrates how to derive an operational semantics for CSP from its algebraic laws in the same way that Section 10.1 did for a sequential language. We will treat prefixing, non-determinism, choice, parallel and sequential composition, hiding and recursion.

The empty transition of an operational semantics is identified with the resolution of possible internal non-determinism of a process. The result can only be equally or more deterministic than the original. As in Section 10.1 we define

$$P \rightarrow Q =_{df} P \sqsubseteq Q$$

The action transition relation of an operational semantics is written

$$P \xrightarrow{a} Q$$

It means that a is a possible initial event for P, and Q is a description of possible behaviour after a. Consequently, the range of behaviours of P does not increase when the possible behaviour of $a \rightarrow Q$ is added as an explicit alternative to P. We therefore define

Definition 10.5.1 (Action transition relation)

$$P \xrightarrow{a} Q \;=_{df}\; P \sqsubseteq (a \to Q) \| P \qquad \square$$

The inequality is required because P may resolve internal non-determinism in a way that may even prevent it from engaging in an initial event a, or from behaving like Q afterwards. The defining inequality may be rewritten as an equation

$$P = ((a \to Q) \| P) \sqcap P$$

which in turn can be rewritten to

$$P = (a \to Q) \| (x \to P) \backslash \{x\}$$

where x is an event name occurring only as shown, and nowhere else. In CCS such an event is encoded as τ; thus

$$P = a.Q + \tau.P$$

The main algebraic laws for the proofs have been given in Section 8.2. The following four lemmas are also required.

Lemma 10.5.2

$$(P \| Q); R \;\sqsubseteq\; (P; R) \| (Q; R) \qquad \square$$

Lemma 10.5.3

$$(P \| Q) \backslash E \;\sqsubseteq\; (P \backslash E) \| (Q \backslash E) \qquad \square$$

Lemma 10.5.4

Let $P = ((a \to R) \| S)$ and $a \notin \mathcal{A}(Q)$. Then

$$P \|_{CSP} Q \;=\; (a \to (R \|_{CSP} Q)) \| (P \|_{CSP} Q) \qquad \square$$

Lemma 10.5.5

Let $P = ((a \to R) \| S)$ and $Q = ((a \to U) \| W)$. Then

$$P \|_{CSP} Q \;=\; (a \to (R \|_{CSP} U)) \| (P \|_{CSP} Q) \qquad \square$$

Using the definition given above, we now proceed to derive the standard operational semantics of CSP [158, 160].

The first step of the process $a \to P$ is to engage in the event a. Afterwards, it behaves like the process P.

(1) $(a \to P) \xrightarrow{a} P$

Proof From idempotence of $\|$. □

Let E be any set of events, and let $Q(x)$ be an expression defining subsequent behaviour for each different x in E. The process $(x : E \to Q(x))$ first offers a choice of any event a in E, and then behaves like $Q(a)$.

(2) $(x : E \to Q(x)) \xrightarrow{a} Q(a), \quad \text{if } a \in E$

Proof From associativity and idempotency of $\|$. □

$P \sqcap Q$ behaves like P or like Q, where the selection between them is arbitrary, without the control of the external environment.

(3) $P \sqcap Q \to P$

$P \sqcap Q \to Q$

Proof $\sqcap$ is the greatest lower bound operator with respect to $\sqsubseteq$. □

If one of the operands of $\|$ proceeds by resolving non-deterministic choice, then the external choice construct performs the same step, and postpones the selection on its alternatives.

(4) $P \| Q \to P' \| Q, \quad \text{whenever} \quad P \to P'$

$P \| Q \to P \| Q', \quad \text{whenever} \quad Q \to Q'$

Proof From monotonicity of $\|$. □

If P and Q can perform an action, then the environment of $P \| Q$ can control which of P or Q will be selected, solely based on the very first action.

(5) $P \| Q \xrightarrow{a} P', \quad \text{whenever} \quad P \xrightarrow{a} P'$

$P \| Q \xrightarrow{a} Q', \quad \text{whenever} \quad Q \xrightarrow{a} Q'$

Proof From associativity and monotonicity of $\|$. □

The first step of the sequential composition $P; Q$ is the same as the first step of its component P.

(6) $P; Q \to P'; Q, \quad \text{whenever} \quad P \to P'$

Proof From monotonicity of ;. □

(7) $P; Q \xrightarrow{a} P'; Q, \quad \text{whenever} \quad P \xrightarrow{a} P'$

Proof From Lemma 10.5.2 and law $(a \to P'); Q \;=\; a \to (P'; Q)$. □

The first step of $SKIP; Q$ is to discard its first component $SKIP$.

(8) $SKIP; Q \to Q$

Proof $SKIP$ is the unit of sequential composition. □

$P\backslash E$ behaves like P except that all occurrences of actions internal to P are concealed, and so is any event in E.

(9) $P\backslash E \to P'\backslash E, \quad \text{whenever} \quad P \to P'$

Proof From monotonicity of hiding. □

(10) $P\backslash E \to P'\backslash E, \quad \text{whenever} \quad P \xrightarrow{a} P' \text{ and } a \in E$

Proof From law

$$((a \to P) \| Q)\backslash(E \cup \{a\}) \sqsubseteq P\backslash(E \cup \{a\})$$ □

(11) $P\backslash E \xrightarrow{a} P'\backslash E, \quad \text{whenever} \quad P \xrightarrow{a} P' \text{ and } a \notin E$

Proof From Lemma 10.5.3 and 8.2**L8**

$$(a \to Q)\backslash E = a \to (Q\backslash E), \quad \text{if } a \notin E$$ □

When P and Q are assembled to run concurrently, events that are in both their alphabets require simultaneous participation of P and Q.

(12) $P\|_{CSP}Q \xrightarrow{a} P'\|_{CSP}Q', \quad \text{whenever} \quad P \xrightarrow{a} P' \text{ and } Q \xrightarrow{a} Q'$

Proof From Lemma 10.5.5. □

However, internal events, and events in the alphabet of P but not in the alphabet of Q, are of no concern to Q.

(13) $P\|_{CSP}Q \to P'\|_{CSP}Q, \quad \text{whenever} \quad P \to P'$

$P\|_{CSP}Q \to P\|_{CSP}Q', \quad \text{whenever} \quad Q \to Q'$

Proof From monotonicity of $\|_{CSP}$. □

(14) $P\|_{CSP}Q \xrightarrow{a} P'\|_{CSP}Q, \quad \text{whenever} \quad P \xrightarrow{a} P' \text{ and } a \in \mathcal{A}(P) \setminus \mathcal{A}(Q)$

$P\|_{CSP}Q \xrightarrow{a} P\|_{CSP}Q', \quad \text{whenever} \quad Q \xrightarrow{a} Q' \text{ and } a \in \mathcal{A}(Q) \setminus \mathcal{A}(P)$

Proof From Lemma 10.5.4. □

(15) $\mu X \bullet P(X) \to P(\mu X \bullet P(X))$

Proof $\mu X \bullet P(X)$ is a solution of the recursive equation $X = P(X)$. □

This operational semantics of CSP is susceptible to analysis by strong or by weak bisimulation. They are both congruences, but they fail to validate the full set of algebraic laws. Solutions to all these problems are given in [158, 160].

We have now given separate operational semantics for a process algebra and for sequential programming. A practical programming language like occam [97] has to combine both sequential and concurrent features. An operational semantics for a combined language consists mainly of a combination of the operators of the two component sublanguages, and of the steps that define how they are to be executed. But unfortunately, it is not so easy to combine theories of programming that have been based on operational semantics. This is because any results that are dependent on induction may also have to be reconsidered. The fragility of induction when languages are extended is a discouragement to the choice of operational semantics as a starting point for unifying theories of programming. In the denotational presentation, all that was necessary was to combine the alphabets of the predicates, and in an algebraic presentation, it is the laws and the healthiness conditions that are combined. Nothing has to be withdrawn and nothing has to be redefined and nothing has to be reproved. That is why this book starts with denotational and algebraic presentations, and ends here with the operational.

Appendix 0: Alphabets

Observables

	SL	**LabP**	**LL**	**ACP**	**CSP**	**DF**	**HL**	**DL**
stable (ok, ok')	$\surd$	$\surd$	$\surd$		$\surd$	$\surd$	$\surd$	$\surd$
waiting ($wait$, $wait'$)				$\surd$	$\surd$	$\surd$		$\surd$
control (l, l')		$\surd$						
program variables (v, v')	$\surd$	$\surd$					$\surd$	$\surd$
question (q), answers (a')			$\surd$					
trace (tr, tr')				$\surd$	$\surd$	$\surd$		
refusal (ref, ref')				$\surd$	$\surd$	$\surd$		
procedure variables (p, p')							$\surd$	$\surd$

- **SL**: Sequential programming language defined in Chapter 5.
- **LabP**: Labelled programs defined in Chapter 6.
- **LL**: Logic programming language defined in Section 7.6.
- **ACP**: Algebra of communicating processes defined in Section 8.1.
- **CSP**: Communicating Sequential Processes defined in Section 8.2.
- **DF**: Data flow processes defined in Section 8.3.
- **HL**: High order language defined in Chapter 9.
- **DL**: Declarative programming language defined in Section 9.4.

Appendix 1: Shared Variables

	Merge relation M	Atomic actions $\mathcal{A}$
stable (ok') (7.1)	$(0.ok \wedge 1.ok) \Rightarrow ok'$	
resource (r) (7.2)	$r' = 0.r + 1.r - r$	$r := r + e$
log (out) (7.2)	$(out' - out) \in$	$out := out^\frown < e >$
	$(0.out - out)\|\|\|(1.out - out)$	
clock ($clock$) (7.2)	$clock' = max(0.clock,\ 1.clock)$	$clock := clock + 1$
input (in, c) (7.2)	$(0.c = 1.c)_\perp; c := 0.c$	$m,\ c := in_c,\ c + 1$
output (out, c) (7.2)	$\bigwedge_{c \le i < 0.c}\ out_i := (0.out_i \| 1.out_i);$	$out_c,\ c := e,\ c + 1$
	$(0.c = 1.c)_\perp; c := 0.c$	
array (A) (7.4)	$A' = A \oplus (r_0 \lhd 0.A) \oplus (s_0 \lhd 1.A)$	$A[i] := e,\ x := f(A[j])$
answers (a') (7.6)	$a' = 0.a^\frown 1.a$	$a := a^\frown < c >$
	$a' \in (0.a\|\|\|1.a)$	
waiting ($wait'$)	$wait' = 0.wait \vee 1.wait$	$wait := true$
(8.1 and 8.2)		$wait := false$
trace (tr')	$(tr' - tr) \in (0.tr - tr)\|\|(1.tr - tr)$	$tr := tr^\frown < c >$
(8.1 and 8.2)	$(tr' - tr) \in (0.tr - tr)\|\|\|(1.tr - tr)$	
	$(tr' - tr) \downarrow AP = (0.tr - tr) \wedge$	
	$(tr' - tr) \downarrow AQ = (1.tr - tr)$	
refusal (ref')	$ref' = 0.ref \cap 1.ref$	$\mathbf{true} \vdash (ref' \cap X = \{\})$
(8.1 and 8.2)	$ref' = 0.ref \cup 1.ref$	
program (X') (9.4)	$X' \sqsupseteq (0.X^\bullet \| 1.X)$	$X' \sqsupseteq P$

Appendix 2: Primitives

	Abort	Skip	Stop	Miracle
SL **LabP** **LL**	**true**	$\mathit{II}_{\{v\}} = \mathbf{true} \vdash (v' = v)$		$\neg\, ok$
ACP **CSP** **DF**	$\mathbf{R}(\mathbf{true})$	$\mathbf{R}(\exists ref' \bullet \mathit{II}_{\{tr, ref, wait\}})$	$\mathbf{R}(\mathbf{true} \vdash wait' \wedge tr' = tr)$	$\mathbf{R}(\neg\, ok)$
DL	$\mathbf{W}(\mathbf{true})$	$\mathbf{W}(\mathit{II}_{\{v\}})$	$wait := true$	$\mathbf{W}(\neg\, ok)$
HL	**true**	$\mathit{II}_{\{p\}} = \mathbf{true} \vdash (p' \sqsupseteq p)$		$\neg\, ok$

where **R** and **W** are defined by

$$\mathbf{R}(X(tr,\, tr')) \;=\; _{df}(tr \leq tr') \;\wedge\; (\mathit{II}_{\{tr, ref, wait\}} \lhd wait \rhd (\textstyle\bigvee_s X(s,\, s^\frown(tr' - tr))))$$
$$\mathbf{W}(X) \;=_{df}\; (STOP \lhd wait \rhd X)$$

Appendix 3: Healthiness Conditions

Sequential programming language (Section 3.2 and Example 4.1.21)

H1 $P = (\neg ok \lor P)$

H2 $[P[false/ok'] \Rightarrow P[true/ok']]$

H3 $P = P; I\!I$

H4 $P; \mathbf{true} = \mathbf{true}$ □

Reactive processes (Section 8.0)

R1 $P = P \land (tr \leq tr')$

R2 $P(tr, tr') = P(<>, tr' - tr)$

R3 $P = I\!I_{\{tr, ref, wait\}} \lhd wait \rhd P$ □

ACP (Section 8.1)

R1–R3

ACP1 $P \land (tr' = tr) \Rightarrow wait'$ □

CSP (Section 8.2)

R1–R3

CSP1 $P \;=\; \neg ok \wedge (tr \leq tr') \;\vee\; P$

CSP2 $P \;=\; P; ((ok \Rightarrow ok') \;\wedge\; (tr' = tr) \;\wedge\; \ldots \;\wedge\; (ref' = ref))$

CSP3 $P \;=\; SKIP; P$

CSP4 $P \;=\; P; SKIP$

CSP5 $P \;=\; P|||SKIP$

Data flow processes (Section 8.3)

R1–R3

CSP1–CSP5

DF1 $P \;=\; IN \gg P \gg OUT$ □

High order language (Section 9.1)

P1 $\mathit{II}_{\{p\}}; P \;=\; P$

P2 $P; \mathit{II}_{\{p\}} \;=\; P$ □

Definedness function (Section 9.3)

D1 $\mathcal{D}e[false/\mathcal{D}x] \Rightarrow \;(\mathcal{D}e)[true/\mathcal{D}x]$

D2 $(\mathcal{D}e)[false/\mathcal{D}x] \;\Rightarrow\; \forall x, \mathcal{D}x \bullet \mathcal{D}(e)$

D3 $\mathcal{D}(\mathcal{D}e)$ □

Declarative language (Section 9.4)

W1 $P \;=\; \mathit{II} \lhd wait \rhd P$

W2 $P \;=\; P \;\vee\; (P \wedge wait' \wedge v' \neq v); \mathbf{true}$ □

Bibliography

[1] M. Abadi and L. Lamport. Composing specifications. *ACM Transactions on Programming Languages and Systems*, Vol 15(1): 73–132, (1993).

[2] M. Abadi and L. Lamport. Conjoining specifications. *ACM Transactions on Programming Languages and Systems*, Vol 17(3): 507–534, (1995).

[3] M.L. Abell and P. Braselton. *Maple V Handbook.* Academic Press, (1994).

[4] S. Abramsky and R. Jagadeesan. Games and full completeness for multiplicative linear logic. *Journal of Symbolic Logic*, Vol 59: 543–574, (1994).

[5] S. Abramsky and C.-H. Ong. Full abstraction in the lazy lambda calculus. *Information and Computation*, Vol 105: 159–267, (1993).

[6] S. Abramsky, D.M. Gabbay and T.S.E. Maibaum. *Semantic Structures.* Handbook of Logics in Computer Sciences, Oxford University Press, (1994).

[7] J.-R. Abrial. *The B-Book: Assigning Programs to Meanings.* Cambridge University Press, (1996).

[8] G. Agha. *Actors: A Model of Concurrent Computation in Distributed Systems.* The MIT Press, (1986).

[9] G. Agha and C. Hewitt. Actors: A conceptual foundation for object-oriented programming. In P. Wegner and B. Shrivers (eds): *Research Direction in Object-oriented Programming*, 49–74, The MIT Press, (1987).

[10] R. Alur and T.A. Henzinger. Logics and models of real time: a survey. *Lecture Notes in Computer Science*, Vol 600: 74–106, Springer-Verlag, (1992).

[11] K.R. Apt and E.-R. Olderog. *Verification of Sequential and Concurrent Programs.* Springer-Verlag, (1991).

[12] K. Arnold and J. Gosling. *The Java Programming Language.* Addison-Wesley, (1996).

[13] R.J.R. Back and K. Sere. Stepwise refinement of action systems. *Lecture Notes in Computer Science*, Vol 375: 115–138, Springer-Verlag, (1989).

[14] R.J.R. Back and J. von Wright. Refinement calculus, Part I: Sequential nondeterministic programs. *Lecture Notes in Computer Science*, Vol 430: 42–66, Springer-Verlag, (1989).

[15] R.C. Backhouse. Factor theory revisited. Technical Report of Edinhoven University of Technology, (1990).

[16] R.C. Backhouse and P. Hoogendijk. Elements of the relational theory of data types. *Lecture Notes in Computer Science*, Vol 755, Springer-Verlag, (1993).

[17] J. Backus. Can programming be liberated from the von Neumann style? A functional style and its algebra of programs. *Communications of the ACM*, Vol 21(8): 613–641, (1978).

[18] J.C.M. Baeten and W.P. Weijland. *Process Algebra.* Cambridge Tracts in Theoretical Computer Science, Cambridge University Press, (1990).

[19] J.W. de Bakker. Semantics and termination of nondeterministic recursive programs. *Proceedings of 3rd International Colloquium on Automata, Language and Programming*, 436–477, Edinburgh University Press, (1976).

[20] J.W. de Bakker. *Mathematical Theory of Program Correctness.* Prentice Hall, (1980).

[21] J.W. de Bakker and W.-P. de Roever. A calculus for recursive program schemes. *Proceedings of 1st International Colloquium on Automata, Language and Programming*, 167–196, North-Holland, (1972).

[22] M. Barr and C. Wells. *Category Theory for Computing Science,* Second Edition. Prentice Hall, (1995).

[23] J. A. Bergstra and J. W. Klop. Algebra of communicating processes with abstraction. *Theoretical Computer Science*, Vol 37(1): 77–121, (1985).

[24] G. Berry. Esterel on hardware. *Philosophical Transactions of the Royal Society of London*, Series A, Vol 339: 87–104, (1992).

[25] G. Berry and G. Gonthier. The Esterel synchronous programming language: design, semantics, implementation. Rapport de Recherche 842, INRIA, (1988).

[26] R.J. Bird and P. Wadler. *Introduction to Functional Programming.* Prentice Hall, (1988).

[27] R.S. Bird. Transformational programming and the paragraph problem. *Science of Computer Programming*, Vol 6: 159–189, (1986).

[28] R.S. Bird and L. Meertens. Two exercises found in a book on algorithmics. In L.G.L.T. Meertens (ed): *Program Specification and Transformations*, 451–457, Elsevier Science Publishers B.V., North-Holland, (1987).

[29] D. Bjørner. A ProCoS project description. *Proceedings of International Conference on AI and Robotics*, North-Holland, (1989).

[30] R.S. Boyer and J.S. Moore. *A Computational Logic Handbook.* Academic Press, (1988).

[31] J.D. Brock and W.B. Ackermann. Scenarios: a model of nondeterministic computation. *Lecture Notes in Computer Science*, Vol 107: 252–267, Springer-Verlag, (1982).

[32] S.D. Brookes, C.A.R. Hoare and A.W. Roscoe. A theory of communicating sequential processes. *Journal of the ACM*, Vol 31: 560–599, (1984).

[33] M. Broy. Semantics of finite and infinite networks of concurrent communicating agents. *Distributed Computing*, Vol 2(1): 13–31, (1987).

[34] M. Broy and C. Lengauer. On denotational versus predicative semantics. *Journal of Computer and System Sciences*, Vol 42(1): 1–29, (1991).

[35] J.R. Burch, E.M. Clarke, D.L. Dill and L.J. Hwang. Symbolic model checking: 10^{20} states and beyond. *Proceedings of 5th IEEE Annual Symposium on Logic in Computer Science*, 428–439, IEEE Press, (1990).

[36] CCITT Blue Book, Vol X-Fasc. X.1, Recommendation Z.100, Geneva, (1989).

[37] CCITT COM X-R 26, part II.3, revised recommendation Z.100, Geneva, (1992).

[38] K.M. Chandy and J. Misra. *Parallel Program Design: A Foundation.* Addison-Wesley, (1988).

[39] A. Church. A formulation of the simple theory of types. *Journal of Symbolic Logic*, Vol 5: 56–68, (1940).

[40] A. Church and J.B. Rosser. Some properties of conversion. *Transactions of the American Mathematical Society*, Vol 39: 472–482, (1936).

[41] P. Coad, D. North and M. Mayfield. *Object Models: Strategies, Patterns and Applications.* Prentice Hall, (1995).

[42] P. Cohn. *Universal Algebra.* Reidel, (1981).

[43] J.H. Conway. *Regular Algebra and Finite Machines.* Chapman and Hall, (1971).

[44] S. Cook and J. Danies. *Designing Object Systems: Object-Oriented Modelling with Syntropy.* Prentice Hall, (1994).

[45] O.-J. Dahl, B. Myhrhaug and K. Nygaard. *SIMULA 67 Common Base Language.* Publication no. S-2, Norwegian Computer Centre, (1968).

[46] R. DeNicola and M. Hennessy. Testing equivalence for processes. *Theoretical Computer Science*, Vol 34: 83–133, (1983).

[47] W.-P. de Roever. Recursion and parameter mechanisms: an axiomatic approach. *Lecture Notes in Computer Science*, Vol 14: 34–65, (1973).

[48] W.-P. de Roever. Recursive Program Schemes: Semantics and Proof Theory. *Mathematical Centre Tracts 70*, Centre for Mathematics and Computer Science, (1976).

[49] E.W. Dijkstra. Cooperating sequential processes. In F. Genuys (ed): *Programming Languages*, 43–112, Academic Press, (1968).

[50] E.W. Dijkstra. *A Discipline of Programming.* Prentice Hall, Englewood Cliffs, NJ, (1976).

[51] E.W. Dijkstra and W.H.L. Feijen. *A Method of Programming.* Addison-Wesley, (1988).

[52] E.W. Dijkstra and C.S. Scholten. *Predicate Calculus and Program Semantics.* Texts and Monographs in Computer Science, Springer-Verlag, (1990).

[53] M. Dincbas, P. Van Hentenryck, H. Simonis, A. Aggoun, T. Graf and F. Berthier. The constraint logic programming language CHIP. *Proceedings of the International Conference on 5th Generation Computer Systems* (FGCS'88), Japan, (1988).

[54] R. Fagin, J.Y. Halpern and N. Meggido. A logic for reasoning about probabilities. *Information and Control*, Vol 87: 78–128, (1990).

[55] M. Fitting. *Intuitionistic Logic, Model Theory and Forcing.* North-Holland, (1969).

[56] M. Fitting. *First Order Logic and Automated Theorem Proving*, Second Edition. Springer-Verlag, (1996).

[57] R.W. Floyd. Assigning meanings to programs. *Proceedings of Symposia in Applied Mathematics*, Vol 19: 19–32, (1967).

[58] S. Fortune and J. Wyllie. Parallelism in random access machines. 10th ACM Symposium on the Theory of Computing, 114–118, (1978).

[59] M. Fowler and K. Scott. *UML Distilled: Applying the Standard Object Modeling Language.* Addison-Wesley, (1997).

[60] N. Francez. *Fairness.* Springer-Verlag, (1986).

[61] M. Fränzle. From continuity to discreteness — five views of embedded control hardware. Technical Report, Kiel University, (1994).

[62] M. Fränzle. A discrete model of VLSI dynamics in hybrid control application. Technical Report, Kiel University, (1994).

[63] D. Gelernter. An integrated microcomputer network for experiments in distributed programming. PhD dissertation, SUNY at Stony Brook, (1982).

[64] D. Gelernter. Generative communications in Linda. *ACM Transactions on Programming Languages and Systems*, Vol 7(1): 80–113, (1985).

[65] D. Gelernter and A. Bernstein. Distributed communications vis global buffer. *Proceedings ACM Symposium on Principles of Distributed Computing*, 0–18, (1982).

[66] J.Y. Girard. Linear logic. *Theoretical Computer Science*, Vol 50: 1–102, (1987).

[67] J. Goguen and T. Winkler. Introducing OBJ3. Technical Report SRI-CSL-88, SRI International, Computer Science Laboratory, (1988).

[68] J. Goguen, J. Thatcher, E. Wagner and J. Wright. Initial algebra semantics and continuous algebra. *Journal of the ACM*, Vol 24(1): 68–95, (1977).

[69] M.J.C. Gordon. HOL: A proof generating system for higher-order logic. In G. Birtwistle (ed): *VLSI Specification, Verification and Synthesis*, 73–128, Kluwer Academic Publishers, (1988).

[70] D. Gries. *The Science of Programming.* Springer-Verlag, (1981).

[71] R.L. Grossman, A. Nerode, A.P. Ravn and H. Rischel (eds). Hybrid Systems. *Lecture Notes in Computer Science*, Vol 776, Springer-Verlag, (1993).

[72] P. Le. Guernic, M. Le Borgne, T. Gauthier and C. Le Maire. Programming real time applications with Signal. In *Another Look at Real Time Programming*, Proceedings of the IEEE, (1991).

[73] C.A. Gunter. *Semantics of Programming Languages: Structures and Techniques.* The MIT Press, (1992).

[74] C.A. Gunter and J.C. Mitchell. *Theoretical Aspects of Object-Oriented Programming.* The MIT Press, (1994).

[75] N. Halbwachs, P. Capsi, P. Raymond and D. Polaul. The synchronous data flow programming language LUSTRE. *Proceedings of the IEEE*, Vol 79(8): 1305–1319, (1991).

[76] D. Harel. Statecharts: a visual formalism for complex systems. *Science of Computer Programming*, Vol 8: 231–247, (1987).

[77] E.C.R. Hehner. Predicative programming, Part 1 and 2. *Communications of the ACM*, Vol 27(2): 134–151, (1984).

[78] E.C.R. Hehner and C.A.R. Hoare. A more complete model of communicating processes. *Theoretical Computer Science*, Vol 26: 105–120, (1983).

[79] E.C.R. Hehner and A.J. Malton. Termination conventions and comparative semantics. *Acta Informatica*, Vol 25: 1–14, (1989).

[80] P. Henderson. *Functional Programming.* Prentice Hall, (1980).

[81] M. Hennessy. Synchronous and asynchronous experiments on processes. *Information and Control*, Vol 59: 36–83, (1983).

[82] M.C. Hennessy. *Algebraic Theory of Processes.* The MIT Press, (1988).

[83] M.C. Hennessy and R. Milner. Algebraic laws for nondeterminism and concurrency. *Journal of the ACM*, Vol 32(1): 137–161, (1985).

[84] T.A. Henzinger, Z. Manna and A. Pnueli. Timed transition systems. *Lecture Notes in Computer Science*, Vol 600: 226–251, Springer-Verlag, (1992).

[85] C.A.R. Hoare. An axiomatic basis for computer programming. *Communications of the ACM*, Vol 12: 576–583, (1969).

[86] C.A.R. Hoare. Procedures and parameters: an axiomatic approach. In *Symposium on Semantics of Programming Languages*, 102–116, Springer-Verlag, (1971).

[87] C.A.R. Hoare. Proof of correctness of data representation. *Acta Informatica*, Vol 1: 271–281, (1972).

[88] C.A.R. Hoare. *Communicating Sequential Processes.* Prentice Hall, (1985).

[89] C.A.R. Hoare. Programs are predicates. *Proceedings of International Conference on 5th Generation Computer Systems*, Tokyo, 211–218, (1992).

[90] C.A.R. Hoare and He Jifeng. The weakest prespecification. *Fundamenta Informaticae*, Vol 9: 51–84, 217–252, (1986).

[91] C.A.R. Hoare and N. Wirth. An axiomatic definition of the programming language PASCAL. *Acta Informatica*, Vol 2: 335–355, (1973).

[92] C.A.R. Hoare *et al.* Laws of programming. *Communications of the ACM*, Vol 30(8): 672–686, (1987).

[93] C.A.R. Hoare, He Jifeng and A. Sampaio. Normal form approach to compiler design. *Acta Informatica*, Vol 30: 701–739, (1993).

[94] G. J. Holzmann and D. Peled. The state of SPIN. *Lecture Notes in Computer Science*, Vol 1102: 385–389, Springer-Verlag, (1996).

[95] P. Hudak, S.L.P. Jones and P. Wadler. Report on the Programming Language Haskell, version 1.2. *ACM SIGPLAN Notices*, Vol 27(5), (1992).

[96] G. Huet. Cartesian closed categories and lambda-calculus. *Lecture Notes in Computer Science*, Vol 242, Springer-Verlag, (1986).

[97] INMOS Limited. *Occam 2 Reference Manual.* Prentice Hall, (1988).

[98] ISO 8807. *Information processing systems — Open Systems Interconnection — LOTOS — a formal description technique based on the temporal ordering of observational behaviour.* ISO standard, Geneva, Switzerland, (1987).

[99] M. Jackson. *System Development.* Prentice Hall, (1983).

[100] J. Jaffar and S. Michaylov. Methodology and implementation of a CLP system. In 4th International Conference on Logic Programming, Australia, (1987).

[101] C.B. Jones. *Systematic Software Development Using VDM.* Prentice Hall, (1986).

[102] B. Jónsson. Varieties of relation algebra. *Algebra Universalis*, Vol 15: 273–298, (1982).

[103] B. Jónsson and A. Tarski. Boolean algebra with operators, Part 1. *American Journal of Mathematics*, Vol 73: 891–939, (1951).

[104] B. Jónsson and A. Tarski. Boolean algebra with operators, Part 2. *American Journal of Mathematics*, Vol 74: 127–162, (1952).

[105] M.B. Josephs. Receptive process theory. *Acta Informatica*, Vol 29(1): 17–31, (1992).

[106] G. Kahn. The semantics of a simple language for parallel processing. In J.L. Rosenfeld (ed): *Information processing '74*, 471–475, North-Holland, (1974).

[107] G. Kahn and D. MacQueen. Coroutines and networks of parallel processes. In B. Gilchrist (ed): *Information processing '77*, 994–998, North-Holland, (1977).

[108] B. von Karger and C.A.R. Hoare. Sequential calculus. *Information Processing Letters*, Vol 53(3): 123–130, (1995).

[109] J.C. King. A program verifier. PhD thesis, Carnegie–Mellon University, (1969).

[110] S.C. Kleene. *Introduction to Meta-mathematics.* Princeton University Press, (1952).

[111] D.E. Knuth. *The Art of Computer Programming.* Addison-Wesley, (1973).

[112] L. Lamport. win and sin: Predicate transformers for concurrency. *ACM Transactions on Programming Languages and Systems*, Vol 12(3): 396–428, (1990).

[113] L. Lamport. A temporal logic of actions. *ACM Transactions on Programming Languages and Systems*, Vol 16(3): 872–923, (1994).

[114] J. Launchbury. A natural semantics for lazy evaluation. Conference Record of 20th Annual ACM SIGPLAN-SIGACTS Symposium on Principles of Programming Languages, 144–154, (1993).

[115] J.W. Lloyd. *Foundations of Logic Programming.* Springer-Verlag, (1984).

[116] S. Mac Lane. *Categories for the Working Mathematician.* Springer-Verlag, (1971).

[117] R.D. Maddux. Fundamental study Relation-algebraic semantics. *Theoretical Computer Science*, Vol 160: 1–85, (1996).

[118] Z. Manna and A. Pnueli. *The Temporal Logic of Reactive and Concurrent Systems: Specifications.* Springer-Verlag, (1991).

[119] A.J. Martin. A general proof rule for procedures in predicate transformer semantics. *Acta Informatica*, Vol 20: 301–313, (1983)

[120] P. Martin-Löf. Constructive mathematics and computer programming. In L.J. Cohen (ed): *Logic, Methodology and Philosophy of Science*, Vol 4: 153–175, North-Holland, (1982).

[121] Mathematics of Program Construction Group, Eindhoven University of Technology. Fixed-point calculus. *Information Processing Letters*, Vol 53: 131–136, (1995).

[122] J. McCarthy *et al.* *LISP 1.5 Programmer's Manual.* The MIT Press, (1962).

[123] W.F. McColl. BSP programming. *Proceedings of DIMACS Workshop on Specification of Parallel Algorithms*, Princeton University Press, (1994).

[124] B. Meyer. *Object-Oriented Software Construction.* Prentice Hall, (1994).

[125] R. Milner. A Calculus of Communicating Systems. *Lecture Notes in Computer Science*, Vol 92, Springer-Verlag, (1980).

[126] R. Milner. *Communication and Concurrency.* Prentice Hall, (1989).

[127] R. Milner. Polyadic π-calculus: a tutorial. Technical Report ECS-LFCS-91-180, University of Edinburgh, (1991).

[128] R. Milner, M. Tofte and R.W. Harper. *The Definition of Standard ML.* The MIT Press, (1990).

[129] C.C. Morgan. *Programming from Specifications*, Second Edition. Prentice Hall, (1994).

[130] J.M. Morris. A theoretical basis for stepwise refinement and the programming calculus. *Science of Computer Programming*, Vol 9(3): 287–306, (1987).

[131] J.M. Morris. Non-deterministic expressions and predicate transformers. *Information Processing Letters*, Vol 61: 241–246, (1997).

[132] P.D. Mosses. *Action Semantics.* Cambridge Tracts in Theoretical Computer Science, Cambridge University Press, (1992).

[133] M. Müller-Olm. Modular Compiler Verification. *Lecture Notes in Computer Science*, Vol 1283, Springer-Verlag, (1997).

[134] P. Naur. Proofs of algorithms by general snapshots. *BIT*, Vol 6: 310–316, (1969).

[135] G. Nelson. A generalisation of Dijkstra's calculus. *ACM Transactions on Programming Languages and Systems*, Vol 11(4): 517–561, (1989).

[136] Van Nguyen, A. Demers and S. Owicki. A model and temporal proof system for networks of processes. *Distributed Computing*, Vol 1(1): 7–25, (1986).

[137] M. Nivat. Nondeterministic programs: an algebraic overview. In S.H. Lavington (ed): *Information processing '80*, 17–28, North-Holland, (1980).

[138] M. Nivat and J. Reynolds (eds). *Algebraic Methods in Semantics.* Cambridge University Press, (1985).

[139] E.-R. Olderog and C.A.R. Hoare. Specification oriented semantics for communicating processes. *Acta Informatica*, Vol 23: 9–66, (1986).

[140] C.-H. Ong. Correspondence between operational and denotational semantics. In S. Abramsky, D. Gabbay and T.S.E. Maibaum (eds): *Handbook of Logics in Computer Science*, Vol 4. Oxford University Press, (1995).

[141] Open Verilog International. *Verilog Hardware Description Language Reference Manual*, Version 1.0, Open Verilog International, 15466 Los Gatos Blvd, Los Gatos, California, (1995).

[142] S.S. Owicki and D. Gries. An axiomatic proof technique for parallel programs. *Acta Informatica*, Vol 6: 319–340, (1976).

[143] S. Owre, S. Rajan, J.M. Rushby, N. Shankar and M. Srivas. PVS: combining specification, proof checking, and model checking. *Lecture Notes in Computer Science*, Vol 1102: 411–414, Springer-Verlag, (1996).

[144] D.M.R. Park. On the semantics of fair parallelism. *Lecture Notes in Computer Science*, Vol 86: 504–526, Springer-Verlag, (1979).

[145] D.L. Parnas, J. Madey and M. Iglewski. Precise documentation of well-structured programs. *IEEE Transactions on Software Engineering*, Vol 20(12): 948–976, (1994).

[146] J.L. Peterson. *Petri Net Theory and the Modeling of Systems.* Prentice Hall, (1981).

[147] C. Petri. Kommunikation mit Automaten. PhD dissertation, University of Bonn, (1962).

[148] C. Petri. Concepts of net theory. *Proceedings of the Symposium and Summer School on Mathematical Foundations of Computer Sciences*, High Tatras, 137–146, (1973).

[149] G.D. Plotkin. Call-by-name, call-by-value and the λ-calculus. *Theoretical Computer Science*, Vol 1: 125–179, (1975).

[150] G.D. Plotkin. A powerdomain construction. *SIAM Journal on Computing*, Vol 5: 452–487, (1976).

[151] G. D. Plotkin. A structural approach to operational semantics. Technical Report, DAIMI-FN-19, Aarhus University, Denmark, (1981).

[152] A. Pnueli. The temporal semantics of concurrent programs. *Theoretical Computer Science*, Vol 13: 45–60, (1981).

[153] V. Pratt. Event spaces and their linear logic. In AMAST'91: Algebraic Methodology and Software Technology, (1992).

[154] J.C. Reynolds. Definitional interpreters for higher-order programming languages. *Proceedings of the ACM Annual Conference*, 717–740, (1972).

[155] J.C. Reynolds. *The Craft of Programming.* Prentice Hall, (1981).

[156] J.C. Reynolds. The essence of Algol. In J.W. de Bakker and J.C. van Vliet (eds): *Algorithmic Languages*, 345–372, North-Holland, (1981).

[157] D.M. Ritchie and K. Thompson. The UNIX timesharing system. *Communications of the ACM*, Vol 17(7): 365–375, (1974).

[158] A.W. Roscoe. Two papers on CSP. Technical Monograph PRG-67, Oxford University Computing Laboratory, (1988).

[159] A.W. Roscoe. Model-checking CSP. In A.W. Roscoe (ed): *A Classical Mind: Essays in Honour of C.A.R. Hoare*, 353–378, Prentice Hall, (1994).

[160] A.W. Roscoe. *The Theory and Practice of Concurrency.* Prentice Hall, (1998).

[161] A.W. Roscoe and C.A.R. Hoare. Laws of Occam programming. *Theoretical Computer Science*, Vol 60: 177-229, (1988).

[162] K.L. Rosenthal. *Quantales and Their Applications.* Pitman, (1990).

[163] L. Saunders and R. Waxman. *IEEE Standard VHDL Language Reference Manual.* The Institute of Electrical and Electronics Engineers, USA, (1988).

[164] D.A. Schmidt. *Denotational Semantics.* Allyn and Bacon, (1986).

[165] D.S. Scott. Continuous lattices. *Lecture Notes in Mathematics*, Vol 274: 97–136, Springer-Verlag, (1972).

[166] D.S. Scott. Data types as lattices. *SIAM Journal on Computing*, Vol 5: 522–587, (1976).

[167] D.S. Scott. Domains for denotational semantics. *Lecture Notes in Computer Science*, Vol 140: 577–613, Springer-Verlag, (1982).

[168] D.S. Scott and Christopher Strachey. Towards a mathematical semantics for computer languages. *Proceedings of 21st Symposium on Computers and Automata*, 19–46, Polytechnic Institute of Brooklyn, (1971).

[169] M.B. Smyth. Power domains. *Journal of Computer and System Science*, Vol 16(1): 23–26, (1978).

[170] M.B. Smyth and G.D. Plotkin. The category-theoretic solution of recursive domain equations. *SIAM Journal on Computing*, Vol 11: 761–783, (1982).

[171] J.M. Spivey. *The Z Notation: A Reference Manual*, Second Edition. Prentice Hall, (1992).

[172] J. Stoy. *Denotational Semantics.* The MIT Press, (1977).

[173] C. Strachey. Fundamental concepts in programming languages. Unpublished lecture notes, International Summer School in Computer Programming, Copenhagen, (1967).

[174] A. Tarski. On the calculus of relations. *Journal of Symbolic Logic*, Vol 6(3): 73–89, (1941).

[175] A. Tarski. A lattice-theoretical fixpoint theorem and its applications. *Pacific Journal of Mathematics*, Vol 5: 285–309, (1955).

[176] R.D. Tennent. The denotational semantics of programming languages. *Communications of the ACM*, Vol 19: 437–453, (1976).

[177] R.D. Tennent. *Semantics of Programming Languages.* Prentice Hall, (1991).

[178] R.D. Tennent. Correctness of data representation in Algol-like languages. In A.W. Roscoe (ed): *A Classical Mind: Essays in Honour of C.A.R. Hoare*, 405–418, Prentice Hall, (1994).

[179] A.M. Turing. Checking a large routine. Report of a Conference on High Speed Automatic Calculating Machines, 67–69, University Mathematical Laboratory, Cambridge, (1949).

[180] D.A. Turner. An overview of Miranda. In D.A. Turner (ed): *Research Topics in Functional Programming*, Addison-Wesley, (1990).

[181] J.T. Udding. Classification and composition of delay-insensitive circuits. PhD dissertation, Eindhoven University of Technology, (1984).

[182] J.D. Ullman. *Elements of ML programming.* Prentice Hall, (1994).

[183] L.G. Valiant. A bridging model for parallel computation. *Communications of the ACM*, Vol 33(8): 103–111, (1990).

[184] G. Winskel. *The Formal Semantics of Programming Languages.* The MIT Press, (1993).

[185] N Wirth and C.A.R. Hoare. A contribution to the development of ALGOL. *Communications of the ACM*, Vol 9: 413–431, (1966).

[186] S. Wolfram. *The Mathematica Book.* Cambridge University Press, (1996).

[187] Zhou Chaochen, C.A.R. Hoare and A.P. Ravn. A calculus of durations. *Information Processing Letters*, Vol 40(5): 269–276, (1992).

[188] J. Zwiers. Compositionality, Concurrency and Partial Correctness. *Lecture Notes in Computer Science*, Vol 321, Springer-Verlag, (1989).

Index